LITERACY AND YOUNG CHILDREN

Solving Problems in the Teaching of Literacy
Cathy Collins Block, Series Editor

Literacy and Young Children
Research-Based Practices

Edited by
DIANE M. BARONE
LESLEY MANDEL MORROW

THE GUILFORD PRESS
New York   London

© 2003 The Guilford Press
A Division of Guilford Publications, Inc.
72 Spring Street, New York, NY 10012
www.guilford.com

Printed in the United States of America

Library of Congress Cataloging-in-Publication Data

Literacy and young children : research-based practices / edited by Diane
M. Barone and Lesley Mandel Morrow.
        p.   cm. — (Solving problems in the teaching of literacy)
Includes bibliographical references and index.
   ISBN 1-57230-820-6 (hardcover) — ISBN 1-57230-819-2 (pbk.)
   1. Reading (Early childhood)—United States.   2. Reading
teachers—In-service training—United States.   3. Literacy—United
States.   I. Barone, Diane M.   II. Morrow, Lesley Mandel.   III. Series.
LB1139.5.R43 L58   2003
372.4—dc21

                                                                    2002010221

About the Editors

Diane M. Barone, PhD, received her doctorate in literacy from the University of Nevada, Reno. She taught at the University of Nevada, Las Vegas, and is currently Professor of Literacy Studies at the University of Nevada, Reno. She teaches courses on early literacy, diversity issues in schools, and qualitative research. Dr. Barone's research centers on children in schools considered at risk. She has followed the literacy learning of children exposed prenatally to crack cocaine. Currently, she is studying 13 children through their entire elementary experience in a school designated at risk to document their literacy learning and instruction. Previously, Dr. Barone was Editor of *Reading Research Quarterly*.

Lesley Mandel Morrow, PhD, is Professor at Rutgers University's Graduate School of Education, where she is also Chairman of the Department of Learning and Teaching. She began her career as a classroom teacher, then became a reading specialist, and later received her doctorate from Fordham University. Her area of research focuses on early literacy development and the organization and management of language arts programs, carried out with children from diverse backgrounds.

Dr. Morrow has more than 200 publications that appear as journal articles, book chapters, monographs, and books, most recently *Literacy Development in the Early Years: Helping Children Read and Write* (4th ed., 2001, Allyn & Bacon), *The Literacy Center: Contexts for Reading and Writing* (2nd ed., 2001, Stenhouse), and *Organizing and Managing the Language Arts Block: A Professional Development Guide* (2003, Guilford Press). She is presently a researcher for the Center for the Improvement of Early Reading Research Achievement. She is also the vice president of the International Reading Association, to be president in 2003–2004.

Contributors

Bonnie Albertson, MA, Delaware Reading Project and Delaware Center for Teacher Education, School of Education, University of Delaware, Newark, Delaware

Diane M. Barone, EdD, Department of Curriculum and Instruction, University of Nevada, Reno, Nevada

V. Susan Bennett-Armistead, BS, College of Education, Michigan State University, East Lansing, Michigan

Renée M. Casbergue, PhD, Department of Curriculum and Instruction, University of New Orleans, New Orleans, Louisiana

Heather Casey, MEd, Graduate School of Education, Rutgers University, New Brunswick, New Jersey

Nell K. Duke, EdD, College of Education, Michigan State University, East Lansing, Michigan

Christine Evans, MI, Delaware Reading Project and Delaware Center for Teacher Education, School of Education, University of Delaware, Newark, Delaware

Irene W. Gaskins, EdD, Benchmark School, Media, Pennsylvania

Courtney Haworth, MEd, Graduate School of Education, Rutgers University, New Brunswick, New Jersey

Marcia Invernizzi, PhD, Reading Education, Department of Curriculum, Instruction, and Special Education, Curry School of Education, University of Virginia, Charlottesville, Virginia

Rachel A. Karchmer, PhD, Division of Teacher Education, School of Education, Virginia Commonwealth University, Richmond, Virginia

Barbara Krol-Sinclair, EdD, Intergenerational Literacy Project, Chelsea Public Schools, Chelsea, Massachusetts

Melanie Kuhn, PhD, Department of Teaching and Learning, Graduate School of Education, Rutgers University, New Brunswick, New Jersey

Lisa Lenhart, PhD, Department of Curriculum and Instructional Studies, University of Akron, Akron, Ohio

Donald J. Leu, Jr., PhD, Department of Curriculum and Instruction, University of Connecticut, Storrs, Connecticut

Marla H. Mallette, PhD, Department of Curriculum and Instruction, Southern Illinois University, Carbondale, Illinois

Lea M. McGee, EdD, Reading Education, College of Education, University of Alabama, Tuscaloosa, Alabama

Gigliana Melzi, PhD, Department of Applied Psychology, New York University, New York, New York

Lesley Mandel Morrow, PhD, Department of Learning and Teaching, Rutgers University, New Brunswick, New Jersey

Jeanne R. Paratore, EdD, Department of Developmental Studies and Counseling, School of Education, Boston University, Boston, Massachusetts

Mary Beth Plauché, MEd, Metairie Park Country Day School, Metairie, Louisiana

Ebony M. Roberts, PhD, College of Education, Michigan State University, East Lansing, Michigan

Kathleen Roskos, PhD, Department of Education and Allied Sciences, John Carroll University, University Heights, Ohio

Judith A. Schickedanz, PhD, Department of Curriculum and Teaching, School of Education, Boston University, Boston, Massachusetts

Steven A. Stahl, EdD, Reading Education, College of Education, University of Georgia, Athens, Georgia

William H. Teale, PhD, Department of Education, University of Illinois at Chicago, Chicago, Illinois

Carol Vukelich, PhD, Delaware Center for Teacher Education, School of Education, University of Delaware, Newark, Delaware

Shelley Hong Xu, EdD, Department of Teacher Education, College of Education, California State University, Long Beach, California

Preface

This edited volume grew out of a preconvention institute at the 2001 annual convention of the International Reading Association. The institute was centered in research-based practices that supported young children's literacy development. We coupled this work with engagement because we wanted to see young learners engaged with meaningful activities as they learned to read and write, not low-level skills-based assignments. A goal of this book is to have teachers see that using practices currently supported in research does not lead to dull and drill-oriented instruction, but rather to language-rich activities that support children's current levels of knowledge while moving them to more complex understandings of literacy. Another goal is to make teachers feel excited about instruction for young learners and to simultaneously provide them with exemplary instructional practices. In this volume we merge scientifically based instruction with descriptions of strategies and activities for carrying them out. However, scientific research does not always take into account individual differences among children and teachers. Therefore, the art of teaching incorporated in this book considers individual differences between children—for example, varying cultural backgrounds, experiences, and abilities. The importance of families, as they engage in literacy experiences with their children, is also emphasized.

Various chapters blend explicit instruction and constructivist problem solving. The authors, all leaders in the field of early literacy, talk about engaging young children in activities that help them learn concepts about books and print and comprehension of text. The authors of this book use a broad lens as they discuss early literacy, and each takes into account research, theory, and practice from the past and present and how it connects to exemplary teaching practices. Examples in the text are drawn from real classrooms, which makes them authentic and credible. Readers, especially teachers, can be assured that the strategies and activities presented here have been tried with real children in their classrooms.

The book is organized into five parts. The first section provides a foundation for later chapters in that it looks at professional development, general questions about early literacy learning and teaching, and a multi-dimensional approach to early literacy instruction. The second section considers the home literacy experiences of children and how teachers can build on these experiences to support students' literacy learning in their classrooms. The third section looks at important elements of early childhood classrooms that center on oral language, phonemic awareness, and the alphabetic principle. The fourth section considers newer research trends in early literacy that center on technology, fluency, and informational text. The book concludes with a chapter that encourages teachers to be thoughtful and cautious as they implement new strategies or activities.

The first four chapters present the foundation or grounding for this book. The chapter by Lesley Mandel Morrow, Heather Casey, and Courtney Haworth leads off. They explore the problems with previous models of staff development and present a newer, more collaborative way of working with teachers over time. They then share a 3-year staff development project that Morrow led, which included in-class support, observations and assessments, and discussion groups. The chapter includes two case studies that provide rich descriptions of how teachers enacted change in their classrooms. William H. Teale's chapter reviews the current state of knowledge about early literacy and suggests key questions that should be asked in four areas of the field: Theoretical Questions, Instructional Questions, Teacher Education Questions, and Policy Questions. He also poses questions that are currently receiving considerable attention but that do not merit such attention. This chapter provides a theoretical framework for considering the current debates about early literacy in research, education, and public policy. In her chapter, Irene W. Gaskins provides descriptions of instructional practices and experiences necessary to meet the learning needs of children acquiring literacy knowledge and understanding. Her multidimensional approach incorporates 12 issues and classroom characteristics—motivation, management, time, resources, variety, instruction, support, interaction, knowledge, practice, evaluation, and home–school communication. Throughout this chapter, research and practice are intertwined. The chapter supports the importance of the teacher in realizing achievement gains for students. Shelley Hong Xu's chapter demonstrates how the use of sociocultural approaches supports the early literacy learning of all children, and in particular those learning English as a new language in all-English classrooms. She presents two children, Qing and Maria, to demonstrate how the learner, teacher, text, and context intersect in learning and teaching. Finally,

Xu discusses research-based practices that facilitate the literacy learning of English language learners.

The next section focuses on the home literacy experiences of children. The chapters in this section provide evidence of the substantial literacy learning that is acquired by children as they interact with their parents and siblings. Lisa Lenhart and Kathleen Roskos tell of the early home literacy experiences of Hannah and Emma in their chapter. They observed that the home environment is powerful in shaping sibling literacy understandings. They also found that literacy served a social function for the sisters, that older siblings share their knowledge of literacy with younger siblings, that the younger siblings' learning was constructivist in nature, and that the younger sibling had a strong desire to become part of the literacy club. Through four conversational exchanges, the process of the sisters' literacy interactions are richly described. In the next chapter, Jeanne R. Paratore, Gigliana Melzi, and Barbara Krol-Sinclair write about the importance of family literacy to school learning success. They share the ways Latino families in one community reported their use of literacy and the factors that influenced these uses. They offer implications for ways in which teachers may build from these experiences to develop home–school literacy connections through the use of a monthly newsletter and a home literacy portfolio and by involving parents as classroom readers.

The third section is composed of three chapters that focus on phonemic awareness, code learning, and book acting. These chapters provide teachers with a repertoire of strategies for children as they learn about sounds and concepts associated with reading, writing, and speaking in English. Judith A. Schickedanz's chapter presents essential components of early literacy that affect a child's later success in learning to read and write. Threaded throughout this discussion are instances in which teachers have provided inadequate instruction, and Schickedanz reasons why this might be so. Her chapter concludes by providing strategies to overcome many of the barriers that hamper exemplary practice. Marcia Invernizzi's chapter is filled with activities to facilitate young children's learning of the concepts and vocabulary of print and sound, alphabet knowledge, and the concept of word. This chapter helps teachers provide concrete experiences to encourage the learning of very abstract language concepts. The last chapter in this section, written by Lea M. McGee, highlights the importance of storytelling and drama in the early literacy classroom. She shares a strategy called "Book Acting," in which children are involved in a story so deeply that they adopt its literary language, explore the characters' motivations, and try out multiple ways of being in a character's role. McGee builds a cogent argument as to why these activities are critical to children's literacy and language growth.

The next section presents the most recent trends in early literacy research, which include technology, fluency, and informational text. Rachel A. Karchmer, Marla H. Mallete, and Donald J. Leu, Jr., encourage teachers to consider the best practices in technology and early literacy and to expand on traditional book literacy understandings in their chapter. They provide strategies and resources to develop multiple literacies, which include reading Internet text, writing Internet text, navigating the Internet, participating in the global community, and evaluating Internet text. Steven A. Stahl's chapter focuses on struggling readers and how teachers can help these students develop fluency and motivation to read. He discusses text difficulty and strategies to support struggling readers that counter the traditional "keep it simple and make it concrete" philosophy. He encourages teachers to use thematic units, provide opportunities for struggling readers to look and feel like readers, and help them become members of the classroom community. Melanie Kuhn's chapter offers pragmatic guidelines so that teachers can provide systematic instruction in fluency for all students. She shares multiple strategies that move from unassisted to assisted interventions. Among the interventions are repeated readings, paired repeated readings, and readers' theater, among others. In the next chapter, Nell K. Duke, V. Susan Bennett-Armistead, and Ebony M. Roberts provide historical background on the use of narrative and informational text. They present an argument for the use of informational text in early childhood classrooms and they dispel several myths relating to the use of such text to support early literacy development. In their chapter, Renée M. Casbergue and Mary Beth Plauché offer teachers support in selecting informational books for young learners. They also provide suggestions to help teachers scaffold children's interactions with nonfiction books. This chapter includes many examples of children's writing in response to informational text. Carol Vukelich, Christine Evans, and Bonnie Albertson write about the organization of informational texts and how students can learn about the various types of organization in their chapter. They describe how teachers can use these texts for analysis and student modeling. They use the text *Outside and Inside Rats and Mice* (Markle, 2001) to give a concrete example of how teachers can foster such learning in their classrooms.

In Part V, the final chapter by Diane M. Barone cautions teachers to introduce new strategies and activities into their classrooms thoughtfully. Barone encourages teachers to consider all aspects of their classrooms as they try new strategies to support their students' literacy learning. She provides exemplary and not-so-exemplary implementations to help teachers think through the process of change.

All of the chapters in this book reflect the most current research-based practices for literacy instruction to foster the learning of young students. Each author shares the theory and research in which a particular practice is grounded. The authors have been careful to connect the research base with its practical applications so that teachers can more easily incorporate these strategies within their literacy instruction repertoires.

Each chapter honors the teacher and his or her value to the learning experiences of students. We all recognize that it is teachers who make a difference in the literacy development of children. It is they who implement research-based practices on a day-to-day basis and adjust these practices to best meet the needs and challenges of their students. It is our hope that this book serves as a valued resource for such exemplary instruction.

DIANE M. BARONE
LESLEY MANDEL MORROW

REFERENCE

Markle, S. (2001). *Outside and inside rats and mice*. New York: Atheneum.

Contents

PART III. PHONEMIC AWARENESS, CODE LEARNING, AND BOOK ACTING

PART IV. RECENT TRENDS IN LITERACY RESEARCH: TECHNOLOGY, FLUENCY, AND INFORMATIONAL TEXT

PART V. CONCLUSION

Part I

Foundations for Early Literacy Learning and Instruction

Part 1

1

Staff Development
for Early Literacy Teachers
A Plan to Facilitate Change

LESLEY MANDEL MORROW
HEATHER CASEY
COURTNEY HAWORTH

Current research dealing with early literacy development has created the need for change in classroom practice. To enable teachers to implement research-based best practices, professional skills should be enhanced regularly (Guskey, 1986). It is important to investigate *what* teachers must know, and *how* they are going to be informed about current information. The answer lies in carefully constructed staff development opportunities.

OBSTACLES IN PROMOTING CHANGE

Staff development programs are a systematic or forward attempt to change professional practice and beliefs for a specified goal. These programs have had only a small impact on bringing research-based practice into classrooms (Griffin, 1983). In the past, staff development programs have not been very effective. This is often blamed on teacher resistance. A teacher's reluctance to change may be part of the explanation, but it is not the only one.

Current research suggests that the practice of simply telling teachers what to do most often does not result in change and can actually foster

3

teacher resistance (Sparks & Loucks-Horsley, 1990). Studies have found that change is more likely to be effected by focusing on the *process* of teacher learning as well as the *product* (Sparks & Loucks-Horsley, 1990).

MODELS OF STAFF DEVELOPMENT

Existing models of staff development fall in three major categories: externally driven, teacher-initiated, and collaborative (Richardson, 1990). Externally driven models are those imposed on teachers, typically training workshops. Teacher-initiated programs are teacher-generated and provide teachers with some degree of control over the changes taking place. Collaborative models involve individuals from various perspectives working together to bring new ideas to the classroom (Richardson, 1990). Collaborative procedures are quite successful, because they give individual teachers control over the changes taking place and provide support and direction from colleagues, administrators, and/or researchers.

Research has shown that all three models can be successful if those in charge take key issues of adult learning theory into account. It has long been established that the goals of staff development include changes in teacher practice, student learning, and teacher beliefs and attitudes. Many staff development programs try to change teacher beliefs and attitudes first. This goes against the natural learning process of humans. Guskey (1986) concluded that the three goals of staff development are indeed important, but that these goals should be addressed in a different order. He recommended the following order.

The first goal staff developers should focus on is *changing classroom practices*. Experts should model the teaching practice they hope will be implemented. When teachers can observe *changes in student learning* as a result of the modeled activities, *changes in teacher beliefs and attitudes* will follow (Guskey, 1986). The theory underlying behind this approach is that changes in the learning outcomes of students may be a prerequisite for significant change in the beliefs and attitudes of teachers (Guskey, 1986).

As the National Staff Development Council (NSDC) and the National Association of Elementary School Principals (NAESP) developed standards for staff development, they incorporated psychological research on human learning about the process of change. The following are the principles of adult learning that the NSDC and the NAESP (1995) have found to be the most relevant for creating successful staff development programs:

- Adult learning experiences must be based on research and proven principles.
- Adult learning is ultimately self-directed.

- Independent and interdependent learning approaches are equally important to adults.
- Adults are motivated by clear and measurable outcomes and ongoing support.
- Change requires time, resources, and support structures.

Supporting teachers through any change is complicated. For staff development to be well received, research must be combined with practical experience when brought into schools. Staff development must address the real details of teachers' daily work lives, and must be in a form that provides intellectual stimulation (Goldenburg & Gallimore, 1991; Sparks, 1988). Staff developers have to understand that they are working with adult learners and must be aware of their needs.

ISSUES IN LITERACY DEVELOPMENT THAT SUGGEST THE NEED FOR CHANGE

Language arts programs must support the development of explicit skills as well as constructivist problem-solving activities. Often referred to as a balanced literacy program, this idea suggests that teachers emphasize both form (phonics, mechanics, etc.) and function (comprehension, purpose, meaning) and recognize that learning occurs effectively in a whole–part–whole context (Gambrell & Mazzoni, in press).

Studies that deal with teachers modeling effective and exemplary practices, specifically in the language arts, have found that these teachers' classrooms have the following characteristics (Morrow, Tracey, Woo, & Pressley, 1999; Pressley, Rankin, & Yokoi, 1996; Ruddell & Ruddell, 1995):

1. Varied teaching strategies to motivate literacy learning
2. High expectations for student accomplishment
3. Varied structures for instruction to meet individual needs, such as whole-group, small-group, and one-on-one settings with the teacher
4. Literacy-rich classroom environment with accessible materials
5. Careful organization and management of materials
6. Opportunities for children to practice skills taught
7. Guidance in structured lessons for acquisition of skills
8. Opportunities for children to work independently or in collaborative groups

This chapter discusses a 3-year staff development project that implemented theory about adult learning to help teachers change their instruction. In addition, the goal was to foster exemplary practice, or a balanced approach, to literacy instruction. Another major purpose of the project was to develop a model of effective staff development for teachers, supervisors, and administrators. Regardless of position or level of authority, all educators interested in facilitating change can find something in this model to implement.

CREATING SUCCESSFUL STAFF DEVELOPMENT IN THE LANGUAGE ARTS

A project was undertaken to identify specific aspects of staff development that seem to promote change in teacher behavior. The project, which was a collaborative effort between a school district and a university in the northeastern United States, emphasized change in literacy practices as a result of a staff development program that focused on the teachers as adult learners.

One of the goals of the staff development program was to help teachers create a balanced approach to literacy instruction through the reorganization of their language arts block. More specifically, there would be a transition from whole-group literacy instruction to small-group guided reading instruction and the development of literacy centers with independent work for students to use while teachers work with small groups. Creating a literacy-rich environment was another goal, through the use of word walls, morning messages, and so forth. The emphasis on classroom environment was for the purpose of supporting instructional practice.

Participants

Ten female teachers participated in the project, ranging in age from age 24 to 54. All taught in the same urban setting in preschool through third-grade classrooms. All had an opportunity to work collaboratively with their colleagues and faculty from a nearby university in an effort to improve the language arts education in their schools.

The university faculty worked with this district on a regular basis. The schools were referred to as Professional Development Schools (PDS). The staff development project was a joint effort between the teachers, administrators, and university faculty. The teachers were to work in collaboration with each other as they moved toward making changes in their literacy programs (Richardson, 1990).

Procedures

The project consultant created a staff development model to support the teachers as learners. The 3-year staff development project used the following techniques:

1. Administrative support for the project prior to beginning
2. Volunteer participation of teachers, to ensure interest in the project

3. A 14-week course on early literacy development to enhance knowledge
4. Goals to be accomplished set by teachers
5. A student aide provided for each teacher to help accomplish goals
6. Classroom observations by the consultant and an assistant to monitor progress
7. Teacher discussion groups to foster collaboration and reflection
8. Encouragement of teachers to become leaders in fostering change

Setting Individual Goals a Part of the Course Requirement

The teachers began their staff development with a 14-week course that met for 3 hours each week. Assignments for the teachers were tailored to fit their needs. The intent of the course was to expand teachers' knowledge of small-group guided reading instruction, assessment in guided reading groups, and center activities for independent learning. Because the teachers varied in personal needs, it was necessary to allow them to set their own goals related to what was being taught.

Facilitating Goals

To facilitate accomplishment of the individual goals of each participant, the teachers were provided with a packet of lesson plans entitled *Organizing and Managing the Language Arts Block* (Morrow, 2002). The plans were designed with the teachers in mind and included the following:

1. Independent activities when children arrive at school
2. The morning meeting
3. Center work
4. Guided reading
5. Assessment
6. Writers' workshop

The teachers selected plans from the packet to help carry out their goals. It was anticipated that each teacher would also draw information from the lectures, readings, discussions, and demonstrations that related to her goal.

In-Class Support

To facilitate the incorporation of goals, each teacher was assigned a student aide from the university who worked with the teacher once a week for 3 hours each time. In addition, there was a graduate student, who was an experienced teacher, who acted as a coach for those who needed further direction.

Observations and Assessments

The researcher and her research assistant observed the teachers regularly. After each observation, they met with the teacher to discuss current strategies and techniques the teacher could be using to create a more balanced literacy program. It was during these meetings that the three also reviewed the materials needed for change.

Teacher Discussion Groups

The teachers and the consultant met once a month for 2 hours after school to discuss and reflect on the changes taking place in their classrooms. After the 14-week course ended, the participating teachers continued meeting to update each other on their progress and to address any issues that arose during the period of classroom change. The teachers also observed one another's classrooms.

Observation Information

Information was gathered through observations of the teachers, from teacher discussion sessions, from individual interviews, and through reflective surveys. Discussion groups were taperecorded, and notes were taken as well. During the first year, teachers were observed every 2 weeks during the language arts block, for a total of 20 hours per teacher. Notes were taken as to the skills taught, the strategies used, the environmental design of the classrooms, and the materials used. There was an effort to note the practices used by the teacher when the program began, what the classroom was like in the middle of the program, and at the end.

The teachers were asked to fill out three reflective surveys. The first survey was designed to obtain information about each teacher's attitude toward change. The second provided a chance for the teachers to reflect on their initial goals and to modify them if necessary. The third and last survey asked teachers how they had changed, what had made them change, and how they would continue to change. The surveys and observations offered a broad picture of each teacher's progress and enabled researchers to examine the types of changes that took place and to what extent they could be considered successful.

What Was Discovered?

The following section presents descriptions of two of the ten teachers with whom we worked. They were selected because they were representative of the two different groups that emerged, based on the observations of all the teachers. These two teachers, like all the others, made changes to their classrooms. The following descriptions illustrate that the goals set by two of the teachers, and their perspectives toward change, were quite different.

One of the teachers was very enthusiastic about the staff development program. She started out with goals that were easily accomplished, but as time went on she became more ambitious with her goals. The second teacher needed only minor work for change, inasmuch as she already used many of the strategies discussed in the staff development program. This teacher, however, was more resistant to change.

The teachers in the group differed in age, years of experience, their attitude toward change, and the types of changes undertaken. Change proved to be very personal. Yet, whether young or old, expert or novice, positive about change or hesitant, teachers did change. As the following case studies trace and analyze the progress each teacher made toward her stated goals, they discuss how the individual teachers handled change and identify the factors that facilitated this change.

CASE STUDY 1: SARAH

Background Information

Sarah is a kindergarten teacher in an at-risk urban setting. In her 24 years as an educator, she has been a classroom teacher and a reading specialist. She is in her early 50s, married, with one adult child. She is an enthusiastic teacher with a lot of patience and energy. Sarah admits, "I'm a bit slow with change, but I'm willing to think about it and then try. If there's an idea I like, I'll try it, but I'm not going with everything. If I see things are not working, I'll try something else."

Sarah will incorporate new ideas into her classroom, but likes to be well informed about the concept and appreciates having a choice as to whether to use different ideas. She admits she needs to be nudged by administrators and colleagues, but it is ultimately her own desire to become a better teacher that has kept her interested in the PDS program. She said, "When I try new things and they work, it makes me feel proud when other teachers ask me about what I am doing in my classroom." It was interesting to watch Sarah over the 3 years. During the first year, she made a few small changes; in the second, she became more willing to listen and try more. In the third year, her change was dynamic.

Sarah's Goals

Although Sarah was always enthusiastic, her goals in the first year were modest. She admitted that she was in the program because her building principal strongly suggested that she participate. Sarah decided that she wanted to enhance her classroom environment with a literacy center that would encourage the students to read or look at books. This became her goal for the first year. To accomplish the goal, she asked her student aide to arrange the books in baskets according to categories. All the changes that occurred were directed by Sarah, but her student aide carried them out.

In her second year Sarah worked on creating a rich literacy environment in her classroom. She labeled materials, created a word wall, and posted class rules. These were all things she had never done before.

In the third year Sarah made major changes. After the first review session at the beginning of the school year, Sarah was definitive about what she wanted to achieve. She announced that her main goal for this year was "To make my classroom a place where students' individual needs are met, where all students develop at their own pace, and to the best of their abilities. I want each of my students to feel confident and capable about literacy and about him- or herself." In the third year of the project Sarah began to see a need to individualize her reading instruction. To achieve this goal, she began to move toward guided reading groups. This led her to focus on creating better center work to keep children on task while they worked independently during the guided reading group period. Finally, Sarah needed to find new and better ways of assessing students. She stated, "I'm learning that there is a lot of stuff that I didn't know, and you can always get better. I didn't see the value of what was being presented when we started. Somehow now it is coming together for me, and it has taken 3 years."

Sarah's Classroom Environment

Before the Program Began

Before she participated in the Literacy Project, Sarah's classroom was a typical kindergarten room, with a dramatic play area, bookshelves for the library, round tables for the students, a block area, a playhouse, and decorated walls. But it was not a literacy-rich environment.

Since the Program Began

Sarah has made changes to her classroom environment since the program began. She has consciously incorporated more literacy materials into the room. For example, she arranged the books in her literacy center to be more accessible. She ordered an open-faced bookshelf to display thematic books. She began to introduce new books regularly to entice children to use the literacy center. Sarah began a word wall to build on with her students throughout the year. She began labeling parts of her room, such as the "Book Nook," and "Helper Chart." She has also added a large erasable board with markers near the Book Nook so that the children can draw and write. Sarah ordered and hung a pocket chart near her literacy center that helps with lessons for sequencing sentences, building words, matching letters with pictures, and the like. She has a bright rug and a big wooden rocking chair that she uses to define an area for whole-group lessons, story reading, or retellings.

Sarah rearranged the seating in the room as well. The children are divided into heterogeneous groups of five at four different tables. She has designated two extra tables for small-group reading instruction. One table is for materials, and one for the children.

Small-Group Reading in Sarah's Room

Before the Program Began

A main goal for Sarah was to become confident in using small-group reading in her classroom. She was accustomed to teaching in a whole-group setting whereby the same instruction was given to the entire class. She commented, "I used to try to teach to the middle level; however, lately I've felt frustrated. I realized that the high-level students were ready for more sophisticated lessons and the lower-level students were struggling to keep up." She recognized that she needed a better format for teaching literacy skills. She noted, "Small-group reading instruction has forced me to look at kids' needs."

Since the Program Began

Through the staff development program, Sarah had access to information and support for implementing reading groups in her classroom. She experimented with this information, read books on the topic, and asked for advice from the consultant and other teachers in the school.

Sarah has begun to group children according to their needs, and as children progress or need more work on specific skills, she *regroups*. Sarah selects her groups by, "putting together students who have similar needs and abilities." Sarah realized that she needed the materials for the guided reading lessons to be easily accessible and well organized, so she created a "guided reading tub." This is a large plastic container in which Sarah stores each group's books and materials. In the tub are leveled books, folders, and manipulative materials, such as magnetic letters, for teaching skills. Small-group reading lessons are of many different forms in Sarah's classroom, because this is kindergarten and most children are not conventional readers. In the following lesson, Sarah is helping a group to match uppercase and lowercase letters.

TEACHER: Let's review the letters *B*, *D*, and *P* that we learned about a while ago. Can you find the upper- and lowercase *B*, *D*, and *P* cards?

(*The children begin to sift through the letters, looking for them.*)

TEACHER: (after the letters are found) Very good! Now I want you to find the big and little letters for your names, so Jose will look for the big *J* and the little *j*, Edward will look for the big *E* and the little *e*, and Nichelli will look for the big *N* and the little *n*.

Again, the children sift through the letters. One child finds another's letter and gives it to him. Sarah commends the student for recognizing other letters. Within a few minutes and with just a little prompting from Sarah ("Oh, you're close to your letter, I can see it"), the children find their letters. She then gives them erasable boards.

TEACHER: Try and write the letters you just found and your first names.

(*The children write their names. She then helps them with their last names by writing them on a 5 × 8 card and then having them copy what she wrote. She takes notes about the children as they are writing.*)

TEACHER: Now write down all the letters of the alphabet that you know, and look around the room at labels that will help you. (*She takes notes while the children write the letters.*) That was great, Jose, I saw you look up at the letter train on the wall to find letters you needed to write.

At first, Sarah found herself constantly being interrupted during her guided reading lessons, and asked for help. Based on input from a colleague and the consultant, Sarah spent time before and in between the guided reading groups, walking around the room talking to students at centers to see that they were on task.

Sarah's goals for guided reading included organizing the groups properly and acquiring more materials such as leveled books. After doing guided reading for a few months, she realized that she needed a better way to keep notes on each group's performance. She created a chart similar to one demonstrated at the staff development sessions, which she filled in after each guided reading session. This system allowed her to keep notes on student progress and plan for future lessons.

Sarah started by having guided reading once a week and now does it three or four times a week. She was concerned that this approach would not go as smoothly without the student aide present, but since the aide left Sarah felt that it is still going well and she really likes doing it. Sarah said,

"Guided reading allows me to have quality time with my students. When you work with them in small groups, you get to know what they know and what they don't know, and what instruction is appropriate. I've found that this year, since starting the guided reading groups, I know more about the children I teach than I ever did before."

Centers in Sarah's Room

Before the Program Began

Sarah originally did not have independent center activities in her classroom. She had several activities that the children worked on in small groups, but they only occasionally incorporated literacy skills. She was concerned about the ability of her students to work independently, stay on task, and be accountable for what they were working on. Sarah was also concerned about the amount of planning time needed and acquiring the appropriate materials for the various centers recommended for the program. However, she said, "I'll give it a try."

Since the Program Began

Sarah has implemented the use of independent center work while she does guided reading. She has four or five independent center activities and one teacher-directed center. Her centers include a book nook, math center, science center, and a computer for writing. One of the centers deals with a concept students are working on at the time. Sarah has a student leader for each center who attempts to resolve problems as they arise. This helps decrease the number of distractions during her guided reading lesson. She said, "Students need to be engaged without the teacher, so activities should be at an independent student level."

Sarah models the activities at each center before assigning students to it. She makes sure that everyone is engaged at his or her center activity and then calls the designated children for their guided reading. Each activity center has four to five children in it, and the activities alternate with guided reading lessons. Sarah said, "I like center activities because they allow the children to be in charge of their learning. They teach students to cooperate with each other and help to develop leadership qualities."

Assessment

Before the Program Began

Before participating in the program, Sarah used daily work samples as her major source for assessment. Feeling she needed more information to reflect student progress, she set a goal of investigating assessment measures.

Since the Program Began

Sarah decided to try portfolio assessment in her classroom, which she learned about in the staff development program. For the portfolios, she now collects daily work samples, observations, and anecdotal records. She collects language samples by taperecording students' story retellings, which she evaluates for sense of story structure and to measure comprehension as well as language development.

Changes Made Through the Staff Development Program

The staff development program helped Sarah with some major changes in her classroom. She said, "Many teachers won't try new things. Sometimes it is because they are burned out and because the district keeps asking them to do so many things without time to learn about them and without the help needed for implementation. The best way to foster change in teachers is to introduce ideas through the use of a consultant and to demonstrate strategies using videotapes of real teachers teaching. The lesson plans we had were very helpful. I also found that visiting other classrooms to see live teachers doing these strategies was extremely valuable. It is very important to realize that change happens slowly. I liked our discussion groups because we needed to talk to each other about change." Sarah went on to say, "The discussion meetings helped me a lot because we talked with our peers, exchanged ideas, and got advice from the consultant."

CASE STUDY 2: TRACI

Background Information

Traci is a second-grade teacher. She is in her early 30s, married, with one child. She has been teaching for 9 years and has taught first, second, fourth, and sixth grades. She has an upbeat attitude and is intent on making her classroom an ideal setting for learning. She hopes to become a "model" teacher, but in spite of the fact that she is an excellent teacher, she does not adjust well to change.

The changes that Traci could make to her program were minimal. Traci's room needed some reorganization of materials. When asked whether she would consider organizing the information on the walls in her classroom, she said, "Don't touch my mess, I like it the way it is." Although she knew her room needed some organizing, she was reluctant to change.

Traci is creative in the activities she plans for her children and in getting the students on task. When she notices that the children seem tired, for example, she pulls out a purple bottle she calls "brain spray" and sprays it into the air to activate and motivate their minds. The bottle is actually air freshener. She enforces class rules but has an excellent affective relationship with her class. She shares her enthusiasm for learning with the children.

Traci's Goals

Originally, Traci did not set any goals. Although these roles were never defined, she became a self-appointed mentor to the other teachers and an assistant to the consultant. She had an open-door policy for project participants. She made herself available for consultation at any time during the day. As mentioned, Traci did not set goals for the first or second year. In the third year she was more open to change.

We realized that Traci needed to notice things that should be changed in her room rather than being told. One staff development session focused on organizing and managing independent work in a way that made children accountable for what they do. We watched videotapes and visited classrooms of teachers with exemplary management skills. Very quietly, Traci took the consultant aside and said, "I think I need to improve the organization of my independent center time when children work on their own. After watching that tape and visiting that classroom, I think my kids aren't on task enough, and it might be that I'm not asking them to be accountable for completing tasks."

Another important goal that Traci set was to work on teaching more skills during guided reading. Traci understood grouping and some guided reading strategies, but she could go further. At the beginning of the staff development program, Traci was a leader in the group. She was already using many of the strategies discussed. As time went on, however, she did not change. During the first year, Traci offered a great deal of help to teachers who were just getting started with some of the strategies. Throughout the second year, she took the same role. During this time, the other teachers were implementing new ideas and continually refining their instruction. In the third year, Traci suddenly realized that she did need to change. She felt she needed to improve skill development in guided reading and to organize her centers so students were more accountable.

Traci's Classroom Environment

Before the Program Began

At the beginning of the program, the centers and furniture in Traci's room appeared to be cluttered. The following was written by her student aide:

> "Traci said that the students didn't seem comfortable in her centers any more and it seemed as if they didn't know where to find things. I suggested that first we reorganize the literacy center. It was too cluttered

and children couldn't sit anywhere and be comfortable and read. Books were not categorized, and they were not leveled to inform students of their difficulty. I helped Traci figure out how to level her books and store them in a categorized system on her bookshelves."

Since the Program Began

During the first two years of the program Traci resisted changing her environment, but during the third year she came to us for help. Once we got her going, Traci was inspired to continue on her own. She reorganized the furniture to display several different, clearly defined centers. The materials were labeled and placed in containers in the math and art centers. The books in the literacy center were divided into levels and genres. She outfitted the writing center with different writing paper and erasable miniboards. The desks were placed in pods of four and angled across the center of the room. Clean pillows replaced the old soiled ones.

These initial changes did improve her classroom, but she didn't stop. During the course of the third year Traci kept moving things on a regular basis to try to make improvements. Each time she worked on the room, it looked more spacious. Her bulletin boards were now defined, and she was reorganizing them regularly to match the theme the class was working on.

Guided Reading

Before the Program Began

Another goal selected by Traci was to improve her guided reading instruction. Traci had been doing guided reading for a while and felt comfortable with it in her classroom. She was aware of the benefits of small-group instruction for individual students. She said, "I like the fact that I get to have the kids in small groups. I really get to focus on individual needs. And I like to see the growth that they're making. I believe that children benefit from guided reading since they have one-on-one attention from the teacher." As a goal, Traci decided to systematize instruction more than she had to be sure she was emphasizing skills.

Since the Program Began

Now when asked about guided reading, Traci says, "I try to provide personal attention that students need in guided reading and get right down to business. I realized recently that I was quite pleased with getting into the structure of doing guided reading, I hadn't thought about the lessons as well. I need to be sure I am teaching skills." The following is an example of how focused her guided reading sessions have become in her second-grade class. Traci read aloud:

> I fell down hard
> And broke a bone
> I got a cast and went back home
> Dad read me books and told me jokes
> I ate a chocolate ice cream cone
> It's not so bad to break a bone!

The students were asked to discover things they knew about the print in the words in the passage before they read. When they finished reading together, they were asked to let the group hear their discoveries.

CHILD 1: There are one-syllable words—*so, bone, bad.*

CHILD 2: There is a title and an author.

CHILD 3: *Fell* has short *e. It's* is a contraction.

CHILD 4: *Books* is a plural.

CHILD 2: *Got* has short *o.*

TEACHER: What words are plural without an *s?*

CHILD 1: *Mice, sheep, feet, fish, people, children, geese, teeth.*

CHILD 2: Bones are inside the body.

CHILD 3: *Read* makes a long *e* sound.

TEACHER: That was excellent, you really found a lot of things in that passage. Now let's take just one of those, the short *o* sound. (*Traci then focused on short o in a mini-lesson.*)

Traci's new guided reading routine of walking the children through the text, using various cues, is based on her exposure to guided reading instruction through the staff development program.

Centers

Before the Program Began

Before participating in the program, Traci did not recognize that her center time was disorganized. She did not have a system for assigning students to centers, and she did not require any accountability for the work done. She also did not know how to ensure that the children would stay on task. It took until the third year of the program for Traci to discover that the staff development program, with its lectures, videos, visits, and discussions with other teachers, was causing her to realize the necessity for change.

Since the Program Began

It is apparent that Traci spent a good amount of time creating the activities for the centers in her classroom during the third year of the program. She has 14 different centers to assign students to: computer, listening, oral language, writing, newspaper, book nook, art, social studies, research, math, pocket chart, science, learning games, and activity sheets. Traci commented, "I love centers. They provide many ways to reinforce skills and meet the individual needs of students. They allow me time to work closely with small groups since the others are working independently."

The staff development program provided Traci with several ideas for organizing the center work. She chose to adopt the idea of the sign-in sheet, which shows which students were at which centers. In addition, she made a center wheel with various colors signifying the various centers that can be used. As students select a center, they put their clothespins with their name on it on the color of the center they are working in. She also chose to use center folders to organize their center work. Periodically, she evaluates the work in the folders to see what the children are accomplishing and what their needs are. She uses this information for report cards.

Before center time begins, Traci informs the students about the areas that are open, how much time they have to work, and the activities available at each center. With this new organization, Traci says, her students enjoy the activities more than ever and almost everyone is on task. She checks on the students during center time to make sure they understand what they are to do.

Traci has incorporated several useful tactics from the staff development program, and her center time is now quite structured. Traci notes, "You really have to teach your kids how to be independent and responsible for completing work."

Changes Facilitated by the Staff Development Program

The staff development program helped Traci to better organize the physical space of her classroom. It also helped her to better organize her instruction during guided reading lessons. Traci reflected:

> "The thing that influenced me to change the most was the realization that my students' needs were not being met and therefore they were not reaching their full potential. Soon after I started to change my instruction, I began to see change. The students were now capable of what was

being asked of them. This was true for my guided reading lessons and in the center work as well."

Reassured by the positive results in her students' achievements, Traci continued to make improvements. Guskey (1986) notes, "When teachers see the effects new instructional techniques have on student achievement, they are more likely to incorporate the techniques into their classroom. Evidence of improvement (positive change) in the learning outcomes of students generally precedes and may be a prerequisite to significant change in the beliefs and attitudes of most teachers" (p. 7). Traci felt assured that the children were making greater gains from the changes she had made in her literacy program, and consequently she was inspired to move forward.

HOW THE PROFESSIONAL DEVELOPMENT PROJECT HELPED TO CREATE CHANGE

It is interesting to note that *significant change* did not happen until the third year of the project. Sarah believed that the consultant's role was necessary to disseminate the information and provide support for change. She also found that it was equally important to work with other teachers in her school. She said:

"I found that it was extremely helpful to have someone observe me and give suggestions based on my needs. Visiting other teachers' rooms and meeting with each other was very beneficial. I enjoyed taking the course and applying the information based on my personal needs. The lesson plans for me to use made change easy."

Sarah spoke most favorably about the information sessions led by the university consultant, in which she was able to learn about best practices and view them in action via videotapes and classroom visitations. She enjoyed sharing the work of her students and discussing the changes in her classroom environment and teaching techniques. For example, Sarah took her children on a field trip to a farm and related this anecdote: "When we got to the farm, the children noticed that the sheep had numbers branded on them. One child said, 'Hey, Mrs. R., those sheep have labels like we label the room, but we put words in our room and they used numbers. That isn't right, they should label the sheep with their names.' " The children were transferring what they were learning in school to other situations.

Overall, Sarah's year was filled with one success after another. The researcher commented, "Sarah had a definite agenda. Once she determined her goals, she did what was necessary to achieve them." At the end of the year Sarah stated that she still felt as though she had a lot to learn about teaching reading through small-group reading instruction, but now thought she had learned a lot, and, more important, had the motivation to keep on learning. She intends to remain active in the Professional Development Project: "I will definitely participate in meetings with the consultant and my peers. I will also be happy to help other teachers who may want to begin guided reading in their classrooms." The skeptic for the first two years had become a believer in the third.

Traci's story was a bit different from Sarah's. First impressions of Traci suggested that she was a leader and a good teacher who was confident in her abilities. This confidence allowed her to act more as a mentor to the other teachers than as a participant in the staff development project. This same confidence, however, got in the way of her implementing change in the first two years.

Traci told us that at the beginning of the project she did not think she needed to change, because what was described as goals for staff development she was already doing. She finally realized that she did need to make some changes when she observed that her colleagues were moving forward while she was standing still. This encouraged her to look more carefully at her own classroom practices. It was then she realized that she had many of the procedures and strategies required for balanced literacy in place, but the disorganization of the physical environment, the mess she loved so much, was impacting her instruction. As Traci began to make both her room and her instruction more orderly, she was delighted with the results. She learned to listen more at meetings and look more carefully at what was being presented by both her colleagues and the consultant. She began to realize that being a good teacher was not just a matter of sharing what *you* did well with others, but was also about being receptive to what others could do well. The teacher-leader of the first two years had become a true learner in the third.

CONCLUSIONS

This project demonstrated that learners of all ages require the same types of experiences to ensure that learning takes place. We know from the literature that teachers need similar contexts for learning as they provide for their students. Therefore, we created learning experiences that have been found to facilitate change. In considering these experiences, the ten teachers listed the following as the elements that were most important in promoting change:

1. Accessible information.
2. Flexible goals.

3. Accessible materials.
4. Collaboration with peers.
5. Administrative support.
6. Working with a consultant.
7. Modeling guides to support change.
8. Time for change to occur.

Although no two teachers rated these factors equally, the breadth of this project enabled each one to find the support needed to change.

Our analysis of the case studies of the 10 teachers in this project demonstrated that motivation for change is highly individual. All of the teachers, regardless of experience, age, and willingness to participate, made changes in their programs. Some were more intrinsically motivated than others, and some needed more extrinsic motivation to learn and change. Those more resistant to change were likely to set goals that appeared easy for them to accomplish and seemed to ensure quick success. These teachers selected activities such as "Morning Message" or creating a word wall as part of their goals. Those that were more confident and able to take risks attempted small-group guided reading and allowed children to work independently in centers. With one success, no matter how small, all of the teachers were willing to continue to take another step.

Investigating the change process in teachers, and in particular in Sarah and Traci, provides further insight for staff developers. Despite their differences in style and previous knowledge, the factors that influenced their changes are quite similar. In both cases, these teachers needed background knowledge, support from the administration and their colleagues, objectives and deadlines, and *time* for peer discussions. Although they started at different points, it took both Sarah and Traci until the third year of this project to make significant changes. Change does not happen overnight, and it cannot be neatly packaged in a single workshop or meeting. Instead, it is a *process* that involves multiple participants and varied experiences.

In our staff development project we were helping teachers to create literacy-rich environments and a balanced language arts program that would be developmentally appropriate, meaningful, interactive, and cooperative as well as independent. We hoped that teachers would use multiple measures for assessing children and offer positive and constructive feedback to them. The teachers moved forward and are continuing to do so in their quest to create a more balanced literacy program. This is a journey that has no end. It will always be necessary to provide staff development in the area of language arts to find the best way for all children to succeed.

The variety of the staff development approaches that the teachers in this project rated as effective suggests that there are many ways to begin, or to continue, the change process. It may not be feasible for every school or district to take on a staff development program of this magnitude. There are pieces of this model, however, that can be implemented with relative ease. Teachers can form study groups with one another to pursue common interests. Supervisors who lack funds for university consultants can arrange time for teachers to visit one another's classrooms. Administrators who do not have access to university students can arrange for interested high school students to become aides. Most important, both supervisors and administrators can provide *support* and *time* for teachers embarking on new endeavors. The possibilities are endless. As this project has demonstrated, there is more than one approach to effective staff development, and all educators, from teachers to administrators, have a role to play in facilitating change.

REFERENCES

Gambrell, L. B., & Mazzoni, S. A. (in press). Principles of best practice: Finding the common ground. In L. M. Morrow, L. M. Gambrell, & M. M. Pressley (Eds.), *Best practices in literacy instruction* (pp. 11–21). New York: Guilford Press.

Goldenberg, C., & Gallimore, R. (1991). Changing teaching takes more than a one-shot workshop. *Educational Leadership, 49*(3), 69–72.

Griffin, G. A. (1983). Introduction: The work of staff development. In G. A. Griffin (Ed.), *Staff development: Eighty-second yearbook of the National Society for the Study of Education* (pp. 1–12). Chicago: University of Chicago Press.

Guskey, T. (1986). Staff development and the process of teacher change. *Educational Researcher, 15*(5), 5–15.

Morrow, L. M. (2002). *Organizing and managing the language arts block: A professional development guide.* New York: Guilford Press.

Morrow, L. M., Tracey, D., Woo, D., & Pressley, M. (1999). Characteristics of exemplary first-grade literacy instruction. *The Reading Teacher, 52*(5), 462–476.

National Staff Development Council & National Association of Elementary School Principals. (1995). *Standards for staff development: Elementary school edition.* Alexandria, VA: NSDC.

Pressley, M., Rankin, J., & Yokoi, L. (1996). A survey of the instructional practices of outstanding primary level literacy teachers. *Elementary School Journal, 96,* 363–384.

Richardson, V. (1990). Significant and worthwhile change in teaching practice. *Educational Researcher, 19,* 10–18.

Ruddell, R. B., & Ruddell, M. R. (1995). *Teaching children to read and write: Becoming an influential teacher.* Boston: Allyn & Bacon.

Sparks, D., & Loucks-Horsley, S. (1990). Models of staff development. In R. Houston (Ed.), *Handbook of research on teacher education* (3rd ed., pp. 234–250). New York: Macmillan.

Sparks, G. (1988). Teachers' attitudes toward change and subsequent improvements in classroom teaching. *Journal of Educational Psychology, 80*(1), 111–117.

2

Questions about Early Literacy Learning and Teaching That Need Asking— and Some That Don't

WILLIAM H. TEALE

Early childhood development and early childhood education are hot items these days. Brain research, Head Start, early education opportunities, early intervention, and many other issues related to funding, policies, facilities, and curriculum for young children seem omnipresent in both professional and public media. During the late 1990s, the Clinton administration initiated a series of White House Conferences on Early Childhood that has continued through the present administration. In July 2001, for example, First Lady Laura Bush hosted the White House Summit on Early Childhood Cognitive Development—Ready to Read, Ready to Learn. Said Mrs. Bush, "The years from the crib to the classroom represent a period of intense language and cognitive growth. Armed with the right information, we can make sure every child learns to read and reads to learn" (*http://www. ed.gov/PressReleases/07-2001/07262001.html*).

In 2000, the Education Commission of the States began a 2-year initiative focused on three key areas: expanding the national dialogue about the importance of early care and learning, providing the best information available on what works in early education policy and programs, and helping states implement their early childhood agendas. That initiative has had significant impact on governors and their education and early childhood policies.

The *Education Week* publication *Quality Counts 2002: Building*

Blocks for Success serves as another example of the considerable attention being paid to early education. This document examines the states' activities in providing early learning experiences for young children, the quality of the experiences offered, and the preparation and pay of early childhood educators, and evaluates the results of early childhood programs. The report is centered on the idea that "when it comes to early learning, quality counts, just as it does in K–12 education" (*http://www.edweek.org/sreports/qc02/templates/article.cfm?slug=17exec.h21*).

Perhaps most influential during the coming years will be President Bush's "No Child Left Behind" policy embodied in the No Child Left Behind Act of 2001 (Reauthorization of the Elementary and Secondary Education Act, ESEA) (*http://www.ed.gov/inits/backtoschool/teachers/index.html*). Literacy education, especially literacy education during the preschool and primary grade years, is a cornerstone of this act. Bush has indicated that he is committed to "promoting the very best teaching programs, especially those that teach young children how to read." The Reading First Initiative focuses both on reading in early grades (getting states to establish a "comprehensive K–2 reading program anchored in scientific research") and on early childhood reading instruction (funding to implement "research-based pre-reading methods" in preschool programs, including Head Start centers) (*http://www.ed.gov/inits/nclb/part2.html*).

Clearly, literacy is figuring heavily in all of this attention to early education and development. Whether it is public preschool or primary grades education as embodied in the ESEA reauthorization, early intervention programs like Reach Out and Read (*http://www.reachoutandread.org/*) or Born to Read (*http://www.ala.org/alsc/born.html*), the HeadsUp! Reading Initiative that provides online professional development in early literacy to Head Start teachers (*http://www.huronline.org*), or the main principle behind the Bush educational agenda—ensuring that every child can read by the third grade—it is clear that the initial years of the 21st century are quickly evolving into an era of public policy that pays considerable attention to early literacy education.

This period can be seen as one that offers unprecedented opportunities for teachers and researchers to promote early literacy. But it should also be recognized that many issues, perspectives, programs, and policies related to early literacy learning and teaching are vying for recognition and endorsement at this time. Although some would have us believe that the *scientific* evidence is abundant and points clearly to what needs to be done to get children off to a proper start in literacy (and thereby significantly raise reading and writing achievement during the primary grades and subsequent years), I believe we have a number of critical questions that need to be asked—and answered—to fulfill such a goal. This chapter offers a perspective on the current state of knowledge about early literacy and suggests a number of key questions, the answers to which can help move us forward professionally and politically to ensure that we make available the best possible early literacy instruction.

The questions that need to be asked are organized into four areas: Theoretical Questions, Instructional Questions, Teacher Education Questions, and Policy Questions. Also discussed is another category of questions—those currently receiving considerable attention but which, for reasons that are discussed, do not seem to merit the degree of attention they are being given. The overall intent of this chapter is to provide a framework for considering current early literacy issues and directions related to research, education, and public policy.

QUESTIONS THAT SHOULD BE ASKED

Theoretical Questions

Theoretical understandings related to early literacy development form the foundation on which practical decisions about issues such as instruction and policy are made. There is a robust theoretical literature in the field of early literacy. It consists primarily of research on oral language development (see, e.g., Bloom, 1993; Wells, 1985), the past 20 years of work in emergent literacy (see, e.g., Teale & Sulzby, 1986b; Yaden, Rowe, & MacGillivray, 2000), and a considerable body of research on beginning reading (see, e.g., Adams, 1990; Ehri, 1994; Snow, Burns, & Griffin, 1998), all of which draw upon contributions from fields such as linguistics, cognitive psychology, child development, and anthropology. Social constructivist perspectives provide a helpful interpretive frame for understanding the body of literature, and both empirical research and ethnographic work contribute to current theoretical understandings in early literacy.

As has historically been the case (Teale, 1995), theoretical differences in the field persist, but the past decade has also seen some consensus arise about the nature of early literacy learning, development, and teaching (see, e.g., Dickinson & Tabors, 2001; Snow et al., 1998; Stanovich, 2000). Still, significant gaps in our theoretical understandings remain. I see three major questions whose answers would help move theoretical knowledge about early literacy forward significantly:

• *What does typical literacy development look like across the early childhood years?* Despite the existing descriptions of literacy development from birth through grade 3 that can be found in reputable sources like *Preventing Reading Difficulties in Young Children* (Snow et al., 1998), *Stages of Reading Development* (Chall, 1996), and the International Reading Association/National Association for the Education of Young Children joint position statement on early literacy (IRA/NAEYC, 1998), the fact is that we have relatively little systematic data on the changes that occur in children's reading and writing development during this time period. Our knowledge base would benefit tremendously from a longitudinal study of a sample of the literacy development of *typical* children as they progress from their early years through third grade. Currently, our descriptions are built mainly on amalgamated results from cross-sectional empirical studies of different children at different ages and from case studies and other observational studies that are of relatively short duration. It is true that we have a handful of longer-term case studies (e.g., Baghban, 1984; Bissex, 1980), but the subjects are almost exclusively children of literacy researchers, a sample that can by no means be thought of as typical. Moreover, some very useful developmental insights have emerged from the Home–School Study of Language and Literacy Development (Dickinson & Tabors, 2001). But a strong longitudinal design that includes carefully gathered demographic data, empirical testing of various literacy concepts and strategies, and strong ethnographic descriptions of children's interactions and developing understandings and uses of reading and writing, would provide much needed insight into the expected literacy learning trajectories of typically developing children. Such information would contribute significantly to improved theoretical understanding of what is involved in early literacy development; it would also shed light on individual differences in literacy learning processes and suggest more perceptive ways of identifying children in need of early intervention for literacy difficulties.

• *What patterns of development characterize children's transition from emergent to conventional literacy?* A phase of development that deserves special attention is the period when young children move from emergent to conventional literacy. What patterns of concept and strategy development are exhibited by children as, for example, emergent storybook reading behaviors (such as those described by Sulzby, 1985) change to conventional reading that involves the coordination of previously disparate processes such as comprehension, sight word recognition, and decoding? Teale and Sulzby (1986a) noted one of the central tenets of emergent literacy theory in stating, "Although children's learning about literacy can be described in terms of generalized stages, children can pass through these stages in a variety of ways and at different ages" (p. xviii). In perhaps no phase of early literacy learning do we know less about these different paths and rates than during the time when children are transitioning from emergent reading and writing to conventional reading and writing. Understanding this transition is especially critical because a significant number of children get hung up in their learning during this time and because what happens during this time seems to have significant influence on children's progress in literacy achievement across later grade levels (Juel, Griffith, &

Gough, 1986). Thus, whereas the theoretical question about early development discussed previously focused on what is typical, this one seeks to gain insight into individual differences and group variations in how children achieve this significant milestone in development. Close observations of different children will help us understand the complexities of this critical phase.

• *What roles do factors like a young child's sociocultural and linguistic background, as well as his or her motivation to learn, play in the literacy learning process?* Learning to read and write is a complex process that involves much in addition to the development of cognitive operations. Unfortunately, the state of our theoretical understanding of this process includes relatively little systematic attention to the roles that personal motivation and sociocultural and linguistic influences, such as language variation, play in learning to read and write in one's native language. As a result, the field has, de facto, acted as though there is a literacy learning process that is essentially acontextual and acultural—or that engagement and culture play only a secondary or peripheral role in a person's becoming literate.

The field of reading has traditionally been most heavily influenced by the discipline of psychology. However, as was found in the 1980s when educational and psychological researchers affected by disciplines such as anthropology and what was then known as cross-cultural psychology, started looking at issues of learning and development in more expansive ways (e.g., Laboratory of Comparative Human Cognition, 1983), it became clear that cognitive processes and thinking strategies can truly be understood only by recognizing that they are part and parcel of the contexts in which they develop and occur. The theory of activity (Wertsch, 1981, 1998) elucidates this idea in the following way: Activities (e.g., baking a cake) are composed of goal-directed actions (read the recipe, mix the ingredients, etc.). Actions are conscious, and different actions may be undertaken to meet the same goal (Grandmother may not use a recipe when she bakes a cake). Actions are implemented through operations (word recognition, comprehension strategies for reading the genre of directions, etc.). Operations do not have their own goals; rather, they provide an adjustment of actions to current situations. The constituents of activity, then, are not fixed but can dynamically change as conditions change.

Thus, one's cognitive processes are intimately linked with one's history as a sociocultural being, as well as with the immediate contextual variables of the situation in which the cognitive processing (such as reading) occurs. In other words, context is an integral part of thinking rather than merely a backdrop that influences thinking. Such a conception has profound theoretical implications for the roles of sociocultural and linguistic factors in learning to read and write. Understanding better what it means to learn to read and write as an African American child, as a child who is not particularly interested in reading, as a speaker of a nonstandard dialect, as a poor child growing up in a rural environment, as a girl, as a boy, and so forth, or understanding what writing is like under various time constraints, when children have different degrees of background knowledge, and so forth, become theoretical investigations central to discerning the nature of literacy learning and the processes of reading and writing. Calling for systematic attention to such issues should not be interpreted as support for theoretical relativism or as a proposal for proliferating reading models or developmental schemata to the extent that they become theoretically meaningless. Rather, it represents an effort to pay much more attention to the central role of factors such as disposition to literacy, language register, and culture in the basic processes of early literacy development.

• *What more can we learn about the link between early childhood vocabulary development and literacy development?* The questions posed thus far have been *big* ones, questions that focus on major patterns in development and learning. This theoretical question zeroes in on one specific aspect of the literacy learning process: coming to know the meanings of words. For many decades now, the connection between vocabulary and reading achievement has been clearly established in the research literature (cf. Anderson & Freebody, 1981; Davis, 1944, 1968). Recently, researchers have focused on elucidating the role that children's oral language plays in early literacy development. A major element of the work on language has been vocabulary. The research of Hart and Risley (1995, 1999) has been especially helpful, providing insight into the relation of children's experience (what parents said to and did with their children) to their vocabulary growth and use. Dickinson, Snow, Tabors, and colleagues have moved the work on vocabulary development even further by examining it from age 3 through the teenage years in both home and school settings. In Dickinson and Tabors (2001) they discuss findings related to early childhood. This study helps us see the extreme importance of language, not only to early literacy learning but to long-term literacy achievement as well. It also provides thoughtful discussion of the relationship between home and school variables related to language and literacy.

Such work is exciting because it contributes to our theoretical understanding in ways that have important implications for home and classroom environments, and therefore for policy and curriculum development related to family literacy and early childhood instruction. But there is still much of interest to be learned. Are there certain corpora of vocabulary words that have more impact on literacy learning than others? Clearly, a child's direct experiences contribute significantly to vocabulary learning, but for children from backgrounds where family financial resources limit their opportunities for travel and other experiences, are there alternative ways to broaden vocabulary? How does nonstandard dialect relate to vocabulary development once factors such as income or family structure are accounted for? In environments where parents have low levels of literacy, can oral language vocabulary be enhanced to facilitate literacy learning? How does a child's vocabulary learning at home relate to vocabulary learning in the classroom—in what ways do the two settings complement, duplicate, reinforce, or contradict each other? These and other questions remain to be investigated and answered as part of this very important topic.

Instructional Questions

Central to the issue of how well children learn to read is what teachers do with children in the classroom to promote literacy. Professional groups and individual scholars have offered various lists and extensive discussions of best or recommended practices for early literacy. These lists include many empirically and practically proven practices. In fact, some have argued that as a result of the recent period of research, we now have a clear indication of what needs to be done in teaching early reading and writing, and we just need to do it (Moats, 1999). There is truth in such a statement—we do know a great deal more about effective early literacy instructional practices than we did a quarter century ago. There are also useful guidelines contained in the descriptions of effective practices that have been offered. But I suggest that we have by no means solved the puzzle of how to teach so that young children are almost universally successful at learning to read and write. Numerous questions remain to be answered. The following six are offered as especially significant ones whose answers have potential to move our instructional practices significantly forward.

• *What kinds of classroom oral language activities contribute significantly to early literacy learning?* Early childhood educators have long recognized the importance of rich oral language experiences to children's development. Findings of recent longitudinal research conducted by Dickinson, Tabors, Snow, and colleagues (e.g., Dickinson & Tabors, 2001) and the work of Hart and Risley (1995, 1999) have highlighted even more strongly the critical contribution of oral language to early literacy development, especially during the preschool years. Despite this longstanding recognition, examination of curriculum materials, actual classroom practices, and the content of teacher preparation programs shows that many preschool and kindergarten teachers, as well as the programs and personnel who provide their training, have paid little systematic attention to vocabulary instructional practices (see, e.g., Patterson, 2002, or McGill-Franzen, Lanford, & Adams, 2002).

Insights from the Home-School Study of Language and Literacy Development (see especially Cote, 2001, and Dickinson, 2001b), suggestions regarding how read-alouds can be conducted to stimulate learning (e.g., Beck & McKeown, 2001; Dickinson, 2001a; Teale, in press), and descriptions of oral language activities outlined in books like *Starting Out Right: A Guide to Promoting Children's Reading Success* (Burns, Griffin, & Snow, 1999) provide research-based ideas for instructional activities. Yet much more systematic classroom-based work needs to be done in order to see what classroom activities effectively develop children's oral language so as to impact literacy learning.

• *How much do independent reading activities help children become capable, comprehending readers—and what kinds of activities are helpful?* An extensive body of research convincingly demonstrates the correlation between a child's reading ability and the amount of time the child spends independently reading connected text (Fielding, Wilson, & Anderson, 1986; National Reading Panel, 2000). But the usefulness of spending instructional time having children engage in sustained silent reading (SSR) in school has been seriously questioned (National Reading Panel, 2000). Teale and Bean (2002) have argued that SSR can be effective instructionally *if* the teacher adopts an active role—conferencing with students, building productive accountability structures into SSR, and making participative response activities such as book talks an integral part of SSR. The instructional importance of SSR is deep-seated in primary grade teachers (Block & Mangieri, 2002). We need more sensitive research that allows us to determine whether or not this more participatory version of SSR, as argued for by Teale and Bean (2002), actually helps children become better and more willing readers—and if so, how?

• *What role should phonemic awareness instruction play in the reading/language arts curriculum?* It has been clear for many years that phonemic awareness (PA) plays a crucial role in learning to read and write (Goswami, 2000). Considerable evidence also indicates that in addition to being immersed in a classroom rich in opportunities for rhyming, language play, and informal phonemic awareness development, some children need to participate in phonemic awareness lessons, especially those that focus on segmenting and blending (NRP, 2000). Finally, the research suggests that development is enhanced if PA instruction is done in conjunction with attention to letter–sound relationships (NRP, 2000).

Observations of classroom practice and instructional materials show that the importance of PA instruction has been clearly recognized by K–1 teachers. These teachers plan PA lessons and use materials specifically designed to develop PA. But there are two potential problems on the PA instructional landscape in K–1. One is the amount of attention given to PA in the curriculum. The zeal with which early literacy reform efforts, such as the Texas Reading Initiative (*http://www.tea.state.tx.us/reading/era.html*) or those based on findings from the National Institute of Child Health and

Human Development (NICHD) research program (Lyon, 1998), have been pursued has often resulted in teachers behaving as if PA is *the* essential element in an early literacy curriculum. Under these circumstances a disproportionate amount of classroom time and instructional energy is put into only one aspect of what children need instructionally.

The other concern related to phonemic awareness in K–1 classrooms is the place of the PA *program* in the context of the overall curriculum. In many circumstances PA instruction has been implemented as an *add-on* or as a separate block of time devoted to this particular skill rather than being developed as a central part of the overall thematic unit or other content framework by which the curriculum has been organized. Thus, the major question in K–1 classrooms is how PA instruction can be made a more integral part of the reading/language arts program to work in concert with the other aspects of early literacy development.

The situation in preschool settings with respect to PA is somewhat different and perhaps even more problematic. In conducting observations during 2001 in a sample of 13 preschool classrooms serving 4- and 5-year-olds, for example, Patterson (2002) found virtually no informal or formal instructional attention being paid to phonemic awareness. Thus, one issue is whether preschool teachers are even promoting appropriate phonemic awareness development among 3- to 5-year-old children. Beyond this arises the same question asked in regard to older children—what is the place of PA instruction in the context of the preschool curriculum?

• *Which types of texts help beginning readers learn to read—and in what ways do they help?* This question has become a significant one in the field over the past few years as beginning literacy instruction has shifted from literature-based programs to programs that emphasize vocabulary control, decodable text, and more explicit word-level skill instruction. This shift has occurred as part of the move to scientifically based reading instruction promoted by the NICHD reading initiatives (Lyon, 1998) and, more recently, by the aforementioned No Child Left Behind Act of 2001 (*http://www.ed.gov/inits/backtoschool/teachers/index.html*). Although the Center for the Improvement of Early Reading Achievement (CIERA) has as one of its focal research areas the characteristics of texts that have the greatest influence on early reading achievement, key instructional questions remain to be answered. Primary among them is whether there is adequate scientific evidence to support the notion of decodability and vocabulary control adopted by states such as California and Texas in regulating the instructional texts the states make available to children and teachers in their classrooms.

Word complexity, text predictability, the degree to which a text engages the reader, and prior instruction (whether or not the orthographic/ phonics patterns of the words that make up the text have been taught) are all factors that affect text readability, and thus the suitability of a text for helping children learn to read. Interestingly, for example, only the last of these factors, the "percent of words introduced that could be read accurately (i.e., pronunciation approximated) through the application of phonics rules that were taught explicitly in the program design prior to the student encountering the word in connected text," was used as a criterion for defining what constituted acceptable decodable texts for the basal reader programs that could be sold in the state of Texas beginning in 2000 (Hoffman & Sailors, 2001). I believe that all early childhood educators think that text characteristics play a key role in facilitating the process of learning to read, and that text characteristics related to decoding and word recognition are of critical importance. But it also is the case that our current knowledge in this area is still significantly lacking in enabling us to understand, in a substantive and scientific way, which types of texts help beginning readers learn to read—and why. This is an instructional question of extreme importance to the field.

• *What types of instruction programs best meet the needs of children of color and children from low-income backgrounds?* This instructional question is closely linked to the theoretical question posed earlier, "What roles do sociocultural factors, linguistic background, and motivation play in literacy learning?" National Assessment of Educational Progress data clearly show a significant gap in reading and writing achievement at the fourth-grade level for poor children and children of color in the United States (Donahue, Finnegan, Lutkus, Allen, & Campbell, 2001; Donahue, Voelkl, Campbell, & Mazzeo, 1999; Greenwald, Persky, Campbell, & Mazzeo, 1999). No comparable national achievement data exist for lower grade levels, but results from state and standardized tests, as well as reports from teachers, make it clear that similar gaps exist among younger children. The reasons that we are not meeting the needs of these children are multifaceted. Some have to do with the structures of our society, and some with limited access to materials and experiences because of income; others are linked more directly to instructional practices. Much has been discussed and proposed in the past quarter century about the need for culturally appropriate literacy instruction for young children. Au (1998) summarized the instructional issues in this area when she wrote about helping students of diverse backgrounds to become excellent readers and writers:

> The answer . . . lies in developing students' understandings of the reasons why people read and write in real life. . . . These reasons are readily grasped by students of diverse backgrounds when they experience literature-based instruction and the readers' workshop, and the process approach to writing and the writers' workshop. . . . A growing body of research shows that these students can and do benefit from constructivist approaches to literacy instruction. (pp. 17–18)

At both the home/community and school levels, we need more attention to how such constructivist approaches can be built in various school settings.

• *What classroom literacy assessment instruments can be made available to teachers so that they can obtain diagnostic information about individual students that enables effective literacy instruction?* Assessment and instruction are frequently seen as separate educational processes, but in effective classrooms they function in complementary and recursive ways. Literacy assessment can provide essential diagnostic information that enables the teacher to offer the best possible developmentally appropriate literacy instruction for children. Within recent years considerably more emphasis has been placed on assessing young children's literacy learning. Too often such efforts result in large-scale assessment policies that rely on standardized instruments that yield virtually no information that teachers can use to make instructional decisions about individual children. Such programs typically end up placing more emphasis on their cost-effectiveness than on their educational effectiveness.

Now that federal and state policies are increasingly mandating assessment of kindergarten, first-, and second-grade children's literacy achievement, it is imperative that substantiated assessments focused on classroom performance samples, rather than on multiple-choice responses, be accessible to teachers. Much of what is currently available in the way of classroom-based literacy assessments either is so time-consuming and cumbersome to use that teachers do not use such instruments, or has undergone little reliability and validity development and is consequently not worth using.

More efforts like the recent program to develop the Illinois Snapshots of Early Literacy (ISEL) (Barr et al., 2002) will be helpful in addressing this question. The ISEL, an instrument created under the auspices of the Illinois State Board of Education in both English and Spanish versions, is designed to (1) provide assessment information for classroom instructional planning, (2) identify children needing an early reading intervention program, and (3) provide pre- and postassessment data on literacy progress. It is given to students individually within the classroom setting, yet is manageable to administer. It is also comprehensive, having subtests on alphabet recognition, story listening (comprehension and vocabulary), phonemic awareness, one-to-one matching and word naming, letter sounds, developmental spelling, word recognition, and graded passage reading.

Care was taken to ensure that the ISEL was scientifically based, and validity and reliability analyses were an integral part of its construction. This type of assessment, which provides both standardized and qualitative data, yields diagnostic information useful to teachers for classroom-based instruction. The ISEL is also reflective of the National Standards for Reading and the Illinois Learning Standards. In short, this approach to an assessment instrument, if replicated to meet the needs of different states or school districts, would go a long way toward answering the question of what kind of classroom literacy assessment instruments help teachers provide effective literacy instruction. And addressing this question is of extreme importance in the current climate emphasizing assessment in early literacy.

Teacher Education Questions

One of the biggest challenges our field faces in the initial decade of the 21st century is finding more effective ways of preparing teachers to teach young children to read and write. At both the preservice and in-service levels, teacher education is falling short in making teachers knowledgeable about and comfortable with teaching in ways that both engage children and help them achieve at satisfactory levels. Results of the latest National Assessment of Educational Progress show that 37% of children in fourth grade are Below Basic in reading achievement, whereas only 8% are at the Advanced level (Donahue et al., 2001). Moreover, first-year primary grade teachers often feel that they are underprepared to teach reading.

Since the year 2000, Linda Labbo, Don Leu, Chuck Kinzer, and I have been conducting the Case Technologies to Enhance Literacy Learning (CTELL) research project to determine whether the use of Web-based video cases—cases of K–3 classrooms that include a 20-minute overview video of the literacy instruction in each classroom, as well as several 5-minute videos of key instructional activities from the room; work samples, running records, and interviews with focal children; interviews with the teacher, principal, other school personnel and parents; demographic and achievement data from the classroom, and other materials—can produce more knowledgeable and effective teachers of literacy at kindergarten through third-grade levels (see Teale, Leu, Labbo, & Kinzer, 2002, or *http://www.edci. uconn.edu/ctell/* for a more complete description).

One part of this project that enabled development of the cases was a comprehensive review of the existing research literature. This review culminated in a set of 12 key principles for effective beginning reading instruction (Teale, Kinzer, Labbo, & Leu, in press). Most of the principles identified were based on practices in long-term use that are robustly supported in the research, but also included were some emerging strategies, promising practices for which a research base is currently being developed. Important also is the fact that the synthesis of existing research showed that no particular method of beginning reading instruction has proven to be clearly superior in the classrooms of teachers who use research-based practices. Using these findings, we proposed that the key to effective early literacy instruction was not learning the procedures of a particular method of teaching, but being able to apply the principles in real classroom settings with real children.

These principles were offered as guidelines for efforts focused on preparing teachers to teach K–3 children to read and write. Our belief, which is being tested in the CTELL project, is that if teachers conduct their instruction according to these principles, teaching will improve and early literacy achievement can be raised significantly.

The question for teacher education, then, is:

- *How do we develop preservice and in-service teacher education programs that enable teachers to . . .*
  - Make principled, insightful instructional decisions for individual children and orchestrate effective instruction for the group of children being taught, rather than apply learned procedures for instruction or follow scripted lesson plans?
  - Base school reading instruction on young children's language, culture, and home backgrounds?
  - Develop basic early literacy concepts, skills, and positive attitudes by immersing young children in literacy-rich classrooms?
  - Foster children's phonemic awareness with developmentally appropriate instruction?
  - Provide effective and engaging phonics instruction?
  - Provide effective and engaging comprehension instruction?
  - Promote children's independent reading?
  - Foster children's reading fluency through appropriate instructional activities and extensive opportunities to read fluently?
  - Integrate writing and reading instruction?
  - Effectively and appropriately integrate technology into early literacy instruction?
  - Monitor children's early literacy development through ongoing classroom assessment and provide instruction based on the diagnostic information obtained, including appropriate instructional intervention for children who fall significantly behind?
  - Teach in ways that foster young children's enthusiasm for and engagement with reading and writing?

The nationwide development of teacher education programs that graduate teachers who teach according to these principles must start with work at the institutional level—a college or university faculty, in collaboration with local schools, committing itself to the creation of courses and fieldwork that enable this kind of early literacy teaching to be done. Alliances with external partners can make these efforts even more effective. For example, useful insights into how to accomplish such aims may come from the International Reading Association's National Commission on Excellence in Elementary Teacher Preparation for Reading Instruction (*http://www.read-*

ing.org/advocacy/commission.html), a 3-year research effort devoted to the study of excellence in eight 4-year undergraduate teacher preparation programs in the United States. Efforts to create a parallel set of principles for instruction at the preschool level can also be productive.

Policy Questions

Policy is what makes things happen in an endeavor like education. Important theoretical ideas, insights about effective practice, research on curriculum materials, information about young children's literacy development—effective policy can help all of these and more to become part of home and school educational practice. The best program or set of practices in the world cannot meet the early literacy needs of our society unless it becomes known and used in the educational community, and this is where policy can help.

Community-based, state-level, and federal policies help early literacy research findings, curriculum materials, instructional techniques, family literacy programs, and other effective practices to be implemented in home, child care, preschool, school, and teacher education settings. Two especially important early literacy policy questions are paramount in the current political and intellectual climate.

• *How can we bring to scale classroom implementation of appropriate, effective early literacy assessment, curriculum, and instruction?* In virtually any community, one can find wonderful preschool or primary grade classrooms in which teachers foster positive dispositions toward literacy among children and significantly enhance the reading and writing abilities of their students. It is substantially harder to find an entire preschool or school about which this can be said. And it is rare indeed to find a school district in which early literacy instruction is of uniformly high quality and the overall K–3 student body can be characterized as highly engaged and successfully achieving in reading and writing. A true challenge for educational policy is building the capacity for high-quality literacy instruction in a much larger percentage of early childhood classrooms in the country. Such a challenge has significant implications for teacher education, both at the preschool and primary grade levels. Furthermore, this challenge applies to in-service professional development as well as to preservice teacher education.

What I believe will not work is an attempt to accomplish such a goal through universal, large-scale testing programs or the imposition of scripted, direct instruction programs in a top-down fashion. Using testing to accomplish education reform typically creates only certain low-level changes related to teaching surface literacy skills.

Such an approach may yield short-term increased test scores but does not lead to true gains in children's reading or writing. Direct instruction focused on scripted lessons merely bypasses the issue of educating competent teachers; moreover, there is little research to indicate that such programs are effective at helping children develop higher-level reading and writing skills from the intermediate grades on.

Serious, large-scale reform of professional preparation for literacy instruction in preschool and the primary grades necessitates that child care personnel and classroom teachers develop deep knowledge about children's literacy development, curriculum components (word study; fluency, comprehension, and writing instruction; development of voluntary reading habits), the benchmarks these components are designed to help students of various ages achieve, systems for aligning benchmarks with assessment practices and associated instructional approaches, and coherent approaches for orchestrating curricular content within available instructional time. In addition, high-quality professional development (that which leads to student learning) is characterized by teachers' participation in and learning to draw on support from peer networks, external professional groups, and site-based professional activities.

How to develop models for making such change on a large-scale basis is a policy question well worth pursuing. The HeadsUp! Reading Initiative, a distance learning course that provides professional development in early literacy to Head Start teachers (*http://www.huronline.org*), is an interesting venture with preschool educators that merits closer studying. The Standards Based Change Process (Au, 2002) being implemented in elementary schools across the state of Hawaii is another large-scale model that may be instructive. It develops local school leadership teams that work with external partners (such as a university or foundation) and with analogous teams in other schools.

Over the years numerous projects have succeeded in accomplishing positive reforms of early literacy education in one or a few schools. Such work is important and informative. A key question in regard to policy is how to extend the limited reach of such reform programs to the large number of preschools and schools that could benefit from more coherent and effective early literacy programs.

• *How can grant funding from both governmental sources and foundations be used more effectively?* Each year in the United States millions of dollars are spent on basic research and program development projects related to early literacy. These funds come from a variety of sources within the public and private sectors. For example, at the federal level, the Office of Educational Research and Improvement; the Office of English Language Acquisition, Language Enhancement, and Academic Achievement for Limited English Proficient Students; and the Department of Special Education, all within the U.S. Department of Education, have funded work in early literacy, as have the National Science Foundation and the National Institutes of Health. In localities across the country, numerous foundations operate independently to support early literacy initiatives for families, in preschool programs, and in elementary schools; in many cases these initiatives overlap with or even duplicate each other.

Although funding for early literacy is perhaps now more abundant than it has ever been, the resources available are certainly limited and, if truth be told, inadequate. Therefore, we have to get smarter about how these funds are used. We are a society with an entrepreneurial spirit, and I do not want to suggest that we move toward a centralized bureaucracy that dispenses monies for early literacy projects to only the anointed few. On the contrary, many of our truly exciting early literacy initiatives started as small projects with a vision. But it seems that combining a more coordinated, strategic approach to funding of early literacy endeavors with opportunities for grassroots start-ups may lead to even more impressive gains for early literacy than currently being experienced. For instance, a few years ago the Heinz Endowments (*http://www.heinz.org*), which focus on development in southwestern Pennsylvania, devised a plan for being more strategic in their giving. Previously, the organization had funded numerous projects related to young children, but as a result of thoughtful planning, it now has a Children, Youth, and Families Program, one focus of which is on Children as Learners. Children as Learners is specifically designated to "improve the literacy status of young children" by enhancing teacher training and professional development programs; expanding after-school, weekend, and summer programming for children grades K through three; and supporting efforts to create linkages between preschool and primary grades. More of this kind of deliberative policy coordination can help in leveraging the limited funding related to early literacy so that it becomes more effective. Thoughtful planning can eliminate duplication, coordinate the labor of similarly intentioned agencies, and create synergy among previously separate initiatives. Collaborative work among professional organizations, foundations, government agencies, and institutions of higher education may provide valuable leadership to answer this important policy question.

QUESTIONS RECEIVING MORE ATTENTION THAN THEY DESERVE

The questions outlined earlier constitute an ambitious agenda for work on early literacy theory, instruction, and policy. Answering them requires considerable effort and resources on the part of professional organizations; schools, preschools, and child care providers; researchers; child advocacy groups; and government personnel. Certainly, we do not want to waste valuable energy or resources pursuing issues that are of peripheral importance or already resolved. In the spirit of preserving our limited early childhood capital and thus being able to tackle what is important, I propose that the field may find it healthier to set the following questions aside, rather than put more effort into answering them:

- *Should early literacy programs include phonics instruction?* Of course. We have decades of evidence clearly indicating that systematic phonics instruction should be an integral part of early literacy instruction. Phonics should not *be* the program, but teaching young children about letter–sound relations must be central to it.
- *How should phonics be taught?* There will always be room in education for good new instructional ideas, and so it is with how to teach children about letter–sound relations. But there are currently plenty of good strategies available for teaching decoding skills so that they are (1) consistent with a developmentally appropriate/balanced approach to early literacy and (2) effective and engaging for children. Scripted instruction and/or the endless, mindless, worksheet–skill 'em–drill 'em–kill 'em approach is neither necessary nor desirable. See, for example, *Words Their Way* (Bear, Invernizzi, Templeton, & Johnston, 2000), Pat Cunningham's ideas on phonics (Cunningham, 2000; Cunningham & Hall, 1997), or *Beyond Traditional Phonics* (Moustafa, 1997) for solid instructional strategies and programs.
- *What about reading aloud as an instructional technique?* Questions have been raised about the effectiveness of reading aloud as an instructional activity in the classroom. Some research even found negative correlations between the amount of time teachers read aloud to their children and the children's reading achievement (Meyer, Wardrop, Hastings, & Linn, 1993; Meyer, Wardrop, Stahl, & Linn, 1994). But as Dickinson's work has shown, reading aloud can have significant positive effects on young children's vocabulary and literacy learning (Dickinson, 2001a; Dickinson & Smith, 1994). In a recent review of research (Teale, in press), I suggested that what made the difference in whether reading aloud to children promoted language and literacy development was why readings were done, what teachers read, and how they read:

> We should never believe that the children in our early childhood classrooms will learn to read merely by being read to—no matter how high the quality of the books or how engaging the reading. There is much more to teaching children to read than simply reading to them. But reading to children *does* help them develop the knowledge, strategies, and dispositions that are fundamental aspects of becoming literate. . . . Like anything we do in our efforts to teach children, it is not the procedures of an instructional activity

that make a difference; it is the principled way in which that activity is woven into the fabric of the classroom and the learning needs of the children that makes it significant. Reading aloud is a valued, and even special, instructional activity for most teachers of young children. It deserves that status so long as we continue to be thoughtful about the whats, whys, and hows of it.

• *Can play contribute to children's literacy learning?* The answer is yes; read Roskos and Christie (2000) and Dickinson (2001b). The real issue in regard to this topic is the degree to which the potential of play for developing early literacy is being realized in preschool and kindergarten classrooms. Patterson (2002), for example, found that the 13 preschool teachers she observed generally did not value or encourage reading or writing in children's dramatic play and that none of the teachers created literacy-related themes within their dramatic play areas or intervened in children's play to suggest the use of reading or writing materials. Dickinson (2001b) noted the differential effects of the various types of interactions teachers have with children during free-play times. Teachers need a better understanding of the value of play for reading and writing development and more preparation with respect to instructional techniques for taking advantage of the kinds of literacy learning opportunities play offers.

• *What should early childhood educators do to get all children reading on grade level by the end of third grade?* I have begun referring to this policy as the Third Grade Mantra. It seems as though some people believe that if you repeat "all children reading on grade level by the end of third grade" often enough, it will happen. It won't. I firmly believe that the early childhood period is crucial for literacy development and that we should be doing everything we can to provide high-quality, rigorous reading and writing instruction during this time. But the third-grade-every-child-on-grade-level notion creates at least as many problems as it solves. Learning to read should not be viewed as a process that is accomplished by age 9 or 10. Much remains to be learned—and should be taught—after grade 3. In addition, people who work directly with children know that instruction is most effective when it is based on a conception of development that *embraces* the idea that there is considerable variation in the time frame during which *normal* children accomplish a complex achievement, such as becoming conventionally literate. Finally, what message do parents and even children themselves get from a policy that dictates reading on grade level by the end of grade 3? If the goal is not accomplished, does that imply that hope is lost? We must be more cautious when we create catchy sayings to represent important educational policies. In this case, a well-founded desire to emphasize the important mission to which we, as educators of young children, should dedicate ourselves—helping all children learn to read and write in early childhood—has been undermined rather than advanced.

CONCLUSION

The initial part of the 21st century has emerged as a period offering unprecedented attention to early literacy. Educators, family advocacy groups, early childhood professionals, foundations, and policy makers on the local, state, and national levels are coming together around the general issue of early childhood education and are focusing especially on early literacy development. Still, a variety of perspectives, programs, and policies are extant in the field, despite the contention by some that the *scientific* evidence clearly indicates what the content and form of early literacy curricula and instruction should be. I hope that the questions posed in this chapter indicate that children and early childhood educators will benefit from continuing rigorous and thoughtful theoretical and field-based investigations. Such work is needed to gain the additional insights necessary to provide the best information and resources to parents that we can, build the best child care and preschool programs that we can, and create the best reading/language arts materials and curricula for primary grade children that we can. The questions discussed in this chapter will not be easy to answer, but they are worth asking.

REFERENCES

Adams, M. J. (1990). *Beginning to read: Thinking and learning about print*. Cambridge, MA: MIT Press.

Anderson, R. C., & Freebody, P. (1981). Vocabulary knowledge. In J. T. Guthrie (Ed.), *Comprehension and teaching: Research reviews* (pp. 77–116). Newark, DE: International Reading Association.

Au, K. H. (1998). Constructivist approaches, phonics, and the literacy learning of students of diverse backgrounds. In T. Shanahan & F. V. Rodriguez-Brown (Eds.), *Forty-seventh yearbook of the National Reading Conference* (pp. 1–21). Chicago: National Reading Conference.

Au, K. H. (2002). Elementary programs: Guiding change in a time of standards. In S. B. Wepner, D. S. Strickland, & J. T. Feeley (Eds.), *The administration and supervision of reading programs* (3rd ed., pp. 42–58). New York: Teachers College Press.

Baghban, M. (1984). *Our daughter learns to read and write: A case study from birth to three*. Newark, DE: International Reading Association.

Barr, R., Blachowicz, C., Buhle, R., Chaney, C., Ivy, C., & Suárez-Silva, G. (2002). *Technical manual—Illinois snapshot of early literacy: Field test year 2000–2001*. Springfield: Illinois State Board of Education.

Bear, D., Invernizzi, M., Templeton, S., & Johnston, F. (2000). *Words their way: Word study for phonics, vocabulary, and spelling instruction* (2nd ed.). Upper Saddle River, NJ: Merrill.

Beck, I. L., & McKeown, M. G. (2001). Text talk: Capturing the benefits of read-aloud experiences for young children. *The Reading Teacher, 55*, 10–20.

Bissex, G. (1980). *GNYS AT WRK: A child learns to read and write.* Cambridge, MA: Harvard University Press.

Block, C. C., & Mangieri, J. N. (2002). Recreational reading: 20 years later. *The Reading Teacher, 55,* 572–585.

Bloom, L. (1993). *The transition from infancy to language: Acquiring the power of expression.* New York: Cambridge University Press.

Burns, S., Griffin, P., & Snow, C. E. (1999). *Starting out right: A guide to promoting children's reading success.* Washington, DC: National Academy Press.

Chall, J. S. (1996). *Stages of reading development* (3rd ed.). Fort Worth, TX: Harcourt Brace.

Cote, L. R. (2001). Language opportunities during mealtimes in preschool classrooms. In D. K. Dickinson & P. O. Tabors (Eds.), *Beginning literacy with language* (pp. 205–222). Baltimore: Brookes.

Cunningham, P. M. (2000). *Phonics they use: Words for reading and writing* (3rd ed.). New York: Longman.

Cunningham, P. M., & Hall, D. P. (1997). *Month-by-month phonics for first grade.* Greensboro, NC: Carson Dellosa.

Davis, F. B. (1944). Fundamental factors of comprehension in reading. *Psychometrika, 9,* 185–197.

Davis, F. B. (1968). Research in comprehension in reading. *Reading Research Quarterly, 3,* 499–545.

Dickinson, D. (2001a). Book reading in preschool classrooms: Is recommended practice common? In D. K. Dickinson & P. O. Tabors (Eds.), *Beginning literacy with language* (pp. 175–204). Baltimore: Brookes.

Dickinson, D. (2001b). Large-group and free-play times: Conversational settings supporting language and literacy development. In D. K. Dickinson & P. O. Tabors (Eds.), *Beginning literacy with language* (pp. 223–256). Baltimore: Brookes.

Dickinson, D. K., & Smith, M. W. (1994). Long-term effects of preschool teachers' book readings on low income children's vocabulary and story comprehension. *Reading Research Quarterly, 29,* 104–122.

Dickinson, D. K., & Tabors, P. O. (Eds.). (2001). *Beginning literacy with language.* Baltimore: Brookes.

Donahue, P. L., Finnegan, R. J., Lutkus, A. D., Allen, N. L., & Campbell, J. R. (2001). *The nation's report card: Fourth-grade reading 2000.* Washington, DC: United States Department of Education, Office of Educational Research and Improvement/National Center for Educational Statistics.

Donahue, P. L., Voelkl, P. E., Campbell, J. R., & Mazzeo, J. (1999). *NAEP 1998 reading: Report card for the nation and the states.* Washington, DC: United States Department of Education, Office of Educational Research and Improvement/National Center for Educational Statistics.

Ehri, L. C. (1994). Development of the ability to read words: Update. In R. B. Ruddell, M. R. Ruddell, & H. Singer (Eds.), *Theoretical models and processes of reading* (4th ed., pp. 323–358). Newark, DE: International Reading Association.

Fielding, L., Wilson, P., & Anderson, R. C. (1986). A new focus on free reading: The role of trade books in reading instruction. In T. Raphael & R. Reynolds (Eds.), *The contexts of school-based literacy* (pp. 149–160). New York: Random House.

Goswami, U. (2000). Phonological and lexical processes. In M. L. Kamil, P. B.

Mosenthal, P. D. Pearson, & R. Barr (Eds.), *Handbook of reading research* (Vol. III, pp. 251–267). Mahwah, NJ: Erlbaum.

Greenwald, E. A., Persky, H. R., Campbell, J. R., & Mazzeo, J. (1999). *NAEP 1998 writing: Report card for the nation and the states.* Washington, DC: United States Department of Education, Office of Educational Research and Improvement/National Center for Educational Statistics.

Hart, B., & Risley, T. R. (1995). *Meaningful differences in the everyday experiences of young American children.* Baltimore: Brookes.

Hart, B., & Risley, T. R. (1999). *The social world of children learning to talk.* Baltimore: Brookes.

Hoffman, J. V., & Sailors, M. (2001, December). *Investigating decodable features of basal texts and first-grade reading performance.* Paper presented at 51st annual meeting of the National Reading Conference, San Antonio, TX.

International Reading Association and the National Association for the Education of Young Children. (1998). Learning to read and write: Developmentally appropriate practices for young children. A joint position statement of the International Reading Association and the National Association for the Education of Young Children. *Young Children, 53,* 524–546.

Juel, C., Griffith, P. L., & Gough, P. (1986). Acquisition of literacy: A longitudinal study of children in first and second grade. *Journal of Educational Psychology, 78,* 243–255.

Laboratory of Comparative Human Cognition. (1983). Culture and cognitive development. In W. Kessen (Ed.), *Handbook of child psychology: History, theory, and methods* (Vol. I, pp. 295–356). New York: Wiley.

Lyon, G. R. (1998). *Overview of reading and literacy initiatives* [On-line]. Available at http://www. nichd.nih.gov/crmc/cdb/r_overview.htm

McGill-Franzen, A., Lanford, C., & Adams, E. (2002). Learning to be literate: A comparison of five urban early childhood programs. *Journal of Educational Psychology, 94,* 443–464.

Meyer, L. A., Wardrop, J. L., Hastings, C. N., & Linn, R. L. (1993). How entering ability and instructional settings influence kindergartners' reading performance. *Journal of Educational Research, 86,* 142–160.

Meyer, L. A., Wardrop, J. L., Stahl, S. A., & Linn, R. L. (1994). Effects of reading storybooks aloud to children. *Journal of Educational Research, 88,* 69–85.

Moats, L. (1999). *Teaching reading is rocket science.* Washington, DC: American Federation of Teachers.

Moustafa, M. (1997). *Beyond traditional phonics: Research discoveries and reading instruction.* Portsmouth, NH: Heinemann.

National Reading Panel. (2000). *Report of the National Reading Panel.* Washington, DC: National Institute of Child Health and Human Development Clearinghouse.

Patterson, J. (2002). *Teacher beliefs and practices in preschool literacy instruction.* Unpublished doctoral dissertation, University of Illinois at Chicago.

Roskos, K. A., & Christie, J. F. (Eds.). (2000). *Play and literacy in early childhood: Research from multiple perspectives.* Mahwah, NJ: Erlbaum.

Snow, C. E., Burns, M. S., & Griffin, P. (Eds.). (1998). *Preventing reading difficulties in young children.* Washington, DC: National Academy Press.

Stanovich, K. E. (2000). *Progress in understanding reading: Scientific foundations and new frontiers.* New York: Guilford Press.

Sulzby, E. (1985). Children's emergent reading of favorite storybooks. *Reading Research Quarterly, 20,* 458–481.

Teale, W. H. (1995). Young children and reading: Trends across the 20th century. *Journal of Education, 177,* 95–125.

Teale, W. H. (in press). Reading aloud to young children as a classroom instructional activity: Insights from research and practice. In A. van Kleeck, S. A. Stahl, & E. Bauer (Eds.), *On reading books to children: Parents and teachers.* Mahwah, NJ: Erlbaum.

Teale, W. H., & Bean, K. (2002, March). *Of SSR, AR, and the notion of independent reading: What's a teacher to do?* Paper presented at 2002 Illinois Reading Conference, Springfield, IL.

Teale, W. H., Kinzer, C., Labbo, L. D., & Leu, D. J., Jr. (in press). *Beginning reading instruction* (Educational Practices Series). Brussels, Belgium & Geneva, Switzerland: UNESCO/International Academy of Education and International Bureau of Education.

Teale, W. H., Leu, D. J., Jr., Labbo, L. D., & Kinzer, C. (2002). The CTELL project: New ways technology can help educate tomorrow's teachers of reading. *The Reading Teacher, 55,* 654–659.

Teale, W. H., & Sulzby, E. (1986a). Emergent literacy as a perspective for examining how young children become writers and readers. In W. H. Teale & E. Sulzby (Eds.), *Emergent literacy: Writing and reading* (pp. vii–xxv). Norwood, NJ: Ablex.

Teale, W. H., & Sulzby, E. (Eds.). (1986b). *Emergent literacy: Writing and reading.* Norwood, NJ: Ablex.

Wells, G. (1985). *Language development in the preschool years.* New York: Cambridge University Press.

Wertsch, J. V. (1981). *The concept of activity in Soviet psychology.* Armonk, NY: M. E. Sharpe.

Wertsch, J. V. (1998). *Mind as action.* New York: Oxford University Press.

Yaden, D. B., Rowe, D. W., & MacGillivray, L. (2000). Emergent literacy: A matter (polyphony) of perspectives. In M. L. Kamil, P. B. Mosenthal, P. D. Pearson, & R. Barr (Eds.), *Handbook of reading research* (Vol. III, pp. 425–454). Mahwah, NJ: Erlbaum.

3

A Multidimensional Approach to Beginning Literacy

IRENE W. GASKINS

Early in my teaching career, in a community dotted with oil refineries, I worked with a first-grade teacher who in just 10 short months regularly taught all her students to read and write. I was intent on discovering the magical materials or commercial program she used. However, as I got to know this resourceful and energetic teacher, I learned that the magic was in what was in her head and heart. She had taken bits and pieces from a variety of programs and approaches and knew just how to weave them together to provide her students with a menu of possibilities for becoming literate.

This first-grade teacher composed stories reinforcing the spelling patterns she was teaching and placed picture cards around the room to cue students about the sounds represented by isolated vowels and consonants. She read high-quality literature to and with students, often engaging them in echo-reading. Students chorally read simple stories from a host of old basals, and they dictated to a volunteer parent their own original stories, which they later read to one another. Students in Mrs. Jones's class were engaged in reading and writing, and in talking about what they read and wrote, at least five hours a day. Some even stayed in during recess to fill more pages with their writing.

What Mrs. Jones knew about teaching literacy more than 40 years ago is exactly what researchers have documented that effective first-grade teachers know and do today. They implement a multidimensional approach to literacy, the approach we believe in at Benchmark School. This chapter outlines the rationale and research that support a multidimensional approach to beginning literacy and provides examples of this approach from Benchmark School, an elementary school for children with average or above average intelligence who are struggling readers.

RATIONALE AND RESEARCH

There is no one best method or set of materials for teaching all children to read, a fact confirmed more than 30 years ago by the first-grade reading studies (Bond & Dykstra, 1967). Children learn differently, therefore a variety of instructional practices and experiences is necessary to meet their needs. This is especially true for beginning readers. Believing that one program fits all guarantees that some students will not learn to read. Instead, effective teachers of beginning literacy engage students in experiences that provide many different pathways for reaching literacy goals (Neuman & Dickinson, 2001). These teachers implement a multidimensional approach to beginning literacy.

Effective teachers of beginning literacy not only understand that children learn differently and thus need a multidimensional approach, they also understand that the very nature of reading is multidimensional—that readers must fluidly coordinate many component skills and strategies in order to recognize individual printed words and comprehend the meaning of the strings of words they identify. Success in beginning literacy is built on a foundation that includes awareness of phonemes and rimes, concepts about print, background knowledge, vocabulary, ability to reason verbally, and some acquaintance with the text structures of literature genres and expository text.

Fortunately, there is emerging consensus about effective practices and experiences that foster the development of beginning literacy. These practices and experiences constitute a multidimensional approach to beginning literacy that addresses 12 issues and classroom characteristics: motivation, management, time, resources, variety, instruction, support, interaction, knowledge, practice, evaluation, and home–school communication. In developing the curriculum at Benchmark School we have tried to keep at the forefront what we have learned from research about these 12 areas, as well as what we know about how the brain works and how development proceeds.

MOTIVATION

A basic ingredient of a successful multidimensional classroom is a school day saturated with motivation (Pressley, 2001). The teacher orchestrates classroom activities so that the basic needs that undergird motivation—competence, belonging, and choice (Deci, 1995)—are met for all students. For example, in presenting the Benchmark Word Identification lessons called Word Detectives (Gaskins, Ehri, Cress, O'Hara, & Donnelly, 1996–1997), teachers quickly become aware of the discoveries each beginning reader has chosen to make about how our language works. This knowledge allows the teacher to call on an "expert" when a specific sound–letter match is needed to decode an unknown word. Children beam with pride when the teacher asks, "Who is *our expert* for the sound represented by . . . ?" These student experts not only feel competent, but they also feel a sense of belonging as contributing members of the class. As a result, they are motivated to stay engaged in the lesson.

Students also love choice, as well as working with other students. They like to participate in partner reading, in which they are allowed to choose stories to read to their partners from among those they have practiced reading with the class and with their parents. Because they have practiced the chosen stories so often, they are able to discover the pleasure that comes from reading like a good reader reads. We have learned that when we orchestrate fluent reading, students begin to believe that they are good readers. This feeling of competence motivates beginning readers to want to read and to make discoveries about how our language works. Choosing what they read, from text they can read competently, and having the opportunity to read with other students provide motivation for students to engage in literacy tasks.

MANAGEMENT

Teachers of classes containing a high percentage of successful beginning readers typically provide well-managed, productive, and focused classrooms in which there is a high level of involvement in learning (Goldenberg, 2001; Pressley et al., 2001). Students in these classes spend a great part of the school day meaningfully involved in literacy tasks. This involvement comes about because expectations are clear, materials are organized, routines are well established, and the teacher has created a caring community of learners (Noddings, 1992).

In addition, well-managed, productive, and focused classrooms are frequently characterized by instruction in which teachers make use of every-pupil-response (EPR) activities. Expecting that every student will respond is in direct contrast to a practice, which research suggests is more widely employed, in which the teacher initiates a question, one student responds, and the teacher evaluates that response while other students may be off task or thinking about something else (Cazden, 1988). An example of using EPR activities to keep every student involved occurs at Benchmark during activities designed to develop phonemic awareness. The technique is called Ready-Set-Show. Students each have a card with a smiling face on one side and a frowning face on the other. The teacher says a pair of words that do, or do not, rhyme. Children are instructed to whisper those words to themselves; then, after the teacher says "Ready-Set-Show," all students hold up their cards at the same time. They show a smiling face if the words rhyme or a frowning face if the words do not rhyme. Each child is required to do his or her own thinking, because all students hold up their cards at the same moment. This enables the teacher to quickly evaluate who does and does not understand the concept of rhyme. Ready-Set-Show is also employed for evaluating students' awareness of the sounds represented by initial consonants, consonant blends, and consonant digraphs.

Teachers of well-managed classrooms are also experts at scaffolding learning activities so that each student employs active-involvement strategies (e.g., predicting, surveying, setting purposes, monitoring for sense) to stay involved and to achieve success on the assigned literacy task. To monitor their understanding, students are asked to "talk to themselves"—initially a difficult concept for our first graders. Early in the school year, we explicitly teach students what to say when they talk to themselves. The first step in the strategy, monitoring for sense, is for students to tell themselves what happened in the portion of text they read. To accomplish this step, students are taught to use the characters' names and to tell, in their own words, what the characters did. The next step is for students to ask themselves: "Does what I read fit with what has happened so far? Does it fit with the pictures? Does it fit with my background knowledge?"

During small-group, guided-reading lessons, and after a story has been introduced, students whisper-read a portion of the text, then talk to themselves about what they have just read. Once students become comfortable with the basic strategy of monitoring for sense, teachers coach them to whisper to themselves about other aspects of constructing meaning—for example, what they have learned regarding their purpose for reading. Teachers may also ask students to jot down on a note card (using invented spelling) some information from the text that they would like to share with the group. The specific response requested varies according to the goal of the lesson; however, a scaffold is always provided to remind students that they are expected to be actively involved, thinking about and responding to what they have read.

When students have independent time because the teacher is working with other students (e.g., teaching a reading group), those in well-managed classrooms understand exactly how they are expected to use their time. Beginning readers at Benchmark use their independent time to read simple texts, then write short responses to what was read. They also make revisions in a draft of personal experience writing. Some students listen to taped books as they follow along and point to the words in their copies of the book. Others may practice reading their Books-in-Bags (see the "Resources" section below). Because the teacher applies consistent and well-thought-out management techniques, there are few occasions when students are not reading, writing, or responding to text.

TIME

In classrooms in which beginning readers make better progress than may be expected, researchers find that an extensive amount of time each day is devoted to literacy instruction and practice (Allington, 2001; Pearson & Duke, 2002). In fact, it is often the case that the children are engaged in reading and writing for most of the school day.

At Benchmark, literacy is the focus of instruction for beginning readers during at least two-thirds of the day. Teachers read high-quality literature to children and model their thinking as they read. They demonstrate how they think about the writing process and directly teach strategies to help children become better writers. Parent-read-aloud books are sent home each day for parents to read to their children. The following day, teachers discuss one of the books individually with each student and the students write summaries of the books. Teachers read and echo-read simple trade books with students, then send the books home for students to practice with parents. These books are later read to an adult or fellow student. Students participate in directed-reading lessons and read on their own during independent time, writing responses about what they read. Children write their own personal experience stories, which they read to classmates. In addition, reading and writing take place during math, social studies, science, and health lessons, occasions when students learn some of the skills and strategies of nonfiction reading.

Literacy is clearly the major focus in these classrooms. Only an occasional fire drill occurs to interrupt the literacy block. Teachers have requested that there be no assemblies, announcements, field trips, parties, or other interruptions (e.g., for lunch count, attendance, or fund-raising promotions) during the time reserved for literacy. Literacy time is sacred time.

RESOURCES

A learning environment rich in reading and writing resources is typical of the classrooms where children make satisfactory progress in literacy (Allington, 2001; Morrow & Gambrell, 2001; Pressley, in press). These resources are not always the newest or in mint condition, but they represent a variety of literacy possibilities. For example, children have access to a wide array of picture books and little books, both fiction and nonfiction. These include books that are decodable, books that are predictable, and books that feature easily memorizable text. There are listening stations where children can listen to a book read to them as they follow in the book or on the screen. Wordless books are also part of the classroom library. These books encourage students to construct their own stories based on the pictures they contain. Read-aloud books are available for children to take home for their parents to read to them. There are computers and keyboarding programs, as well as books with blank pages to be filled with students' stories.

Beginning readers at Benchmark participate in a Books-in-Bags program. Each night they take home two resealable plastic bags of books for independent reading. One bag contains five little books, usually with very few words on a page, such as those published by Wright Group and Rigby. The books are leveled according to difficulty; thus, books written at the same level of difficulty are placed in one bag. The second bag they take home contains stories featuring the spelling patterns that have been introduced in Word Detectives lessons. During the school day students read in many materials, including basal readers, literature readers, student-composed language experience stories, decodable texts, and predictable rhymes.

The availability of many resources that support literacy instruction provides a wealth of opportunities for students. However, resources in the absence of a knowledgeable teacher yield small returns.

VARIETY

Classrooms in which most students learn how to read tend to feature a wide variety of curriculum and instructional approaches (Allington, 2001; Pearson, 2001; Pressley et al., 2001). It is clear that in these classrooms teachers present no one favorite approach that they believe will work for all students. They know that children learn differently, thus they provide more than one way for children to learn to read, as well as more than one type of text. Their instruction meets the needs of their students. For example, instruction is provided that is a match for students who initially find it easier to acquire a sight vocabulary by memorizing individual words or by relying on context clues rather than by blending isolated sounds into words. Instruction is also provided for those students who prefer to match sounds with a letter or letters (e.g., /n/ to KN), because this seems to work better for them. Further, these teachers provide the option for learning words by analogy, using a known word for each spelling pattern (the vowel and what follows) to unlock unknown words with the same spelling pattern (e.g., using *NOT* to decode *COT*). They do not insist on one way as the right way to learn words. They teach students a menu of word-learning options from which they can choose.

Benchmark teachers provide students with an opportunity to learn to read words by incorporating components from a variety of approaches into their instruction, including pieces of a structured language experience approach; a literature-based approach; a basal reader approach; a synthetic, analytic, or analogy approach (via Word Detectives); or any combination of approaches. However, no matter what approach a student chooses to use to correctly pronounce a word, the central issue is always, "What makes sense?" In Benchmark classes the emphasis is on meaning. Presenting students with a variety of options for word learning, as well as a variety of texts, provides opportunities for all students to achieve success in reading.

INSTRUCTION

Direct, explicit, and systematic instruction in how to complete the assigned classroom activities is the hallmark of a successful teacher of beginning reading (Allington, 2001; Goldenberg, 2001; Hiebert, 1994; Pressley, in press). For example, systematic and explicit instruction in decoding, with a focus on how sounds in words are represented by letters, is essential for children to learn to read (Gaskins et al., 1996–1997; Goldenberg, 2001; NRP, 2000; Taylor, Anderson, Au, & Raphael, 2000). Further, students need instruction in comprehension strategies, such as monitoring understanding, summarizing, inferring, and identifying patterns in text (Gaskins, Anderson, Pressley, Cunicelli, & Satlow, 1993; Pearson, 1993; Pressley et al., 1992, 2001).

The teacher of Benchmark's 6-year-old beginning readers, Mrs. Cress, talks to students about "what you have to do in your head" when you are learning how to read and write. The "what you have to do in your head" is the implementation of active-reader strategies. For example, Mrs. Cress would explain to students that she is going to teach them to use words they know to decode words they do not know. She would go on to tell them *why* this strategy is important:

> "It is important because it would be hard to memorize individually all the words in the dictionary. However, once you know a few words with common spelling patterns, you can use those words to decode other words with the same spelling pattern. Using words you know to figure out words you don't know is more efficient than memorizing individual words."

Mrs. Cress next explains *when* students can use the strategy. She says that this is a good strategy to use any time you come to a word you do not know. You can figure out a word that has the same spelling pattern as a word that you do know. The *how* is to use words you know how to pronounce to decode words that you do not know how to pronounce (e.g., use *CAR* and *HER* to decode *BARTER*).

Each day Benchmark teachers place a *college* word in a sentence on the chalkboard and model how to decode that word using high-frequency, known words. Students love to work with the teacher in decoding the word and feel a great sense of accomplishment in being able to decode difficult words. For example, the sentence on the chalkboard may be "There is a lot of wind in a *cyclone*." The teacher reads aloud: "There is a lot of wind in a blank." The teacher models the process, using known key words to decode *CYCLONE*:

> "The first thing I must do is decide how many spelling patterns there are in the word. I know that each spelling pattern must have a vowel. I see the vowels *Y*, *O*, and *E*, but *E* at the end of a word usually does not represent a sound. Thus, there will be two vowels that represent sounds, so I know the word has two chunks and two spelling patterns. The first spelling pattern is *Y* by itself. The second spelling pattern is *O-N-E*. The key word I know for the spelling pattern *Y* is *MY*. The key word I know for the spelling pattern *O-N-E* is *PHONE*. If I know *MY*, then I know *CY*. If I know *PHONE*, then I know *CLONE*. The word is *CY-CLONE*."

During the rest of the Word Detectives lesson the teacher scaffolds the students' practice, using known words to decode unknown words.

At Benchmark, the teaching of comprehension strategies is also direct, explicit, and systematic. For example, if teachers expect beginning readers to monitor their understanding by summarizing what they have just read, they explicitly teach them a strategy for summarizing. To do this, teachers of beginning readers may teach students to identify the common pattern in narrative text, the pattern of characters, the setting, the story problem, and the resolution. After students have become successful in identifying these story elements, teachers model how they can summarize a story by telling about the main characters, the setting, the central story problem, and the resolution of the problem. Over time, with a decreasing amount of scaffolding, students are expected to use this strategy as one way to monitor their understanding of a selection. All comprehension strategies are taught explicitly, with modeling and guided practice, until the students can apply them independently. At Benchmark, instruction means explicitly teaching students how to do what you expect them to do.

SUPPORT

Teachers of successful beginning readers provide a great deal of support in the form of modeling and scaffolding (Pressley, in press). This support allows teachers to meet each student where she or he is, thus promoting the student's feeling of competence.

For example, to their continuing surprise, Benchmark teachers of beginning readers find that they must frequently model for students the thought process that goes on when one monitors for sense. Too often it is a beginning reader's tendency to keep right on reading even though he or she has mispronounced a word, which results in a sentence not making sense. To make this point, Mrs. Cress read a sentence on the chalkboard, misreading one word, "The girl put *pudding* in the pumpkin costume to make it look round." Mrs. Cress stopped reading and told the class that what she just read didn't make sense; she couldn't imagine using pudding to fill out a pumpkin costume. She went on to say, "I'd better reread the sentence to see if I read all the words correctly." When she finished reading, she wrote the word *pudding* on the chalkboard. At this point, students gleefully told Mrs. Cress that she misread the word *padding*. Mrs. Cress asked the class what she did when she read the sentence that did not make sense. Students replied that she reread to see whether she had read all the words correctly. The students concluded that when they read, they need to think about what they are reading and take action when what they read does not make sense. They decided that one action they could take is to reread.

Scaffolding entails giving students just the right amount of support to enable them to be successful. For example, Benchmark teachers find that the statement, "What have you tried?" may be sufficient scaffolding for success when students ask a teacher to solve a problem for them such as, "How do you pronounce this word?" Asking, "What have you tried?" reminds students that they know strategies that they can use independently before relying on a teacher.

Another instance in which scaffolding is appropriate is when a student expresses frustration at being unable to find information in the text that supports his or her inference. The teacher may begin by asking what strategy the student has learned for making inferences. This may cue the student to remember that inferences are the result of combining relevant information from the text and from one's background knowledge. A teacher can scaffold the formation of the student's response by asking what facts in the selection are related to the inference and what background knowledge the student has about those facts. For example, the student may need to find out when a story took place. The facts in the story may be that the sun was just coming up and some members of the family were still in bed. Once the teacher guides the student to identify the facts that relate to the question, the teacher may ask, "What time of day is it when the sun comes up, yet some people are still in bed?"

Modeling and scaffolding support students in such a way that they learn how to navigate reading and writing while also feeling competent. Support of just the right kind, at just the right time, is characteristic of teachers of achieving beginning readers.

INTERACTION

Successful teachers of beginning literacy provide opportunities for small-group interaction (Hiebert & Taylor, 2000; Taylor, Pearson, Clark, & Walpole, 2000), including guided writing (Taylor, Anderson, et al., 2000) and meaningful talk about text (Goldenberg, 2001; Pearson & Duke, 2002; Pressley, in press). These teachers realize that learning is a social activity, thus students profit from interacting about text.

An opportunity for meaningful interactions occurs during writing instruction. Benchmark's beginning readers enjoy writing personal experience pieces and sharing them with their classmates. In response to a student reading his or her piece to the group, students are taught to tell at least one thing they liked about the piece; then, if appropriate, they ask clarification questions. Based on the clarification questions, writers usually gain information about how they can improve their next draft. To enhance this process, teachers often write question marks on yellow adhesive notes and place them on a student's text at points where classmates have suggested that clarification may be needed. These yellow notes are used to trigger ideas for revision.

Talking about text is a frequent occurrence in Benchmark classes. Students enjoy discussing the literature teachers read to them, as well as the text that they read on their own. To initiate interaction, a teacher may ask a question calling for interpretation or critical analysis, then suggest that each student work with a partner to discuss the question and form a response to share with the group. We find that students are more likely to become actively involved in discussions if they are allowed to talk with a partner before sharing their ideas with the group.

Students' interactions with one another can fulfill their need for belonging, as well as increase their knowledge of the perspectives of others. Thus, the result of providing opportunities for students to interact with other students is often more motivated and better informed students.

KNOWLEDGE

Teachers of successful beginning readers and writers facilitate their students' acquisition of age-appropriate knowledge and concepts that will form the foundation for further learning (Anderson, Wilson, & Fielding, 1988; Neuman, 2001; Neuman & Celano, 2001; Stanovich, 1986). Children's understanding of what they read is based on their experiences and knowledge; thus, teachers must do whatever they can to help children fill the gaps in their background knowledge. One way we accomplish this at Benchmark is by choosing to read aloud to children both fiction and non-fiction that will provide background information for the topics they will be discussing not only in their literacy program, but also in social studies, science, and health classes. When a gap in background information is noted, a teacher may also select simple picture books on the topic for students to read. In addition, Benchmark teachers select parent-read-aloud books that they know will provide background knowledge for the topics that will be read about or discussed in class. Teachers also lend families videotapes that will provide schemas for important understandings. In addition, teachers send home parent-read-alouds that are illustrative of genres that may be unfamiliar to some children. Knowing that organized knowledge is easier to recall and use, Benchmark teachers further facilitate the acquisition of knowledge by guiding students to notice the patterns and structure in the knowledge they are acquiring. What a child knows is a scaffold for the acquisition of additional knowledge. Thus, teachers must do whatever they can to help students acquire age-appropriate concepts and knowledge.

PRACTICE

Students who become successful readers are usually those who have been given opportunities to practice reading. Research confirms the fact that voluminous reading, including repeated reading, in a wide variety of text supports the development of reading fluency (Allington, 2001; Hiebert, 1994; Pressley et al., 2001). It is also true that voluminous writing supports students' development as writers (Hiebert & Taylor, 2000).

Year after year Benchmark students demonstrate that children who read the most books, written at a level that allows for fluent reading, make the most progress in reading. Benchmark's beginning readers are expected to read no less than 20 minutes each evening. An incentive for doing lots of easy reading is an autograph program. Beginning readers read to as many people as possible and obtain an autograph each time they read a "little book" to someone. They may read each book as many times as they like, as long as they point to each word as they read. Students are also asked to analyze the words in stories they are reading and make discoveries about how our language works. They dictate these discoveries to a parent, who records them; the students then share their discoveries the next day in class.

It is a well-accepted fact that to improve in any area, one must practice. If teachers accept this premise, it is shocking that they plan for their students to read only a few pages of text each day, sometimes spending as much as a week reading one five- or six-page basal story. Benchmark students prove every year that the number of words read, in books at an appropriate level, correlates with progress in reading.

EVALUATION

Systematic evaluation of each student's progress is characteristic of classrooms in which students make the most progress (Hiebert & Taylor, 2000; Taylor, Pearson, et al., 2000). Such evaluations are usually both formal and informal. Formal evaluations include standardized tests, usually administered at the beginning and end of each school year, and informal evaluations are those that teachers perform on a daily basis as they teach. At Benchmark we call the latter process *diagnostic teaching*. The cardinal rule at Benchmark is to give no tests or evaluations that will not be used to improve instruction.

Benchmark teachers teach diagnostically to determine which skills, strategies, and concepts each beginning reader has acquired and which he or she needs to develop. Initially, teachers are interested in book handling, concept of word, phoneme awareness and segmentation, and meaning—all are developmental milestones on the road to reading.

For example, with respect to book handling, does the student move through text from front to back and across a page from left to right? With respect to concept of word, does the student understand that white spaces separate words? Can he or she point to the first, next, and last word on a page? Can the student point to words in a familiar text, such as "Happy Birthday," when it is read aloud?

With respect to evaluating phoneme awareness and segmentation, can the student identify words that begin with the same sound? Can the student identify words that rhyme and words that do not rhyme? Can the student supply words that begin with the same consonant sound and produce rhyming words for a given word? Can he or she segment one-chunk words into their component sounds and match letters to sounds? Can the student write using appropriate invented spelling? Does he or she notice and discuss consistencies in the matches between sounds and letters?

Comprehension at this level may be evaluated by noting whether the student expects the text to make sense. Does the student monitor understanding and take remedial action when necessary? Can he or she construct meaning from text?

As students begin to decode words and acquire a sight vocabulary, teachers continue diagnostic teaching, noting the strategies that work best for each student in acquiring a sight vocabulary and in constructing meaning. Further, they note each student's strengths and needs with respect to learning words and constructing meaning from text.

To facilitate diagnostic teaching, some teachers keep a grid on a clipboard nearby, with each student's name across the top and concepts to be learned down the side. As the teacher interacts with students, he or she makes notes about areas of strength and need. These notations provide information about possible instructional goals for the next day.

Benchmark teachers administer achievement tests at the beginning and end of each school year. Decoding, spelling, and comprehension tests are included. Informal reading inventories and/or reader-level tests are administered several times a year to evaluate progress.

Constant evaluation of students' growth and needs alerts teachers to what seems to be working for each student and makes them aware of students who may need more scaffolding in a specific area or who may respond better to a different approach. Evaluation reminds teachers that when a student is not responding to instruction as expected, it is the teacher who must do the changing.

HOME–SCHOOL COMMUNICATION

Productive home–school communication and collaboration are commonplace in schools where students make average or better progress in literacy (Goldenberg, 2001; Taylor, Pearson, et al., 2000). Teachers keep parents informed about classroom goals and how parents can support the achievement of these goals. Parents keep teachers informed about issues that may influence their children's response to instruction. Teachers and parents collaborate to develop systems that enhance achievement.

Teachers of beginning readers at Benchmark meet individually with each student, and with each student's parents, in September prior to students meeting as a whole class. This allows the teacher to learn a little about each student before beginning with the entire class, and it allows parents to share any concerns or special requests with the teacher. During one evening of the first week of school there is a New Parent Coffee for parents new to the school. At this meeting each new parent meets his or her "buddy parent," a veteran Benchmark parent who serves as the new parent's contact person throughout the child's education at Benchmark. At the New Parent Coffee parents hear a talk by the principal about the values that undergird the Benchmark program. A week or two later, at a Back-to-School Night meeting, parents meet in the classroom with their child's teacher and learn about the curriculum for the year. They also learn about the experiences parents can provide for their children that develop background information for topics to be discussed during the school year. At the end of September there is a Fall Get-Together on a Sunday afternoon. This provides an opportunity for students and parents to meet and form friendships with the families of other students in each classroom, as well as with families throughout the school. October and November feature once-a-week morning coffee-and-discussion sessions for parents who are new to the school. At these coffees, parents tell of their successes and challenges and learn how other new parents are coping with the vagaries of supporting a beginning reader. Also during October, the classroom teachers of beginning readers hold an evening meeting to provide information about the Word Detectives Program and to coach parents in ways they can support their children. Individual parent conferences are held three times a year to apprise parents of their children's progress and to set goals for the next trimester. Additional conferences are held as needed.

In addition to meetings, there are other forms of communication between parents and the school. Parents and teachers collaborate via a homework checklist that goes back and forth in a homework folder on a daily basis. On this checklist the parent notes how much time his or her child spent engaged in reading, making discoveries, practicing a word ring, planning for writing, and listening to a parent read aloud. There is also a space for parent and/or teacher comments. Another form of paper communication is provided by the Wednesday Announcements. This is a packet that is sent home each Wednesday to inform all parents about happenings in the Benchmark community. In addition, some teachers send home monthly letters noting specific goals and how parents can reinforce these at home. Phone communication is also common. Parents often write a note on the homework checklist, requesting that a teacher call at a specific time. It stands to reason that beginning readers will respond best to instruction if their parents support the program the teacher is presenting. Communication is essential to gaining parental support.

FINAL THOUGHTS

None of the research-based characteristics of a multidimensional classroom is in itself sufficient to produce successful beginning readers. It is the teacher's ability to adroitly manage the complexities of all 12 of these factors that determines which students will move on to second grade as fluent and knowledgeable readers. No published program can make this happen. Successful beginning readers, especially those who achieve beyond expectation, are the products of extraordinary teachers who skillfully manipulate the time and tools available to ensure that students' literacy abilities will develop to the fullest extent possible.

REFERENCES

Allington, R. L. (2001). Teaching children to read: What really matters. In B. Sornson (Ed.), *Preventing early learning failure* (pp. 5–14). Alexandria, VA: Association for Supervision and Curriculum Development.

Anderson, R. C., Wilson, P., & Fielding, L. (1988). Growth in reading and how children spend time outside of school. *Reading Research Quarterly, 23*, 285–303.

Bond, G. L., & Dykstra, R. (1967). The cooperative research program in first-grade reading instruction. *Reading Research Quarterly, 2*, 5–142.

Cazden, C. B. (1988). *Classroom discourse: The language of teaching and learning.* Portsmouth, NH: Heinemann.

Deci, E. L. (1995). *Why we do what we do: The dynamic of personal autonomy.* New York: Putnam's Sons.

Gaskins, I. W., Anderson, R. C., Pressley, M., Cunicelli, E. A., & Satlow, E. (1993). Six teachers' dialogue during cognitive process instruction. *Elementary School Journal, 93*, 277–304.

Gaskins, I. W., Ehri, L. C., Cress, C., O'Hara, C., & Donnelly, K. (1996–1997). Procedures for word learning: Making discoveries about words. *The Reading Teacher, 50*, 312–327.

Goldenburg, C. (2001). Making schools work for low-income families in the 21st century. In S. B. Neuman & D. K. Dickinson (Eds.), *Handbook of early literacy research* (pp. 211–231). New York: Guilford Press.

Hiebert, E. H. (1994). Reading recovery in the United States: What differences does it make to an age cohort? *Educational Researcher, 23* (9), 15–25.

Hiebert, E. H., & Taylor, B. M. (2000). Beginning reading instruction: Research on early interventions. In M. L. Kamil, P. B. Mosenthal, P. D. Pearson, & R. Barr (Eds.), *Handbook of reading research* (Vol. III, pp. 455–482). Mahwah, NJ: Erlbaum.

Morrow, L. M., & Gambrell, L. B. (2001). Literacy-based instruction in the early years. In S. B. Neuman & D. K. Dickinson (Eds.), *Handbook of early literacy research* (pp. 348–360). New York: Guilford Press.

National Reading Panel (2000). *Teaching children to read: An evidence-based assessment of the scientific research literature on reading and its implications for reading instruction: Reports of the subgroups.* Washington DC: National Institute of Child Health and Human Development.

Neuman, S. B. (2001). Essay Book Review: The role of knowledge in early literacy. *Reading Research Quarterly, 36*, 468–475.

Neuman, S. B., & Celano, D. (2001). Access to print in low-income and middle-income communities. *Reading Research Quarterly, 36*, 8–26.

Neuman, S. B., & Dickinson, D. K. (2001). Introduction. In S. B. Neuman & D. K. Dickinson (Eds.), *Handbook of early literacy research* (pp. 3–10). New York: Guilford Press.

Noddings, N. (1992). *The challenge to care in schools: An alternative approach to education.* New York: Teachers College Press.

Pearson, P. D. (1993). Teaching and learning reading: A research perspective. *Language Arts, 70*, 502–511.

Pearson, P. D. (2001). Life in the radical middle: A personal apology for a balanced view of reading. In R. Flippo (Ed.), *Reading researchers in search of common ground* (pp. 78–83). Newark, DE: International Reading Association.

Pearson, P. D., & Duke, N. K. (2002). Comprehension instruction in the primary grades. In C. C. Block & M. Pressley (Eds.), *Comprehension instruction: Research-based best practices* (pp. 247–258). New York: Guilford Press.

Pressley, M. (2001, December). *What I have learned up until now about research methods in reading education.* Oscar Causey Address at the National Reading Conference, San Antonio, TX.

Pressley, M. (in press). Effective beginning reading instruction: A paper commissioned by the National Reading Conference. *Journal of Literacy Research.*

Pressley, M., El-Dinary, P. M., Gaskins, I. W., Schuder, T., Bergman, J. L., Almasi, J., & Brown, R. (1992). Beyond direct explanation: Transactional instruction of reading comprehension strategies. *Elementary School Journal, 92*, 513–555.

Pressley, M., Wharton-McDonald, R., Allington, R., Block, C. C., Morrow, L., Tracey, D., Baker, K., Brooks, G., Cronin, J., Nelson, E., & Woo, D. (2001). A study of effective first-grade literacy instruction. *Scientific Studies of Reading, 5*, 35–58.

Stanovich, K. E. (1986). Matthew effects in reading: Some consequences of individual differences in the acquisition of literacy. *Reading Research Quarterly, 21*, 360–406.

Taylor, B. M., Anderson, R. C., Au, K. H., & Raphael, T. (2000). Discretion in the translation of research to policy: A case from beginning reading. *Educational Researcher, 29*(6), 16–26.

Taylor, B. M., Pearson, P. D., Clark K., & Walpole, S. (2000). Effective schools and accomplished teachers: Lessons about primary-grade reading instruction in low-income schools. *Elementary School Journal, 101*, 121–165.

4

The Learner, the Teacher, the Text, and the Context

Sociocultural Approaches to Early Literacy Instruction for English Language Learners

SHELLEY HONG XU

Qing, speaking limited English, came with his parents from China to the United States in early August. He was enrolled in an all-English kindergarten class and in a pullout ESL class for 45 minutes daily. In early spring, I noticed him browsing through a Chinese newspaper in the playhouse center. I asked him in Chinese what he was reading. He replied in Chinese, "To learn what is going on in China." I then asked him whether he knew how to say *newspaper* in English. He took me to the environmental print center and pointed at the label *newspaper* beside the English newspapers and said the word. He then showed me a Chinese menu and an English menu. When I asked him in Chinese what they were for, he responded in Chinese, "You choose what you want to eat from here." A minute later, Qing ran to his teacher, Ms. Smith, and gave her the Chinese menu and showed her the English menu. Ms. Smith pointed at the name of the restaurant, asking Qing, "Name of the restaurant, right?" Qing responded in English, "Right!" pointing at the name of the restaurant on the top of the English menu. Ms. Smith then asked me to tell Qing in Chinese that she wanted to know how to say the name of the Chinese restaurant in Chinese. After I translated Ms. Smith's words for him, Qing beamed, saying in Chinese, "Really?"

Maria arrived in the United States from Mexico a year ago and spoke limited English. She was enrolled in an all-English kindergarten class and in a pullout ESL class for 1 hour daily. Maria and her peers spent 30 minutes each day copying letters and words from a chalkboard into their wordbooks. Maria always finished her copying after her peers. After several observations, I discovered that she did not immediately copy letters and words when her teacher, Ms. Jones, had finished writing on the board; instead, she first looked back and forth between her peers' wordbooks and the board for a few minutes, and then she started copying. One day in late winter, I stopped at her table and told her, while pointing to the board, "Copy the letters and words." She responded, "What's *copy*?" I then realized that Maria did not understand the concept of *copy*. She had followed what her peers were doing. I copied down the word *the* on a piece of paper. I then took Maria to *the* board and put the paper next to *the* on the board. I moved my finger from *the* on the board to *the* on the paper, saying, "Copy." Maria responded, "Oh." After school, when I asked Ms. Jones, "Why didn't Maria know the concept of *copy*?" Ms. Jones responded, "I cannot believe that! We have been doing copying since September!"

Qing and Maria are among the more than 4 million students in the United States who speak a language other than English at home. This number reflects a 100% increase between 1989 and 2000 in the population of Limited English Proficient students (National Clearinghouse on Bilingual Education, cited in Freeman & Freeman, 2000). Yet very few teachers in all-English classrooms have been prepared to teach English language learners (Faltis, 2001). The U.S. Department of Education projects that there are fewer than 3% of teachers who have knowledge of another language (National Center for Education Statistics, 1999). With the rapid growth in the population of English language learners and the small number of teachers who have been prepared to teach English language learners, students like Qing and Maria are likely to be in all-English classrooms and taught by European American teachers who have had limited experiences with other languages and cultures (Grant, 2001; Ladson-Billings, 2000; Schmidt, 1998; Xu, 1996, 2000).

This chapter discusses research-based practices of early literacy instruction for English language learners in all-English classrooms. It begins with research on sociocultural approaches to literacy and second language acquisition. A number of vignettes are then presented, and I discuss how the learner, the teacher, the text, and the context interdependently play out in Qing's and Maria's classroom literacy experiences. Finally, I discuss research-based practices that involve the learner, the teacher, the text, and the context.

THE SOCIOCULTURAL APPROACHES TO LITERACY

In the last decades of the 20th century, research on literacy teaching and learning has advanced our understandings of literacy and acquisition of literacy. Apart from the traditional view of literacy that focused on mere cognitive abilities to decode and comprehend words, the sociocultural approaches to literacy acknowledge that literacy is culturally and socially embedded. Children learn how oral and written language serves various purposes within their environments; learning is thus contextualized (Cummins, 1989; Goodman, 1985; Heath, 1983; Purcell-Gates, 1995; Teale & Sulzby, 1986; Wong-Fillmore, 1991). That is, children develop knowledge of language and literacy (1) through many observations of literate persons' use of language and literacy, such as by watching their parents write a check to pay a bill; (2) through extensive interactions with print, such as by reading environmental print—for example, *McDonald's*, to learn that this is a place to buy hamburgers; and (3) through frequent literacy practices, such as by listening to a storybook read and later reading it.

Literacy practices vary greatly from one community to another. In her seminal study, Heath (1983) documented how children in Trackton, an African American working-class community, and those in Roadville, a European American working-class community, practiced literacy in different ways. Children in Trackton, for example, were encouraged to discuss with others what they had read. They could use their personal experiences or share group experiences in constructing the meanings of the text. Children in Roadville, however, were taught to comprehend a written text only from the written words. It was implicit that the author of the text had the right meaning of the text; children's personal interpretations of the text were not allowed.

Variations in literacy practices in different communities are also reflected in mismatches between children's home and school literacy experiences. Studies with a focus on African Americans (Heath, 1983), Asian Americans (Schmidt, 1998; Xu, 1999), Hawaiians (Au & Mason, 1981), Hispanics (Delgado-Gaitan & Trueba, 1997; Volk, 1997), and Native Americans (Philips, 1983) have suggested that children's home literacy practices are not always similar to school-type literacy practices and are not often supported in school literacy learning. Volk's (1997) study showed that both Hispanic children and their parents initiated learning tasks at home, whereas at school they experienced only teacher-initiated learning tasks. Yan, a Chinese American boy receiving instruction in English as a Second Language (ESL), was included in Xu's (1999) study. He was always behind in completing his worksheets, because he was not skillful at doing such assignments. At home, Yan spent most of his time watching TV and reading both Chinese and English books. The rich literacy knowledge he developed through his home literacy experiences was not supported by his classroom literacy experiences.

The sociocultural approaches to literacy are aligned with the research on second language acquisition. Researchers (Cummins, 1994; Krashen, 1982b) have long viewed the goal of second language acquisition to be learners' communicative competence in a language. Krashen's (1985) notion of comprehensible input suggests that language to which English language learners are exposed must be situated in meaningful contexts. Similarly, Cummins's (1994) notion of contextualized language also posits that a meaningful context provides learners with "interpersonal and situational cues" for constructing meanings (p. 4). For Qing, introduced earlier, the cues included the Chinese newspaper, both Chinese and English menus, and his interactions with his teacher and me. The recent theories of second language acquisition (Lantolf, 1999) reinforce language learning as a social practice rather than a mere process of learners acquiring linguistic abilities (Roberts, Byram, Barro, Jordan, & Street, 2000). It is argued that proficiency in English should be measured by how well English language learners function effectively in an English-speaking society.

Furthermore, research on the literacy development of English language learners suggests that language literacy knowledge and skills acquired through learners' native language can be transferred to their English language learning, although degrees of transfer may vary, depending on individual learners and their native languages (Allen, 1994; Cummins, 1989; Hudelson, 1987). Moreover, the process of language and literacy development that English language learners go through is very similar to that of their native English-speaking counterparts. That is, children learn any language best within a rich and meaningful context in which (1) reading, writing, listening, and speaking are integrated and (2) learners use language for real communicative purposes rather than for doing language exercises (Altwerger & Ivener, 1994; Barone, 1996; Perez, 1998). Finally, many pedagogical practices that are effective with native English-speaking students can be also effective, with some modification, for English language learners (Hudelson & Serna, 1997; Perez, 1998).

LOOKING CLOSELY AT THE LEARNER, THE TEACHER, THE TEXT, AND THE CONTEXT

Who Is the Learner?

Qing and Maria were English language learners in all-English kindergarten classrooms, who had different cultural and linguistic experiences. Qing was growing up in a family with a unique Chinese culture and spoke Chinese, a nonalphabetic language that uses characters instead of alphabetical letters.

Maria was part of a Mexican family with a unique Mexican culture and spoke Spanish, an alphabetic language with some similarities to English. Qing and Maria had different literacy experiences in their classrooms. Qing continued to have some contact with Chinese, which was comprehensible and familiar to him. Because of his familiarity with the Chinese newspaper, Qing was able to link its Chinese label to its English label. Furthermore, his experience with a Chinese menu allowed him to discover the similar function of an English menu. His discovery also motivated him to explore with his teacher both Chinese and English menus. The Chinese and English environmental print helped Qing see a connection in the functions and forms of Chinese and English.

Conversely, Maria's literacy experience seemed less personally connected to her as she did not initiate the task of copying. Although she had done copying since the beginning of the school year, she had not grasped the concept of *copy*. The act of copying was decontextualized for Maria, as the letters and words did not seem to be meaningful to her. Maria also lacked an opportunity to demonstrate her understanding of these letters and words and of the connection between English and Spanish. I wonder whether Maria would have learned the concept of *copy* if she had not asked me, "What's *copy*?"

WHO IS THE TEACHER?

Ms. Smith and Ms. Jones were European-American women who did not speak their English-learning students' native languages. Ms. Smith had taught for 3 years and had learned, through her university course work some theoretical and pedagogical principles for teaching English language learners. She believed in providing classroom support for English language learners. When I asked her, "How?" she responded, "You just have to believe in what they can do and provide a context for them to shine." Ms. Jones had taught for 15 years and had taken the school district's professional development courses on teaching English language learners. Ms. Jones believed that Latino culture and language were so similar to mainstream American culture and English that Latino students should not have great difficulty in learning English, adding, "If their parents are supportive of school learning."

The difference between Ms. Smith's and Ms. Jones's beliefs about English language learners was clearly reflected in the different literacy experiences that Qing and Maria had in their classrooms. Ms. Smith encouraged Qing to use his knowledge and experiences of Chinese in the process of learning English. She also showed her interest in learning about Chinese and engaged Qing in verbal and nonverbal conversation about the Chinese and English menus. Although Ms. Smith and Qing had limited knowledge about each other's native language, the conversation was carried out smoothly, because it occurred in the rich context of Qing's wanting to know about the English menu and the similarities and differences between the Chinese and English menus.

Ms. Jones's beliefs also affected her ways of teaching literacy to Maria. When Ms. Jones used the same method to teach the same content to Maria and her native English-speaking peers, she decontextualized Maria's learning to pure acquisition of English letters and words, rather than functions and forms of the English language. Furthermore, Ms. Jones suggested an attitude of blaming victims when she implied a wish for more support from Maria's parents.

What Is the Text?

In this chapter text is defined in a broad sense; that is, it includes both print (e.g., books and environmental print) and nonprint (e.g., TV shows and conversations) text. Both Qing and Maria interacted with text, although the quality and quantity of the text varied to some extent. Qing was reading self-selected Chinese environmental print that was familiar and meaningful to him; he was also exposed to English environmental print, to which he made a connection through his Chinese environmental print. Moreover, Qing was able to interact with me and with his teacher. Both English and Chinese texts made sense to him in terms of their functions, and he was also learning about their forms when he pointed to the name of the restaurant on the English menu.

Conversely, Maria did not have any exposure to Spanish in her classroom. Ms. Jones selected the letters and words for Maria to copy. Maria had been mechanically practicing penmanship since the beginning of the school year. The letters and words seemed to make less sense to Maria than to her native English-speaking peers, because they had rich contact with oral English, which Maria lacked. There were also no interactions between Ms. Jones and Maria during the task of copying.

What Is the Context?

As described in the preceding vignettes, the context for Qing and Maria included their all-English classrooms and the instructional and sociocultural contexts. In Qing's case, the instructional context was learner-centered: He was permitted free exploration of environmental print in both Chinese and English and was able to interact with his teacher. Qing was an active participant, and his teacher was a co-participant. The sociocultural context was present in the Chinese environmental print (i.e., the menu and newspaper) and the Chinese language that Qing was encouraged to speak. Ms. Smith indirectly created the sociocultural context that was familiar to Qing. In Maria's case, the instructional context was teacher-centered: Maria was doing seatwork that was unfamiliar and meaningless to her. Maria was not an active participant nor could she interact with both Spanish and English. A sociocultural context for Maria was evidently absent from her classroom. She was simply asked to copy what her teacher had written. Maria did not have any interaction with her teacher during the task of copying.

RESEARCH-BASED PRACTICES OF EARLY LITERACY INSTRUCTION FOR ENGLISH LANGUAGE LEARNERS

The discussion of the learner, the teacher, the text, and the context, in regard to the vignettes presenting Qing and Maria, shows that the process of English language learners acquiring English literacy is not a mere process of learning the linguistic codes. Rather, the process is dynamic, cultural, and social, and it involves not just the learner but, equally important, the teacher, the text, and the context. The instructional materials and strategies used by teachers of English language learners do not always reflect best practices. Early literacy instruction for English language learners must be situated within a broad social and cultural context, which includes learners' outside-school sociocultural communities. Teachers do not simply teach literacy; they teach literacy *to* and *with* English language learners. The following sections, with a consideration of the learner, the teacher, the text, and the context, discuss what teachers can do to support English language learners.

Become Active in Self-Examining Beliefs and Misconceptions about English Language Learners

Lisa Delpit (1988) states, "We do not really see through our eyes or hear through our ears, but through our beliefs" (p. 297). Before teachers ask themselves what they can do to best support the literacy development of English language learners in all-English classrooms, they must first examine their own beliefs and misconceptions about the cultures of English language learners and the effects of their own cultural and linguistic experiences on the development of such beliefs and misconceptions (Grant, 2001; Ladson-Billings, 2000; Schmidt, 1999). Just as English language learners bring to the classrooms their unique cultures, teachers' own cultures color the way they teach. It is important to discover how learners' cultures differ from those of their teachers, to constantly examine the way in which teachers react to such differences, and to pay special attention to the differences.

In particular, teachers must challenge the misconceptions and stereotypes about English language learners. During conversations with teachers of Asian English language learners in all-English classrooms, I often hear comments glorifying the learners: "They are *so* smart!" But few teachers know that in the Asian culture it is believed that if one works hard, one can accomplish one's goal. So instead of attributing Asian students' success to intelligence, teachers should praise the students for their diligence. The teachers' praise thus becomes relatively fitting to Asian students' culture.

To examine their own cultures and beliefs, as well as misconceptions about other cultures, teachers can begin by writing their autobiographies (Florio-Ruane, 1994; Ladson-Billings, 2000), which can allow them to become aware of how their own cultures shape who they are. Teachers can then interview their English language learners about their cultures. The next step is for them to look for similarities and differences between their own cultures and their students'. Finally, teachers can reflect on how they feel about the differences and how their attitudes toward such differences have affected their teaching English language learners (Schmidt, 1999). If an English language learner is not ready to communicate in English during the interview, the teacher can interview parents or people from the learner's community. An alternative is to ask someone to act as an interpreter during the interview.

Become Active in Learning about Learners' Native Language and Culture

Show Your Interest in Learners' Native Language

It is virtually impossible for teachers to learn a student's native language in a short period of time, but it is possible to learn *about* it. The next time you hear English language learners talking in their native language, pay closer attention to their talk. Try to understand the talk as much as you can. This process can put teachers in the position of students who are learning a new language (English). Even if you do not understand the talk, smile and nod instead of frowning and walking away. Students are always thrilled to learn that their teachers want to know about their native language.

Ask English language learners and their parents to bring to class print materials written in their native language. Read the materials and try to discover similarities and differences between English and the native language. Use the Chinese text in Figure 4.1 to see how many similarities and differences between Chinese and English you can discover. Through this experience, you may develop some knowledge about Chinese and thus have a better understanding of what can and cannot be transferred from Chinese to English. Your own discovery about native language is important, as young English language learners often cannot describe the specific details of their native language.

Chinese	English
小红： 你好！知道你今年回上海很高兴。小弟这月来北京把你的E-Mail地址给我了。想给你寄一张照片，可是找了半天也没找到一张全家福，只能给你寄两张老照片。 　给我寄一张你家的照片给我看看。 　你的个人主页，我怎么找不到？是这个地址吗：www. tltc.ttu.edu/Xu。 　　　　叔周彬文	Xiao Hong: Hello! I was glad to learn that this year you came back to visit Shanghai. This month Xiao Di came to Beijing and gave me your e-mail address. I thought I could send you a photo of our family, but could not find one at all. I had to send you just two pictures that were taken a long time ago. Please send me a photo of your family. I would like to see it. How come I couldn't find your home page? Is this the right address: *www.tltc.ttu.edu/Xu*? Uncle Zhou Binwen

FIGURE 4.1. A Chinese and English text.

Encourage Your Learners to Use Their Native Language

Encourage learners to bring something from home that can help to demonstrate their knowledge of their native language. For example, during Show and Tell, learners can bring environmental print, print materials, toys, and photos that are familiar to them. Because of the personal significance of these cultural artifacts, students are more likely to show and tell about them. It is OK if your students just want to show, but not talk about, their artifacts. It is especially true for English language learners who are at the silent stage of their language development where they are observing the functions and forms of language rather than using language to communicate (Krashen, 1982a). Just showing the artifacts can give learners a sense of participation. If learners are ready to show *and* tell, encourage them to talk about their artifacts in the language with which they feel most comfortable. Remember to model for learners what to do in Show and Tell, as it may not be a common literacy activity in the schools of their home country.

"Visit" Learners' Outside-School Sociocultural Context

To learn about your learners' culture, you can read books and talk with parents and others from that culture. A more effective way of learning, however, is to have contact with that culture, such as by attending a cultural event (e.g., Cinco de Mayo) and visiting the learners' sociocultural context (i.e., the community and the home). With consent from school administrators and parents, take a walk with your learners through their neighborhood (Orellana & Hernández, 1999). Encourage your learners to be your tour guides. Ask them about environmental print in English and in the native language, if any. Also ask them to describe life in the neighborhood, such as after-school activities. Their descriptions can help you understand your learners' unique literacy practices. During my interviews with Chinese parents and children who did not live in my neighborhood, I learned that children did not often play outside their apartments because of crime in the neighborhood. Instead, they spent after-school hours in a church studying the Bible and Chinese. Even without the company of your learners, you can take a walk through their neighborhood, observing what is similar to and different from your neighborhood. A neighborhood walk can allow a teacher to get a broader sense of their learners' sociocultural context.

To gain a deeper sense of the sociocultural context in which learners' unique literacy practices occur, teachers should conduct home visits. During a home visit, bring an open mind and a note pad. First, jot down whatever you have observed. Pay special attention to (1) the presence of print and nonprint, school materials in English and in the native language, (2) the availability of school supplies (e.g., pencils, paper), (3) any display of the learner's work completed at school or at home, and (4) the use of the native language between the learner and the parent(s) or others.

Then have a casual conversation with the parents and the learner about literacy practices that occur at home. Focus the conversation on:

1. School-related literacy practices (e.g., reading a book related to what has been read at school) that the learner initiates, that the parent initiates, and that the learner and the parent co-initiate.
2. Non-school-related literacy practices (e.g., looking at a supermarket advertisement to decide what to buy) that the learner initiates, that the parent initiates, and that the learner and the parent co-initiate.
3. Parents' beliefs about teaching and learning and the educational system in the home country.

Finally, ask parents and the learner to demonstrate for you one school-related and one non-school-related literacy practice. Through the demonstration, you may witness how parents and the learner carry out a literacy practice very differently from the way you do it at school. In my observations of Chinese parents, I learned that the main purpose of reading books to a child was to help the child learn new words and moral lessons; book enjoyment was less important, as it would not help with improving the child's academic achievements. Thus, the parents' purpose of reading to children may be very different from many teachers' preconceptions. Consequently, Chinese students may lack experiences of responding to books. Chinese students thus may need their teachers to provide more frequent

modeling for them on how to respond to a book read and additional opportunities for responding to books.

Become an Effective Kidwatcher of Your Learners

Although all English language learners are required to be assessed at the beginning of a school year, the assessment data do not always accurately reflect what learners know about English and their native language (García
& Pearson, 1994). In many cases, teachers do not obtain any information
about learners' language and literacy skills in the native language. Therefore, teachers must conduct an ongoing informal assessment of learners
throughout a school year. Becoming a "kidwatcher" (Goodman, 1985) of
English language learners is an effective way to get to know about the
learners' language and literacy development in both English and the native
language. Make sure to allow 10 to 15 minutes every day to kidwatch your
learners interacting with print, with peers, and with you in various settings.
Christie, Enz, and Vukelich (1997) provide a guide for kidwatching. While
kidwatching, teachers must first focus on the setting, the participants, and
the event and then interpret what has been observed. The following is an
example of kidwatching Qing using the guide by Christie and colleagues
(p. 4):

1. *The setting*: Where and when does the observation occur?

    In early spring, while I was visiting Qing's all-English kindergar-
    ten class, I noticed Qing browsing through a Chinese newspaper in
    the playhouse center in his classroom. There were many literacy-
    related play props in the center, such as environmental print and
    newspapers in English and in Chinese, a calendar, and containers
    for food.

2. *The participants*: Who is involved in the event you are observing?

    I was observing Qing, a kindergartner who came from China to
    the United States in early August. He spoke limited English and was
    enrolled in a pullout ESL class for 45 minutes daily.

3. *The event*: What did you observe? Try to record the exact dialogue.

    SHELLEY: (*in Chinese*) What are you reading?

    QING: (*in Chinese*) To learn what is going on in China.

    SHELLEY: (in Chinese) Do you know how to say "newspaper" in
    English?

    QING: (*pointing at the label "newspaper" beside a stack of English
    newspapers*) Newspaper.

4. *Interpreting the event*: What does the child understand about lan-
    guage and literacy?

Qing understood the informative function of a newspaper. He was able to locate an English label for a newspaper by reading English environmental print at the environmental print center. He also demonstrated his knowledge of environmental print both in Chinese and in English.

Keep records of your kidwatching and examine patterns that emerge across a period of time. These patterns become rich assessment data that provide you with details on what the learner knows about language and literacy in English and in the native language. This information can also guide you in modifying your teaching to support the learner's strengths and address his or her needs.

Become Skillful at Selecting Texts

When making texts available to English language learners, keep in mind these guiding principles: (1) Texts should value learners' native language and culture (Altwerger & Ivener, 1994; Freeman & Freeman, 2000), (2) texts should help lower learners' anxiety about learning English (Krashen, 1982a), and (3) texts should help to maximize learners' engagement in constructing meaning. The illustrations of the texts should be appealing and supportive of the texts (Au, 1993; Freeman & Freeman, 2000).

Texts of Learners' Native Language and Culture

The presence of a learner's native language in an all-English classroom adds familiarity and provides comfort to English language learners (Freeman & Freeman, 2000). Print materials in the native language continue supporting a learner's exploration of the functions and forms of that language (Allen, 1994). The knowledge gained through exploration can be transferred to English learning. Encourage learners to read print materials in their native languages and ask them to talk about these materials to the class. In so doing, you can provide opportunities for learners to demonstrate what they know about the functions and forms of language. It is possible to obtain texts written in a student's native language or in a bilingual format from various publishers (e.g., Scholastic). Ask your students and parents to bring print materials written in their native language or in a bilingual format. You can also ask parents or anyone from the learner's community to translate the learner's favorite English book into his or her native language.

Texts on learners' linguistic and cultural experiences (see Figure 4.2 for a list of books) also help to create a familiar and comfortable classroom environment for English language learners. When reading such texts, learners can use their own similar linguistic and cultural experiences to build up

Ada, A. F. (1997). *Gathering the sun: An alphabet in Spanish and English*. New York: Lothrop.

Anholt, C., & Anholt, L. (1998). *Big book of families*. Cambridge, MA: Candlewick.

Bang, M. (1997). *Diez, Nueve, Ocho*. New York: Morrow.

Bartoletti, S. C. (1997). *Dancing with Dziadziu*. San Diego: Harcourt Brace.

Bercaw, E. C. (2000). *Halmoni's day*. New York: Dial.

Bertrand, D. G. (1997). *Sip, slurp, soup soup*. Houston, TX: Pinata Books.

Bloom, V., & Axtell, D. (1997). *Fruits: A Caribbean counting poem*. New York: Holt.

Chavarria-Chairez, B. (2000). *Magda's tortillas*. Houston, TX: Pinata Books.

Davol, M. (1997). *The paper dragon*. New York: Atheneum.

dePaola, T. (1989). *Tony's bread*. New York: Putnam.

Doodley, N. (1991). *Everybody cooks rice*. Minneapolis, MN: Carolrhoda Books.

Garza, C. L. (1996). *In my family*. Danbury, CT: Children's Press.

Hausheir, R. (1997). *Celebrating families*. New York: Scholastic.

Hopkins, J., Gillespie, I., & Wong, R. (1999). *Hide and seek in Hawaii*. Honolulu, HI: Mutual Publishing.

Levine, E. (1989). *I hate English!* New York: Scholastic.

Low, W. (1997). *Chinatown*. New York: Holt.

McDermott, G. (1997). *Musicians of the sun*. New York: Simon & Schuster.

Miller, J. (1997). *American Indian families*. Danbury, CT: Children's Press.

Morris, A. (1997). *Light the candle! Bang the drum!* New York: Dutton Books.

Morta, P. (1992). *A birthday basket for Tia*. New York: Macmillan.

Olawsky, L. A. (1997). *Colors of Mexico*. Minneapolis, MN: Carolrhoda Books.

Pomeranc, M. H. (1998). *The American Wei*. New York: Albert Whitman.

Rosa-Casanova, S. (2001). *Mama Provi and the pot of rice*. New York: Aladdin.

Russell, C. Y. (1997). *Moon festival*. Honesdale, PA: Boyds Mills.

Say, A. (1993). *Grandfather's journey*. Boston: Houghton Mifflin.

Soto, G. (1993). *Too many tamales*. New York: Putnam.

Soto, G. (1999). *Snapshots from the wedding*. New York: Putnam.

Tchana, K. H., & Pami, L. T. (1996). *Oh, no, Toto!* New York: Scholastic.

Waters, K. (1990). *Lion dancer: Ernie Wan's Chinese New Year*. New York: Scholastic.

Yem, S. S. (1997). *All kinds of families*. Birmingham, AL: New Hope Publishing.

Zamorano, A. (1999). *Let's eat!* New York: Scholastic.

FIGURE 4.2. Books on English language learners' linguistic and cultural experiences.

background knowledge. Such background knowledge can make the texts more personally connected to learners and make their comprehension of the text less challenging (Freeman & Freeman, 2000). Thus, learner engagement is maximized, and comprehension of the text can become easier. Native English-speaking students in the class can also learn about other cultures and languages from these texts.

Wordless Texts

Because of the absence of words in wordless texts (e.g., wordless books and photos), English language learners feel less intimidated while reading, as they can tell a story based solely on illustrations (Flatley & Rutland, 1986). Using wordless texts (see Figure 4.3 for a list of wordless books) also allows learners to demonstrate their knowledge of text structures both in English and in a native language. Because wordless texts are subject to interpretations, it is possible for English language learners at different stages of English acquisition to benefit from reading them.

Teachers can use the Language Experience Approach to teach literacy skills through authentic texts learners have produced from wordless books. Specifically, a learner browses through a wordless book and the learner talks about the book read. The teacher records the learner-produced talk on chart paper and then reads it to and with the learner. Next, the teacher and the learner talk about different aspects of the produced text, such as the main ideas of the text and concepts of print. Later, the teacher types the learner-produced text on a computer and cuts the text into sentence strips. The learner uses the sentence strips to label the illustrations in the wordless book. The process of making print–illustration matches may assist the learner to note missing information in the produced text. Thus, revising the text becomes a meaningful literacy activity. The teacher and the learner can

Bang, M. (1980). *The gray lady and the strawberry snatcher.* New York: Simon & Schuster.

Briggs, R. (1978). *The snowman.* New York: Random House.

Carle, E. (1971). *Do you want to be my friend?* New York: HarperCollins.

dePaola, T. (1978). *Pancakes for breakfast.* New York: Harcourt.

Goodall, J. S. (1998). *Creepy castle.* New York: Margaret McElderry.

Goodall, J. S. (1999). *Midnight adventures of Kelly, Dot, and Esmeralda.* New York: Margaret McElderry.

Goodall, J. S. (1999). *Naughty Nancy goes to school.* New York: Margaret McElderry.

Goodall, J. S. (1999). *The surprise picnic.* New York: Margaret McElderry.

Goodall, J. S.(1999). *Naughty Nancy.* New York: Margaret McElderry.

Hoban, T. (1986). *Shapes, shapes, shapes.* New York: William Morrow.

Hoban, T. (1988). *26 letters and 99 cents.* New York: Greenwillow.

Hoban, T. (1994). *What is that?* New York: Greenwillow.

Hoban, T. (1994). *Who are they?* New York: Greenwillow.

Hoban, T. (1997). *Is it larger? Is it smaller?* Glenview, IL: Scott Foresman.

Hoban, T. (1999). *Construction zone.* New York: Greenwillow.

Hutchins, P. (1987). *Changes, changes.* New York: Aladdin.

Mercer, M. (1992). *A boy, a dog, and a frog.* New York: Dial.

Rathmann, P. (1996). *Good night, gorilla.* New York: Putnam.

Rohmann, E. (1994). *Time flies.* New York: Crown.

Spier, P. (1982). *Rain.* Garden City, NY: Doubleday.

Spier, P. (1996). *Christmas.* Garden City, NY: Bantam Doubleday Dell.

Tafuri, N. (1984). *Have you seen my duckling?* New York: Greenwillow.

Wiesner, D. (1991). *Tuesday.* Boston: Houghton Mifflin.

FIGURE 4.3. A list of wordless books.

visit the wordless book, and the original and revised learner-produced texts, many times, during which the learner can engage in various literacy activities (e.g., adding details to the produced text).

If a learner produces a text in his or her native language for a wordless book, the teacher tape-records it for someone literate in that language to translate. The bilingual text is then pasted as a caption for a picture onto the wordless book. Then the bilingual text allows the learner to learn about the native language and English. Teachers should save learner-produced texts as powerful assessment data for the learner to note later in regard to his or her growing knowledge of language and literacy in both English and the native language.

Texts That Share a Universal Knowledge Base

Young children are always inquisitive about their environment. Regardless of what native languages English language learners speak or where they have lived, they tend to ask similar questions about their environment (e.g., animals). Texts that share a universal knowledge base include *ABC* books, concept books (e.g., numbers, shapes, and senses), and other informational books (e.g., dinosaurs). These texts can help learners bring their prior knowledge of their environment to the process of comprehending the text (Freeman & Freeman, 2000). When selecting books for English language learners, teachers need to make sure that texts are written at a level comprehensible to the learners and that the illustrations/photos are supportive of the texts.

Texts with Linguistic Patterns

English language learners need to have multiple exposures to the same linguistic patterns in order to master the patterns (Boyle & Peregoy, 1990; Farnan, Flood, & Lapp, 1994). Pattern books provide English language learners with predictable text structure and with multiple opportunities to visit a linguistic pattern. When a pattern book is also an informational book, reading it becomes more meaningful, authentic, and rewarding, as language learning occurs through content learning (Freeman & Freeman, 2000). Teachers can assess learners' mastery level of a linguistic pattern through learners' patterned writing. For example, a teacher can ask learners to substitute a few words in the patterned sentence from *I Went Walking* (Williams, 1989): "I went walking. What did you see? I saw a black cat looking at me." Learners can use a different color word in the sentence ("I saw a *yellow* cat looking at me"), a different animal ("I saw a black *sheep* looking at me"), and a different verb ("I saw a black cat *smiling* at me").

Texts Based on TV Shows

Many children's books are based on TV shows (e.g., *Blue's Clues*). Several shows promote English language learners' native language and culture. The characters in *Dora, the Explorer* on the Nickelodeon channel speak both Spanish and English. Furthermore, many TV shows are part of the popular culture of children, which can be universal. When I first met Qing, *Pokémon* was the topic that started our conversation. I later learned that Pokémon had been very popular in China before it appeared in the United States. I felt that Qing's talking about Pokémon gave him a sense of pride, as he told me in Chinese, "I still can talk in here, even if I don't speak English." If the teacher provides tapes and books of favorite TV shows, learners have opportunities to both watch a show and read a book about it. Because learners are already familiar with and interested in the show, they are more likely to use their prior knowledge in comprehending the book and to have more active interactions with the book, peers, and the teacher.

Many books based on TV series have the same characters, similar plot, and similar text structure (e.g., *Clifford*). These features make the book series more predictable and thus reduce the level of difficulty with the language for English language learners. After learners read the first several books in a series, they become familiar with characters, plot, and text structure. Such familiarity allows learners to use their background knowledge in reading subsequent books in a series; they thus continue reinforcing linguistic and comprehension skills.

Become a Master of Strategies and Contexts

Research on English language learners' successful literacy experiences in all-English classrooms has indicated that teachers can modify some instructional strategies that they use with native English-speaking children to teach English language learners (Au, 1993; Freeman & Freeman, 2000; Perez, 1998; Xu, 1999). Although a teacher's knowledge of instructional strategies matters to the success of learners, how well a teacher orchestrates and modifies multiple strategies to meet learners' unique needs matters more. For example, after reading aloud to the whole class, the teacher can provide English language learners with additional experiences with the book before their independent reading of the book. The teacher re-reads it with English language learners so that they have more exposure to oral English language. Next, the teacher lets learners listen to the book on tape. Throughout the week, the teacher encourages native English-speaking students to read the book to and with English language learners. Through multiple exposures to the oral version of the book, learners can experience less difficulty during their independent reading.

In addition to having knowledge of the learners, texts, and strategies, teachers of English language learners must also become masterful at creating authentic, meaningful, and print-rich contexts in their all-English classrooms (Altwerger & Ivener, 1994). Specifically, teachers need to ensure the following:

1. English language learners have a familiar and comfortable environment in which their native language and culture is present and valued. Texts written in the native language and about native culture are available. Teachers encourage learners to share with the class their native language and culture. Use of native language in literacy activities is encouraged.
2. English language learners have easy access to a wide range of texts of various topics and interests. The texts allow learners to actively use their prior knowledge in comprehension and demonstrate their growing knowledge about language and literacy and about specific content topics.
3. English language learners work with native English-speaking peers in small and large collaborative groups. There are various levels of student–student and student–teacher interactions during literacy activities. The teacher explicitly models strategies and scaffolds learners' learning.
4. English language learners experience reading, writing, listening, speaking, valuing, and interpreting through literacy activities that have personal significance and interest to them. Learners use language and literacy for authentic, meaningful, and communicative purposes rather than for mere practicing of linguistic codes.

CONCLUDING REMARKS

I began this chapter with Qing's and Maria's literacy experiences in their all-English classrooms and then used the sociocultural approaches to literacy in discussing how the learner, the teacher, the text, and the context play out in their classroom experiences. The presentation of research-based practices for English language learners focused on what the teacher can do for learners. Specifically, I stressed that teachers have the responsibility and power to help learners (by including their native language and culture) feel welcomed, respected, and valued in the classroom. They are also responsible for making the text supportive of learners' language and literacy learning in both English and their native language, and for making the context most conducive to learners' engagement in literacy activities and to their demonstration of growing knowledge in language and literacy. I hope that teachers of English language learners see themselves playing a far more important role in learners' successful literacy experiences than the instructional strategies and materials they provide.

REFERENCES

Allen, V. G. (1994). Selecting materials for the reading instruction of ESL children. In K. Spangenberg-Urbschat & R. Pritchard (Eds.), *Kids come in all languages: Reading instruction for ESL students* (pp. 108–131). Newark, DE: International Reading Association.

Altwerger, B., & Ivener, B. L. (1994). Self-esteem: Access to literacy in multicultural and multilingual classrooms. In K. Spangenberg-Urbschat & R. Pritchard (Eds.), *Kids come in all languages: Reading instruction for ESL students* (pp. 65–81). Newark, DE: International Reading Association.

Au, K. H. (1993). *Literacy instruction in multicultural settings.* Fort Worth, TX: Harcourt Brace.

Au, K. H., & Mason, J. M. (1981). Social organizational factors in learning to read. *Reading Research Quarterly, 17,* 115–152.

Barone, D. (1996). Whose language? Learning from bilingual learners in a developmental first-grade classroom. In D. Leu, C. Kinzer, & K. Hinchman (Eds.), *Literacies for the 21st century: Research and practice: Forty-fifth yearbook of the National Reading Conference* (pp. 170–182). Chicago: National Reading Conference.

Boyle, O. F., & Peregoy, S. F. (1990). Literacy scaffolds: Strategies for first- and second-language readers and writers. *The Reading Teacher, 44,* 194–2000.

Christie, J., Enz, B., & Vukelich, C. (1997). *Teaching language and literacy: Preschool through the elementary grades.* New York: Addison-Wesley.

Cummins, J. (1989). *Empowering minority students.* Sacramento: California Association for Bilingual Education.

Cummins, J. (1994). The acquisition of English as a second language. In K. Spangenberg-Urbschat & R. Pritchard (Eds.), *Kids come in all languages: Reading instruction for ESL students* (pp. 36–61). Newark, DE: International Reading Association.

Delgado-Gaitan, C., & Trueba, H. (1997). *Crossing cultural borders: Education for immigrant families in America.* New York: Falmer Press.

Delpit, L. (1988). The silenced dialogue. *Harvard Educational Review, 58,* 280–298.

Faltis, C. J. (2001). *Joinfostering* (3rd ed.). Upper Saddle River, NJ: Merrill.

Farnan, N., Flood, J., & Lapp, D. (1994). Comprehending through reading and writing: Six research-based instructional strategies. In K. Spangenberg-Urbschat & R. Pritchard (Eds.), *Kids come in all languages: Reading instruction for ESL students* (pp. 135–157). Newark, DE: International Reading Association.

Flatley, J. K., & Rutland, A. D. (1986). Using wordless picture books to teach linguistically and culturally different students. *The Reading Teacher, 39,* 276–281.

Florio-Ruane, S. (1994). The future teachers' autobiography club: Preparing educators to support literacy learning in culturally diverse classrooms. *English Education, 26,* 52–66.

Freeman, D. E., & Freeman, Y. (2000). *Teaching reading in multilingual classrooms.* Portsmouth, NH: Heinemann.

García, G. E., & Pearson, P. D. (1994). Assessment and diversity. *Review of Research in Education, 20,* 337–391.

Goodman, Y. (1985). Kidwatching: Observing children in the classroom. In A. Jaggar & M. Smith-Burke (Eds.), *Observing the language learner* (pp. 9–18). Newark, DE: International Reading Association.

Grant, C. A. (2001). Teachers and linking literacies of yesterday and today with literacies of tomorrow: The need for education that is multicultural and social reconstructionist. *National Reading Conference Yearbook, 50,* 63–81.

Heath, S. (1983). *Ways with words.* New York: Cambridge University Press.

Hudelson, S. (1987). The role of native language literary in the education of language minority children. *Language Arts, 64,* 827–834.

Hudelson, S., & Serna, I. A. (1997). Optimizing oral language learning experiences for bilingual and second-language learners. In J. Christie, B. Enz, & C. Vukelich, (Eds.), *Teaching language and literacy* (pp. 108–113). New York: Addison-Wesley.

Krashen, S. D. (1982a). *Principles and practice in second language acquisition.* New York: Pergamon.

Krashen, S. D. (1982b). *Second language acquisition and second language learning.* Oxford, UK: Pergamon.

Krashen, S. D. (1985). *Input in second language acquisition.* Oxford, UK: Pergamon.

Ladson-Billings, G. (2000). Fighting for our lives: Preparing teachers to teach African-American students. *Journal of Teacher Education, 51,* 206–214.

Lantolf, J. (Ed.). (1999). *Sociocultural theory and second language learning.* Oxford, UK: Oxford University Press.

National Center for Education Statistics. (1999). *The condition of education 1999.* Washington, DC: U.S. Department of Education.

Orellana, M. F., & Hernández, A. (1999). Talking the walk: Children reading urban environmental print. *The Reading Teacher, 51,* 612–619.

Perez, B. (Ed.). (1998). *Sociocultural contexts of language and literacy.* Mahwah, NJ: Erlbaum.

Philips, S. U. (1983). *The invisible culture.* New York: Longman.

Purcell-Gates, V. (1995). *Other people's words: The cycle of low literacy.* Cambridge, MA: Harvard University Press.

Roberts, C., Byram, M., Barro, A., Jordan, S., & Street, B. (2000). *Language learners as ethnographers.* Clevedon, UK: Multilingual Matters.

Schmidt, P. R. (1998). *Cultural conflict and struggle: Literacy learning in a kindergarten program.* New York: Peter Lang.

Schmidt, P. R. (1999). Know thyself and understand others. *Language Arts, 76,* 332–340.

Teale, W., & Sulzby, E. (1986). *Emergent literacy: Writing and reading.* Norwood, NJ: Ablex.

Volk, D. (1997). Questions in lessons. *Anthropology and Education Quarterly, 28,* 22–49.

Williams, S. (1989). *I went walking.* Orlando, FL: Harcourt.

Wong-Fillmore, L. (1991). Second-language learning in children. In E. Bialystok (Ed.), *Language processing in bilingual children* (pp. 49–69). Cambridge, UK: Cambridge University Press.

Xu, H. (1996). A Filipino ESL kindergartner's successful beginning literacy learning experience in a mainstream classroom. In D. J. Leu, C. K. Kinzer, & K. A. Hinchman (Eds.), *Literacies for the 21st century: Research and Practice: Forty-fifth yearbook of the National Reading Conference* (pp. 219–231). Chicago: National Reading Conference.

Xu, H. (1999). Reexamining continuities and discontinuities: Language minority children's home and school literacy experiences. *National Reading Conference Yearbook, 48*, 224–237.

Xu, H. (2000). Preservice teachers in a literacy methods course consider issues of diversity. *Journal of Literacy Research, 32*, 505–531

Part II

Home Literacy Experiences of Children

5

What Hannah Taught Emma and Why It Matters

LISA LENHART
KATHLEEN ROSKOS

Emma, who is 2½ years old, is standing in the kitchen when her 5-year-old sister, Hannah, enters. Hannah is wearing a sweatshirt with her name embroidered across the front in big, multicolored block letters. Emma notices and comments, "Hannah, I like your ABCs." Hannah explains, "Those aren't ABCs, Emma. That spells Hannah. See— *H-A-N-N-A-H*. If you had one of these it would say, *E-M-M-A*. Emma."

The late-20th-century discovery that children's literacy development begins at a very early age has profoundly affected our understanding of early literacy learning and the contexts in which it occurs. Once reserved for the first grade in school (and first grade teachers), learning to read and write is now seen as a matter for families, communities, child service agencies, *and* schools. These different places, and the people in them, provide all kinds of opportunities for young children to encounter writing and reading in their early days. It is out of the particulars of these literacy experiences— their mundane purposes and tiny details—that children's first wonderings become organized into literacy understandings and skills that pull children forward.

Our chapter continues this brief history of closely observing children's early literacy, which exposes the riches of their capabilities. Its content draws on a year-long observational case study that describes the literacy interactions of two sisters—Hannah and Emma—in their natural home environment (Lenhart, 2000). We first provide the background of this case study, highlighting how observations were made and documented by their mother (Lenhart) in the flow of everyday life. We then examine four literacy episodes as examples of sibling teaching and learning. Applying a Vygotskian (1978) lens, our goal is to show how Hannah, the older sister, imparts knowledge to Emma, demonstrates literacy skills, and shapes her emergent attitudes toward print and books. She, too, is Emma's first teacher along with her parents. And Emma is a willing pupil, although (as we soon see) she has quite a mind of her own.

BACKGROUND OF THE CASE STUDY

Like Piaget before them, several notable parent-researchers have used the case study approach to observe and document the literacy learning of their own children (Baghban, 1984; Bissex, 1980; Lass, 1982, 1983; Schickedanz, 1990). Admittedly a parent first and foremost, and thus subjective, the formally trained parent nonetheless (as a disciplined researcher) brings a keen insight to the task of observation. Under these circumstances, "no other person will ever know the child, the context of the child's life, and the particular research situation so completely as the parent" (Baghban, 1984, p. 8). Because of a parent's relationship and proximity to the child, Bissex (1980) argues, the documentation of literacy through the inherent "enlightened subjectivity" of the parent offers a depth of insight and understanding that outsiders cannot achieve (p. vi). And much has been learned about the foundations of literacy development through the critical eyes of parent-researchers. It was Lass (1982, 1983), for example, who observed her son's literacy development from birth and found that he appeared to have certain reading behaviors early in life, suggesting that systematic instruction was unnecessary for some things. She concluded that teachers have much to learn from parents and recommended that teachers try techniques used in the home, such as following the child's lead, identifying words and symbols in the environment, and repeated readings. Baghban (1984) revealed that *readiness for reading* is an inappropriate term. She observed that the language arts are mutually reinforcing systems, that early reading and writing are social, and that learning language is easier with a model. After observing her child, Schickedanz (1990) proposed that children come to understand the alphabetic principle through multiple inventions and social interaction with responsive adults, suggesting that children construct this knowledge over a long period of time.

From these case studies we glimpse the powerful role parents play in the early literacy education of their children and the environmental potential of the home in creating conditions for literacy acquisition. In each case, the children demonstrated that literacy learning is indeed complex. The children created their own knowledge, interacted and interpreted their own worlds, and demonstrated that learning takes place within a social context (the home) and with strong adult–child interaction.

But many homes include family members other than parents who certainly may be influential in the literacy development of young children. Siblings, too, can play an important role in the literacy learning and achievements of one another. Research on children playing school with younger brothers and sisters, for example, shows that the younger siblings have an easier time learning to read in school (Norman-Jackson, 1982). In their examination of sibling teaching–learning exchanges, Azmitia and Hesser (1993) observed that older siblings gave more spontaneous guidance, more explanations, more feedback, and more learner control to younger siblings, as compared with equally competent older peers. In addition, they found that younger siblings, given a problem to master, were likely to learn more when an older sibling was available to guide them and from whom they might seek assistance, than when they had access to an older peer. Finally, Durkin (1966), in her study of early readers, noted that siblings helped by playing school, identifying words, talking about letters, reading to the younger sibling, and by printing and spelling words for them. The role of siblings in the process of learning to read, she commented, should not be underestimated.

As compared with the evidence of how parents or other adults function as young children's first literacy teachers, however, we understand little about how siblings help one another to achieve literacy. Even as we know siblings teach one another games, tricks of the trade, jargon, and important information on a need-to-know basis, we have not scrutinized their interactions for evidence of literacy instruction that communicates literacy knowledge and skill. The case study that we describe in the following section investigates this sibling teaching–learning process as it occurs between two sisters who are about 4 years apart in age. The study focuses the observational lens on those sibling exchanges that involve literacy—which is to say, talk and demonstrations related to reading words, reciting the alphabet, writing words or letters, sharing storybooks, singing songs, saying rhymes, and the like.

A CASE STUDY OF SIBLING LITERACY TEACHING AND LEARNING

The Family and Its Home Print Environment

Hannah, the older sibling (5 years, 1 month, at the onset of the study), and Emma, her younger sister (17 months old at the onset of the study), live with their biological parents in a suburb of a large midwestern city. Both parents are professionals: The girls' father is a swimming coach at a local university, and their mother an assistant professor at another. At the time of the study their mother was completing her doctoral degree; the case study provided the basis for her doctoral dissertation.

Over the course of the 1-year study, Emma grew from babbling, cooing baby to effective talker and listener and full conversational participant in family exchanges. She also discovered books and print as objects and experimented with reading and writing as *things to do*. Emma did not spend as much of her free time playing with books as Hannah, her big sister, did in her earlier years. Rather, Emma preferred to interact with and try to keep up with her older sister. For example, when Hannah was using markers to draw a picture, Emma was right beside her creating masterpieces too. When Hannah was studying the pictures in a book on sign language, Emma was imitating her hand movements. She disdained the toddler swing in the backyard and the booster seat at the table that were especially for her; she refused these baby accommodations and insisted on sitting at the table or swinging on a big swing "like Hannah." Upon entering preschool age, however, Emma spent more time with books as things. She sat and looked at books occasionally; she enjoyed being read to; she began to choose a book from the shelf before bedtime and insist that her choice be read.

Already a skilled verbal communicator when the study began, Hannah progressed as a reader and a writer, moving from that emergent phase in which she understood basic concepts about print (e.g., book orientation) and recognized a few high-frequency words (e.g., *the, I, love*), to an early reading and writing phase in which she read predictable storybooks, knew a basic stock of sight words, and composed her own written texts using invented spellings (International Reading Association and the National Association for Education of Young Children Position Statement, 1998; Rees, 1994). From infancy, Hannah literally loved books—objects that were as endearing to her as cuddly stuffed animals and toys. In fact, in her toddler stage, books were her favorite toys. She would sit for long periods of time in front of her bookshelf, pulling books off the shelf one by one. She would look through them, point and babble at pictures, and then move on to another. Hannah maintained this passion for books and reading into her preschool years—a passion rivaled only by her keen interest in writing tools and supplies. As a busy 5-year-old, she insisted on a clipboard like her dad's and a grade book like her mom's. After watching her mother write checks, using the checkbook, Hannah wanted—no, desired and absolutely had to have—her own checkbook with a fabric cover. During the period of the study, she constantly carried around a three-ring binder with folders in it; she delighted in stationery, note cards, and tablets of all kinds.

The girls' home—where they each first encountered literacy—was abundant with print and alive with reading and writing as everyday activities. Their bedrooms, where each child spent many hours getting up, going to bed, playing, and passing time, were filled with books of various genres: chubby board books; books that played music; pop-up books; children's dictionaries and Bibles; informational books on animals, insects, artists, authors, and concepts; and children's magazines. In addition, ample supplies of pens, paper, pencils, crayons, markers, cards, and envelopes were easily accessible to the girls. Both rooms had cozy, pleasant places for reading or writing, and from their earliest days (and nights), the sisters were allowed to take books to bed with them to read before falling asleep. Often, they could be found sound asleep amid a pile of books.

From their bedrooms outward into the other rooms of the house, the girls encountered books, print, reading, and writing. There were shelves of books in the living room, books on the nightstands of both parents, cookbooks in the kitchen, magazines and books in the bathrooms, and an office filled with professional books for each parent. In the kitchen, the front panels of the refrigerator served as a bulletin board, dotted with pictures of family; snippets of print collected from here and there: quotes, reminders, cartoons, Bible verses, school calendars, lunch menus; magnetic letters to play with and magnetic words to form phrases and sentences.

The nightly routine of bedtime reading was typical in the home, but reading was done at other times too and extended beyond the physical boundaries of the house. Books were never far away, tucked in diaper bags, car pockets, and backpacks, and were often used to fill time in restaurants, doctors' offices, and wherever else waiting is required of young children. The literate environment of the home fostered interest in and curiosity about written language, supporting the children's efforts to become readers and writers both within and beyond its walls.

Case Study Data Sources and Analysis

Two data sources were used to construct this case study of sibling teaching and learning: systematic observations and the collection of literacy artifacts. Observations were obtained via video recordings and field notes. Video was the primary observational source because it allowed the capture of many aspects of the siblings' interactions to finer degree than direct observation alone, including vocalizations, gestures, eye gaze, and use of materials. Video is a flexible, adaptive medium that permits repeated viewing of scenes for purposes of accuracy, objectivity, and verification—qualities especially important in a parent-researcher study. As to procedures used in the study, when it appeared that the girls were about to read together the camera was positioned and turned on, after which the parent left the room. One camera was left on a tripod in the family room, another was available on the second floor near the bedrooms. Most ensuing literacy episodes were signaled by Hannah in some way, such as when she would ask, "Do you want me to read to you?" Hearing this, or a similar invitation, the parent then set up the video camera in a nearby location. Although cumbersome and intrusive at first, the girls quickly grew accustomed to the procedure and ignored the camera once they were left alone together.

Yet video is a tricky medium to work with for observational purposes. It is physically intrusive, and it limits what can be seen—a video camera is either wide angle or close up, but not both, which means that the camera eye misses the near–far density interaction and context that the human eye would not (Roskos & Nolan, 1997). Thus, field notes were also used in this study to supplement video-based observations or to capture an interaction when the presence of the video camera disrupted the flow of events. Field notes also served as the primary source for documenting literacy interactions that occurred in the car, during errands, on vacation, in the doctor's office, or at other places outside the home. Every effort was made to describe what was observed in detail. Field notes contained the researcher's understanding of the context, what went on, the setting, who initiated the exchange and how it unfolded, and significant interactions and impressions. Whether via the camera or in the field notes, the presence of an alert observer was critical, however, inasmuch as literacy interactions between the sisters occurred spontaneously and sporadically in space and time.

Literacy artifacts provided another valuable data source. For purposes of this study literacy artifacts were represented by written notes, cards, signatures, and drawings produced by the girls. As these became available, they were collected, dated, and then attached to the field notes, which provided information regarding the meaning of the artifact. For example, if the girls were making birthday cards together at the table and Hannah showed Emma how to form a letter on her card, Emma's card was collected, dated, and attached to the field notes describing this interaction.

Forty-eight literacy events were selected for data analysis, chosen because they were captured in their entirety, a necessity to answer one of the original research questions regarding how exchanges were initiated. The data analysis strategy used for the study was the constant comparative method (Glaser & Strauss, 1967). Verbatim transcriptions were made of all videotaped exchanges between the girls. Once this process was complete, initial impressions were noted in a column to the right of the transcription. As patterns emerged, groups were formed and then condensed. This level of analysis was done in conjunction with ongoing data collection, contrasting tentative categories that captured recurring patterns. Comparisons were constantly made within and between levels of analysis. The interrater reliability process was employed as an effort to strengthen validity. Two fellow doctoral students were trained in the interrater process. Each rater received a sample of data to demonstrate categories under each of the major themes

(themes came from the research questions), a list of characteristics that were associated with each category, and an example from the data that exemplified that category. Each interrater was given 20% of the data for each category. The accuracy rates (94%, 92%) drawn from this process demonstrated that the categories were mutually exclusive and distinguishable from each other, thus demonstrating a high degree of consistency.

Descriptive Observations and Hypotheses

A case study is the "study of the particular" that tells a story, describes the uniqueness of a situation, or articulates an issue (Stake, 1994, p. 240). From case studies we learn lessons about the particular—the specific child, home, classroom, curriculum—which brings insights and also raises new, more piercing questions. What particulars about literacy were gleaned from this case study of sibling interaction around books, print, reading, and writing? In brief, five observations and two hypotheses emerged.

One observation—not new—was the powerful role of the home environment in shaping sibling literacy interactions. It is the physical and social resources of the home that give rise to literacy activity and determine its nature. Parents, for example, as the richest social resource in the environment, play a pivotal role in encouraging literacy activity between siblings. This case study showed that it was often the parent who distracted the girls from the television or redirected them by telling them to "go read a book." At other times the catalyst for interaction was a parent–child reading session with one or both girls that sparked the interest and drive to continue literacy activity in the parent's absence. Occasionally, literacy activity between the siblings would start because Emma wanted to be read to and both parents were either in the middle of a project or were just too tired: "Ask Hannah to read it." Emma, easy to please, would reply, "OK. Hannah. Oh, Hannah. You read this?"

Adults' urgings, modeling, and guidance within the environment are in turn buttressed by physical resources that support reading and writing activity. In this home setting, access to books and writing materials throughout the house coupled with a standard to value reading as an interesting, worthwhile, and exciting activity created conditions for virtually all of the literacy events in the study. Hundreds of books on numerous topics, interests, and reading levels paved the way for the natural onset of literacy experiences between the siblings. This rich environment was influential, demonstrating not only what print looks like, but what it means and the many situations in which it is used daily.

A second observation was the extent to which literacy served a social function for the sisters; it was used daily to connect and build relationships between them through shared interests or play activity. Intimacy was expressed when the girls shared stories, wrote, or sang songs together. It gave them an opportunity to be close, interactive, and personal with each other. They sometimes spontaneously hugged each other or verbally expressed pride in each other's attempts. The sisters often sat in close proximity and explored mutual interests, such as kittens, through books. They shared their thoughts and told stories by using language and learned about spoken and written language in ways that connected them to each other and to the life around them.

A third observation was that older siblings know a great deal about literacy and can share their knowledge with their younger sibs in ways that are instructive, sensitive, and enjoyable. Hannah was a great support to Emma's literacy attempts. She demonstrated a considerable amount of accommodation when she accepted Emma's babbling, utterances, and gestures as communication and then acted on them, signaling to Emma that she understood. When Emma was just 18 months old, she climbed on the couch next to Hannah, picked up a book, and mumbled "Mmm" as she handed the book to Hannah. Hannah accepted it, then began reading. Emma responded by rocking back and forth excitedly. Throughout this session Hannah would ask a question, such as "What color is it?" and each time Emma would point to the book and say, "Zee" or "Eee." Hannah would then affirm her utterance by answering the question, "It's yellow." She created zones of proximal development for Emma, scaffolded instruction, and demonstrated that older siblings can be important and effective first teachers for their younger siblings. From these exchanges, Hannah learned to adjust her teaching to meet her student where she is, and she learned that an utterance or babble is a baby's way of talking. As Emma got older, Hannah learned that you have to break down difficult concepts into digestible parts, such as when Emma could not open a flap on a book and asked, "Hannah, can you help me?" Hannah responded by showing her how to bend the page just a little to pop the flap open and said, "See? Here is what you do." Again, while she was trying to teach Emma a song one day, Hannah realized that her technique, singing the song and hoping Emma would simply catch on, was not working, so she decided to try a different method, "Wait. Wait, Emma. I'll sing it first, then you sing it back to me."

Another time Hannah wanted to teach Emma "Hickory Dickory Dock." She sang the nursery rhyme first in its entirety, then worked on it line by line, having Emma repeat each line. Hannah was a teacher who listened to and learned about what her student required of her at each stage of development. She appeared to know intuitively how to make adjustments and accommodations in her teaching as she worked to meet her student where she was developmentally.

The case study data also suggested (fourth observation) that Emma's learning was constructivist in nature. This was especially evident when she made sense of new information by piecing it together with what she already knew. Noticing that Hannah had letters embroidered across her sweatshirt, Emma said, "Hannah, I like your ABCs." Even though the letters spelled "HANNAH," to Emma, they were the ABCs. Hannah explained, "Those aren't ABCs, Emma. That spells Hannah. . . . If you had one of these it would say *E-M-M-A*. Emma." Here is another example of bridging the known with the new: The girls were looking at a book about kittens and discussing how cute they were. Emma looked at a picture of the kittens and assigned each a part: "Look at the babies. And that's the mommy." Drawing on her knowledge of family life, Emma brought her own meaning to the illustration and wove it into the discussion and story. She also made sense of written language in other ways as she used literacy tools and supplies, such as paper, books, and pencils, and engaged in reading and writing activities.

The fifth and final observation described Emma's strong desire to be part of the "literacy club" (Smith, 1985), which proved to be highly motivating and may have advanced her literacy development. She clearly saw herself as a reader and writer, declaring, "I write" or "I read, too." Often Emma had to remind family members that she was indeed a reader and should not be interrupted. "I'll read this for me," Emma said as the girls were lying in the backyard tent with a pile of books. When Hannah told Emma to do something, Emma shouted, "Just a second! I'm reading!" This strong desire to belong, to fit in, to be a member, to participate, to do it, may—in the end—constitute the *most important* element of early literacy learning and a powerful reminder for those who wish to teach it.

The particulars of a case study also elicit questions and the need to know more, thus forming the basis of hypotheses for further research. This case study generated two hypotheses that warrant examination. First, it is proposed that the physical and social resources of the home environment form a bounded system that shapes the quantity and quality of sibling teaching–learning related to literacy knowledge and skill. As a system of sibling literacy interaction, it has parts and features, is purposive, integrated, and patterned; it may or may not work well. Second, the case study suggests that sibling interactions may create a zone of proximal development for literacy activity that may be mutually beneficial to younger *and* older sisters and brothers as participants. The nature of the sibling relationship creates a natural zone for teaching and learning in the everyday lives of children, which can be played out in the home if the environment supports this type of learning. (See also Gregory, 2001, for further explication of this synergy.)

SIBLING LITERACY TEACHING AND LEARNING: A CLOSER LOOK

In this section we present four literacy exchanges excerpted from the case study data. Our intent is to put them under the lens, so to speak, and examine them for evidence of Hannah's teaching and Emma's learning about reading and writing. We view each exchange as a construction zone—a special place where sibling minds meet, where the search is for a common ground of understanding, where competence is shared and also created (White, 1993, pp. ix–xii). We preface each exchange as to its context and then describe the interactional processes that inform and explain and also provoke new meanings between the girls.

Excerpt 1: The Puppies: Learning That Reading (and Counting) Is Fun

The setting of the first selection is Hannah's bedroom. It is a Sunday morning, and both girls are sitting on the bed and looking at books. Hannah is 5 years old and Emma is 19 months. Hannah asks Emma whether she wants to read, which is a familiar routine between the girls. As you become acquainted with the girls through this exchange, take note of Hannah's specificity about what the pair will read, as well as her instructional style. The pleasure introduced into the experience is also special and worthy of close attention.

HANNAH: Want to read a counting book, Emma? (*Emma nods positively.*) Stay there. I'll get one. Stay there, OK? (*Hannah leaves and gets a book; Emma waits.*) Arf! Arf! Do you like puppies? (*Emma nods.*) Oh! Look at the stars. Do you want to count the stars? (*Hannah counts the stars; Emma watches both Hannah and the book.*) Now, do you want to count footprints? Let's count footprints. (*Hannah counts. Then she pushes a button on the book for the barking sound to play. Both girls laugh.*) Do you want to hear that again? (*Emma nods. Hannah plays it again.*) Do you want to hear that again? (*Emma nods, and Hannah plays it again, this time tickling Emma with the barks. Emma giggles.*) Do you like that puppy? (*Emma nods*). Do you want to hear it again? (*Plays the barking sound again as they continue to look at the book. Hannah then tickles Emma, and she shrieks with delight.*)

Immediately interesting in this excerpt is the fact that Hannah is specific about the book she will share. It is a counting book—not just any kind of book, which in a subtle way signals Emma that there are different kinds of books in the first place. Moreover, this is an informational genre, a concept book that sets out to teach. Hannah then deftly engages Emma in this instructional moment by asking (not without sound effects), "Arf! Arf! Do you like puppies?" And she knows, of course, that Emma indeed loves puppies and will eagerly participate in looking at them in a book. Before asking Emma to count all by herself, Hannah demonstrates, then invites Emma to try. As teachers of reading we quickly recognize the rudiments of the shared book routine emerging here—I read/do; we read/ do; you read/do. And we can surmise how repeated book encounters between Hannah and Emma will solidly establish this routine, which will serve Emma well as she takes on learning to read in school. Finally, Hannah appeals to the toddler's sense of fun and need for repetition: She plays and replays the barking sound and then punctuates it with a playful tickle. As a consequence, Emma gets the idea (and the feeling) that looking at books is fun, counting is worth sitting still for, and that puppies, stars, and footprints are indeed objects in this world that can be counted—one by one.

Excerpt 2: "I Write": Learning That Writing Takes Concentration

It is a spring day; Hannah is almost 6 years old, and Emma is just 2 years. The girls are in the kitchen, with Emma near the refrigerator and Hannah writing at the table. The refrigerator is a busy, bright bulletin board of print dotted with messages, notices, a calendar, the girls' work, and so on. A picture recently drawn by Emma captures her attention, and she decides to write. Notable here is Emma's intention and the concentration it rallies. Also interesting is Hannah's scaffolding, which reaches beyond Emma's zone of proximal development yet also shows some sensitivity to it.

EMMA: I write Hannah.

HANNAH: OK. You can write an *H*. Then make an *A*, the *N*, the *N*, the *A*, the *H*. (*Hannah gets up from the table and comes over to where Emma is at the refrigerator.*) Want to show me how to write my name? (*Emma is busy writing on the picture on the refrigerator. Hannah looks, then walks back to the table and goes back to her writing.*)

In her powerful declaration, "I write," Emma tells us that she already has some fundamental ideas about literacy: It is a distinct activity; it involves certain tools and actions; it is a way to express oneself. Her declaration, however, is misinterpreted by Hannah who thinks that her younger sib is going to attempt to write her sister's name—Hannah. So she plunges into Emma's writing activity and spells out the letters of her own name, crisply and clearly enunciating each letter—H-A-N-N-A-H. But her plunge is too forceful, extending beyond Emma's zone. Emma's lack of response signals Hannah that Emma is not paying attention and prompts her to adjust her scaffolding. She physically approaches Emma with the intention of demonstrating how to write her name (thus reducing the complexity of the task and reentering the zone). Consider for a moment the instructional sensitivity of Hannah, almost 6 years old. She does not remain seated; she does not repeat the letters of her name; she does not quit. Rather, she adjusts the task demands and offers more assistance. These moves, however, are not still enough to engage Emma, who remains absorbed in her interpretation of writing. At this point, though, Hannah shows extraordinary good sense by exiting the learning space and allowing Emma her own personal meaning-making. More than a teacher, she is a respectful big sister.

Excerpt 3: Emma Makes an A: Learning That Writing Takes Skill

The girls are passing time while waiting for their mother to finish some work in her office before the trio go to the zoo. Both girls are drawing: Hannah is making butterflies, and Emma is tracing around coins.

EMMA: Mom, can you write my name? (*Hannah steps in before Mom can help.*)

HANNAH: OK. Make an *A*, Emma. Make an *A*. OK? (*Hannah makes an A for Emma to trace. She next holds Emma's hand in hers. Together, they draw an A.*) EMMIE!! I helped her! I helped her!

EMMA: (*to Hannah*) There. I want to make for you. (*She works on the A some more, and then puts little marks beside it.*) [See Figure 5.1.]

FIGURE 5.1. Hannah "teaches" Emma how to write an *A*.

Among the case study examples of sibling exchanges, this is a treasure. Its simplicity offers a wealth of material for observation. Emma's request for her mother to write her name is transformed into a lesson in which Hannah teaches and Emma learns how to make an *A*. Note the sequence of events here and its pedagogical soundness. It starts with the goal—make an *A*—which is twice announced. It continues with Hannah physically guiding Emma's mind's eye by placing her hand on Emma's and assisting her in making the *A*. Next, Hannah exuberantly praises Emma for her accomplishment with a resounding pronouncement of her name—Emmie! And she also compliments herself as teacher with "I helped her." Note in particular the scaffolding features employed by this 5-year-old. She works jointly with Emma to achieve a goal; she strives to arrive at a shared understanding with her; she structures the task (guiding Emma's hand); she is warm and responsive; she stays within the zone, yet challenges Emma with achievable tasks; and she provides assistance with instructional talk "Make an *A*, OK?" (Berk & Winsler, 1995). This exchange closes with Emma's "I want to make for you," demonstrating the desire to offer something back to her teacher, a willingness to please her. This final comment illuminates how the girls are connected to each other through literacy as well as how literacy serves as a social function and a way to build their sibling relationship.

Excerpt 4: We Don't Rip Books!: Learning That Books Are Precious

Emma, now nearly 3 years old, went to bed with a pile of books beside her as usual. For some reason, though, while lying about, she tore the flaps off the pages of an interactive book entitled *Elmo's Big Lift-and-Look Book* (Ross, 1994). The next day she confesses to Hannah, who is now 6½, as follows:

EMMA: Hannah, I tore this. (*Emma shows Hannah the book.*)

HANNAH: Awwww, Emma. EM-MA! We don't rip books! (*Hannah takes the book, puts it in her closet on a shelf.*) (*to Mom*) There. She can't get it. (*She goes and sits next to Emma.*) Emma, let me tell you something. You can't rip things, OK? It's sad.

EMMA: It's not sad.

But clearly it was sad and the lesson was learned, for a few days later Emma reprimanded Oreo, the cat, for walking across some books scattered on the floor: "Oreo! Oreo! We don't rip books!"

This final excerpt that begins with Emma's declaration of guilt is telling, for it reveals the implicit literacy values and expectations—the literacy

standards, so to speak—of this household. Neither her early morning con-
fession nor her admonishment of Oreo the cat would have occurred if
books, print, and reading were of little significance and meaning in this
family. Tearing pages in books and risky paws on book covers, however,
were transgressions against objects that held high status and represented
the significance of literacy to the family. Hannah knows that the literacy
practices of the home reflect certain cultural norms about books and their
treatment and that books must be preserved for future use, because literacy
is something that happens daily in many ways in this home. This exchange
represents not only Hannah's understanding of the value of books in this
family culture, but her responsibility as a member to teach this to the youngest. It is through social interaction that Hannah passes knowledge to the
less knowledgeable, Emma, teaching her the literacy values of the family
unit. Emma, in turn, does the same when she addresses the cat.

When Hannah takes the book to her closet and places it on a shelf out
of Emma's reach, it brings to mind adults putting away precious objects beyond a little one's reach. In this home, books are as special as precious
breakables, and this exchange highlights their importance. Hannah's response to Emma is significant too. Although she at first expresses disap-
pointment, she shows compassion, maturity, and appropriateness when she
addresses Emma on her level, sitting next to her and gently saying, "Let me
tell you something. You can't rip things, OK? It's sad." Finally, Emma
shows some understanding of the lesson learned when she transfers the
message to Oreo, the cat.

WHY SIBLING TEACHING AND LEARNING MATTERS

That parents are their children's first literacy teachers is a mere aphorism,
and indeed numerous studies over the past three decades affirm the significance of the parental role in children's literacy development. Yet, although
we know far less about this relationship, sisters and brothers who play and
work together may also assume this role, pushing forward the literacy development of one another. Gregory (2001), for example, argues for a
unique reciprocity between older and younger siblings in which a different
kind of scaffolding and collaborative learning apply. Her descriptions of sib
dyads' storybook reading and play activities show how the older sibling
teaches the younger, but also learns through the transaction, and how
knowledge building is personalized between the sib pair, differentiating it
from adult scaffolding and peer collaboration. On the basis of such descrip-
tive accounts, sibling teaching (and learning) bears watching, because it reveals another kind of access to literacy knowledge and skills in the family
setting. Likewise, the case study excerpts presented here highlight the liter-

acy potential within sibling relationships and interactions along three lines worthy of further exploration.

One consideration is the increase in *opportunity* for literacy learning that siblings can afford one another in the comings and goings of family life. Communicating in shared reading and writing activities that are a regular part of their day, siblings have a chance to talk the talk of literacy to one another and to try out skills (practice) in situations of meaning for them (e.g., playing school). The sheer repetition of acts of reading and writing between siblings allows each to clarify basic concepts about print, to elaborate and extend these ideas into subtler meanings and understandings, and to translate official information (e.g., letter names) into personal interpretations that build literacy knowledge. In addition, through their literacy encounters siblings can help one another to regulate their literacy behaviors, gearing them to specific goals and adapting them to the demands of the task.

A second consideration is the *importance* attached to literacy activity that older siblings can communicate and model for their younger brothers and sisters. Along with information and details about the stuff of reading and writing, such as words, letters, how-to information, and tools, older sibs teach the household standards that apply to literacy and its role in life. Through modeling talk and interaction, older siblings teach the younger ones many things, including values surrounding books and other print in the home. This transferring of cultural norms takes place in many ways among family members daily and has implications for the classroom. Just as Hannah saw it to be her responsibility as a member of the family culture to pass knowledge on to the less knowledgeable, teachers can create conditions in their classroom culture whereby children in mixed groups are allowed to interact with and around literacy daily. It is through these informal opportunities with literacy tools that the importance attached to literacy can be conveyed.

A third consideration, not yet well explored, is what we can learn about the origins of *interest* and the motivation it fuels for tackling the intellectual work of learning to read and write. Here an enduring principle of sibling relationships applies: What older brothers and sisters do, younger brothers and sisters try to do. Thus, if older siblings model literacy and engage in literacy, finding it pleasurable and worthwhile, then their younger sibs are sure to follow—which has significance for their school readiness and the development of a strong disposition toward literacy and literacy activity. We observed that the siblings in this study had fun with the process of reading ("Arf! Arf! Do you like puppies?"). We also saw evidence of accomplishment and the satisfaction that comes from a job well done ("I helped her! I helped her!") as well as feelings of mastery and self-control ("There. I want to make for you"). Although these conversations may seem like child's play, as educators we need to be mindful regarding the pure fun—the playfulness—that surrounds these interactions. Such enjoyment is the wellspring of interest in reading and writing and the bedrock of dispositions that become reading habits.

Pursuing these lines of inquiry more deeply and more thoroughly can contribute to a fuller understanding of the home environment as a site for literacy development and acquisition. We can readily observe from even these brief case study excerpts, for example, that a literate, accessible environment supports and nurtures sibling interactions by setting standards and values for literacy. When reading and writing are perceived as fun, positive, interesting things to do, children perceive that reading with a family member or making homemade cards for friends is time well spent. When literacy materials are readily available in the environment, children naturally explore and interact with them. Like Hannah and Emma, children tend to pick up these items and engage in the literacy activities they engender, just as they might pick up a toy and act on its potential. As part of their real world, literacy objects and tools in the immediate environment stimulate activity that lays the groundwork of literacy knowledge (i.e., Emma noticing letters on a shirt or the print on the refrigerator). In short, literacy is available for children to handle, to hold, and to grasp.

We see, too, that siblings can be literacy teachers, and quite effective ones at that. Siblings generally spend large amounts of time together, and adults are wise to create a ripe environment for their sharing in literacy activities together, thus facilitating siblings' talk about and around literacy. In our four excerpts we noted that a supportive relationship between siblings paves the way for brave reading and writing attempts that the younger sib might not otherwise try. Here the older sister, Hannah, used instructional talk and was remarkably sensitive to her young tutee, adjusting instruction to meet her needs. We could see and hear her teach concepts about print: information about different kinds of genres ("It's a counting book") or how to spell a word ("You can write an *H*. Then make an *A* . . . "). Finally, using spoken language, children have opportunities to regulate each other's behaviors in relation to literacy ("Let me tell you something. You can't rip things, OK?"), which helps young children to think about and reflect on their actions in relation to this activity and its significance in everyday life.

One final observation—and perhaps the most insightful—is the joy and pleasure that literacy interactions between siblings can bring to their everyday lives. What fun to share a book with a few tickles here and there, and what delight to make an *A* under the gentle hand of a big sister. We must not forget the power of emotion in literacy encounters and its motivational potential, not to mention the familial bonds it forges. As educators and teachers of literacy, we need to support these kinds of literacy interactions between children and encourage them in families. Siblings can teach one another a lot about literacy, and our hope is that what they impart builds not only literacy knowledge and skill, but also strong, loving family relationships.

Not long ago, the milestone of learning to read and write was reserved for the first-grade classroom and placed largely in the hands of the first-grade teacher. This is no longer the case; we now grasp the significant role of parents and caregivers in children's earliest literacy learning. In fact, we are beginning to look beyond the parent as the child's single, first literacy teacher to other members of the family unit who may also assume this role. How siblings teach, shape, guide, invite, cajole, and otherwise enjoin one another to participate in literacy activity to their mutual benefit is fertile ground for further research. This chapter highlights just some of what awaits when we begin to look closely at what goes on in the way of reading and writing between brothers and sisters.

REFERENCES

Azmitia, M., & Hesser, J. (1993). Why siblings are important agents of cognitive development. *Child Development, 64,* 430–444.

Baghban, M. (1984). *Our daughter learns to read and write: A case study from birth to three.* Newark, DE: International Reading Association.

Berk, L. E., & Winsler, A. (1995). *Scaffolding children's learning: Vygotsky and early childhood education.* Washington, DC: National Association for the Education of Young Children.

Bissex, G. L. (1980). *Gnys at wrk: A child learns to read and write.* Cambridge, MA: Harvard University Press.

Durkin, D. (1966). *Children who read early.* New York: Teachers College Press.

Glaser, B. G., & Strauss, A. L. (1967). *The discovery of grounded theory.* Chicago: Aldine.

Gregory, E. (2001). Sisters and brothers as language users and literacy teachers: Synergy between siblings playing and working together. *Journal of Early Childhood Literacy, 1,* 301–322.

International Reading Association and the National Association for the Education of Young Children. (1998). *Learning to read and write: Developmentally appropriate practices for young children: A joint position statement of the International Reading Association and the National Association for the Education of Young Children.* Newark, DE: International Reading Association.

Lass, B. (1982). Portrait of my son as an early reader. *The Reading Teacher, 36,* 20–28.

Lass, B. (1983). Portrait of my son as an early reader II. *The Reading Teacher, 36,* 508–515.

Lenhart, L. (2000). *"Do you want me to read to you?": A case study of sibling interactions during literacy events.* Unpublished doctoral dissertation, Kent State University, Kent, Ohio.

Norman-Jackson, J. (1982). Family interactions, language development and primary reading achievement of black children of low income. *Child Development, 53,* 349–358.

Rees, D. (1994). *Reading developmental continuum.* Portsmouth, NH: Heinemann.

Roskos, K., & Nolan, H. (1997). Video as a methodological tool with examples from early literacy research. In C. Kinzer, K. Hinchman, & D. Leu (Eds.), *Inquiries in literacy theory and practice: Forty-sixth yearbook of the National Reading Conference* (pp. 519–532). Chicago: NRC.

Ross, A. (1994). *Elmo's big lift-and-look book.* New York: Random House.

Schickedanz, J. A. (1990). *Adam's righting revolutions: One child's literacy development from infancy through grade one.* Portsmouth, NH: Heinemann.

Smith, F. (1985). *Reading without nonsense.* New York: Teachers College Press.

Stake, R. (1994). Case studies. In N.K. Denzin & Y.S. Lincoln (Eds.), *Handbook of qualitative research* (pp. 236–247). Thousand Oaks, CA: Sage.

Vygotsky, L. (1978). *Mind in society: The development of higher psychological processes.* Cambridge, MA: Harvard University Press.

White, S. (1993). Forward. In D. Newman, P. Griffin, & M. Cole (Eds.), *The construction zone: Working for positive change in school* (pp. ix–xii). New York: Cambridge University Press.

6

Learning about the Literate Lives of Latino Families

JEANNE R. PARATORE
GIGLIANA MELZI
BARBARA KROL-SINCLAIR

Current school reform efforts are largely united in their goal to have all children acquire basic reading skills by the end of grade 3. Toward that end, in addition to a concerted effort to improve the quality of the instruction children receive during the school day, many policymakers, administrators, and teachers emphasize the importance of the role parents play in children's school success. As a result, in communities where the rate of reading failure is particularly high, home–school partnership programs are increasingly implemented as part of the effort to improve rates of reading achievement. Although most educators agree on the potential benefit of home–school collaborations, there are some who caution that for such programs to be successful, we need to have a full understanding of the literacy routines and practices present in the lives of families different from those of the mainstream and of how the activities that teachers advocate may intrude on important daily routines present in family lives (Bronfenbrenner, 1979; Taylor, 1997; Valdés, 1996).

The purpose of this chapter is threefold: to present the ways Latino families in one urban community reported using literacy during the course of their daily lives, to discuss the factors that influenced their uses of literacy, and to suggest how teachers might think about family literacies and how they may attempt to build home–school literacy connections.

STEPPING BACK: THE FOUNDATION FOR THE BELIEF
THAT FAMILY LITERACY MATTERS

That parents play an important role in their children's school success is a long-held belief. Among the most widely cited work is that of Dolores Durkin (1966), who reported that children who entered first grade as readers had had common experiences prior to school entry: They had parents who read with them, answered their questions about print and responded to requests for help, and demonstrated the importance of reading in their own lives. Durkin's early work was supported with similar findings by many others (e.g., Briggs & Elkind, 1977; Clark, 1976; Dunn, 1981; Mason, 1980; Morrow, 1983). In 1985 the federally appointed Commission on Reading, charged with the task of reviewing existing research related to how children learn to read, concluded in its report, *Becoming a Nation of Readers*, that "the single most important activity for building the knowledge required for eventual success in reading is reading aloud to children" (Anderson, Hiebert, Scott, & Wilkinson, 1985, p. 23). This report, read widely by both professionals and the lay public, intensified the focus on the role of parents in their children's reading success.

In the years since, although the strength of the relationship has been questioned (Scarborough & Dobrich, 1994), most researchers and practitioners have continued to view parent–child storybook reading as a critical factor in children's reading achievement. Notable among recent studies is the work of Bus, van IJzendoorn, and Pellegrini (1995). In their reanalysis of 29 studies of parent–child joint storybook reading, they reported substantial effects on children's language and literacy development. They presented their findings as evidence of the need to support parent–child storybook reading, and in particular, as "straightforward support for family literacy programs" (p. 15).

At present there are few who question the importance or relevance of these findings—most agree that a foundation in storybook reading is important for children's success in school. However, there is also a potential downside to this understanding. The evidence of the importance of family storybook reading has led some educators to practice a sort of *means* test for families as their children enter school: Absence of parent–child storybook reading is often taken as evidence that the child has been reared in a low-literate home and is therefore at risk for reading difficulty. Subsequently, family literacy programs are often focused on instilling an understanding of and skill in family storybook reading and promoting daily reading among family members (Tao, Khan, Gamse, St. Pierre, & Tarr, 1998).

The emphasis on such school-like literacy behaviors is not necessarily negative, but many argue that such instruction often occurs with little understanding of the literate traditions that are already present in families. As a result, opportunities to build on existing literacies may be squandered. Evidence to support this point of view is found in the landmark work of Shirley Brice Heath (1983), who reported compelling evidence of the mismatch between the literacy profiles teachers expect of children and the literacy profiles some children outside the cultural and linguistic mainstream may have as they enter school. Heath argued that the children she studied were not illiterate but, rather, that their family and community interactions led to the development of literacies different from those that were known to prepare children for success in school. Many subsequent studies have lent support to Heath's conclusion (see, e.g., Purcell-Gates, 1995; Taylor & Dorsey-Gaines, 1988; Valdés, 1996; Vasquez, Pease-Alvarez, & Shannon, 1994.) As a result, many educators believe that the combination of the *missing* literacies and the absence of any attempt by teachers to build on the literacies that children do bring to school contributes to the difficulty in learning to read that many linguistically and culturally different children experience.

In some ways, the idea that different families practice different literacies is widely accepted. For example, in the report of the most recent National Assessment of Educational Progress (Donahue, Finnegan, Lutkus, Allen, & Campbell, 2001), the authors noted that "families use print for various activities on a daily basis, and different cultural groups have unique ways of integrating oral and written language with daily social life" (p. 54). Despite the acknowledgement and recognition evident in this statement, in practice it often seems that little is done to uncover in any degree of detail the specific literacies practiced in diverse home settings or to build on home literacies in systematic ways. In our visits to urban primary-grade classrooms, we have been told repeatedly that the children "come with nothing" and that teachers are doing "the best they can" with children who enter as "empty slates." We find these comments to be in conflict with our observations of parents in a local family literacy project. In the section that follows, we describe what we learned from the parents in our community and how we think the information may be applied to early literacy practices and to the development of home–school literacy connections.

THE FAMILIES AND THE COMMUNITY

We work with parents in an intergenerational literacy project situated within an urban community in which 75% of public school students speak a first language other than English. Immigrant parents attend classes 3 to 4 days per week for 2 hours each day to learn about ways to improve their own English literacy and ways to support their children's success in American schools. The instructional emphasis is on helping parents situate liter-

acy experiences within the fabric of their daily lives, rather than on the creation of school-like contexts in the home setting. Parents are encouraged to
join with their children in multiple uses of literacy, including reading and
writing oral histories, composing letters to friends and family members,
journal writing, and story writing and publishing. A second area of emphasis is on storybook reading, with routine modeling of read-aloud strategies
and discussion of book selection. Parents are also taught how to help their
children with homework, the types of questions they might ask the classroom teachers to learn about their children's progress, and the types of
questions they might ask their children to learn about the school day.

   Since its inception, the Intergenerational Literacy Project (ILP) has
served more than 1,600 parents and other adult family members. Learners
include parents, grandparents, aunts, uncles, and siblings. Mothers are the
most likely family members to participate, representing 65.2% of all participants. The most common ethnicity of participants is Latino (78.2%), although the program has served families from 57 different countries in Central America, South America, Asia, Europe, Africa, and North America
since it began. On average, parents who participate have completed 8 years
of formal schooling; however, this varies widely, from learners who have
never attended school to those who have completed college.

THE WAYS THE FAMILIES USE LITERACY AT HOME

As part of the daily classroom routines, ILP teachers ask parents to record
their home literacy activities on a Literacy Log. The log is a two-sided form
on which parents record literacy activities of personal interest on one side
and literacy activities they share with their children on the other side. Literacy teachers introduce the Literacy Logs during the first week of each instructional cycle (semester), they explain that the logs should be used to record literacy activities in which learners engage outside their class, and they
discuss the types of events parents might record. At least once a week parents share and discuss the entries they have recorded in their logs.

   To learn more about the family literacy routines among our participants, we collected all Literacy Logs completed by 69 mothers over their
entire period of participation in the project. The length of participation varied among these parents, ranging from two to nine cycles. So that we could
study the influence of years of schooling on family literacy routines, we
formed two groups of mothers: one with high levels of education (9 to 12
years) and one with low levels of education (8 or fewer years).

   Mothers recorded their entries in the language of their choice. Some
were in Spanish, some in English, and, in many cases, in both Spanish and

English. A total of 5,427 Literacy Log entries were analyzed, 3,434 that had been recorded by mothers in the high-education group and 1,993 that had been recorded by mothers in the low-education group. We examined the entries using a modification of the literacy domains proposed by Teale (1986). Table 6.1 shows the categories we used and some examples of unedited reports of activities that we included in each.

Our results (reported in detail in Melzi, Paratore, & Krol-Sinclair, 2000) led to three major findings:

TABLE 6.1. Domains of Literacy with Examples

Literacy for the sake of teaching/learning literacy	
Mother's Schooling and Learning	Yesterday I read about the First AID and CPR because yesterday I began une curs [a course] about this.
Children's Schooling and Learning	Yesterday I read the Alfabet with my son and help with his homework.
Viewing for Teaching and Learning	Last night I watched the movie called the chick and the Fox and spoke with my children about it.
Literacy Reflections	When I want to read a book to my son he don't listen only wants to play and pay attention to the color book.
Daily literacy	
Daily Living	Yesterday I read instruction to order the [school] picturs for my children. I wrote a chek to pay the order of my children's pictures.
Information Networks	Yesterday I read a magazine article about children.
Interpersonal Communication	I wrote one letter for the teacher of Mason.
Work	Yesterday I read the orders of what I have to do for my work.
Religion	I read BIBLE.
Literacy in leisure activities	
Mother's Book Reading	I read a book called Homeless Bird.
Storybook Time	Yesterday I read a book with my children the title is *Why Plane Can Fly*.
Entertainment	I listened to music and an interesting program on the radio.

• Mothers in both the high- and low-education groups reported spending more time in literacy activities that were deliberately and explicitly intended to advance their children's learning than in any other type of literacy activity. We interpreted this as evidence that mothers were interested in and dedicated time to helping their children with literacy learning. Typical interactions related to children's learning included both school-generated assignments, such as homework, and activities generated by the mothers themselves, such as writing letters to family members, teaching their children early learning concepts, such as colors and numbers, or learning songs and chants.

• The amount of time mothers spent in reading with their children was not influenced by mothers' years of formal education. It was, however, influenced by length of participation in the family literacy project; that is, the longer mothers attended literacy classes, the more likely they were to read with their children. We took this as indicative of two important points. First, level of formal education is not a reliable indicator of parents' interest in or ability to engage children in family storybook reading; and second, participation in a family literacy project was helpful in increasing the frequency of family storybook reading.

• Mothers with high and low levels of education engaged in different types of literacy events in the course of their daily lives. Those with high levels of education most commonly used information networks, such as reading newspapers and magazines; activities of this type were rarely reported by mothers with low levels of education. Instead, mothers with low levels of education most commonly engaged in literacy activities related to interpersonal communication, such as writing notes and letters to family members.

APPLYING WHAT WE LEARNED
TO SCHOOL-BASED AND CLASSROOM-BASED PRACTICES

There are three assumptions that often influence the ways many family literacy programs, in particular, and home–school partnership efforts, in general, are planned and implemented (Yaden & Paratore, 2002). First, many teachers and administrators assume that in families in which parents are undereducated or have low levels of English literacy and English education, there is an absence of any form of literacy. Second, many assume that in homes in which parents are undereducated, have low levels of literacy, or have low levels of English language proficiency, parents are uninterested in or unable to support their children's success in school; and third, many assume that parents who are uneducated or have low levels of English literacy also lack effective parenting skills.

The results of our work specifically challenge the first two assumptions. The parents in our study with diverse levels of education and with low-to-moderate levels of English proficiency reported engaging in routine and diverse literacy events at home. They read prayers, books, and environmental print of all sorts. They sang songs, engaged in finger play, and talked about daily experiences; they wrote letters and drew illustrations. They engaged in literacy events primarily with their children, but in some cases also used literacy to achieve personal goals and needs.

In addition, although results indicate a correlation between level of education and frequency of literacy events in general, among this sample of parents who were participating in a family literacy program, we found no such relationship between level of education and parent–child storybook reading. Instead, we found that parents with limited formal education and little knowledge of English can and will engage in read-alouds with their children. However, we also found that length of participation in the family literacy project correlated with frequency of parent–child storybook reading, and we interpreted this as evidence of the importance of explicit and relatively long-term training in parent–child storybook reading. The need for clear and consistent read-aloud training and support programs is further underscored when one considers the nature of our sample. The parents who participated in the family literacy project enrolled in the program because they chose to, and by so doing showed themselves to be already interested in some form of shared literacy activity. It is important to note that even with this predisposition, storybook reading routines were often embedded within the families' daily lives only after parents had regularly participated in the family literacy program for several months. A campaign of telling parents to read aloud or a practice of sending home classroom books for parent–child reading is unlikely to have helped the parents in our study. These parents already possessed the interest and motivation to support their children, but they lacked the knowledge of the particular strategies and routines that could help their children succeed in an American school.

Drawing from these findings, as well as from the work of Edwards (1991) and Krol-Sinclair (1996), we concluded that parent–child storybook reading intervention programs are more likely to be successful when they are explicit and detailed in the presentation of the types of literacy behaviors they wish parents to use during storybook reading and when they are long-term in the support of parents' acquisition and implementation.

In response to what we learned, we set out to develop classroom routines that would help us accomplish two goals: to discover ways that parents could learn more about what children learn and do in school and to help teachers uncover the range of literacy experiences children have at home. We reasoned that these reciprocal goals would help teachers to better understand the children they teach and their parents and would help parents to more fully understand what children do and are expected to do in school and, as a result, to more effectively support their children's school success.

To accomplish our goals, we established three home–school partnership initiatives: the monthly publication of a project newsletter, the development of home literacy portfolios, and a classroom storybook reading project. Each of these efforts is described in the following sections.

The Monthly Newsletter

The purpose of the monthly newsletter was to share with parents the details of classroom themes and activities and to elicit from them information about how the focal themes or activities connected to children's experiences outside of school. In a recent example, children in the Early Childhood Learning Center (a component of the Intergenerational Literacy Project) had just completed a unit on winter. In the monthly newsletter (see Figure 6.1) the Early Childhood teachers described the classroom activities, suggested activities for each age group that parents and children might do together at home, and showcased children's artwork and writing. The teachers also used the newsletter to let parents know that the upcoming unit would focus on transportation and to suggest transportation-related books that parents might read and discuss at home. The teacher posted a request in the newsletter that parents tell her about any transportation-related events their children had experienced.

The parents, all participants in the Intergenerational Literacy Project, were asked by their adult literacy teachers to bring the newsletter to their literacy class. Here they read and discussed the newsletter and worked in small groups to generate a list of the transportation-related events experienced by their children. They also discussed books, poems, nursery rhymes, songs, or chants that they commonly shared with their children that might relate to the transportation theme. The list of transportation experiences was given to the Early Childhood teacher. (The list of activities elicited from one group of learners is displayed in Figure 6.2). Throughout the month the teacher used what she had learned about children's home experiences to build connections as they read, talked, and wrote about transportation.

We have found the newsletter to be helpful in our effort to meet both of the goals we set out to achieve. It is a useful vehicle for conveying to parents what children are studying and doing in school. By informing parents of the particular books and making them available in a home-lending library, teachers ensure that children have common reading experiences at home and at school. By using the newsletter as a reading text in the adult literacy classroom, parents who might otherwise be reluctant to respond to

FIGURE 6.1. Monthly newsletter.

ILP Children's Program Newsletter
February 2002

Winter and Clothing

The second semester has begun successfully. The children have been learning about winter and clothing. Some key concepts have been:

- Winter is the coldest season of the year.
- In Massachusetts, the weather in winter is different from the weather during other times of the year. It is colder.
- Precipitation often is snow or sleet, rather than rain.
- Cold weather means that we have to wear different clothing than we do in warm weather.
- For example, we wear hats, mittens, gloves, coats, and scarves when it's cold.

Books

The children have enjoyed focusing on the book of the week. For this unit, they have listened to or read:

- *The Mitten* by Jan Brett
- *The Three Little Kittens* by Lorianne Siomades
- *Chicken Soup with Rice* by Maurice Sendak
- *Snowballs* by Lois Ehlert
- *The Dress I'll Wear to the Party* by Shirley Neitzel
- *The Jacket I Wear in the Snow* by Shirley Neitzel

We have extra copies of these books in the ILP library. Please borrow a copy to read with your child at home.

Writing

The children have made books based on the book *Chicken Soup with Rice*. Please stop by and read the books with your children.

Art

The children have made mittens, snowflakes, and snowpeople from a variety of art materials.

Drama

In the evening, the children acted out the story *The Mitten* by Jan Brett. They took turns pretending to be the different animals in the story.

(*continued on next page*)

FIGURE 6.1. (*continued*)

Suggestions for home

Ages 0–2:

- Read a book and sing a simple song with your child every day.
- When you help your child dress, talk about his/her clothing. "Let's put on your shirt. Would you like to wear the blue one or the red one? How many buttons does this shirt have?"

Ages 3–5:

- Read a book and sing a song with your child every day.
- Have your child practice cutting at home. Make sure the scissors your child uses are made for children and have *rounded edges.*
- When you're outside, talk about the weather with your child. "Is it colder today than yesterday?"

Ages 6 and up:

- Read a book and sing a song with your child every day.
- Keep a journal of the local weather/temperature for a week, using information from the newspaper or TV forecast, or by making observations with your child.

Coming next

Beginning the week of February 18, we will be studying transportation. Here are some of the books we will read:

- *Freight Train* by Donald Crews
- *Firefighters A to Z* by Chris L. Demarest
- *Little Toot* by Hardie Gramatky
- *Tina's Taxi* by Betsy Franco
- *City Sounds* by Rebecca Emberley

We have copies of all of these books in the library. Borrow one to share with your child at home.

We want to learn from you. What transportation-related experiences have your children had? Please write to us and tell us about them.

Children's Gallery

Each newsletter will include writing and pictures by different children attending the morning and evening classes.

Lacing
by Madina, age 4

Alphabet
by Dzenana, age 4

FIGURE 6.1. (*continued*)

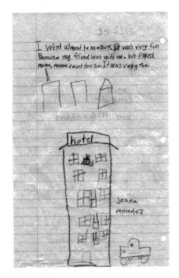

It's snowing in the house.
My dad and my sister and
my mom and me live in
this house.

by José, age 6

I went almost to New York. It was
very fun because my friend was
with me. We played Mama, Mama,
Can't You See. It was very fun.

by Joana, age 8

teachers' requests for information are supported by their adult literacy teacher and their peers in doing so. As a result, the newsletter helps us to achieve our second goal—to help teachers learn more about families and their routine literacy-related and non-literacy-related experiences.

The Home Literacy Portfolio

Like the monthly newsletter, the Home Literacy Portfolio represented an attempt to engage parents and teachers in reciprocal learning. It provided an opportunity for parents to share and explain home literacy practices with teachers and for teachers to share and explain school literacy practices with parents.

To accomplish this, during the adult literacy classes teachers explained and demonstrated how parents might observe their children's uses of literacy at home. Teachers discussed how many parents were already documenting their children's use of literacy by saving items in scrapbooks or memory boxes, and they related this family practice to the types of records

Transportation Experiences Our Children Have Had

- *T train* from East Boston to downtown Boston very often—Ramón
- *Bus* from Chelsea to East Boston to see relatives every week—Dimas
- *Bus* from Chelsea to Haymarket and then took T [subway] to Medical Center—Jeimy
- *Boat* in El Salvador to sightsee—Encarnación
- *Boat* to see Boston Harbor Islands—Dina
- *Plane* from Germany to Boston—Senija
- *Car* from Bosnia to Germany—Sevida
- *Car* from Everett to Chelsea every day—María
- *Car trip* from Chelsea to Bangor, Maine (7 hours)—Brankica
- *Truck* from Everett to Rhode Island to visit family—Silvia
- *Swan Boats* in Boston in the spring—Lilian
- *Bicycle* at Revere Beach—Ceferino
- *Bicycle* at McDonald Park in Medford—Dora
- *Horse* in Honduras going to my sister's town—Clarit

FIGURE 6.2. List of children's transportation experiences elicited from parents.

teachers keep in school. Teachers explained that parents' records of children's uses of literacy at home may add to what classroom teachers already know and, by so doing, may provide teachers with useful information about how children are developing as readers and writers.

Parents were given a special folder to use as a family literacy portfolio and were asked to document their children's uses of literacy outside school by collecting samples of their children's literacy activities and saving them in the folder. Teachers and parents discussed the types of materials to collect. Emphasis was placed on the importance of including samples of children's written work (e.g., drawings, stories, and letters) as well as parents' own written observations. The artifacts that commonly made their way into home literacy portfolios were varied; a few examples are provided in Figures 6.3, 6.4, and 6.5. Figure 6.3 presents a coupon filled out by a kindergarten child while her mother was in the drugstore. The mother annotated it in the bottom right-hand corner. Figure 6.4 is a letter a child wrote, again annotated by the mother. Figure 6.5 is a mother's written observation of her child's literacy behavior.

In addition to encouraging and showing how to document children's uses of literacy at home, the adult literacy teacher also discussed ways parents might share the home literacy portfolios with teachers during informal meetings and conferences. Because most teachers had at least one conference with every child's parents, and some had several more, the parent–teacher conference provided an ideal venue for parents to show their documentation of children's uses of literacy at home.

To prepare parents to share the portfolios with their children's teacher, they were first introduced to the context of parent–teacher conferences. During adult literacy classes, parents were provided short articles about

FIGURE 6.3. Home literacy portfolio sample: A discount coupon completed by a kindergarten child while waiting for her mother in the drugstore.

parent–teacher conferences to read and discuss. Conversations related primarily to three questions: Why are parent–teacher conferences important? What information should a parent bring to the conference? What questions should a parent ask of the teacher during the conference? These discussions generally ended with parents and teachers summarizing important points that parents should remember. Although these differed from class to class, a typical list is displayed in Figure 6.6.

When possible, the adult literacy teachers also met with the children's classroom teachers to explain the home literacy portfolios being assembled by families participating in the ILP. Teachers were asked to encourage parents to bring the portfolios to parent–teacher conferences and to provide time during the conference for parents to share the portfolios and discuss how children's uses of literacy at home connect to uses of literacy in the classroom.

We conducted a number of studies of the ways in which the home portfolios influence the conversations between parents and teachers during conferences (Paratore et al., 1995; Paratore, Hindin, Krol-Sinclair, & Durán, 1999; Paratore, Hindin, Krol-Sinclair, Durán, & Emig, 1999), and in conjunction with that work we collected numerous transcripts of parent–teacher conferences. We learned that parents and teachers used the portfolio artifacts to build on and reinforce each other's point of view. This practice of validating or confirming what was said was reciprocal between parents and teachers—teachers affirmed parents' beliefs and understandings and parents affirmed teachers' beliefs and understandings.

We also found that the conversations were notably collaborative and

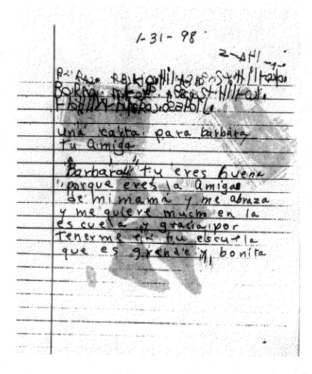

FIGURE 6.4. Home literacy portfolio sample: A letter written by a child to her mother's friend.

supportive, and, according to teachers and parents who participated, these interactions were different from those in earlier conferences, described by one parent as "deeper" than they had been before. Parents were not alone in perceiving a difference in the conversational climate. Teachers, too, commented that the portfolio seemed to change the interaction, even to shift the balance of power. One teacher worded it this way: "Since she [the parent] had something to contribute, too, we came in on a more even level."

There is also evidence that the exchange of home and school literacy practices led to increased learning opportunities at home and at school. As parents described home literacy practices, teachers often offered suggestions for ways they might further support their children's literacy development.

Our work with home literacy portfolios suggests that they may provide a useful context in which parents and teachers can exchange what they know about children's reading and writing, and by so doing, can co-construct an understanding of the child as a literacy learner.

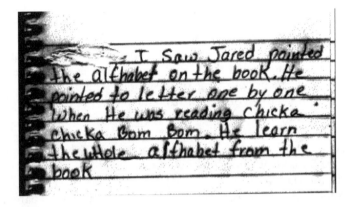

FIGURE 6.5. Home literacy portfolio sample: Mother's written observation of child's literacy behavior.

Parents as Classroom Storybook Readers

The purpose of the Parents as Classroom Storybook Readers project was to help parents enter into partnerships with teachers by bringing into the classroom what they were learning to do at home—shared storybook reading. Parents participated as storybook readers in their children's prekindergarten to second-grade bilingual and general education classrooms.

To help prepare parents, many of whom had never before entered their children's classrooms, to read aloud to a group of children, we provided them with intensive and ongoing training in book selection and read-aloud techniques. In their initial training session the teacher offered a description of the classrooms in which parents would read, described a typical storybook reading session, and modeled and discussed particular strategies, such as holding the book so that it can readily be seen by the students, stopping along the way to invite children to comment and make predictions, and en-

Guidelines for a Parent–Teacher Conference

- Before the conference, write down what you want to talk about.
- Introduce yourself.
- Be on time.
- Be prepared—you have only a short time to talk.
- Bring the family literacy portfolio and ask whether you can share it with the teacher.
- Let the teacher know that you are willing to communicate with him or her.
- Ask the teacher whether and how you can contact him or her when you need to.
- Remember that teachers expect parents to help at home.

FIGURE 6.6. Parent-generated guidelines for parent–teacher conference.

couraging children to chime in on chants and repetitive phrases. Following the discussion, the teacher modeled reading aloud, explaining her use of particular strategies. She then presented the parents with a selection of children's books, summarizing the stories and discussing specific features of each book (e.g., the use of rhyme or repetition). The parents selected their books from among those offered or from the program library and discussed strategies for sharing them with the class. Finally, each parent rehearsed the chosen book one or more times, with suggestions and support offered by the teacher and the other participants. Parents were then asked to practice reading the book they had selected with their children at home before they went into the classroom.

Upon entry to the classroom, the teacher introduced the parent to the class. Students were seated on a rug in a story corner at the beginning of each session, and the parent sat or stood in front of them. Parents used big books for reading a story and left small copies of the books in the classroom after the session.

This sequence of activities was repeated each week as parents prepared new books for reading aloud; each training session emphasized a different read-aloud strategy. Included among these were eliciting predictions before and during reading, engaging children in choral reading of chants or repetitive refrains, questioning techniques, encouraging response during and after reading, and eliciting retellings.

As we did with the Home Literacy Portfolio project, we conducted formal investigations of the outcomes of the Parents as Classroom Storybook Readers project (Krol-Sinclair, 1996; Paratore & Krol-Sinclair, 1996). Evidence showed that over the course of their participation, all of the parents incorporated effective read-aloud strategies that they had not used in their initial sessions. Each of the parents used some strategies consistently in each read-aloud. All of them initiated some type of prereading, during-reading, and postreading activity into each session. Most of the parents were consistently responsive to the children's comments as they read. An added bonus was that tape-recordings of at-home parent–child storybook reading sessions indicated that parents used the strategies they had learned for classroom storybook reading with their own children at home. More informally, parents reported to us that they especially liked this opportunity. One father, in fact, who had agreed to read in his daughter's class, eventually read in seven different classrooms. It is noteworthy that most of the parents who participated in the Classroom Storybook Reading project were among those most likely to be labeled as not supportive of their children's learning. They spoke little English, and they had little experience with formal education. With support, however, they were able to participate in a meaningful and effective way in their children's classrooms.

CONCLUSION

The perception that children whose parents are poor, undereducated, and proficient in languages other than English are generally raised in home settings with few opportunities for literacy learning is widespread and persistent. Our experiences combine with those of others to tell us that it is also untrue. Teachers' awareness and recognition of parents' interest in their children's schooling, and of the multiple literacies that characterize most home settings, are critical in the development of home–school partnership programs to be built on reciprocity of learning between parents and teachers. As such, parent–teacher partnerships will have the potential to make a difference in helping poor, linguistically and culturally different children experience greater success in American schools. There are many strategies that can provide parents and teachers an opportunity to learn from each other. We hope that the three we describe here—the monthly newsletter, the home literacy portfolio, and parents as classroom storybook readers—will provide adult literacy, elementary education, and early childhood teachers a place to start in building effective literacy learning partnerships with parents.

REFERENCES

Anderson, R. C., Hiebert, E. H., Scott, J., & Wilkinson, I. (1985). *Becoming a nation of readers.* Washington, DC: U.S. Department of Education, National Institute of Education.

Briggs, C., & Elkind, D. (1977). Characteristics of early readers. *Perceptual and Motor Skills, 44,* 1231–1237.

Bronfenbrenner, U. (1979). Who needs parent education? In H. J. Leichter (Ed.), *Families and communities as educators* (pp. 203–223). New York: Teachers College Press.

Bus, A. G., van IJzendoorn, M. H., & Pellegrini, A. D. (1995). Joint book reading makes for success in learning to read: A meta-analysis in intergenerational transmission of literacy. *Review of Educational Research, 65,* 1–21.

Clark, M. (1976). *Young fluent readers: What they can teach us.* London: Heinemann.

Donahue, P. L., Finnegan, R. J., Lutkus, A. D., Allen, N. L., & Campbell, J. R. (2001). *The nation's report card: Reading 2000.* Washington, DC: U.S. Department of Education, Office of Educational Research and Improvement.

Dunn, N. E. (1981). Children's achievement at school-entry age as a function of mothers' and fathers' teaching sets. *Elementary School Journal, 81,* 245–253.

Durkin, D. (1966). *Children who read early.* New York: Teachers College Press.

Edwards, P. A. (1991). Fostering early literacy through parent coaching. In E. H. Hiebert (Ed.), *Literacy for a diverse society: Perspectives, practices, and policies* (pp. 199–213). New York: Teachers College Press.

Heath, S. B. (1983). *Ways with words: Language, life, and work in communities and classrooms.* Cambridge, UK: Cambridge University Press.

Krol-Sinclair, B. (1996). Connecting home and school literacies: Immigrant parents with limited formal education as classroom storybook readers. In D. J. Leu, C. K. Kinzer, & K. A. Hinchman (Eds.), *Literacies for the 21st century: Research and practice* (pp. 270–283). Chicago: National Reading Conference.

Mason, J. M. (1980). When do children begin to read: An exploration of four-year-old children's letter and word reading competencies. *Reading Research Quarterly, 15,* 203–227.

Melzi, G., Paratore, J. R., & Krol-Sinclair, B. (2000). Reading and writing in the daily lives of Latino mothers participating in an intergenerational literacy project. *National Reading Conference Yearbook, 49,* 178–193.

Morrow, L. M. (1983). Home and school correlates of early interest in literature. *Journal of Educational Research, 76,* 221–230.

Paratore, J. R., Hindin, A., Krol-Sinclair, B., & Durán, P. (1999). Discourse between teachers and Latino parents during conferences based on home literacy portfolios. *Education and Urban Society, 32,* 58–82.

Paratore, J. R., Hindin, A., Krol-Sinclair, B., Durán, P., & Emig, J. (1999, December). *Deepening the conversation: Using family literacy portfolios as a context for parent–teacher conferences.* Paper presented at the National Reading Conference, Orlando, FL.

Paratore, J. R., Homza, A., Krol-Sinclair, B., Lewis-Barrow, T., Melzi, G., Stergis, R., & Haynes, H. (1995). Shifting boundaries in home and school responsibilities: Involving immigrant parents in the construction of literacy portfolios. *Research in the Teaching of English, 29,* 367–389.

Paratore, J. R., & Krol-Sinclair, B. (1996). A classroom storybook-reading program with immigrant parents. *School Community Journal, 6,* 39–51.

Purcell-Gates, V. (1995). *Other people's words: The cycle of illiteracy.* Cambridge, MA: Harvard University Press.

Scarborough, H. S., & Dobrich, W. (1994). On the efficacy of reading to preschoolers. *Developmental Review, 14,* 245–302.

Tao, F., Khan, S., Gamse, B., St. Pierre, R., & Tarr, H. (1998). *National evaluation of the Even Start family literacy program* (1996 Interim Report ED 418 815). Bethesda, MD: Abt Associates.

Taylor, D. (1997). *Many families, many literacies: An international declaration of principles.* Portsmouth, NH: Heinemann.

Taylor, D., & Dorsey-Gaines, C. (1988). *Growing up literate: Learning from inner-city families.* Portsmouth, NH: Heinemann.

Teale, W. H. (1986). Home background and young children's literacy development. In W.H. Teale & E. Sulzby (Eds.), *Emergent literacy: Writing and reading* (pp. 173–206). Norwood, NJ: Ablex.

Valdés, G. (1996). Con respeto: *Bridging the differences between culturally diverse families and schools.* New York: Teachers College Press.

Vasquez, O., Pease-Alvarez, L., & Shannon, S.M. (1994). *Pushing boundaries: Language and culture in a Mexicano community.* New York: Cambridge University Press.

Yaden, D., & Paratore, J. R. (2002). Family literacy at the turn of the millenium: The costly future of maintaining the status quo. In J. E. Flood, D. Lapp, J. Jensen, & J. Squire (Eds.), *Research in English and the language arts* (pp. 532–545). Mahwah, NJ: Erlbaum.

Part III

Phonemic Awareness, Code Learning, and Book Acting

7

Engaging Preschoolers in Code Learning
Some Thoughts about Preschool Teachers' Concerns

JUDITH A. SCHICKEDANZ

Almost everyone recognizes the important contributions of early experience to a child's later success in school. It is now practically taken for granted by policymakers and the public at large that preschool education is an essential rung on the educational ladder, especially for children who traditionally have experienced difficulty with academic achievement once they enter elementary school. Ensuring adequate achievement in the foundation areas of numeracy and literacy is, of course, of greatest concern to everyone.

This chapter outlines some of the essential components of early literacy for a child's later success in learning to read and write. It also reviews briefly data from some research indicating that many preschool teachers provide inadequate literacy instruction in their classrooms. Reasons for the relatively meager literacy instruction found in many classrooms are discussed, and some suggestions are made for how preschool teachers may be helped to incorporate more literacy instruction, including code-related experiences, into their programs. Code-related components of early literacy consist of phonological awareness, letter name knowledge, knowledge of sound–letter associations, and the insight that letters function to represent sounds in words (i.e., the alphabetic principle).

ESSENTIAL EARLY LITERACY EXPERIENCES

Much has been learned about early literacy development over the past three decades. A considerable amount of research now informs us about the early experiences in language and literacy that are related to later success in reading and writing. The range of knowledge and skills that children must acquire if they are to become literate is extensive (Adams, Treiman, & Pressley, 1998; Dickinson & Tabors, 2001; Snow, Burns, & Griffin, 1998), and the interactions among various components are quite complex.

In *Beginning Literacy with Language* (2001), Dickinson and Tabors identify several language and literacy experiences during the preschool years that foretell achievement in kindergarten. Critical classroom experiences include hearing rare words used by teachers, having one's comments extended through questioning, hearing books read, and having one's attention focused on analysis of books. It is also important for children to be engaged frequently in intellectually challenging conversations and to be provided a solid curriculum and environmental support for writing. In *Preventing Reading Difficulties in Young Children* (1998), Snow and her colleagues outline additional components of preschool literacy programs, including those related to code learning. These components are also reviewed by Adams and her colleagues (Adams et al., 1998) in Volume 4 of the *Handbook of Child Psychology*.

As a consequence of these and other recent publications and of additional efforts that have spanned the last three decades, literacy instruction, designed to enable children to acquire certain kinds of experience, has found its way into preschool programs. Yet one still finds significant differences in the literacy experiences included in preschool programs and in the specific kinds and levels of experiences provided by individual preschool teachers. The experiential opportunities provided to preschool children in the areas of language and literacy are remarkably uneven across classrooms, because in many programs literacy instruction is woefully inadequate.

Interestingly, even among teachers who believe that reading books is the most important literacy activity for a preschool classroom, reading sometimes turns out to be infrequent. Dickinson (2001a) found that children in about one-third of the classrooms he studied listened to books read in large groups for only 25 minutes or less each week. In another 25% of the classrooms, children listened to stories in large groups for 50 minutes or less each week. In only about 25% of the classrooms did children listen to stories in large groups for more than 50 minutes each week. Reading to children individually and in small groups was also rare in the classrooms studied. Even when teachers reported a goal to read to individual and small groups of children, most rarely managed to do it (Dickinson, 2001a).

Children's opportunities for writing in many preschool classrooms are as variable, and often as minimal, as book reading. In some classrooms, writing centers are provided and children and teachers use them relatively extensively. In other classrooms, there is no writing center at which children can explore and play with writing, or, if a writing center is provided, teachers spend little or no time in it (Smith, 2001). Likewise, extensive opportunities related to code learning are included in some programs and are provided by teachers in some classrooms, whereas virtually no code-related experiences are included in other programs and classrooms. Moreover, the nature of code-related experiences provided can vary quite dramatically across classrooms.

EXPLAINING THE VARIABILITY FOUND ACROSS PRESCHOOL CLASSROOMS

A number of factors influence preschool teachers' behavior and thus account both for the alarming absence of essential literacy experiences in some preschool classrooms and for the inadequate quantity of literacy experiences in others. Among these factors are such things as the teacher–child ratio in a classroom and the length of the school day. Less favorable ratios and shorter school days make it more difficult for teachers to engage in extensive conversations with children across a variety of classroom settings, to give individual children adequate time to speak, to plan and implement small-group activities, and to join individual children or small groups in a book area or writing center (Dickinson, 2001b). Yet structural classroom features do not tell the whole, or apparently the most important, story about what influences preschool teachers' behavior in language and literacy instruction.

Of more consequence, according to Dickinson (2001b), are (1) a teacher's understanding of early literacy development and (2) a teacher's view of his or her place in children's learning. The preschool teachers of children who did relatively well on the kindergarten assessment used in the Home–School Study of Language and Literacy Development (Dickinson & Tabors, 2001) placed importance on child attentiveness during group times, for example, and expended effort in obtaining and maintaining children's attention. They also deliberately planned and implemented more small-group and individual activities than did teachers whose students did not do as well on the kindergarten assessment (Dickinson, 2001b). Finally, children from classrooms in which teachers reported that they thought academic as well as social goals were important in preschool programs, did better on the kindergarten assessment than children from classrooms in which teachers believed that the primary goal of the preschool experience is socioemotional development and that academic instruction might even do harm.

To summarize, the level of support that preschool teachers in this study provided for literacy learning in their classrooms appeared to be closely related to whether they were *intentional* in their instructional efforts "to push children's thinking and support their literacy development" (Dickinson, 200lb, p. 286). Instructional intentionality, in turn, rested on teacher beliefs about the purposes of preschool education and about the importance of the teacher in children's literacy learning.

THE SOURCES OF PRESCHOOL TEACHERS' BELIEFS

Some basic tenets of traditional, mainstream early childhood (i.e., preschool) education support teacher beliefs that conflict with beliefs and actions related to better literacy outcomes (Dickinson, 2001b). Consider these remarks in the preface of a current training guide on emergent literacy (Trans-Management Systems Corporation, 1999, 2001):

> This technical guide is about emerging literacy—the gradual, ongoing process through which children naturally make sense of oral language (listening and speaking) and written language (reading and writing). This process is supported by caring families and attentive teachers who respond to children's communications and provide children with the time, space, and materials to make their own literacy discoveries. . . . This guide will help participants develop skills. . . . These skills encourage children's emerging literacy by responding to their interests and efforts rather than by providing direct instruction. Most children will make many discoveries about language on their own, when families and Head Start staff . . . watch, listen, and respond to children's gestures and words; talk with children and encourage children to talk with their peers; read aloud to children regularly and talk with children about the characters, plots, settings, and information in books; provide reading and writing materials that children can use by themselves; and show children through their actions that reading and writing are important. . . . (pp. 1–2)

Although the practices enumerated are known to benefit greatly the development of infants, toddlers, and preschoolers, the preface conveys three interrelated and problematic messages. First, code-related literacy activities are excluded from the language and literacy experiences highlighted in the preface, which implies that these are not critical components of early literacy development. Second, learning in the young child is portrayed as a natural process, largely a matter of independent discoveries. Third, teachers are directed to respond to children's interests and efforts and to avoid direct instruction.

All three of these pronouncements are in agreement with assertions made in the first National Association for the Education of Young Children (NAEYC) document, *Developmentally Appropriate Practices in Early Childhood Programs* (DAP) (Bredekamp, 1987). They are not, however, consistent with the current NAEYC *Developmentally Appropriate Practices* document (Bredekamp & Copple, 1997), the *Joint Position Statement on Learning to Read and Write: Developmentally Appropriate Practices for Young Children* (International Reading Association and the National Association for the Education of Young Children [IRA/NAEYC], 1998), and the report prepared by the National Research Council's Committee on Early Childhood Pedagogy (*Eager to Learn*; Bowman, Donovan, & Burns, 2001). Chief among the revisions and clarifications of original DAP philosophy is a caution against taking *to the extreme* such things as the importance of children's play and self-selection of activities, and relying on developmental categories as a basis for curriculum and assessment to the exclusion of subject-matter content considerations. In addition, there is a caution in *Eager to Learn* against interpreting constructivist theory so narrowly that it disallows direct adult guidance of children's learning. This caution is also stated explicitly in the *Joint Position Statement on Learning to Read and Write* (IRA/NAEYC, 1998, p. 6): "The ability to read and write does not develop naturally, without careful planning and instruction." These revisions should help to move preschool educators' thinking beyond the limitations on both program components and instructional practices that the first DAP document and traditional early childhood beliefs imposed.

Of course, it is difficult to change beliefs and the ways of behaving that are linked to them. Old and new beliefs and practices often exist side by side for many years, as new ideas make their way readily into some quarters but are rejected in others. Sometimes we are torn in our own minds between ideas. This occurs when a teacher thinks each of a number of ideas is good, but then, in actual practice, two or more good ideas come in conflict. That is, teachers can find themselves in situations where providing one opportunity for children seems to undermine their ability to take advantage of another opportunity. As a consequence, children choose among opportunities for learning as they come into competition with each other during the preschool day. The schedule and expectations in many preschool programs lead inevitably to a conflict between many good literacy opportunities, and they reduce the chances that every child in a classroom will receive the benefits that a program might actually offer.

HOW LITERACY GOALS PLAY OUT IN PRESCHOOL CLASSROOMS

Suppose that story reading is on almost every preschool teacher's list of very good and important things for children to experience. Suppose further that teachers think it important to provide an attractive book area in the classroom that is accessible to children each day during free-choice activity periods. Suppose also that many preschool teachers believe they should read to individual and small groups of children each day when children gather in the book area. And suppose that many preschool teachers believe in giving children considerable choice about their participation in activities, even in those, such as story time, that are planned for a group of children.

Now imagine that two teachers in charge of a typical preschool class of 20 3- and 4-year-olds set aside a specific 15- to 20-minute time each day for large-group story reading. These teachers allow children to choose whether they will join the group for the scheduled story time. If children choose not to join the story group, they may work quietly with puzzles or other manipulables at a nearby table, or they may join the second teacher in an adjoining room to help with midmorning snack preparations. Children who do join the group story time know that they may leave at any time they wish to join one of the other activity options.

Let us also suppose that on a given day, during the free-choice activity period, these two teachers also find themselves in circumstances that require them to do the following: (1) Help children with a finger painting project at the art table, (2) calm children whose excitement leads to carelessness in keeping water *in* the water table, (3) intervene to support resolution of several quarrels between children, (4) comfort a distraught child whose block building collapsed when another child accidentally bumped into it, (5) join a small group of children playing "let's go to the supermarket" in the dramatic play area in order to help a child with delayed language stay afloat in the play, (6) assist a child who has asked for help in locating a missing puzzle piece, which is preventing him from finishing a jigsaw puzzle, (7) wipe a child's bottom after the child has used the toilet, (8) change the clothing of a child who did not get to the bathroom in time, and (9) apply a Band-Aid after a child has picked the scab off a week-old scratch, causing it to bleed.

Given the specific arrangements in this classroom for book reading, it would not surprise anyone to learn that 6 of the 20 children in the class did not join the large-group story reading session, or that neither of the teachers found even a moment during this particular day to read books to children in the book area during the free-choice activity period. It also would not surprise anyone to learn that, across a week's time, a consistent core group of 11 children chose most days to listen to books read at group story time, but that group story time attendance of the remaining 9 children ranged from 0 to 4 days. Nor would it come as a surprise to learn that the record of children's visits to the book corner for the week looked like this: Eight children visited at least once each day, six children visited at least once on three different days, one child visited once on two days, and the five remaining children made no visits at all during the week. Finally, no one would be shocked to learn that on three days of the week neither of the teachers could find time to go to the book area to read to individuals or small groups of children, and that on each of the remaining two days only one teacher joined children in the book area, once for 10 minutes, and once for 15.

Fortunately, not all days in a preschool classroom are as hectic as the one portrayed here. Sometimes a teacher can translate his or her good intentions for children's learning into action, although it is never a sure bet. The day described here is typical of what happens in many preschool classrooms on all too many days. Under such circumstances, there is no guarantee that even book reading, the language/literacy activity that has achieved perhaps the broadest and most enthusiastic acceptance among preschool teachers, will reach every child in a classroom on any consistent basis. For code-related literacy instruction, the situation is probably worse.

BELIEF BARRIERS TO CODE-RELATED LITERACY LEARNING

The barriers to a child's access to book reading in a preschool classroom do not compare in number or kind to the barriers that often exist with respect to code-related learning. The barriers are greater for code-related aspects of literacy because, in addition to the barriers created by beliefs about choice and other accepted practices of preschool program organization, there is much less acceptance by preschool educators of the very idea that there are benefits to preschoolers in code-related experiences. Moreover, among preschool educators' beliefs are those about associations between code-related experiences and direct or explicit instruction, and formal learning.

To illustrate the barrier created by resistance to code-related learning at the preschool level, consider alphabet letter learning (i.e., naming). An established undergraduate text on early childhood education (*Preschool Appropriate Practices*, 1996, pp. 158–159) contains the following assertions about alphabet letter instruction ("Letter Awareness," not "Letter Instruction," are the specific words used in the section heading):

> If children are surrounded by letters, letter games, alphabet books, computer alphabet programs, and other letter activities, they will eventually learn to distinguish a number of alphabet letters. It is neither necessary nor appropriate to teach your children the letters of the alphabet in any formal sense. Let them play around with letters, words, and writing in your Writing Center and elsewhere in the classroom. If they ask you how to make a letter, show them. If they ask you the name of a certain letter, tell them. Thus they will teach themselves to recognize the letters they need to know as they use them playfully and seriously in the activities they pursue. (Beaty, 1996, p. 159)

These claims give the impression that letter learning must truly be optional, something for which preschool children must take the initiative. It is true that when preschool teachers read stories, they often give children a choice about participating. But once teachers are reading, there is no counterpart to the caution one finds in relation to code-related skill learning to avoid teaching in "any formal sense." There is, of course, the research on story reading styles, such as the work done by Dickinson and Smith (1994), in which teachers are cautioned against using a didactic, low-level, cognitive talk approach, which does not support the development of vocabulary and comprehension to the same extent as other styles. But this is not of the same order as cautioning teachers against *initiating* story reading each day at a designated story time as if doing so might constitute too formal an approach. In short, preschool teachers are never told, "Provide books in a book center, and then leave it to the children to determine whether you will read, to whom you will read, and when. *Never* read to children unless they explicitly ask you."

It is odd, considering the nature of these introductory claims, that the activities suggested in this book for promoting letter knowledge in preschool children are very good. The suggestions include using alphabet books, plastic and wooden letters, computer software programs, and various games that involve use of letters. One problem, of course, is that any reader (individual teacher) is free to pick and choose among the many activities offered. The strength of the suggestions, however, rests not only on the merits of each individual one, but on combining them during the course of a year in a preschool program. This programmatic use is not ensured simply because a book presents a list, and, of course, children's participation in any of these activities is likely to depend on each child's choice, given mainstream early childhood practices. An additional problem is that many teachers surely would hesitate to join too enthusiastically in whatever code-related activities they offer, when children choose to participate in them, given the cautions against engaging in direct instruction. It is frequently the case that readily available information that *could* strengthen language and literacy components of preschool programs often turns out to influence very little the educational opportunities of some, even many, children.

To add to our understanding of the uneasiness found among many preschool educators about code-related instruction, we can use as a yardstick of general expectations the list of developmental accomplishments provided in *Preventing Reading Difficulties in Young Children* (1998). According to this report, the successful 3- to 4-year-old child (preschooler) will be able to "identify 10 alphabet letters, especially those from his or her name" (Snow et al., 1998, p. 61). With respect to phonological awareness, knowledge of sound–letter associations, and insight into the alphabetic principle, the successful preschooler, according to the volume by Snow and colleagues (1998, p. 61), will "pay attention to separable and repeating sounds in language (e.g., Peter, Peter, Pumpkin Eater, Peter Eater)" and "may begin to attend to beginning or rhyming sounds in salient words." With respect to writing, the successful preschool learner is expected only to "'write' (scribble) messages as part of playful activity" (Snow et al., 1998, p. 61).

The kindergarten child (5-year-old), on the other hand, should be able to "recognize and name all uppercase and lowercase letters" and should know that the sequence of sounds (phonemes) in a word relates to the sequence of letters in the printed form of the word. In addition, a kindergarten child should recognize words that rhyme or start with the same sound; be able to generate new words to match rhyming word targets; learn a number of letter–sound associations; and invent phonemic-based spellings, using phonemic segmentation skills and letter name knowledge (Snow et al., 1998, p. 80).

The authors of this report write that these lists identify "a set of particular accomplishments that the *successful* learner is likely to exhibit during the preschool years" (italics added) that the lists "are neither exhaustive nor incontestable," and that "the timing of these accomplishments will to some extent depend on maturational and experiential differences between children" (Snow et al., 1998, pp. 60, 80). These qualifying statements certainly leave open the possibility that some committee members thought that the list underestimated the preschool child's potential for accomplishing code-related developmental milestones. Of course, the cautionary statements also leave open the possibility that some committee members thought even these meager code-related expectations for preschoolers were too demanding. It is hard to imagine that anyone would take such a position, but the cautionary statements invite that conclusion.

OVERCOMING THE BARRIERS

Increasing all children's access to important language and literacy experiences in preschool classrooms hinges on making some adjustments in common preschool practices that are based on deep-seated if unconsidered beliefs. It is possible to improve the situation in many preschool classrooms without asking teachers to abandon their beliefs completely.

Simple Changes Can Make a Difference

Imagine, for example, a simple change of offering children only one other option at the time that group story reading is scheduled, and making the second option the opportunity to go to the book area to look at books.

One teacher is assigned to read stories to the group; the second teacher is assigned to join the children in the book area (and will probably read to one or more children there upon request). This change still gives children a choice (more limited than before, to be sure), but the alternatives are confined to two different book opportunities. If a preschool teacher cannot refine his or her belief that children must always be given a choice in what to do, the teacher can apply that belief in ways that will increase children's access to story reading and books.

I would prefer two story-reading groups, with children assigned on a regular basis to each one, with no choice about whether to attend. Of course, teachers should accommodate, in the many ways that skilled preschool teachers know how, legitimate refusals, such as may occur early in a school year when some children are reluctant even about staying in their new day-care center or preschool. Other children are reluctant to stop playing with puzzles or blocks at cleanup time, or they go to these play areas when it is time for story group. Sometimes it works best to ignore such a child at first, and to read to the children (usually most) who have gathered. We have noticed in our own program that a child in this situation often turns to look and listen to the story, even though he or she has decided to stay at the puzzle table. Often, within a day or two, the child has joined the story group without teachers having forced him or her to leave the puzzles.

In our preschool, teachers simply assume that a 3-year-old does not know that the blocks or the puzzles or some other favorite material or activity will be available at school on subsequent days. How is a child to know that, even if a teacher says so? (And the teacher does.) With the passage of a few days, the child learns from experience that there is plenty of time in a school day to engage in favorite activities *and* to listen to stories as well (which often becomes a favorite activity as the child gains more experience with it). Establishing a set routine of story time does not require teachers to be heavy-handed with preschoolers or to abandon kind and considerate understanding and treatment of young children's feelings.

Code-Related Literacy Instruction Requires Considerable Change

Overcoming barriers to code-related literacy instruction requires more drastic changes, but some of these would not require teachers to abandon deep-seated beliefs (e.g., that children should always have choices about what they will do). Some of the most basic beliefs underlying teachers' reluctance to provide code-related instruction actually derive from the incompleteness of available evidence and information. For example, many preschool teachers believe that young children can make important literacy discoveries on their own if they are provided with a print-rich environment. Many preschool teachers also apparently believe that all children, when ready in a maturational sense, will become phonemically aware. In the not-too-distant past, even more preschool educators held these beliefs, because evidence showing their pedagogical inadequacy had not yet been systematically gathered and published (or the teachers did not know how to test the effectiveness of their practices). Now the evidence confirms that children do indeed acquire some literacy understanding through their own discoveries and inferences, but that they cannot learn everything this way.

Examples of discoverable literacy knowledge may include the following:

- Writing is used for a number of purposes, in many different contexts.
- Each book contains a specific story, which is why, no matter who reads a particular book, the same story is heard.
- Graphic patterns that people refer to as "writing" are organized in lines; graphic patterns that people refer to as "pictures" are arranged differently.
- Graphic symbols used to write are made of combinations of straight and curved lines.
- Some symbols differ greatly from others. Some are so similar that they may very well be different versions of the same thing.

To be sure, even these discoveries require exposure to certain forms of instruction. The point is that experiences of stories, print, and pictures contain the information from which children make these discoveries (assuming that the children are attentive). Above and beyond providing the general experience, an adult need not point out explicitly, nor instruct directly, on most of these matters. (Children will, of course, learn more quickly to distinguish among all 26 of the alphabet letters if adults point out that very small differences found among highly similar letters are essential and should be honored.)

Some literacy understandings, however, are not discoverable. To say they are distorts the common meaning of the word. For example, letter names, in contrast to their graphic features, are not discoverable at all. Some human being, some animated character on a television screen, or some computer program must supply a name or label for each one and must do so in a way that links the appropriate label to each graphic design. Given that the design of many alphabet books makes explicit the links between graphic symbols and verbal labels, some parents and teachers think they have done nothing but read books to children and that the children have *discovered* letter knowledge, all on their own. In fact, the teaching has been explicit if the adults have read quite a number of alphabet books, or the same few many, many times. How much more explicit can one get than to say, "*A* is for acorn. *B* is for barn. *C* is for carrots that grow on the farm.

D is for dentist, for dog, and for drama. *E* is for eggs that are cooked by your mama."

Add to the reading the kind of pointing that is typical (i.e., to the letters that often appear in big, bold print), and it won't take many readings before a preschooler will learn the names of most letters. Add to alphabet book experience a bit of play with magnetic letters on the refrigerator door (or wall of the preschool), and just listen in. Suppose a few letters fall to the floor and are not noticed by the child. The parent stops by, picks up the letters, and says, "Oh, looks like the letter *A* and the letter *L* have fallen onto the floor. We'll put them right back up here. Do you want them next to the *E* up here, or should we put them down here by the *X*?" Often, considerable explicit teaching takes place in these contexts without the adult ever realizing it. It is not *formal* instruction, but it is both explicit and direct. Children do not discover the names of alphabet letters, because the conventions of language and alphabet cannot be discovered. Someone must tell them in ways that link each name to a specific letter.

Children also cannot discover that spoken words can be conceived of as a series of individual sounds. We now know that, "acoustically speaking, phonemes do not exist" (Adams et al., 1998, p. 282). To make matters worse, children, like the rest of us, focus on meaning when they listen to language. Early on, getting and sending meaning is the sole purpose of what language is for the child (Huttenlocher, 1964). Setting meaning aside—setting aside the basic use or function of language—and focusing on its structural properties is simply not something that a young child does. Doing so would require the child to "treat language as an object of thought" (Snow et al., 1998, p. 111).

When a young child is using language, the child's attention is elsewhere (i.e., on meaning), which is perhaps why songs and texts that use rhyme, alliteration, and abrupt changes in intonation are so entertaining to a young child. That is, when listening to a nursery rhyme, the child hears rhyming words and words that start with the same sound, as well as abrupt changes in intonation. Amazing perceptual ability makes a baby especially sensitive to both visual and auditory input and wonderfully capable of noticing changes from the normal and familiar. The child perceives that nursery rhymes differ from the language that he or she usually hears. As a consequence, the language a child hears in a nursery rhyme disrupts his or her typical focus on meaning and directs it to the sound and rhythm of the language—to aspects of its form. Like any pleasant novelty, such language captures the baby's attention and leads to delight. (Perhaps there is a rare 10-month-old who delights at hearing a skillful performance of "Hickory Dickory Dock" or some other nursery rhyme because he or she understands completely the meanings of the words, but I have never met one. The child's delight springs from the sound of the language and from the excitement caused by a parent's fingers running up and down the baby's chest and tummy in time with the cadence of the recitation.)

Noticing the sound, as distinct from meaning, in such language play is only a very first step on the path of acquiring code-related knowledge. Lucky indeed is the child who is given this kind of experience with language starting in infancy. During the preschool years, while language play, of the very same kind that many parents and caregivers offer to babies and toddlers, is extended and broadened, children must also be engaged in word games, such as thinking of words that rhyme with, or begin with the same sound as, a target word, and listening to adults sound out words that they or the children wish to spell. Phonemic level awareness, on which the alphabetic insight so indispensable to reading rests (although not the only critical understanding/skill on which reading rests, it is essential nonetheless), is not discoverable by children in any normal sense of that word. Rather, adults must bring children to this awareness by behaving in very specific ways in the context of experiences of a certain kind.

The relationship between oral language and print must also be brought to the child's attention. Anyone who has worked with preschoolers knows that their first written words consist of strings of letters. The strings resemble words, but are not actual words (Schickedanz, 1999). Young preschoolers do not have the slightest idea of just how, or even that, graphic symbols and speech are related. The alphabetic insight does not come suddenly, with a certain level of physical and neurological maturation, nor can it be discovered. It rests on tutoring of a very specific kind.

Preschool-level teachers, as well as teachers at other levels, have been led, unfortunately, to the mistaken belief that the child's acquisition of letter name knowledge, phonemic awareness, and sound–letter association knowledge require formal and direct instruction and that formal instruction is the same as, or inseparable from, direct instruction. It is true that direct instruction is required. But formal instruction is not. The term *formal schooling* does have a specific meaning, narrowly played out in practice. It means that a teacher (or, more commonly, a program developer or writer) plans a very specific program of instruction, which consists of an organized series of lessons that are spelled out in great detail and placed in a specific sequence. The integrity of the program of instruction is delivered by using the lessons, in the way they are set forth, and in the sequence established. The content (i.e., skills, knowledge, strategies, and so on) included in a formal program of instruction is usually decontextualized, sometimes to an extreme, which means that clutter of any kind (i.e., anything not directly related to the skill or knowledge at hand) is excluded from the program. The teacher is to exercise no discretion in delivering the program. So conceived, formal instruction discards the intelligence and experience of the teacher and therefore limits the opportunities of the child. It is far different from direct instruction.

If we take letter name learning as an example, a highly formal program of instruction may teach children to recognize, name, and write all of the letters (by the time children finish the formal program) through use of flash cards and work sheets, without ever engaging the children with letters in the context of words. Even something such as reading alphabet books to children may not be included. (Certainly, the use of alphabet books *can* be included in a formal program of instruction aimed at teaching children alphabet letters, but there are instructional programs for alphabet learning that do not include them.)

Formal instruction almost always includes direct instruction, because those who think that what is to be learned must be cut apart, packaged in specific lessons, and delivered in a specific sequence, also make other assumptions about children. Chief among these is the assumption that both teachers and children have very few robust cognitive powers, such as the power to deduce or discover much of anything. Many advocates of formal instruction think that all of children's learning, or at least any important part, must be explicit and direct and must be delivered without distraction (i.e., decontextualized).

Of course, not all formal programs of instruction are so narrowly designed, and not all of the designers make these assumptions. The point, however, is that some formal programs of instruction can be described fairly in this way, and that in many preschool teachers' minds, formal *programs of instruction* and *direct instruction* are indivisible. As a consequence, teachers often want nothing to do with *either one of them*. If avoiding direct instruction (i.e., explicit teaching of something by pointing it out to children or by providing specific information or demonstrations) is the only way to avoid formal instruction, out it goes. Avoidance of direct instruction in all contexts diminishes preschool children's code-learning opportunities, because some of the understandings and skills to be acquired do inescapably hinge on explicit, direct instruction.

What Teachers Can Do to Increase Code-Related Learning

The transcripts of two different situations involving children who wanted to spell "Daddy" (see Table 7.1) show the differences between a beginning teacher who is reluctant to provide correct information for fear that she will hurt the child's feelings, make the child worry about making mistakes, and so on, and an older, more experienced graduate student who had been engaged in many discussions about appropriate literacy instruction in various seminars and other contexts. Both transcripts are prototypical rather than actual; that is, they are composites of several situations involving the same goal and the same kind of child and teacher behavior. The different teachers' interactions provide the children with different code-learning op-

TABLE 7.1. Teaching Code-Related Literacy Components: Explicit and Direct but Not Formal

---

Beginning teacher's approach

CHILD 1 [3-year-old]:   I'm writing a letter to my daddy. How do you write "Daddy?"

TEACHER: Well, maybe you can figure out what it starts with.

CHILD 2 [5-year-old]: (*Child is also sitting at the table.*) *D.* It starts with a *D.*

CHILD 1: *D.* Does it (*looking at the teacher*)?

TEACHER: Yes, I think that would work OK.

CHILD 1: How does a *D* go?

TEACHER: Well, just try. Do you know what *D* looks like?

CHILD 1: Yes, but I can't make one.

TEACHER: Sure you can. Just try. It doesn't have to be perfect. We'll know what it is, no matter how you write it.

CHILD 2: I know how. I'll show you. (*Gets up from his chair and puts his arm down next to the child's paper, indicating that he is ready to demonstrate.*)

TEACHER: (*quickly*) No! Let her do it herself (*said to Child 2, as the teacher uses her hand to move Child 2's hand away from Child 1's paper*). However she makes it, it is OK.

CHILD 1: (*Puts marker to her paper and makes a circle. Returns marker to the left side and moves it up and down to try to flatten this side.*)

TEACHER: That's very good.

CHILD 1: What is next?

TEACHER: What do you think might be next?

CHILD 1: I don't know.

CHILD 2: (*Child 2 has abandoned his own picture by this time, and has been watching and listening to Child 1 and the teacher.*) I think I know.

TEACHER: Well, let's just let her think about it. We aren't going to tell her.

CHILD 1: Does *D* come next? (*Child has thought for a while and has said the word "daddy" softly to herself several times.*)

CHILD 2: No . . . (*cut off by teacher*).

TEACHER: I think that would work just fine.

CHILD 2: (*Looks at teacher with an expression of puzzlement at first, as if he's thinking about this and considering whether it is correct. Then, his expression turns into a smile, and he nods his head as he looks at the teacher, in a way that says, "Oh, I see what you are doing. It's OK if she doesn't get it right. You want her to do it all by herself."*)

CHILD 1: OK. (*Turns her attention to her paper to make a* D, *much as she had made the first one.*) What comes next?

TEACHER: I think you might be able to figure that out by yourself.

(*continued on next page*)

TABLE 7.1. (*continued*)

CHILD 1: (*Displays thoughtful expression for a while, and again says the word to herself. Doesn't come up with a letter suggestion.*)

CHILD 2: (*Child has been attentive and watchful throughout.*) /i/. Get it? /i/.

CHILD 1: E?

TEACHER: I think that would work!

CHILD 1: (*Writes E fairly well, but makes five horizontal lines rather than only the three that are required.*)

TEACHER: OK. You have written "Daddy." (*Uses her finger to underline the child's writing.*)

CHILD 1: (*Smiles broadly.*)

CHILD 2: (*Smiles in a knowing way at the teacher, suggesting the message, "She doesn't know and that's OK. She's just 3. When she grows up and is 5 like I am, then she'll know better." He even winks.*)

Graduate teaching assistant's approach

CHILD 1 [3-year-old]: I'm writing a letter to my daddy. How do you write "Daddy"?

TEACHER: Well, let's think about that. /d/, /d/, /d/. What letter do you think we might use to write /d/?

CHILD 2 [5-year-old]: D!

TEACHER: Yes. We do use D, but let's let Ana (fictitious) think about it. She's the one who is writing the word. If she needs help, I'll tell you and then you can tell me what your idea is.

CHILD 2: OK.

CHILD 1: I can't make a D.

CHILD 2: I can. I will show you. (*Gets up from his chair and puts his arm down next to the child's paper, indicating that he is ready to demonstrate.*)

TEACHER: Well, actually, wait just a minute. I'll grab the chart. (*Reaches toward an alphabet letter chart that is hanging from a hook on the side of the paper display shelf in the writing center*).

CHILD 2: But I know how. I can show her.

TEACHER: I know that you know how, but Ana might like to know how you learned it, and she might like to know that this chart can show us how, so we'll just take a quick look at it, and, Allen (fictitious), get another piece of paper, honey. Let's not do our demonstration on Ana's paper. She'll write her own D after we show her how.

CHILD 2: (*Draws a straight, vertical line, very deliberately on his paper.*)

CHILD 1: (*Watches Child 2 with eyes wide and bright.*)

TEACHER: OK, that's just great. Now, Ana, you make that part of the D on your paper. Where was it you thought you wanted to write "Daddy"?

CHILD 1: (*Points to the middle of her paper.*)

TEACHER: OK, you want it down here in the middle. OK, start a little over here (*gesturing to the left side of the paper, across from where the child had pointed*) so that you will have enough room for all of the letters we'll need to write "Daddy."

CHILD 1: (*Moves to the spot indicated by the teacher's finger and draws a pretty good straight, vertical line.*) Now what?

TEACHER: Well, now, there's a curved line that comes out like this (*uses index finger to trace curved line in the D on the chart*), and then it goes back in to touch the line down here. Allen is going to show you how to do that on the *D* he is making on his paper.

CHILD 2: (*Draws the curved line very carefully to complete the* D.)

TEACHER: OK, now you can add that curved line to finish your *D*. Start right up here at the top of the vertical line you have already drawn, and then move your marker out this way and then gradually down to touch the line down here (*uses finger to trace the path*).

CHILD 1: (*Draws curved line.*) Now what?

TEACHER: Well, let's see. *D* /ae/, /ae/, Daddy. That's a really hard sound to know how to write.

CHILD 2: No, it isn't. My name starts with that sound.

TEACHER: That's right, it does, and you know what's really funny? Ana's name also starts with that sound, and the sound in her name is spelled with the same letter as the sound in your name. What a coincidence! (*Said as if she had just noticed this herself and thought that it was a remarkable discovery.*)

CHILD 2: *A*!

CHILD 1: *A*?

TEACHER: Yes, A. Just as in (*says both names, one after the other, isolating the first vowel phoneme in each name before saying the rest of it.*)

CHILD 1: I know how to write *A*! (*Proceeds to do it.*) Now, what is next?

TEACHER: Da /d/, /d/ . . .

CHILD 1: *D*?

TEACHER: Yes, there are two of them.

CHILD 1: I already did one.

TEACHER: Well, I mean there are two more in the middle.

CHILD 1: (*Writes the two D's.*)

TEACHER: (*Offers verbal guidance to support recall of lines needed and their direction.*)

CHILD 1: OK. Now what?

TEACHER: Daddy, Dadd /i/.

CHILD 1: *E*! (*Child begins to position her marker to begin making an E.*)

TEACHER: Well, the sound is /i/, but we write it with the letter *Y*. Let me show you one on the chart. (*Same process as was used before is used to instruct Child 1 on making Y and then to help Child 1 to make one of her own.*) OK, that says "Daddy." (*Underlines it with her finger.*) Did you want to write something else?

CHILD 1: No, I'm finished.

portunities. The more informative teaching by the more experienced teacher confirms that preschool teachers need not use formal programs of instruction to improve preschool children's code-related learning. Some preschool teachers, however, will need to provide some explicit or direct instruction (not formal instructional programs) if they are to get closer to the kinds of interactions that are required for code-related aspects of literacy learning. Amount of experience per se does not foretell which of these prototypical interactions will occur. It is the *kind* of experience a teacher has had that tells, as well as the nature of the teacher's previous exposure to various early childhood education beliefs, practices, purposes, and rationales.

I am confident that preschool educators can begin to use practices such as those demonstrated by the more experienced teacher in the example, and can figure out other ways to reconcile their essential beliefs with the need to provide more adequate language and literacy instruction for children in their classrooms. It is important that preschool educators continue to give careful thought to how they might improve code-related literacy learning, and that the benefits of such consideration reach children without delay.

REFERENCES

Adams, M. J., Treiman, R., & Pressley, M. (1998). Reading, writing, and literacy. In W. Damon (Ed.) & I. E. Sigel & K. A. Renninger (Vol. Eds.), *Handbook of child psychology* (5th ed.): *Vol. 4. Child psychology in practice* (pp. 275–355). New York: Wiley.

Beaty, J. J. (1996). *Preschool appropriate practices* (2nd ed.). New York: Harcourt Brace.

Bredekamp, S. (Ed.). (1987). *Developmentally appropriate practices in programs serving children from birth through age 8*. Washington, DC: National Association for the Education of Young Children.

Bredekamp, S., & Copple, C. (Eds.). (1997). *Developmentally appropriate practices in early childhood programs* (Rev. ed.). Washington, DC: National Association for the Education of Young Children.

Bowman, B. T., Donovan, M. S., & Burns, S. (Eds.). (2001). *Eager to learn: Educating our preschoolers*. Washington, DC: National Academy Press.

Dickinson, D. K. (2001a). Book reading in preschool classrooms. In D. Dickinson & P. Tabors (Eds.), *Beginning literacy with language* (pp. 175–203). Baltimore: Brookes.

Dickinson, D. K. (2001b). Putting the pieces together. In D. K. Dickinson & P. Tabors (Eds.), *Beginning literacy with language* (pp. 257–287). Baltimore: Brookes.

Dickinson, D. K., & Smith, M. W. (1994). Long-term effects of preschool teachers' book-readings on low-income children's vocabulary and comprehension. *Reading Research Quarterly, 29* ,104–122.

Dickinson, D. K., & Tabors, P. O. (Eds.). (2001). *Beginning literacy with language.* Baltimore: Brookes.

Huttenlocher, J. (1964). Children's language: Word–phrase relationship. *Science, 143,* 264–265.

International Reading Association and the National Association for the Education of Young Children. (1998). *Learning to read and write: Developmentally appropriate practices for young children: Joint Position Statement.* Washington, DC: National Association for the Education of Young Children; and Newark, DE: International Reading Association.

Schickedanz, J. (1999). Young children and writing. In J. Schickedanz (Ed.), *Much more than the ABCs* (pp. 97–133). Washington, DC: National Association for the Education of Young Children.

Smith, M. W. (2001). Children's experiences in preschool. In D. Dickinson & P. Tabors (Eds.), *Beginning literacy with language* (pp. 149–174). Baltimore: Brookes.

Snow, C. E., Burns, M. S., & Griffin, P. (Eds.). (1998). *Preventing reading difficulties in young children.* Washington, DC: National Academy Press.

Trans-Management Systems Corporation. (1999, 2001). *Training guides for the Head Start community: Emerging literacy: Linking social competence to learning* [Online]. Available at www.headstartinfo.org/publications

8

Concepts, Sounds, and the ABCs
A Diet for a Very Young Reader

MARCIA INVERNIZZI

When children begin first grade, they are expected to know the difference between a sentence, a word, a letter, and a sound. Moreover, they are expected to know what each of these things are, both conceptually and functionally, as units in print. As simple as these terms appear to grownups, in reality they are quite abstract and many of their linguistic attributes overlap. The fact that sounds can be represented by letters that combine to form words that are strung together to form sentences is obscured by the process of making meaning. And the fact that word units are superimposed on other linguistic units like syllables, morphemes, and phonemes doesn't help. As a result, children often confuse the meanings of these terms and find it difficult to orchestrate them in matching their speech to print.

Learning to read entails a process of matching oral and written language structures at several different levels: the macro-level of meaningful phrases or sentences, the lexical level of words within phrases, and the micro-level of sounds within words and syllables. There is not always a one-to-one correspondence between spoken and written language at any of these levels. Mismatches exist because of the frozen configuration of print versus the fluid, dynamic nature of speech. To learn to read, children must synchronize the structures of written and spoken language at the level of phrases and sentences, words within phrases, and sounds within words. Such an undertaking involves a complex interplay of concepts, sounds, and the ABCs.

This chapter describes the essential ingredients of a nourishing literacy diet that enables emerging readers to sort out these concepts of written language. The chapter addresses four facets of early literacy instruction: (1) the concepts and vocabulary of print and sound, (2) phonological awareness, (3) alphabet knowledge, and (4) concept of word. By the end of the chapter, readers will see how the various components of the early literacy diet intermingle and become amalgamated through developmental knowledge of the written word.

CONCEPTS AND VOCABULARY OF PRINT AND SOUND

The concepts and vocabulary of print and sound have to do with children's understanding of the words teachers use to talk about language, storybooks, print, sounds, and writing. This language is used to describe what we do when we talk, sing, make silly rhymes, match speech to print, or when we try to label a picture. There are many ambiguous terms in the language of print, such as in the words *sentence, word*, and *letter*. Other words necessary to communicate about literate matters involve the language of sound, words like *syllable, rhyme*, and *beginning sound*. This section of the chapter describes hands-on, performance-based activities that teachers can use to build children's conceptual understanding of these essential vocabularies.

Young children approach learning through the tangible and sensory attributes of things, and teachers can capitalize on this fundamental learning mode by asking them to categorize examples of terms like *sentence, word*, and *letter* into groups that go together by size. For example, after chanting and playing with the refrain from a favorite storybook like *The Fat Cat* (Kent, 1971), teachers can copy recurring sentences on paper and cut them into sentence strips. The sentence, "What have you been eating my little cat?" would be a good sentence to choose because it recurs on every other page throughout the book and because it is closed by a question mark at the end. Individual words from these sentences can also be copied. Simple nouns and adjectives such as *cat, pot*, and *old* are small enough to be obviously different from a sentence in size, but large enough to be differentiated from a single letter. Individual letters can also be written on little squares of paper. Teachers can model how to sort these sentences, words, and letters into groups, taking care to read and discuss the form and function of each example before placing it in the proper group. Using the word *I* could spark some interesting discussion about one-letter words and result in an oddball category.

After modeling this sorting at the board or on the rug, teachers can give children little envelopes with cut-up sentence strips, words, and letters to sort out and paste into sentence, word, and letter groups on their own.

The children do not actually have to be able to read in a conventional sense to participate in this activity. Teachers can read the sentences aloud to them, and they will already be familiar with what they say from the previous demonstration. The size of each unit will also provide the scaffolding needed for children to understand that the terms *sentence*, *word*, and *letter* refer to different sized units of print. Categorizing them into separate groups makes these differences concrete and explicit.

The concept that sentences usually contain more than one word and that words usually contain more than one letter is best developed through similar concrete experiences. In an activity called "Be the Sentence," for example, the teacher writes a sentence on the board such as "Today is Wednesday" and reads it to the students. The teacher then writes each word from the sentence on a large card, gives each word card to a child, and names the child by the word (e.g., "Kaleigh, you are the word *Today*. Jacob, you are the word *Wednesday* . . . "). Students work together to arrange themselves into the sentence. Another student can read the sentence to check for direction and order. Each "word" can step forward as it is read. If more than one sentence has been constructed, students can discuss which sentence was longer by counting the number of students or words in the lineups (Bear, Invernizzi, Templeton, & Johnston, 2000).

"Be the Nursery Rhyme," an adaptation of "Be the Sentence," adds another concept and vocabulary term to the mix—*syllable*. In this variation, children learn a nursery rhyme and recite it together several times, perhaps over several days. The teacher writes the nursery rhyme on large chart paper and points to the words as the class chants in unison. Once the nursery rhyme is known by heart, the children sit in a circle on the floor. This time one child stands up in the circle as each word is deliberately spoken. In the line "The cow jumped over the moon," for example, six children would stand up, one for each word. If two children stand up for the word *over*, this mistake can be discussed in relation to the word's meaning and with reference to its printed form on the chart paper—*one* printed word unit (*over*) meaning *one* thing ("above and across from one end to the other"), despite the fact that the word has two syllables.

A similar approach can be taken using cut-up sentences. In this variation, sentences are taken from familiar texts or nursery rhymes. A sentence is written on a sentence strip, and students reread the sentence while touching each word. Next, the students cut apart the words in the sentence, mix them up, and then reorder them to reconstruct the sentence. Groups of students can be given different sentences from the same rhyme or story, and after the reconstruction they can count the words to see which sentence is longer. Hands-on activities such as these demystify linguistic terms like *sentence* and *word* and make them more concrete.

Of course sentences have meaning too, and their function for telling something about somebody or something should be made clear. Some teachers explain that a sentence is like a very short story, "and just like a story, a sentence has to tell something and has to name who or what it is telling about" (Adams, Foorman, Lundberg, & Beeler, 1998, p.40). In other words, a sentence has two parts; one part tells something (lost a tooth) and the other part tells who or what that something is about (Jenni). By using children's names as subjects, students can generate predicates in the form of statements about their classmates ("Lavon has a new back-pack"). Sentences can be generated orally, then built with Unifix cubes using one cube for each word in the sentence. As children share their Unifix cube sentences, they can repeat the sentence while touching each cube. Cubes can be counted to compare the length of the sentences to reinforce the notion that more words result in longer sentences.

The Unifix cube idea comes in handy also for sorting out differences between syllables and words. As children build the sentence, "I put my book bag in my cubby," they will, no doubt, add two cubes for the word *cubby*. Here is an opportunity to directly show that *cubby* means *one* thing (a small compartment or closet), even though it has two syllables (*cub-bee*). Teaching children to clap for each syllable in a word also helps them sort out the difference; cubby would have two claps even though it is just one word. By removing the extra Unifix cube and modeling how to point to each cube as the words of the sentences are spoken, a teacher can build the concept that sentences are composed of words that may or may not be composed of more than one syllable.

Issues related to size and one-to-one correspondence may confound other concepts about print and sound as well. For example, very young children often associate the size of the thing they are talking about (the referent) with the size of the printed word. They expect a word that refers to something large to be bigger than a word that refers to something smaller. Using this logic, young children expect the word *bus*, for example, to be longer than the word *motorcycle* because buses are bigger than motorcycles.

Teachers can provide opportunities for children to observe that the length of a printed word bears no relationship to the size of its referent. One way to do so is to write the names of various animals on word cards and have the children sort them into two groups according to printed word length. This simple activity might end up with the words *bee* and *cow* in one category and the words *butterfly* and *elephant* in another. Matching pictures to these words (with a little help with reading the words) will quickly reveal that there is no consistent relationship between the length of a printed word and the size of its referent. Discussing the size of the animal in relation to the size of the word goes a long way toward dispelling some erroneous assumptions about the relationship between the written word and its meaning and begins to build a conceptual framework for word as a linguistic abstraction independent of meaning.

Historians claim that the defining moment in the development of literacy came when humans realized that symbols could be used to communicate the *name* of something as opposed to merely representing the thing itself. It took 40,000 years of human experience to make this conceptual leap and presaged the origin of writing as distinct from the pictograph (Gelb, 1963). Like the early humans, children must come to realize that although a drawing of the sun can represent the sun, the drawing does not actually say "sun." Writing is necessary to express words, and the writing must have some connection to sound, specifically, the speech sounds produced when pronouncing the name of the referent, such as "sun."

At a conceptual level, one of the most powerful ways to teach young children that print communicates through sound is by recording children's experiences as they narrate them. Allowing children to dictate accounts of classroom experiences helps them link speech to print and to see that writing is talk written down. This approach has been traditionally referred to as the Language Experience Approach (LEA; Stauffer, 1970). Playground episodes, art projects, cooking activities, field trips, guest speakers, and birthdays—all provide children with opportunities for discussion around a shared experience. Comments can be recorded next to each child's name (e.g., Jacob says, "The ice cream was cold!") and used to reinforce ideas and vocabulary as well as important linguistic concepts associated with *beginnings*—the *beginning* of the sentence, the *beginning* of the word, the *beginning* sound. Each child can be asked to locate his or her name at the beginning of a sentence and then find a word within the sentence that begins with a certain letter or sound. Rereading each child's dictated sentence further highlights the connection between speech and beginning sounds in print.

The conceptual framework and terminology associated with sounds are particularly challenging for young children because of overlapping boundaries. Phonemes, the smallest units of speech sounds, are particularly difficult because one sound begins before the previous one ends. Unlike rhyming sounds, which are always at the ends of words, phonemes can occur in any location. Knowing what various speech sounds are called, what they consist of, and where they are located is called *phonological awareness*. Phonological awareness is a broad construct that encompasses linguistic features as expansive as the syncopation of stress across syllables (IN-ver-NIZ-zi) or as contained as syllables within words. Phonological awareness also refers to sound features within syllables like alliteration, rhyme, and individual phonemes.

Children become confused about various speech sounds, not because they cannot hear them, but because they do not know what the terms refer to or where they can be found. Directions such as "Listen for the first sound" can really throw them. In response to the question, "What does *car* start with?" for example, one baffled child timidly replied, "Vroom?" As teachers, we can help children understand these abstract concepts through physical activities that play with language.

A fun way to sensitize children to syllable stress in oral language is to play an adaptation of the hand game, "One Potato, Two Potato." Sitting on the rug in groups of three to five, children can take turns tapping their partners' fists held out in the circle as all recite together, "One, two, buckle my shoe. Three, four, shut the door. Five, six, pick up sticks. Seven, eight, lay them straight. Nine, ten, start again!" Children actually shriek with delight at the last line as they anticipate who gets the next turn. Tapping to the rhythm of the nursery rhyme, a child achieves one-to-one correspondence between the stressed syllable or word and his or her fist. Every meaningful word (or at least its stressed syllable) is tapped in this activity. Stressed syllables are an important segue to the most important concept of all—beginning sounds.

What is challenging about beginning sounds is not the sound but its location. Understanding place or location is of critical importance in learning to read. Children cannot pay attention to the beginning sound if they do not know where the beginning is.

Fortunately, location is the perfect setup for variations on the theme of Elkonin boxes (Elkonin, 1973), such as "Beginning-Middle-End: Finding Phonemes in Sound Boxes" (Bear et al., 2000). To play this game, the teacher hangs three large paper pockets next to each other on the blackboard or the wall and labels the pockets "beginning," "middle," and "end," in that order. Next, the teacher chooses a simple three-phoneme word like *cat* and hides large letter cards inside the corresponding pockets: C in the beginning pocket, A in the middle pocket, and T in the end pocket. The students are told that the first word is *cat*, and their job is to decide where the [k] sound is—at the beginning, the middle, or the end. To the tune of "Frère Jacques," children sing, "Where's the [k] sound, where's the [k] sound? Beginning, middle, end? Beginning, middle, end?" One child is then selected to come forward to choose the pocket in which the [k] sound in the word *cat* is hiding. The child chooses the first pocket, reaches in to retrieve the letter card, and then looks to see whether he or she is correct by turning over the card to see the letter C. Research suggests that the beginning sound is most salient for young children, followed by the ending sound. Middle sounds are the most difficult and should not be attempted until children are facile with beginning and ending sounds (Morris, 1993).

The vocabulary of speech and print implies a one-to-one correspondence that is more myth than reality. In speech, words are not distinct; they are not clear, separable units bound by anything finite. Sometimes words even run together, like the letters *LMNOP*. Many children are surprised to find out that it's "The Wizard of Oz" and not "The Wizard of Voz," as they thought. Moreover, it is difficult to match speech units to words because of their overlap with syllables. Because of this lack of one-to-one correspondence between units of speech and units of written language, children often get off track when pointing to written text. To learn to read, children must attain the concept of a written word and distinguish the word *word* from other structures such as *letter* or *sentence*. Phonological awareness and alphabet knowledge allow emergent readers to track words in text by pointing to the beginning sound of each word as it is pronounced.

PHONOLOGICAL AWARENESS

There is a natural division in English written words between the beginning consonant elements (if present) and the vowel and what follows, and this division corresponds roughly to beginnings and ends (Henderson, 1990). Linguists call the beginning consonant elements *onsets*. The ending chunk is called the *rime* (spelled *rime* to differentiate this linguistic unit from nursery *rhymes*). Children are in a better position to deal with the mechanics of beginning reading instruction if they have a working knowledge of onsets and rimes (Stahl & Murray, 1998).

Teachers can build a strong foundation for early reading success by focusing on onsets and rimes and their location within words. Once children understand the location and linguistic function of these two subsyllabic sound units, they are well positioned to listen for similarities and differences between them. Knowing that *boy, bug, ball*, and *bite* all start with the [b] sound signaled by the letter *B*, and that *man, Mom, mop*, and *mud* all start with the [m] sound signaled by the letter *M*, is the first giant step toward knowing where words begin within a line of text. Onsets call attention to beginnings. Rimes call attention to ends.

Many of the instructional approaches to teaching beginning sounds involve alliteration. Alliteration usually refers to a series of two or more words that begin with the same sound. Activities that feature alliteration focus children's attention on beginning sounds that mark the onset of word boundaries both in print and speech. Knowledge of beginning sounds is necessary to separate the speech stream into individual words.

Picture sorts are at the heart of beginning sound instruction and entail categorization routines for classifying onsets by similarity and difference. Beginning-sound picture sorts cross over into the learning of alphabet and letter sound correspondences because as children sort picture cards into groups that all start with the same sound, they place them in columns headed by a letter that represents that sound. Phonological awareness does not have to precede or follow letter-sound instruction, or any other component of early literacy instruction for that matter. Awareness of sounds is heightened by print, and for this reason, is an ongoing, reciprocal by-product of learning to read. Teachers should strive to make connections between beginning sounds and letters whenever possible.

In sorting pictures according to beginning sounds, it is best to start with two very different sounds to avoid confusion. Some teachers choose the sounds [m] and [s] for their first lesson because they are both *continuants* or sounds that can be held onto continuously with out distortion. They are also articulated at different places in the mouth; [m] is articulated by pressing the lips together, whereas [s] is articulated by pressing the tongue to the tip of the roof of the mouth just behind the teeth. The different feel of these sounds in different parts of the mouth make it easier for children to tell them apart and to judge their similarity when they occur in an alliterative sequence (e.g., *man, moon, mop* vs. *sun, sock, six*). It is best not to start out with two sounds that are made at the same place in the mouth, like [p] and [b], especially when they also look so similar. To ensure a successful first picture sort, start with obvious contrasts first (Purcell, 2002).

Picture sorts always contrast at least two sounds at the same time. The same key picture is used consistently to head each sound category along with the letter that represents that sound. The teacher models the sorting routine by saying, "Here is a sock. *Sssssock* begins like *ssssun*. *Sssssock, sssssun*—both start with the sound [s] made by the letter *S*, so I will put it under the picture of the sun and the letter *S*. Here is a picture of a man. *Mmmmman* begins like *mmmouse*. *Mmmman, mmmmouse*—both start with an [m] sound, so I'll put it under the picture of the mouse and the letter *M*." After modeling several pictures, the teacher gives the deck of picture cards to the children to finish categorizing, providing direct supervision and feedback.

Once children become accustomed to categorizing pictures and objects by their beginning sounds, they can participate in many other variations of the activity. In the game "Beginning Sounds Go Fish," familiar pictures with two to three different beginning sounds are cut out and fastened to construction paper (cut into the shape of a fish) with a metal paper clip. The pictures are put in a washtub or within a circle on the floor, and children are equipped with a fishing pole with a magnet at the end of the fishing line. The children fish for pictures. When a child catches a fish, the picture is named and the beginning sound is identified. The child then places the picture in a kettle of fish that share the same beginning sound (Invernizzi & Meier, 2001).

The letters in one's name are among the first letters learned and serve as a good springboard into other phonological insights, such as beginning sounds (Bloodgood, 1999). Teachers can take advantage of children's intrinsic interest in their own names by devising instructional activities that focus on their letters and beginning sounds. To set the stage, a teacher might first read the book *A My Name Is Alice* (Bayer, 1992). Then, using student photographs as personal identifiers, children write sentences beneath their own photograph that model the book's pattern, "____, my name is _____." Using magazine and catalog pictures that have been precut and presorted by beginning sounds, each child then cuts and pastes pictures to complete a second sentence, "My name begins like. . . . " During group time the children can play guessing games to guess whose name starts with the beginning sounds in the magazine pictures displayed.

Another name-related activity that features beginning sounds is "Silly Greetings" (Fitzpatrick, 1997). In "Silly Greetings," the teacher changes the first sound of everyone's name to a different sound—a [t] sound, for example—and then greets everyone upon arrival with his or her new silly name. Sarah, Johnny, and Patrick become Tarah, Tohnny, and Tatrick. These silly greetings call attention to the first sound in everyone's name and create quite an alliterative classroom.

Isolating the beginning sound can also be practiced through segmenting and blending games that are played with puppets, dolls, or stuffed animals that like to talk in a funny way. Pat the Puppet, for example, likes to talk by dividing words into two parts—the beginning sound and the rime that follows. Instead of saying, "Fish," for example, Pat the Puppet says "f-ish." Children repeat what Pat the Puppet says, then blend the onset and rime together to get "fish." Later, children take turns talking in puppet talk. The puppet talk practices the process of isolating the beginning sound and segmenting it from the rest of the word. This is precisely what children must do when they begin to read and spell. The directions to these, and other phonological awareness games supporting beginning sound learning through children's names, can be found at *http://curry.edschool.centers/go/Pals.*

Early childhood educators know that every minute counts if we are to move all our students forward in literacy. That is why teachers need a large repertoire of short and engaging tasks that require little advance preparation. Activities like "Snap" are the perfect solution for those ubiquitous moments of line time: waiting for recess, lunch, or dismissal. In "Snap," the teacher says two one-syllable words in succession. If the words begin with the same sound (*dog, door*), the children snap their fingers or clap their hands. "Snap" can also be played with ending sounds. Riddles and "I Spy" games are quite versatile as well. At any time, at any place, teachers can play "I'm Thinking of Something" (Adams et al., 1998) to focus children's attention on beginning sounds or rhymes. For example, "I am thinking of something you are doing right now that starts with the [r] sound. Can you guess what it is?"

ALPHABET KNOWLEDGE

Words are made of syllables that contain even smaller units of sound, such as onsets, rimes, and phonemes. Letters of the alphabet represent this nested hierarchy of sound structures within words, but sorting out the relationships among them takes time. In speech, consonant and vowel sounds overlap, and this co-articulation makes them difficult to separate. The liquid nature of the [l] sound in *bell*, for example, makes it difficult to hear the vowel in the middle as a separate sound. Through experience and instruction, children learn how the alphabet divides the sounds within syllables.

Alphabet knowledge includes letter naming, letter recognition, letter sounds, letter production, and connecting letters and sounds through invented spellings. There is a lot more to alphabet knowledge than singing the "Alphabet Song"—though that is an excellent place to begin.

Among the prereading skills that are traditionally studied, that which consistently predicts later reading success on its own is accurate, rapid letter naming (Snow, Burns, & Griffin, 1998). Learning the names of the letters is an important first step toward learning letter–sound correspondences. Most of the letter names already include the sounds associated with them. The letters *B*, *K*, and *Z* contain their sounds at the beginning of their names (bee, kay, zee), and the letters *F*, *L*, and *S* have their sounds at the end (eff, ell, ess). The names of the vowels contain their tense, or long-vowel sounds. These letter names are applied quite literally when children begin to write, as in the spelling of *pz* for peas.

The alphabet is learned the same way that other concepts and vocabulary about print and sound are learned—through hands-on explorations of the relationships among all of its facets: letter names, letter sounds, letter formation, what letters look like, and the equivalence between upper- and lowercase forms.

Like activities highlighting beginning sounds, many alphabet activities begin with children's names. Writing, building, reconstructing, or copying their own names is intrinsically appealing to young children and provides the perfect venue for alphabet instruction and writing. Children feel a real sense of ownership over the letters in their names. *K* becomes Keyana's letter and should definitely not be in Derrick's name!

Comparing and contrasting several letters at a time is the best approach to alphabet instruction. The presentation of one letter a week does not allow enough time or practice for children to acquire the alphabetic principle. Letters must be matched and sorted according to similarities and differences in all aspects of their identity.

For children to acquire letter recognition, letters must be matched: uppercase to uppercase, lowercase to lowercase, and finally, uppercase to lowercase. There are many traditional games that involve this basic matching concept. "Bingo," "Concentration," and letter puzzles like "Alphabet

Eggs" are all based on the process of matching. Many of these games are also downloadable from the activity pages of the PALS website (*http:// curry.edschool.centers/go/Pals*). A writing component can be added to many of these games to practice letter formation. For example, in "Letter Spin," children write the letter in addition to picking up the matching letter tile (Bear et al., 2000).

Letter-matching activities can develop basic letter recognition, but this alone is not sufficient. Children must learn letter–sound correspondences and must have plenty of experience in applying letter–sound knowledge in the context of reading and writing. Ultimately, we want children to be able to see the first letter of a word in text and have that letter cue its beginning sound immediately. The beginning-sound picture sorts described in the preceding section, "Phonological Awareness," teach letter sounds by having children categorize initial sounds into groups labeled by the letters that represent those sounds. Picture and object sorts, in combination with writing and reading letters, provide the hands-on learning experiences that young children need.

Alphabet tracking activities can simulate the process of reading and give children practice in achieving one-to-one correspondence between what is said and what they see as they touch the print. Learning the ABC song to the tune of "Twinkle Twinkle" is relatively easy, but singing the song and tracking the letters on an alphabet strip as it is sung at the same time, is hard. Alphabet strips, alphabet posters, the inside jacket of *Chicka Chicka Boom Boom* (Martin, Archambault, & Ehlert, 2000) all provide appropriate materials for alphabet tracking. Alphabet tracking can also occur when children construct the alphabet with "Link Letters" or letter puzzles.

Letter reading is also an important component in alphabet instruction and approximates real reading. Alphabet books that feature alliteration offer opportunities for letter reading and other alphabet activities as well. *Curious George Learns the Alphabet* (Rey, 1963) is particularly useful because the first letter of each word in an alliterative sequence is highlighted. The original *Dr. Seuss's ABC* (Seuss, 1963) is beneficial for teaching upper- and lowercase equivalence in addition to letter sounds. It features upper- and lowercase letters in bold print, as well as alliteration and rhyme. When a parent or teacher pauses at these highlighted or bold letters, children can join in the reading. When choosing alphabet books, it is important to look for clear examples of each beginning sound. To a child who cannot yet read, words like *endive* and *Indian* start with an [n] sound, not a short *e* or short *i*.

An all-time favorite classroom activity that involves children in recognizing, naming, and reading letters is called "Zip Around." In "Zip Around," twenty-six 8-by-4 index cards are passed out. Each one says, for example, "I have *R*, who has *G*?" Each child reads a card that prompts another. When at last someone reads, "I have *J* who has *Z*?" some very lucky child gets to respond, "I have *Z*! It's Zip Around!" This whole-class activity can be adapted to feature uppercase letters, lowercase letters, or letter sounds. The cards are downloadable from the PALS website.

Letter formation instruction and writing for sounds is an often neglected aspect of learning the alphabet. In writing for sounds, children are encouraged to use their letter sound knowledge to label words and write simple messages. Writing for sounds requires children to segment their speech into individual words and sounds and to match those segmented sounds to letters. Teachers model the segmentation process by stretching out the sounds in words and teaching students to do the same. Some teachers ask children to write teacher-made sentences that feature a particular sound or contrast (e.g., "*She shops for shoes*"). Writing for sounds exercises young children's alphabet knowledge and provides opportunities for instruction in letter formation.

Some children are reluctant to write. They may not know how to form the letters, or they may not know they can use letter names to represent the sounds they are trying to write. "Push and Say It" (Johnston, Invernizzi, & Juel,1998) strategies can provide just the support they need to get going. "Push and Say It" is an adaptation of the "Say-It-and-Move-It" procedure for teaching students how to segment individual phonemes within words (Blachman, Ball, Black, & Tangel, 2000, p. 3). The procedure uses letter tiles that are similar to Scrabble squares made of paper or plastic. Teachers model how to segment individual sounds within words by deliberately pronouncing the word in an elongated fashion and stretching out the sounds without distorting them. As each individual sound is pronounced, the teacher pushes a letter tile representing that sound forward on the table. The letter tile provides a concrete symbol for each phoneme. "Push and Say It" strategies are particularly useful for teaching children how to write in invented spelling. By pushing a letter at the same time the sound is produced, teachers demonstrate phoneme–grapheme or sound-to-letter correspondences. In cases where two letters represent one sound, such as the case with the consonant digraphs SH, CH, or TH, it is best to put both letters on one tile. Each tile represents only one sound. The word *chip*, for example, would have three tiles despite the fact that it has four letters in its spelling: *ch/i/p*. Adaptations of the "Push and Say It" activities can be just the ticket for youngsters who are uncertain about how letters work. For example, one stymied preschooler confided that he didn't know how to write his aunt's name on the valentine he was making. When his teacher asked what his aunt's name was, she quickly made two paper letter squares and pushed up the *L* while saying "ell," then pushed up the *N* next to it while saying "en." A lightbulb went on in that child's head, and he eagerly wrote *LN* for *Ellen* and many other names without further ado.

CONCEPT OF WORD

Acquiring a concept of word requires the parallel development of beginning sound awareness and alphabet knowledge. When children are learning about letters and sounds at the same time they are touching words and reading familiar nursery rhymes and other simple texts, there is a reciprocal process at work. Learning one gives logic and purpose to the other (Bear et al., 2000).

A *concept of word* refers to the emergent reader's ability to match spoken words to written words as he or she reads a familiar rhyme, poem, song, or text. A concept of word allows children to hold onto the printed word in their mind's eye and scan it from left to right, noting every sound in the beginning, middle, and end positions. Prior to attaining a solid concept of word in print, children have great difficulty identifying individual phonemes below the level of onsets and rimes, and words slip easily from memory without the support of context (Morris, 1993).

As a result of direct instruction and ongoing teacher support in matching speech to print, children's finger-point reading behaviors change over time, and observing these changes can inform other aspects of literacy instruction. At first, children may track rhythmically across the page, pointing to words as if keeping time for each stressed beat in the recitation. As they learn that words have to match up to speech sounds, their finger pointing is executed more carefully and they achieve a closer match to words and syllables. At this point, the children's finger pointing may still get off track on two-syllable words. They may point to the word *the* while pronouncing the second syllable of the word *over* in the line "the cow jumped over the moon," for example. As recognition of beginning sounds and the letters that represent them becomes more automatic, children finally realize that when they say the word *moon*, they should be pointing to the M word at the end of the sentence. Self-corrections during finger-point reading signal the onset of a concept of word in print.

The best way for children to achieve a concept of word is to point to the words in simple texts and to reread these texts many times over while simultaneously learning how the alphabet represents beginning sounds. In addition to nursery rhymes and language experience approaches (LEAs), simple texts might consist of picture captions, simple patterned books, or excerpts from favorite stories. Once these texts become familiar, children should be encouraged to memory-read them, touching each word as it is spoken.

Picture captions provide a rich opportunity to connect speech to print and to model the writing-for-sounds process. First, children draw a picture of their favorite toy, Halloween costume, or weekend activity. As they are finishing their drawings, the teacher walks around the room, asking each child to tell something about his or her picture. Choosing a key sentence from the child's explanation, the teacher repeats that sentence and writes it verbatim beneath the picture, stretching out the words to emphasize the beginning and ending sounds and calling attention to letters. The teacher then reads the picture caption back to the child, pointing carefully to each word. The child then reads it with the teacher, who models the finger pointing once again. Finally, the child reads the caption alone while touching each word. If the child gets off track on a two-syllable word like *Lego*, it is best to explain that *Lego* is one word that means one thing, but the word has two claps when we say it (*Leg-go*). Children can practice rereading their picture captions to their families and friends.

Simple patterned books provide another handy medium for cultivating a concept of word. Rhyming patterns are particularly appealing to young children and, like picture captions, easily memorized. Some rhyming books are so repetitive and simple that children can read them on their own in short order. The simplest of these highlight hink-pinks, such as *sky-pie* or *sun-fun*, and provide stunning illustrations or photographs to prompt the child's response. After listening to these books read aloud several times, children can touch the words accurately as they read them all by themselves. After a book has been read aloud several times, the teacher can cover up the rhyming word with an index card and leave only the first letter visible as a clue. Children will eagerly supply the missing word and will delight in anticipating the next one. This modified cloze procedure can also be applied to copies of *Rhymes for Reading* (Bear et al., 2000). Copies of familiar rhymes can be pasted in children's personal reader with only the beginning sound of the rhyming words showing. As children practice rereading these rhymes, they can fill in the missing rime using the initial consonant or onset as a clue. "One, two, buckle my shoe," for example, may be copied as follows: "One, two, buckle my sh____. Three, four, shut the d____." Thirty different nursery rhymes featuring the phonograms or rimes first identified by Richard Wylie and Donald Durrell in 1970 are downloadable from Laura Smolkin's website at *www.virginia.edu/go/will*. Other games centering on nursery rhymes may be found in Ericson and Juliebo's *Phonological Awareness Handbook for Kindergarten and Primary Teachers* (1998).

Children pay closer attention to the details of printed words when they see them out of context all by themselves. For this reason, after multiple rereadings, simple but interesting words from their rhymes, patterned books, and LEA dictations, should be copied onto little word cards to be examined in more detail. If children cannot recognize these words in isolation, teachers guide them to match the words to their counterparts in text by using the beginning sound and letter as their guide. This activity can also be conducted in small groups with the use of a chart. Each child can be given a self-adhesive note tag with a word on it; he or she then goes to the chart and attaches the tag to the same word on the chart.

A convenient procedure for honing in on individual words is "I'm Thinking of a Word" (Invernizzi & Meier, 2001). Here, teachers focus on one particular line or sentence in context and say, "I'm thinking of a word in this sentence that begins just like the word *dog*. What word am I thinking of?" Children come up to a chart to point to the word *door*, for example, and the teacher asks, "How did you know?" Prompting children to articulate the clues and strategies they use to figure out words encourages them to use these strategies again. In "I'm Thinking of a Word," teachers focus on alliteration and rhyme, the beginnings and ends of words in context.

BRINGING THE INGREDIENTS TOGETHER

Combining activities into cohesive lessons with a discernible purpose and forward momentum is a challenge and the reward of teaching. It is important that instructional activities flow together in a logical way. For example, texts selected to be read aloud and to be used for concept of word work may include recurring examples of the beginning sounds being studied. The words children are asked to write should also contain the same features. Repeated and deliberate work with words and texts will provide children with the practice they need to evolve into real readers. A focused description of a 20-minute lesson for kindergartners concludes this chapter.

Ms. Purcell's students rotate through carefully structured centers so that she can work directly with a small group of children for 20 minutes at a time. Group work begins with the children tracking the alphabet while singing the ABC song. Alphabet strips are glued to the back of each child's folder, and the children touch each letter while singing. At the song's conclusion, Ms. Purcell plays "I'm Thinking of a Letter." "I'm thinking of a letter that makes the sound ___," she says, and the children put their fingers on the letter that makes that sound. After several rounds of this game, Ms. Purcell hands out envelopes labeled with each child's name printed clearly on the front. Inside are little squares of paper with uppercase letters on them, which, when reassembled, spell each child's name. Using the envelope as a model, the children take out the letter squares and reconstruct their names. A second envelope is quickly passed out, and the children then match each lowercase letter in this envelope to its uppercase counterpart. After checking with Ms. Purcell, the children quickly scoop up the letters and return them to their proper envelopes.

The children then gather together to listen to a read-aloud of a carefully selected text, *That Cat* (Peterson, 1997). Ms. Purcell has chosen a short rhyming-pattern book that features the recurring rimes *at* and *an*. Ms. Purcell introduces the book by calling attention to its cover and the title and invites the children to tell about their observations and experiences. After a short book walk, she asks the children to predict how the story will go. Before she reads, she reminds them to watch her as she points to each word in a sentence. As Ms. Purcell reads *That Cat* out loud, she pauses periodically to think aloud about the rhyming pattern and story line. At the end of the reading, she revisits the text, pointing out certain words and other print features the children have studied before. The children then chorally reread the story, which Ms. Purcell has previously prepared on chart paper. Handing out individual word cards, Ms. Purcell calls on individual students to come to the chart and find and match their word cards to the same words on the chart. As the children do so, Ms. Purcell is careful to ask them how they knew that the word they selected was the same word, so that others can hear the strategy they used—mainly beginning sounds cued by the beginning letter and the predictable rhyming pattern.

In a few days, Ms. Purcell will hand out individual text-only copies of the story so that the children can paste them in their personal readers and practice finger-point reading the story to their friends. Today she follows the chart activity with a *Make-a-Word* demonstration in the pocket chart, showing the children how they can change the word CAT to MAT by removing the C card and substituting the M card. She calls on several students to come to the pocket chart to make other words with the letters she has available: S for SAT, B for BAT. After this brief activity, Ms. Purcell picks up Pat the Puppet from behind her chair, and the children giggle with delight. Pat the Puppet talks in a funny way (she says *m-at* instead of *mat*), and the children love correcting her. After a few rounds with Pat the Puppet, Ms. Purcell passes out small dry-erase boards, and the children write the letters that correspond to the onsets and rimes that Pat the Puppet speaks. The children then pass up the dry-erase boards while Ms. Purcell gives them envelopes with pictures inside. The children sort the pictures into three groups according to beginning sounds (*M, S,* and *B*) then paste them into the already labeled columns in their notebooks. When they are finished sorting and pasting, the children label each picture with their own writing. They know Ms. Purcell will insist that they spell the beginning sound correctly and encourage them to do the best they can with the rest of the word. Ms. Purcell leaves the group to finish their work independently and makes her rounds to the centers to check the work of the other children before the groups switch places.

All of this took place in 20 minutes. Within that amount of time, Ms. Purcell's students participated in many difference activities focused on concepts and vocabulary, phonological awareness, alphabet and letter sounds, concept of word, and writing.

This nutritious diet for her very small readers yielded results. By the end of kindergarten, they were beginning to read.

REFERENCES

Adams, M. J., Foorman, B. R., Lundberg, I., & Beeler, T. (1998). *Phonemic awareness in young children: A classroom curriculum.* Baltimore: Brookes.

Bayer, J. (1992). *A my name is Alice.* New York: Penguin Putnam.

Bear, D., Invernizzi, M., Templeton, S., & Johnston, F. (2000). *Words their way: Word study for phonics, vocabulary, and spelling instruction.* Upper Saddle River, NJ: Prentice-Hall.

Blachman, B. A., Ball, E. W., Black, R., & Tangel, D. M. (2000). *The road to the code: A phonological awareness program for young children.* Baltimore: Brookes.

Bloodgood, J. (1999). Children's name writing and literacy acquisition. *Reading Research Quarterly, 34,* 342–367.

Elkonin, D. B. (1973). U.S.S.R. In J. Downing (Ed.), *Comparative reading* (pp. 551–580) New York: Macmillan.

Ericson, L., & Juliebo, M. F. (1998). *The phonological awareness handbook for kindergarten and primary teachers.* Newark, DE: International Reading Association.

Fitzpatrick, J. (1997). *Phonemic awareness: Playing with sounds to strengthen beginning reading skills.* Cypress, CA: Creative Teaching Press.

Gelb, I. J. (1963). *A study of writing.* Chicago: University of Chicago Press.

Henderson, E. H. (1990). *Teaching spelling.* Boston: Houghton Mifflin.

Invernizzi, M., & Meier, J. (2001) *Phonological Awareness Literacy Screening (PALS).* Charlottesville, VA: University Printing.

Johnston, F. R., Invernizzi, M., & Juel, C. (1998). *Book buddies: Guidelines for volunteer tutors of emergent and early readers.* New York: Guilford Press.

Kent, J. (1971). *The fat cat: A Danish folktale.* New York: Scholastic.

Martin, B., Archambault, J., & Ehlert, L. (2000). *Chicka chicka boom boom.* New York: Aladdin Picture Books.

Morris, D. (1993). The relationship between children's concept of word in text and phoneme awareness in learning to read: A longitudinal study. *Research in the teaching of English, 27,* 133–154.

Peterson, P. (1997). *That cat.* Parsippany, NJ: Modern Curriculum Press.

Purcell, T. (2002). *Articulating attributes of letter sounds: Considering manner, place, and voicing for kindergarten instruction.* Unpublished doctoral dissertation, University of Virginia, Charlottesville.

Rey, H. A. (1963). *Curious George learns the alphabet.* Boston: Houghton Mifflin.

Seuss, Dr. (1963). *Dr. Seuss's ABC.* New York: Random House.

Snow, C. E., Burns, M. S., & Griffin, P. (Eds.). (1998). *Preventing reading difficulties in young children.* Washington, DC: National Academy Press.

Stahl, S. A., & Murray, B. A. (1998). Issues involved in defining phonological awareness and its relation to early reading. In J. Metsala & L. C. Ehri (Eds.), *Word recognition in beginning literacy* (pp 65–88). Mahwah, NJ: Erlbaum.

Stauffer, R. (1970). *The language-experience approach to the teaching of reading.* New York: Harper & Row.

WEBSITES

www.virginia.edu/go/will

http://curry.edschool.virginia.edu/go/pals

9

Book Acting

Storytelling and Drama in the Early Childhood Classroom

LEA M. McGEE

With claims that millions of schoolchildren—including more than half of all inner-city children—cannot read with even basic proficiency, why should young children and their teachers spend time retelling stories or dramatizing narrative accounts that they find in informational books? Why not focus on the important basics, such as acquiring phonemic awareness, learning alphabet letter names, practicing how to apply phonics understandings to decode text, and using comprehension strategies such as predicting, visualizing, and summarizing?

At no time in our history has the public eye been more intently focused on children's reading and writing achievement and classroom instruction in reading and writing. The decisions that teachers make about literacy instruction are more visible than ever before. There is intense pressure for teachers to *justify* instructional activities in light of test scores, to correlate each instructional activity with standards found in curriculum guides, and to abandon any techniques that are not research based. Many teachers respond to such pressures by focusing on paper-and-pencil activities with narrow objectives and direct correlation to the multiple-choice questions so prevalent on achievement tests. A less sensible response seems to be to push back the desks, dust off the puppets, and practice retelling a story as simple as "Little Red Riding Hood." Yet there is a clear role for storytelling and drama in the classroom. The ability to engage children in a story so deeply that they adopt its literary language, explore the motivation of the characters, and try out multiple ways of being in a character's role, *is* effective in promoting children's literacy and language growth.

RESEARCH ON STORY RETELLING AND DRAMA

We have ample research to show that retelling and dramatizing stories increases children's language and literacy concepts. Children's participation in many forms of dramatizing stories is related to the acquisition of a variety of language and literacy concepts. Preschoolers and kindergartners who frequently engage in thematic fantasy play (in which children act out stories that have been read aloud to them) have better vocabularies, use more complex language, and have better story comprehension than children who only draw or talk about stories (Pelligrini & Galda, 1982; Saltz & Johnson, 1974). Children's understanding of stories deepens when adults guide story dramatizations by providing suggestions for how the children should act, model how to compose dialogue, or take a role in the children's dramatizations (Pelligrini, 1984; Williamson & Silvern, 1991). However, older children and children familiar with a particular story need less adult support (Williamson & Silvern, 1991). Adults also provide support for children's story dramatizations by rereading stories frequently and demonstrating how and when to use drama props (Martinez, Cheyney, & Teale, 1991). Children are more likely to enact stories that teachers have read repeatedly. They are more likely to enact stories with repetitive actions and refrains and when props are available for retelling. They are also more likely to enact stories that they have seen older children dramatize or retell (Martinez et al., 1991).

Children who have disagreements with other children about what a character does or says during a drama seem to have more detailed remembrances of stories than those who dramatize stories with few peer disagreements (Williamson & Silvern, 1991). Similarly, children who use more meta-language (language about the actions and dialogue that will occur during drama) acquire more emergent literacy concepts than children who use less meta-language (Galda, Pelligrini, & Cox, 1989).

Even drama that is only loosely related to acting out stories increases children's language development (Levy, Wolfgang, & Koorland, 1992). Kindergartners who have opportunities to learn about themes through field trips and listening to stories and information books and then engage in sociodramatic play, acquire more vocabulary and use more complex sentence structures than children who engage in free play. Adult support during sociodramatic play, such as thematic fantasy play, enhances language development.

Becoming storytellers and retelling familiar stories and informational books is also related to literacy development. Interactive sharing of story-books, in which children take on the role of storyteller rather than passive listener, improves preschoolers' expressive language development (White-hurst et al., 1994a, 1994b, 1999). Similarly, kindergartners who repeatedly listen to and then retell information contained in stories recall more infor-mation and use the particular structures of language found in written infor-mational texts (Pappas, 1991, 1993; Pappas & Brown, 1988). Repeated retelling of storybooks, with teacher guidance and feedback, also facilitates children's comprehension (Morrow, 1984, 1988; Morrow & Smith,1990). Practice in retelling stories improves upper-grade children's comprehension as well (Gambrell, Koskinen, & Kapinus, 1991). Group size is an impor-tant factor in using retelling to improve children's comprehension. Kinder-gartners who retell stories in small groups of three make greater gains in comprehension than those who retell one-on-one with the teacher or in whole groups (Morrow & Smith, 1990). Preschoolers make greater lan-guage gains when teachers share books in small groups of four children than when they read to larger groups (Whitehurst et al., 1994a).

It is clear that engaging children in playful retellings and dramatiza-tions of stories and informational books has multiple benefits. Storytelling and drama lead children to make inferences, integrate information across an entire text, use unique literary and content-specific vocabulary, and speak in sentences with more complex grammatical structures. Such in-volvement also influences children to use the kind of language found in books (termed *decontextualized language, written language register, or book language*), rather than the kind of language used in everyday conver-sation. Dramatization or retelling with other children adds more complex-ity, both cognitively and socially. The children must engage in negotiations with peers, learn to incorporate others' perspectives, and integrate more complex dialogue provided by supportive adults and peers into their own conception of the story. Research has documented that engaging in these cognitive and language activities results in better comprehension of the sto-ries enacted or retold, better recall of new stories (not retold or drama-tized), acquisition of more new vocabulary words, both included in stories told as well as other words not included in target stories, and use of more complex grammatical constructions.

Research on retelling and story drama suggests that adults play at least five roles in supporting children's retellings and dramatizations. First, teachers select appropriate books to use in retelling and dramatizing activi-ties. Appropriate book selections include those with repetitive phrases and favorite books that are reread on several occasions. Second, teachers read stories or informational books aloud in interactive or dialogic ways. Children are encouraged to comment, ask questions, and answer questions. Teachers ask open-ended questions so that the children seem more like storytellers. During interactive read-alouds, teachers provide complex language models as they make comments and respond to children; they expand the children's language, provide feedback, and extend the conversation. Teachers' ability to respond to all children with ample opportunities to expand their language is related to their third function: selecting children who will participate and organizing the classroom for small-group instruction. Small-group interactive read-alouds, followed by retelling or dramatizing, produce better results than interacting only with larger groups of children. Fourth, adults provide props for retelling and dramatizing. These can be simple realistic toys to represent story or informational book characters, or clothing that prompts children to take on a character's role. Finally, adults encourage retelling and dramatization through coaching and demonstrating. Demonstrations of how to use retelling or dramatization props, in ways that are sanctioned in the classroom and not disruptive of other children's play, seem particularly important in encouraging children's spontaneous reenactments of books. Coaching can occur outside the play, as adults take on the role of director, or inside play when adults take on one character's role or act as narrator. The most effective coaching follows from and elaborates upon the children's initial dramatic impulses.

The rest of this chapter describes a four-step teacher-directed method of engaging young children in retelling and dramatizing literature. This method is based on research and has been refined through several years of practice with children from preschool through third grade. In the following section, I make suggestions on how to select books, make and select props, and assess children's learning. In the next section, I briefly discuss the equally important practice of allowing young children opportunities to initiate and direct their own play around books. I describe some techniques for supporting child-directed retelling and dramatizing in the early childhood classroom.

TEACHER-INITIATED RETELLING AND DRAMA

Although retelling and drama are not precisely the same thing, I usually blend the two. Traditionally, retelling implies that one storyteller will tell the entire story, with the other children acting as an audience. Storytelling does not require props, but children often retell more detailed and complex stories when they are prompted by simple props, such as small objects or pictures. In contrast, drama implies that several children will act out a story, with each child taking on the role of one character. Simple props can also be used in drama, which include various kinds of puppets, items of clothing, masks, and even special costume collars. Retelling and drama are blended through the use of props. As props change in the retelling, the storyteller also changes. Therefore, distributing retelling props among children naturally assigns each child a portion of the story to retell. The nature of the props used with a particular book determines whether the enactment will be more like a retelling or a drama. Thus, I call this blended retelling/drama activity "Book Acting."

I usually follow four steps in Book Acting. The first step includes preparing for the activity by selecting a book, preparing props, and making decisions about how to conduct the enactment. The second step involves multiple read-alouds of the book in order to familiarize the children with the story or narrative portion of an informational book. Then I model and guide children through the enactment and discuss how to use the props during independent retelling or drama. The final step is to observe the children, for assessment purposes, as they engage in independent retelling or drama.

Preparing

Preparing involves selecting a book, gathering or making props, and making decisions about Book Acting. Book selection depends on the children's age, their experience with Book Acting, and the classroom curriculum. Younger preschool children need very simple versions of familiar stories or short sections of information books with few characters and events. Older children relish books with more subtle events and well-developed characters.

Teachers I have worked with in Book Acting have used both stories and informational books. Informational books that have strong narrative threads and at least one character are good choices. Appropriate stories have several of the following characteristics: two or three major characters, repetitive dialogue or actions, two or three major settings, well-rounded characters, and memorable language. Folktales make excellent selections for Book Acting because of their natural connection to storytelling. Figure 9.1 presents a list of stories and informational books I recommend for Book Acting.

Once a book is selected, I make decisions about props. The best props are simple, easily obtained or made, and easy to manipulate. I generally use six types of props and adapt these basic types depending on the book. Props can include pictures for a story clothesline or story stick, small objects, items of clothing, puppets, collars, and masks. I simply read the story or informational book and think about objects or clothing I might have or can obtain inexpensively. If certain objects or items of clothing are not readily available, I consider whether it would be easier to make pictures, collars, or masks.

Picture props can be used with either a story clothesline or a story

FIGURE 9.1. Recommended books for book acting.

International folklore

Borreguita and the Coyote	Verna Aardema
Clever Tortoise: A Traditional African Tale	Francesca Martin
The King and the Tortoise	Tololwa M. Mollel
Nine-in-One GRR! GRR!	Blia Xiong
Why Mosquitoes Buzz in People's Ears	Verna Aardema

Versions of favorite folklore

Cat Goes Fiddle-I-Fee	Paul Galdone
Fiddle-I-Fee	Melissa Sweet
The Emperor's New Clothes	Nadine Bernard Westcott
The Principal's New Clothes	Stephanie Calmenson
The Dinosaur's New Clothes	Diane Goode
King Long Shanks	Jane Yolen
The Enormous Carrot	Vladimir Vagin
The Enormous Potato	Retold by Aubrey Davis
The Enormous Turnip	Kathy Parkinson
The Gingerbread Boy	Paul Galdone
The Pancake Boy	Lorinda Bryan Cauley
The Runaway Tortilla	Eric Kimmel
Goldilocks and the Three Bears	Bernadette Watts
Goldilocks and the Three Bears	Retold by Jan Brett
Deep in the Forest	Brinton Turkle
Somebody and the Three Blairs	Marilyn Tolhurts
Goldilocks and the Three Hares	Heidi Petach
Goldilocks Returns	Liza Campbell Ernst
Henny Penny	Paul Galdone
Foolish Rabbit's Big Mistake	Rafe Martin and Ed Young
The Story of Chicken Licken	Jan Ormerod
I Know an Old Lady Who Swallowed a Fly	Nadine Bernard Westcott
I Know an Old Lady Who Swallowed a Pie	Alison Jackson
There Was an Old Lady Who Swallowed a Fly	Simms Taback
There Was an Old Lady Who Swallowed a Trout!	Teri Sloat
The Little Red Hen	Paul Galdone
The Little Red Hen	Lucinda McQueen
The Little Red Hen (Makes a Pizza)	Retold by Philemon Sturges
Cook-a-Doodle-Doo!	Janet Stevens and Susan Stevens Crummel
Little Red Riding Hood	James Marshall
Little Red Riding Hood	Trina Schart Hyman
Little Red Riding Hood	John Goodall
Little Red Riding Hood	Beni Montressor
Ruby	Michael Emberly
Little Red Ring Hood: A Newfangled Prairie Tale	Lisa Campbell Ernst

The Mitten	Adapted by Jan Brett
The Mitten	Alvin Tresselt
The Old Man's Mitten	Retold by Yevonne Pollock
The Woodcutter's Mitten	Loek Koopmans
The Three Billy Goats Gruff	Paul Galdone
The Three Billy Goats Gruff	Retold by Janet Stevens
Three Cool Kids	Rebecca Emberley
The Three Little Pigs	Paul Galdone
The Three Little Pigs	James Marshall
The Three Little Pigs	Gavin Bishop
The Three Little Pigs and the Fox	William H. Hooks
The Three Little Javelinas	Susan Lowell
The True Story of the Three Little Pigs	Jon Scieszka
Ziggy Piggy and the Three Little Pigs	Frank Asch
Three Little Pigs	David Wiesner
Wiley and the Hairy Man	Molly Garrett Bang
Wiley and the Hairy Man	Retold by Judy Sierra

Information and informational story books

Bread Bread Bread	Ann Morris
Chipmunk at Hollow Tree Lane	Victoria Sherrow
Cranberries	William Jaspersohn
The Emperor's Egg	Martin Jenkins
Giving Thanks: The 1621 Harvest Feast	Kate Waters
Iditarod Dream	Ted Wood
Munching, Crunching, Sniffing, and Snooping	Brian Moses
Our Skeleton	Brian and Jillian Cutting
Plants and Seeds	Colin Walker
Surprise Puppy!	Judith Walker-Hodge
Pumpkin Pumpkin	Jeanne Titherington
Red Fox Running	Eve Bunting
See How They Grow Penguin	Neil Fletcher
Seeds, Seeds, Seeds	Brian and Jillian Cutting
Slinky Scaly Snakes!	Jennifer Dussling
Wetlands	Marcia Freeman
What Will Float?	Fred and Jeanne Biddulph

stick. A story clothesline is a length of clothesline tied between two sturdy pieces of furniture, such as the teacher's chair and an easel. Six to ten pictures are created or selected from the book to depict the major events. I have used magazine pictures, clip art, and actual pictures cut from an extra copy of the book. When a book's illustrations are simple and easily copied, I have occasionally sketched pictures and finished them with watercolor, cut construction paper, or felt. Where appropriate, I laminate the pictures and then clip them to the clothesline as children retell the story. The best pictures for a story clothesline are approximately 6 inches square or larger.

When the pictures are smaller, I use a story stick rather than a clothesline. A story stick is constructed by attaching several small squares of Velcro to a yardstick. I also attach a small square of Velcro to the back of each picture and then attach the pictures to the stick as I retell the story. Figure 9.2 shows a teacher telling a version of *Henny Penny* with the story clothesline.

The easiest props to obtain are small objects that represent the characters and important events. I often tell *The Three Bears*, using three small teddy bears, spoons of three sizes, paper cups of three sizes, and three pieces of cloth—small, medium, and large—to match the size of the bears. The spoons represent eating the porridge, the cups represent the chairs, and the cloth is used to represent the three beds. Objects can be used alone or in combination with items of clothing. I use a vest, several scarves, an old-fashioned blouse, an apron, a small quilt, and a tablecloth for retelling *Mirandy and Brother Wind* (McKissack, 1988), along with a pepper mill, a small bucket, a crock, a stuffed rooster, and a child-sized plastic cake.

Collar props are quite easy to make. I use 12″ × 18″ construction paper, folded in half so that each half measures 9″ × 12″. I cut an oval opening for the neck in the fold. In the back, I cut from the neck opening to the bottom of the paper (like the opening in the back of a blouse), which allows a

FIGURE 9.2. Using a story clothesline to retell a version of *Henny Penny*.

child to put the collar on and take it off easily (see Figure 9.3). I cut the collar into a shape appropriate for the character and glue on additional construction paper details as needed. Collars can be laminated for extra durability, I use collar props for example, in dramatizing *The Enormous Turnip*. The farmer wears a collar that resembles a workshirt and the top of bib overalls, his wife wears a decorated shirt, and the daughter has a blouse with a pearl necklace. The dog, cat, and mouse all have collars that look like the animals' faces.

Masks are also easy to make. Instead of cutting out holes for eyes and a mouth, I have found that the easiest masks for young children are made from paper plates with the entire inside cut out. The outside of the paper plate is decorated to represent the character. Children often want to decorate their own masks. String or yarn can be stapled to the sides of the mask and used to tie the mask onto the child. *Henny Penny* and *The Enormous Turnip* can easily be dramatized with mask props.

Several kinds of puppets make excellent Book Acting props. These props take more time to construct and can be more delicate. I use them rarely, but they make a welcome addition to classrooms rich in Book Acting. The easiest puppets to make are pictures of characters stapled to plastic straws. Wooden spoons also make excellent puppets. I have used wooden spoons with cut-out felt details to construct puppets for *The Three Billy Goats Gruff*.

Once the props are gathered or made, I must decide how to introduce the book to the children, what language from the book I will emphasize, both during book introduction and during Book Acting, and how to conduct guided Book Acting. Each of these decisions is more thoroughly discussed in the following sections.

FIGURE 9.3. Collar props.

Familiarizing Children with the Book

Although research suggests that the most effective read-alouds with young children occur in small groups, I usually introduce stories or informational texts in large groups, followed by more extensive explorations in small groups. I have found that teachers are more comfortable introducing a new story and using story props with the whole group rather than a small group. I use two techniques when I introduce a story or informational text for Book Acting. I either read the book aloud interactively or tell the story. I usually tell the story when I know the story is already familiar to the children (such as *The Three Bears*) or when the book is really too complex to be read for a first introduction. For example, I love to use the story *Chrysanthemum* (Henkes, 1991) in a Book Acting activity with 4-year-olds. Yet, for many children, the book is too long, and the pictures are too small to use effectively with a group of preschoolers (especially in classrooms where some or many of the children have home languages other than English), so I tell the story using props the children will use later.

The purpose of a book introduction is for the children to have multiple opportunities to talk about the story or informational book in ways that will extend their understanding of basic concepts and themes. I help children discover character traits and motivation and elaborate on concepts introduced in the story or informational book. For example, the *Three Billy Goats Gruff* is a story about greed and trickery. The troll in the story is not merely hungry, or he would have simply eaten the first Billy Goat. The Billy Goats know that the troll is especially greedy (they are very clever indeed), and they use their knowledge of this trait to trick him into letting the two smaller Billy Goats cross the bridge unharmed.

Other favorite folktales are less dramatic and offer comments on everyday relationships. *The Three Little Kittens* involves children's attempts to please their mother and a mother's gentle punishment and reward. It explores basic concepts of lost/found and clean/dirty. During an interactive read-aloud of *The Three Little Kittens*, I make comments and ask questions such as, "Oh, no, they lost their mittens." I usually pantomime a panicked look and frantic searching all around me. I invite the children to put on their pretend mittens, then to lose their mittens, and declare, "Oh, no. I've lost my mittens." I prompt the children's comments by asking my own questions and making connections to my life. Then I invite them to think about their own connections to the story. I might say, "I wonder where they lost their mittens? I lost a pair of gloves in my car. I think they fell out. Where is a place you might lose your mittens?"

Selecting certain portions of the story for discussion takes some thought. Before reading aloud, I consider character traits, motives, themes, and concepts. I try to think of how these connect to the children's experiences. Then I select five or six places in the story to stop and make comments or "I wonder" statements. My favorite "I wonder" statement for *The Three Little Kittens* is "I wonder what kind of pie Mother has baked." In addition to stopping to let children expand concepts and detect character traits or motives, I also stop to savor the language of stories. Children love to say again and again, "Mother dear, Mother dear. My mittens I have lost."

Guiding Practice in Book Acting

The first step in guided practice involves the teacher's modeling how to use the props and retell the story. I do this in one of three ways. Sometimes I model retelling the story with the props. This works well when the props are to be hung on a clothesline or attached to a story stick. For example, I use the clothesline for *The Gingerbread Man* Book Acting. I retell the story as I clip each picture on the line. I pause just before saying any repetitive parts, to allow the children to chime in. Later, each child will be given a picture and will retell the portion of the story associated with that picture.

Another way in which I model retelling is to allow the children to handle the props as I do the retelling. I pass out the props to the children, then retell the story. I model how the children should use their props while I am retelling. This works well when a number of props can be gathered for each child. I have prop bags that I use with children when retelling *The Three Little Kittens*. Each child has a plastic bag with a small section of clothesline, four clip clothespins, a tin pie plate, and two mittens sewn from inexpensive cotton. I retell the story, model using the props, and help the children to keep track of and manipulate their props.

Sometimes I model how to think through a retelling before using props. I use this approach with second- or third-grade children when the Book Acting will involve several episodes. For example, I help children notice that *Borreguita and the Coyote* (Aardema, 1991) has four major settings. We look through the book and remind ourselves of what events happened at each setting. Then I help the children to retell the dialogue that happened in the first setting. I model creating dialogue and then prompt the children to improvise their own dialogue. I am careful to insert some of the literary language in my dialogue, although I never memorize a story. I repeat the dialogue, praise the children and expand on their dialogue, point out the effective use of props, and make suggestions for handling the props.

After this initial book introduction and modeling of Book Acting, I make decisions about further guidance in small groups. I always provide small groups of children opportunities to relisten to books read aloud and to practice retelling. For example, there are many fine picture book versions of *The Three Bears* and other favorite folktales. I may read different versions of the story to different small groups of children. We continue to use the same props for retelling the story, but retell it in ways that connect it with the version we are reading together. Although not appropriate for preschoolers, older primary grade children especially like spoof versions of favorite tales in which animal characters take on human character roles or a boy character takes on a girl character role.

With small groups, I discuss how to use the story props in the classroom Book Act Center. The Book Act Center has several copies of books we have recently shared, as well as the props for those books. During small-group time, I model how to use a particular book and the props we are using in the Book Act Center. Experience has shown that children sometimes have difficulty in sharing props and selecting portions of the story to tell, so we model several ways to solve this problem. Another difficulty I have found is that children often manipulate the props silently rather than retell the story to someone else. Therefore, I assign at least two children to the Center and have the children model how to take turns being the teller and the audience. Older children who have begun reading often want to read the book as they manipulate the props, rather than tell the story. Re-reading books is a practice I want to encourage, but the purpose of the Book Act Center is for retelling rather than rereading. I have found that if I gather multiple copies of the book and place copies in the library center, in the children's rereading or browsing baskets, and in the retelling center, the children are more likely to retell than reread. However, I do model how to reread the story and then close the book for retelling.

Observing and Assessing during Independent Book Acting

The final step in Book Acting is to provide opportunities for the children to engage in Book Acting on their own. During guided Book Acting, teachers provide models of complex and literary language use, prompts for language and prop use, and feedback for the children's attempts. In the Book Act Center children guide their own enactments and make their own decisions about how to divide retelling responsibilities and use the props. Teachers can observe children as they participate in the Center, to make assessments of their language and story comprehension. I usually observe one child at a time for 2 or 3 minutes and take notes on what I observe.

I specifically notice the use of book language, length and complexity of sentences, and completeness and accuracy in retelling. I consider book language any language from the text that children appropriate and use. I do not try to make the children memorize the words of any book. But repeated readings and attempts at constructing dialogue allow the children opportunities to remember and use language from the book. I try to write verbatim one or two sentences spoken by a child. I listen for sentences that are especially complex and that include vocabulary from the book. This gives me a good indication of sentence length and complexity and of book language use. Finally, if I can, I listen to each child tell a story all the way through. This provides me with an indication of whether the child is retelling in rich detail, with some detail, or has captured at least the bare bones of a story. I keep in mind that the ability to retell stories in sequence, with detailed completeness and accuracy, is an important literacy skill that improves with practice through the primary grades.

CHILD-DIRECTED STORYTELLING AND DRAMA

In classrooms in which teachers frequently use Book Acting, the children often find ways to move beyond the books and props they are provided. They discover imaginative ways to reuse props in new stories or add improvised props and events to favorite stories. This is not surprising, inasmuch as children are already familiar with acting out stories even when Book Acting is not a part of their curriculum. During the preschool years children frequently engage in fantasy play. They play with action figures, dinosaurs, and Harry Potter dolls. It seems natural, then, that children's independent interactions with books spontaneously lead them to retelling or dramatizing events or episodes. Several researchers have described children's unprompted dramatic responses to literature (Rowe, 1998; Voss, 1988; Wolf & Heath, 1992). Although it seems intuitive that such sustained and rich interactions around books should support children's literacy development, we know less about the contributions of these independent enactments to children's language or literacy growth than about more teacher-directed drama and retelling.

Despite the fact that we have less research about child-initiated book drama, we have some indications that these activities are important. Rowe (1998) has suggested that children's search for objects that can represent characters is important in helping 2- and 3-year-olds understand stories. To select objects to represent characters, children had to determine the qualities that defined the characters. Thus, allowing children to collect or construct their own props may be more intellectually challenging than providing them. Meier (2000) has argued that teachers should support and model moving beyond the confines of retelling a book using language like that found in the book. He suggested that such retellings or dramatizations force children to use the voice of the author, rather than develop their own literate voices. This seems to be an important concept to consider. Meier found that helping preschoolers retell their own stories, only loosely modeled on stories read aloud to them, was an important pathway for children's understanding of text and for seeing themselves as literate.

I have found that having a prop box in the classroom promotes children's own dramatizations. Clothes or objects related to stories or informational books we have read are put in a plastic crate. After reading *Little Rabbit Who Wanted Red Wings* (Bailey, 1987), I put several objects related to the story into the prop box, including two headbands with rabbit ears, acorns, plastic sunglasses, two pairs of rubber gardening boots, a mirror, several head scarves, and a pair of fairy wings. The children were invited to use the prop box to become Little Rabbit. This open-ended and nondirective invitation spurred a week of intense drama around the story. Most dramatizations included portions of the story itself, but mixed in with these scenes were many child-developed innovations.

CONCLUSION

Historically, the purpose of many early childhood instructional experiences was to strengthen children's language development. In fact, until the late 1980s language development, rather than literacy development, was the central focus of preschool and kindergarten experiences. During the last two decades researchers have intensified their investigations of young children's literacy development. As a result, we have a far richer understanding of emergent literacy, effective beginning reading instruction, and early predictors of reading failure and success. Three components of early literacy emerged as the best predictors of reading: print knowledge (including alphabet letter recognition and concepts about print), phonemic awareness, and language (including memories for short stories and expressive vocabulary) (Snow, Burns, & Griffin, 1998). Although the focus of early childhood experiences has shifted from an emphasis on language to an emphasis on literacy development, children's language ability is still one of the best predictors of later reading achievement. However, research has demonstrated that certain experiences with particular kinds of spoken language have the strongest relationships with later reading and writing. Experiences that provide opportunities for children to use written language structures, vocabulary, and linguistic features characteristic of written narrative and information text have been shown to be related to literacy development. In addition, language used to talk about text, such as when children negotiate what they will do and say during retelling or drama, is also related to literacy growth. Thus, retelling and dramatizing stories and information books should be an important part of the early childhood curriculum.

REFERENCES

Aardema, V. (1991). *Borreguita and the coyote.* New York: Knopf.

Bailey, C. (1987). *The little rabbit who wanted red wings.* New York: Platt & Munk.

Galda, L., Pellegrini, A. D., & Cox, S. (1989). A short-term longitudinal study of pre-schoolers' emergent literacy. *Research in the Teaching of English, 23*, 292–310.

Gambrell, L. B., Koskinen, P. S., & Kapinus, B. A. (1991). Retelling and the reading comprehension of proficient and less-proficient readers. *Journal of Educational Research, 84*, 356–362.

Henkes, K. (1991). *Chrysanthemum.* New York: Greenwillow.

Levy, A. K., Wolfgang, C. H., & Koorland, M. A. (1992). Sociodramatic play as a method for enhancing the language performance of kindergarten age students. *Early Childhood Research Quarterly, 7*, 245–262.

Martinez, M., Cheyney, M., & Teale, W. H. (1991). Classroom literature activities and kindergartners' dramatic story reenactments. In J. Christie (Ed.), *Play and early literacy development* (pp. 119–140). Albany: State University of New York Press.

McKissack, P. C. (1988). *Mirandy and Brother Wind.* New York: Knopf.

Meier, D. R. (2000). *Scribble scrabble—Learning to read and write: Success with diverse teachers, children, and families.* New York: Teachers College Press.

Morrow, L. M. (1984). Reading stories to young children: Effects of story structure and traditional questioning strategies on comprehension. *Journal of Reading Behavior, 16*, 273–288.

Morrow, L. M. (1988). Young children's responses to one-on-one readings in school settings. *Reading Research Quarterly, 23*, 89–107.

Morrow, L. M., & Smith, J. K. (1990). The effects of group size on interactive storybook reading. *Reading Research Quarterly, 25*, 213–231.

Pappas, C. C. (1991). Young children's strategies in learning the "book language" of information books. *Discourse Processes, 14*, 203–225.

Pappas, C. C. (1993). Is narrative "primary"? Some insights from kindergartners' pretend readings of stories and information books. *Journal of Reading Behavior, 25*, 97–129.

Pappas, C. C., & Brown, E. (1988). The development of children's sense of the written story language register: An analysis of the texture of "pretend reading." *Linguistics in Education, 1*, 45—79.

Pellingrini, A. (1984). Identifying causal elements in the thematic fantasy play paradigm. *American Educational Research Journal, 21*, 691–701.

Pellegrini, A. D., & Galda, L. (1982). The effects of thematic fantasy play training on the development of children's story comprehension. *American Educational Research Journal, 19*, 443–452.

Rowe, D. W. (1998). The literate potentials of book-related dramatic play. *Reading Research Quarterly, 33*, 10–35.

Saltz, E., & Johnson, J. (1974). Training for thematic-fantasy play in culturally disadvantaged children: Preliminary results. *Journal of Educational Psychology, 66*, 623–630.

Snow, C. E., Burns, M. S., & Griffin, P. (Eds.). (1998). *Preventing reading difficulties in young children.* Washington, DC: National Academy Press.

Voss, M. M. (1988). "Make way for applesauce": The literate world of a three-year-old. *Language Arts, 65,* 272–278.

Whitehurst, G. J., Arnold, D. S., Epstein, J. N., Angell, A. L., Smith, M., & Fischel, J. E. (1994b). A picture book reading intervention in day care and home for children from low-income families. *Developmental Psychology, 30,* 679–689.

Whitehurst, G. J., Crone, D. A., & Zevnbergen, A. A., Schultz, M. D., Velting, O. N., & Fischel, J. E. (1999). Outcomes of an emergent literacy intervention from Heat Start through second grade. *Journal of Educational Psychology, 91,* 261–272.

Whitehurst, G. J., Epstein, J. N., Angell, A. L., Payne, A. C., Crone, D. A., & Fischel, J. E. (1994a). Outcomes of an emergent literacy intervention in Head Start. *Journal of Educational Psychology, 86,* 542–555.

Williamson, P. A., & Silvern, S. B. (1991). Thematic-fantasy play and story comprehension. In J. Christie (Ed.), *Play and early literacy development* (pp. 69–90). Albany: State University of New York Press.

Wolf, S. A., & Heath, S. B. (1992). *The braid of literature: Children's worlds of reading.* Cambridge, MA: Harvard University Press.

Part IV

Recent Trends
in Literacy Research:
Technology, Fluency, and
Informational Text

10

Early Literacy in a Digital Age

*Moving from a Singular Book Literacy
to the Multiple Literacies of Networked
Information and Communication Technologies*

RACHEL A. KARCHMER
MARLA H. MALLETTE
DONALD J. LEU, JR.

It is becoming widely accepted that information and communication technologies (ICT) such as the Internet are rapidly redefining the nature of literacy (International Reading Association, 2001; Leu, 2000; Mikulecky & Kirkley, 1998). With this acceptance comes greater attentiveness and interest in researching how these two constructs, literacy and technology, converge (Leu & Kinzer, 2000). For example, the recent International Reading Association position statement on literacy and technology (2001) calls for much greater responsibility on the part of educators and researchers to explore the best methods of preparing students to become proficient in the literacies that emerge from ICT. Journals such as *The Reading Teacher*, *Reading Research and Instruction*, and *Reading and Writing Quarterly* have dedicated entire issues to the topic of literacy and technology, publishing the most recent research in the field specifically related to the Internet. In addition, the International Reading Association has pioneered the development of an online journal, *Reading Online (http://www.readingonline.org)*, which focuses on the new literacies emerging with Internet technologies. Yet despite this considerable focus on ICT in the broader literacy community, there seems to be a lack of similar attention to these important changes within the early literacy community.

It is clear that the nature of early literacy has undergone substantial transformation in the past 20 years (McGee & Purcell-Gates, 1997). Young children, once viewed as preliterate, are now more widely perceived as emergent readers and writers. That is, there is no formal time in which literacy acquisition begins; rather, a recursive, fluid process of literacy development takes place from the time children are born (Labbo & Kuhn, 1998).

Although the groundbreaking work of scholars such as Clay (1975) and Teale and Sulzby (1986) provided a foundation for understanding the nature of early literacy, McGee and Purcell-Gates (1997) have suggested that such work offered only a solid *beginning* to our knowledge in this field. Furthermore, they have suggested that the field of early literacy is still emerging as researchers seek to better understand early literacy from a more comprehensive perspective. Rather than exploring myopic aspects of early literacy, there is a need to synthesize the existing work so as to be able to better articulate research-based theories. Such work has been accomplished through the efforts of the International Reading Association and the National Association of Education for Young Children (1998). Their joint position statement on learning to read and write clearly articulates a coherent approach to the understanding of early literacy from the standpoint of developmentally appropriate practice. A similar comprehensive approach has been attempted in the *Handbook of Early Literacy Research* (Neuman & Dickinson, 2001), a work that the editors suggest represents the "now-and-future phase of work in early literacy" (p. 3). Striking, however, within these comprehensive bodies of research and theory, is the absence of any conversation about the role of technology, especially ICT, in early literacy.

In juxtaposing these two constructs (i.e., the convergence of literacy and technology and the nature of early literacy as a complex, multifaceted process) with the modest amount of research in early literacy and technology, it becomes apparent that research in this area is lagging substantially behind theory. That is, from a theoretical perspective, the convergence of technology and literacy highlights the complexity of multiple literacies (e.g., Bolter, 1991; Bruce, 1997; Leu, 2000; The New London Group, 2000; Reinking, 1998; Reinking, Labbo, & McKenna, 1997). Yet, in sharp contrast, what little research has been conducted in early literacy and technology has focused almost exclusively on how technology may be used to support a singular book literacy. This work assumes that technology functions to support the acquisition of the traditional and unidimensional literacy required by book technologies. To what extent, for example, does the use of talking storybooks assist young readers in acquiring word recognition skills? Or to what extent does a program such as Accelerated Reader increase the amount of children's reading and their ability to comprehend narrative structures?

There are at least two problems with this approach. First, it moves the field of early literacy back to the assumptions inherent in a reading readiness perspective, placing strong emphasis on the acquisition of specific skills. Technology is seen as a way to support students' acquisition of separate skills, not the complex and interdependent act of literacy. Second, this perspective assumes the primacy of a singular book literacy; that is, technology is used to teach the skills required to read a book. It fails to recognize that new technologies transform the very nature of literacy, requiring new skills, strategies, and insights to read, write, and communicate that transcend those required to be literate with traditional book technologies. Thus, in considering best practices in technology and early literacy, we have framed this chapter around the question, Is literacy defining the ways in which we use technology, or is technology defining the ways in which we use literacy?

SINGULAR LITERACY: PHONOLOGICAL AWARENESS AND WORD RECOGNITION SOFTWARE

Over the past 20 years, researchers have studied the effects of technology on reading and writing (see Okolo, Cavalier, Ferretti, & MacArthur, 2000, for a review). With older students (grades 4–12) there has been considerable work in the areas of comprehension (Harper & Ewing, 1986; Keene & Davey, 1987), vocabulary development (Johnson, Gersten, & Carnine, 1987; Reinking & Rickman, 1990), instructional practices (Boone & Higgins, 1993), study strategies (Anderson-Inman, Knox-Quinn, & Horney, 1996; Higgins & Boone, 1990), and writing (MacArthur, Graham, Hayes, & DeLaPaz, 1996; Stoddard & MacArthur, 1992). However, much of the research in the area of early literacy and technology has focused instead on software programs that support students' basic literacy skills such as phonological awareness and word recognition.

Phonological awareness, the ability to segment speech, is one of the best predictors of early reading achievement (Blachman, 2000), and several researchers have examined the use of software designed to reinforce this much-needed skill (e.g., Barker & Torgeson, 1995; Foster, Erickson, Foster, Brinkman, & Torgeson, 1994; Jones, Torgeson, & Sexton, 1987; Roth & Beck, 1987). For instance, Barker and Torgeson (1995) studied the effectiveness of phonological awareness computer programs on at-risk first-graders' reading skills. The software, DaisyQuest and Daisy's Castle, were game-like programs in which students engaged in various phonological awareness tasks, such as rhyming, counting numbers of phonemes in isolated words, and pairing words based on similar initial, medial, or ending sounds. Using a variety of postassessments to measure students' abilities to segment, blend, and recognize words, the researchers found that students' phonological awareness improved after using the software. Likewise, in their study of preschool and kindergarten students' reading skills, Foster and colleagues (1994) found that using similar phonological awareness software programs positively affected these young students' reading skills.

Another major goal of successful reading achievement is automatic word recognition, the ability to immediately recognize words on sight. Struggling readers tend to have difficulty with this skill and often rely on peers or teachers to provide unknown words. Computer-digitized speech, a feature of many software programs, can provide struggling readers the support they need when interacting with new or difficult text. Several researchers have examined the effectiveness of such software in various contexts (e.g., McKenna & Watkins, 1994, 1995, 1996; Reitsma, 1988; Scrase, 1997; van Daal & Reitsma, 1993; Wise, 1992). For example, Reitsma (1988) studied young children's use of digitized speech during independent reading. He found that students' fluency increased and the number of reading miscues decreased with the use of a computer with digitized speech, as opposed to their performance in oral reading of the same text with the teacher. Wise (1992) examined the effects of four types of digitized speech on first- and second-graders' word identification: whole word (*cat*), morphemic units (*cat-s*), onset-rime (*c-at*), and single grapheme-phoneme (*c-a-t*). He found that whole-word feedback was just as helpful as morphemic units and more effective than onset-rime and single grapheme-phoneme digitized speech.

Talking books are electronic texts that incorporate digitized speech. Readers can activate the digitized speech when they encounter unknown words or if they want a complete oral reading of the text. Medwell (1998) studied young children's use of talking books and assessed word recognition through running records. She found that although the children's comprehension of the stories seemed to increase, their word recognition was not greatly affected. Medwell suggested that rather than learning new words from the digitized speech, the children used syntactic and semantic cueing systems to recognize words. McKenna and Watkins (1994, 1995, 1996) also conducted studies of K–1 students' use of talking books and the effects of digitized speech on their word recognition. In these studies, the talking books helped readers connect unknown words to known words by way of analogy. However, it was also found that the talking books did not increase students' word recognition capabilities. Furthermore, the authors suggested that talking books may be best used as reinforcement to systematic decoding instruction, rather than a means of primary instruction.

Hastings (2001) explored a more complex set of relationships in a series of case studies with talking storybook software. She looked at relationships between self-efficacy, reading achievement level, and word recognition knowledge. Among young children labeled as learning disabled, she found that, for certain students, storybook software increases both self-efficacy and word recognition skills. She argued that some students benefit from the control they find in using talking storybook software, as this increases their self-efficacy as well as their word recognition skills.

Although this type of literature is important to gaining a better understanding of the role of technology in early literacy, we posit that these studies and others that concentrate on the reinforcement of a particular reading skill focus squarely on a singular literacy. In turn, the technology (software, in these instances) is defined by the literacy skill that is being reinforced. The technology, then, supplants typical classroom instruction by providing instruction that could be done with paper and pencil or with teacher–student interaction. We argue that this application of technology in early literacy does not prepare early readers and writers to engage in the new, multiple literacies of their futures.

In contrast, we see much more powerful ways to define technology's role in early literacy. In the remainder of this chapter we draw attention to some of the important literacies necessary for effectively using the Internet, and we provide suggestions for supporting them with early readers and writers. We highlight the work of both researchers *and* teachers who have approached their studies from the perspective that ICT, such as the Internet, generates new literacies required to effectively use these technologies for reading, writing, and communicating. This perspective suggests that ICT supports not only the skills of a singular literacy, but also those skills and strategies that aid a reader in becoming a thoughtful consumer and producer of multiple literacies.

MULTIPLE LITERACIES: THE CONVERGENCE OF EMERGENT LITERACY AND INFORMATION COMMUNICATION TECHNOLOGIES

Several scholars suggest that rather than viewing literacy as a singular construct, it may be best to consider multiple literacies (Gee, 2000; Luke, 2000a; The New London Group, 1996, 2000). The New London Group (2000) describes "multiliteracies" (p. 9) in relation to the literacies necessary for communication within a global community. Luke (2000a) describes multiple literacies as drawing on a range of knowledge to make meaning of the linguistic, audio, and visual representations created by new technologies. Clearly, the Internet, a powerful example of ICT, embodies the notion of multiple literacies that involve a variety of important skills.

When examining specifically those related to early literacy, we focus on general skills, beginning with more basic literacies (e.g., reading Internet text) and leading to more sophisticated ones (e.g., evaluating Internet text). Although we examine these literacies separately, it is most important to remember that these skills are interwoven and used simultaneously when interacting with the Internet; thus we describe them as multiple literacies. Furthermore, although it is easy and far too familiar to say that early readers and writers are too young to understand such complex literacy skills, we argue that the integration of the Internet in schools requires teaching young children how to read, write, navigate, interact, and evaluate Internet information and, moreover, that it is decidedly inappropriate to delay such instruction.

Reading Internet Texts

The inclusion of hyperlinks, graphics, digitized speech, animation, and sound with electronic text, ways in which we communicate over the Internet, create challenges for readers. Readers must be able to make important choices about the paths they follow as they interact with nonlinear structures of electronic text, and they must be able to gain meaning not only from the written words, but also from the seamless incorporation of audiovisual features (Reinking et al., 1997). Mitra and Cohen (1999) explain: "The text no longer presumes that the reader will gain the same meaning from the text. . . . In the case of hypertext . . . the reader is liberated to produce whatever text the reader pleases" (p. 186).

In considering young children's literacy development in relation to these complex characteristics of the Internet, it makes sense to be cautious. Are early readers able to synthesize the various types of information available on websites, or will they get lost in the web of hyperlinks, graphics, and other features? Eisenwine and Hunt (2000), first-grade literacy teachers, created talking books to be used with their primary-grade readers. Although their initial intention was to reinforce one-to-one word correspondence, through the use of Hyperstudio they extended the technology's capabilities from reinforcing this singular literacy to supporting multiple literacies. In addition to digitized speech, the authors included animated figures and sounds that added visual and extra auditory components to the text. The program also had interactive capabilities so that students could type in their names and add their own sounds to the existing text, creating personalized stories that could be read back to the students by the computer. Furthermore, the students could take part in retellings by typing their perceptions of the major events of the story into the word processing program. The computer would then read back the retelling, providing the opportunity for students to hone their listening and sequencing skills. According to Eisenwine and Hunt (2000), the incorporation of such interactive features aided their students' reading as they learned to use the digitized speech, animation, and sound to better make meaning of the text.

Furthermore, Karchmer (2001b) found that primary-grade teachers preferred to use websites with their students that had graphics, sound, animation—anything that supported the written text. They viewed these features as textual aids, much like those found in expository text. Conversely, it was the written text itself that seemed to cause more concern, as the primary teachers believed that the readability of most text on the Internet was too difficult for their students. To alleviate this challenge, they found sites with less text and more textual aids, and they used many sites created by other primary-grade classes to ensure readability.

The practice of having students reading other students' work may not be a new one; however, it has definitely become more prevalent as the Internet is used more in classrooms around the world (Leu, Karchmer, & Leu, 1999). One must only view Susan Silverman's website (*www.kidslearn.org*) to see how elementary teachers and students are learning from each other via the Internet. Susan Silverman, the instructional technology integration teacher for a school district in New York, is also the creator and coordinator of more than 13 Internet collaborative projects. Each academic year, Ms. Silverman creates at least two new projects that support literacy skills in conjunction with the New York Standards of Learning. The projects often focus on a piece of children's literature. For instance, her latest project, Cinderella Around the World, co-created with Patty Knox, was introduced during the fall of 2001. Teachers who signed up for the project agreed to have their students read one version of Cinderella and then complete one of several writing activities such as book reviews, Cinderella comparisons, graphic organizers depicting the story, or poems reflecting the plot. Once these activities were completed, the students' work was sent to Ms. Silverman and Ms. Knox and posted on the Internet project site (*http:// viking.stark.k12.oh.us/~ptk1nc/cinderella/*) for other classes to view and learn from. Susan Silverman's site and others like it are powerful examples of the ways in which technology can define how we use literacy and how literacy can define the ways in which we use technology.

Writing Internet Texts

Writers of electronic text must be able to create cohesive products by incorporating audiovisual features that add meaning to their work and provide hyperlinks that logically connect to the meaning of the text. In addition, they must be able to communicate their messages to a greater audience as the Internet makes their work accessible to the outside world. In terms of children writing electronic text, research has examined how children engage in what Labbo and Kuhn (1998) call "electronic symbol making" (p. 79), using word processing and multimedia tools to create symbols that represent meaning. Specifically, Labbo (1996) examined how kindergartners used the artistic and word processing features on Kidpix 2, a software program, to represent play, art, and writing. She found that the students were aware of audience and made important decisions about which symbols were appropriate for the situation. Labbo also noted that students who engaged in electronic symbol making learned to assign meaning to the graphic representations and understood that they "served as a personal record, or memory, of that experience" (p. 380).

For many years hypermedia software (i.e., programs that allow writers to connect various texts via links) has been used in primary classrooms. For example, Lachs and Wiliam (1998) studied inner-city primary children's authoring of hypermedia text. They suggested that in order for a reader's interaction with such text to be meaningful, the reader must be "absorbed and [have] active attention and participation" (p. 59). Likewise, in order for a writer's interaction with hypermedia text to be meaningful, he or she must be an active participant and have opportunities to extend traditional writing to incorporate the interactive capabilities of multimedia software including graphics, sound, and animation. In this study, students created nonlinear text, first by drawing maps of their intended stories and then creating the stories and subsequent links with the software. The researchers found that the students worked well with nonlinear text as they transferred their handwritten maps to the software and then engaged in "swapping from graphics to text and back again to sound, animation, programming, design and back to sound" (p. 68). Furthermore, they found that the students relied heavily on the software's audiovisual capabilities, resulting in these features (i.e., sound, animation, and graphics) being integral components of the text (Reinking & Chanlin, 1994). For instance, students chose which pictures to include before deciding on text, concerning themselves with what the images, in combination with the text, communicated to the reader. Similarly, when the students incorporated sound, it was for the purpose of adding meaning to the story by providing explanations, sound effects, or musical accompaniments rather than just repeating the written text.

Although the students' work in Labbo's study (1996) and in the study by Lachs and Wiliam (1998) was not posted on the Internet, many primary-grade teachers are taking that step by making online publishing a regular practice in their classrooms (Leu & Leu, 2000). Karchmer (2001a) described three types of students' writing that teachers tend to publish on the Internet: (1) traditional writing assignments, (2) collaborative writing projects, and (3) multimedia presentations. The latter two, collaborative writing projects and multimedia presentations, incorporate the types of skills found in the two studies described earlier, namely, creating symbols to represent meaning and using hypermedia to integrate links, graphics, sound, and animation.

The International Reading Association's Miss Rumphius Award website (*http://www.reading.org/publications/journals/RT/rumphius.html*) provides numerous examples of how classroom teachers are publishing student work. The Miss Rumphius Award was established to recognize teachers who create outstanding Internet resources. Many recipients include student work on their web pages, such as the traditional writing assignments at *The Sunnyside School Primary Class* website (*http://www.psd267.wednet.edu/ ~kfranz/index.htm*), the collaborative writing projects at Mary Kreul's second-grade website (*http://www.geocities.com/marykreul/2Kschool/ index.html*), and the multimedia presentations at Terry Hongell and Patty Taverna's second-grade website (*http://www2.lhric.org/pocantico/vietnam/ vietnam.htm*). These exemplary sites can be used as models for primary-grade educators who are new at Internet implementation.

Among the many benefits of publishing students' work on the Internet is the increased quality of their written products when they know their work will be published online for others to see (Leu & Leu, 2000). Calkins (1994) argued the importance of identifying the audience with students before they begin the writing process so they can match their writing style and message to those who will read their work. Because anyone with an Internet connection and the appropriate Internet address can view a classroom website, the audience for Internet-published writing has shifted away from teachers to include a potentially much greater audience beyond school boundaries. Students, including young children, understand the consequences of such communication (Karchmer, 2001b). However, Baker (2000) cautions that students often have the impression that a glitzy presentation is more important than one with substance. Students can easily underestimate the effort it takes to create a multimedia writing assignment, focusing more on the electronic features than the meaningfulness of the work. It is crucial that students be taught how to use the unique features of electronic text so that they are integral to the transmission of knowledge communicated via their written products, rather than supplementary bells and whistles.

Reading and Writing Internet Texts

For young readers and writers, the Internet broadens the construct of early literacy. That is, rather than focusing on the notion that print carries meaning, the Internet opens up a semiotic maze in which meaning is constructed through multiple sign systems. As students begin to read and write Internet text, they should be afforded opportunities to learn how to work with multiple sign systems. Within this broader construct, instruction can no longer focus on reading and writing linear text. Instead, instruction must be centered on the thoughtful integration of semiotics and hypertext.

For example, as students begin to write Internet text, they require direction in learning how and when to use hyperlinks, sound, animation, digitized video, and pictures. Thus, the beginning conceptualization of Internet writing extends the stage of brainstorming beyond a web or outline to the creation of storyboards whereby students can visualize and develop the intricacies of the Internet text they are creating.

Similarly, the focus of instruction for reading Internet text should be on constructing meaning from all the sign systems available. Interestingly, although young children are drawn to illustration long before they attend to written text, early literacy instruction tends to focus young children on the written text. In Internet reading, however, written text is only one of the sign systems that require attention, suggesting that early readers will have to learn how to construct meaning from all the sign systems incorporated in electronic text.

Clearly, reading and writing Internet text requires a more thorough view of early literacy. In this sense, early literacy is far more than understanding narrative text structure read in a linear fashion. Internet text is diverse; it spans all genres, creates new ones, and requires skill in negotiating multiple sign systems in nonlinear ways.

Navigating the Internet

Finding information on the Internet can be frustrating, and especially difficult for young children, because of the many skills necessary for navigating the Internet successfully. First, when using a search engine, one must be able to narrow a topic to succinct key terms to conduct a search. Second, upon finding possible related websites, one must review them for accuracy, readability, and related information. Third, while reviewing the sites, one must be able to navigate the nonlinear structure and use the audiovisual components to gain meaning from the site. These skills are highly sophisticated and can be overwhelming, particularly for young children. Thus, we argue it is crucial that students begin to learn how to navigate the Internet as early as possible in the most developmentally appropriate ways (Gerzog & Haugland, 1999).

When speaking with teachers of young children, we have noted that one of the most frequently discussed issues regarding Internet use is their fear of students uncovering inappropriate websites. We agree that child Internet safety is a noteworthy concern. However, we strongly believe that following certain precautions and, more important, teaching students how to surf the Internet safely will help to ensure positive navigating experiences.

Search engines designed for children's use effectively focus Internet navigation on acceptable websites. For example, when researching a topic, children can send questions to the search engine *Ask Jeeves for Kids* (*www.ajkids.com*). This site is a natural language search engine, meaning that students can use basic phrases or key words to narrow down their topic. It is especially helpful because it significantly eases the navigation process. Shortly after a submission to *Ask Jeeves*, students will receive links to G-rated websites that answer their questions. Only sites that have been screened for child safety, content, and readability are recommended. *Yahooligans* (*www.yahooligans.com*) is another search engine designed for children. At this site, key words can be used to find related kid-friendly sites. A site like *Ask Jeeves for Kids*, to which questions can also be posed, is *Ask Earl* (*www.yahooligans.com/content/ask_earl/*), which responds to queries daily. Sites of this type not only help ensure that students view acceptable material, they also make time spent navigating the Internet more efficient.

In addition to search engines, directory sites specifically created for children's use are wonderful resources and are screened for child safety and accuracy. Directory sites compile information on certain topics within directories. Location is manageable and relatively easy because all of the information is connected with hyperlinks. Examples of directory sites include *Great Sites*, maintained by the American Library Association (*http:// www.ala/org/parentspage/greatsites/amazing.html*), and *Berit's Best Sites for Children* (*http://www.beritsbest.com/*), maintained by Berit Erickson, a librarian. These sites are recommended because their content has been reviewed and rated specifically for its appropriateness for children (Leu & Leu, 2000). For instance, the latter site's rating system evaluates websites based on the following criteria: (1) content, (2) organization, (3) ease of use, (4) appearance, (5) bells and whistles, (6) audience, (7) credibility, (8) fees, and (9) privacy. Sites are given a ranking between 1 and 5, and only sites that score 3 or higher are included. Directory sites like these provide support for navigation of the Internet by teachers and children.

Along with modeling think-alouds, vocabulary strategies, and fluent reading for our students, we recommend that teachers model how to navigate the Internet. This modeling should begin early and continue throughout the school year as students become more proficient navigators. One way to teach Internet navigation is to project the computer screen on a larger area so that all students can watch as the teacher models the search process. In addition, Internet scavenger hunts, which present opportunities for students to search various specified sites for specific content, are also beneficial, as they provide navigation practice (Leu & Leu, 2000). Furthermore, it is extremely important to make the school and classroom guidelines on acceptable Internet use clear and available to students. These guidelines will eliminate any misconceptions related to proper navigation and the consequences for conducting improper searches.

Obviously, the most effective way of eliminating the dangers associated with students' navigation of the Internet is to restrict it completely. To implement Internet use in the classroom, teachers shoulder the responsibility of finding appropriate sites for students to view. Software such as Web Whacker, a program that allows you to download websites onto the computer's hard drive, provides an alternative to live Internet surfing. Students are able to explore the downloaded site but are unable to go beyond it. Internet filters such as Net Nanny are also available. These filters restrict the transmission of inappropriate websites to a computer. Although it is not possible to eliminate all uncertainty about the Internet, we believe that proper modeling and precautionary measures can help in protecting students from the negative aspects of the Internet.

Participating in the Global Community

The Internet provides opportunities to interact with people and places around the globe. With these opportunities comes the responsibility of understanding how to communicate with people of different cultures, religions, and ideologies. Luke (2000a) argues that "intercultural communication" (p. 73) is one of the many literacies expanded upon as the Internet becomes more integral to our way of life. Similarly, The New London Group (2000) suggests that it is important for all cultures to participate in the global community created by information technologies. Fortunately, many such opportunities are already available in our schools.

E-mail may be one of the most popular classroom uses of the Internet. Literacy experts have argued for years for the importance of providing students with opportunities to engage socially in conversations related to what they read and write (Allington, 1998; McKeon, 2001). Furthermore, literature in the areas of response logs (Rasinski & Padak, 1996) and dialogue journals (Staton, 1988) supports the belief that while reading and writing can be considered private activities in some cases, it is beneficial to share ideas and thoughts about text with others (Kasten, 1997). For many educators, e-mail provides avenues for engaging their students in the types of social collaboration researchers have proposed.

Many teacher educators see the benefits of such e-mail communication and have integrated e-mail projects in their education courses (e.g., Curtiss & Curtiss, 1995; McKeon, 2001). For instance, Curtiss and Curtiss (1995) documented their experience when they wrote about how they both wanted to find more engaging ways of getting their respective groups of students to interact with text. Pam Curtiss, a children's literature university instructor in Iowa, and Kerry Curtiss, a second-grade teacher in Nebraska, decided to pair their students, university and elementary, for the purpose of creating relationships to dialogue about the books the students read in class. The education students learned how to implement reading workshops, to communicate with elementary students, and, perhaps most important, to appreciate young children's views of the text they read in school. The second graders involved in the project were given a greater audience for their work, emphasizing the importance of clear and concise writing as well as proper spelling and grammar. Although various obstacles did arise throughout the project, for the most part both the elementary and university students found the experience valuable.

As McKeon (2001), a teacher educator who conducted a similar project with 9- to 10-year-olds and university students, suggested, "The opportunity to send and receive e-mail introduces [students] to a powerful, personal, technological thinking tool. Given its one-to-one nature, e-mail within or between classrooms may one day add a new dimension of humanism to the art of teaching" (p. 704). In addition, the use of e-mail in teacher education, as described earlier, provided preservice teachers opportunities to learn about literacy from young children. Participating in the global community allows all members to be equal participants; that is, the community of literacy learners transcends age barriers.

Collaborative Internet projects like those discussed earlier in this chapter also provide students with opportunities to appreciate the social context of the Internet. Specifically, they help to improve all students' understanding and appreciation of other people and cultures. For example, key pal projects, an online version of traditional pen pal correspondence, are widely used in classrooms around the world. Through word of mouth or online registries such as *The Lightspan Network Internet Project Registry* (*http://www.gsn.org/*) and *Classroom Connect's Teacher Contact Database* (*http://www.connectedteacher.com/teacherContact/search.asp*), teachers pair their students with students in other classes, and they communicate via e-mail about personal and academic issues (Garner & Gillingham, 1996). Because of the Internet's capabilities, students can learn about other places and cultures through the written voices of their peers who are experiencing those places and cultures firsthand; this is a very different experience from learning second- or thirdhand from a book. As we have suggested elsewhere (Leu, Mallette, & Karchmer, 2001), it is with these types of experiences that the Internet allows us "to construct a global village that values the many benefits that diversity provides" (p. 269).

Evaluating Internet Texts

Evaluating information found on the Internet may be one of the most important and most difficult literacies to teach young children. Until recently, teachers of every grade level relied heavily on the books in their classrooms and school libraries. Although these books often become outdated quickly and inconsistencies in information do arise, they also provide quality assurances such as the review of authors and information before publication. Information on the Internet is much different; its author can be anyone with a computer and an Internet account. This condition makes it crucial that students, especially young children, be equipped with critical literacy skills, those that will help them make decisions about the types of information they regularly encounter on the Internet.

In regard to evaluating Internet sources, Karchmer (2001b) found that primary-grade teachers were concerned about their students' ability to evaluate the accuracy of material found on the Internet. Although the teachers in her study had discussed inaccurate information with their students prior to using the Internet, the teachers believed that the issue became much more prevalent in gathering information from websites. Thus, there was a greater need to thoroughly model and reinforce evaluation skills in these earlier grades.

Although assessing the appropriateness and quality of websites is a subjective judgment, many organizations and educators provide guidelines that help define what excellent sites should include. The American Library Association (ALA) has compiled a list of criteria on its website (*www.ala.org/parentspage/greatsites/criteria.html*) that includes (1) authorship/sponsorship, (2) purpose, (3) design and stability, and (4) content. Within each category there are specific components to examine, such as whether the author or sponsor should be listed along with sources of information and an avenue for communicating questions or comments to the author. In addition to offering criteria similar to those of the ALA guidelines, the Haugland/Gerzog Developmental Scale for Web Sites (Gerzog & Haugland, 1999) includes antibias criteria, focusing on the importance of reflecting the diversity of our society. Representation in areas such as age, ability, cultural diversity, gender and role equity, and family diversity are all ranked.

Many teachers have created their own criteria for students to follow when using the Internet (Karchmer, 2001b). For example, Tammy Payton, a first-grade teacher and web editor of her district's website in Indiana, constructed a page that includes Internet evaluation rubrics that can be used with students of various ages (*http://www.siec.k12.in.us/~west/online/eval.htm*). In addition to evaluating a site for its design, technology components, and content, she suggests students review a site for (1) the contact person's name and e-mail address, (2) the name of the host school or institution, and (3) an announcement of when the page was last updated.

It is also important to recognize the commercial nature of many websites found on the Internet. Advertisements, whether they are banners across the top of the main page or interactive boxes that appear at various stages of navigation, can be found on all types of sites, including those that are education related. Thus, as Luke (2000b) suggests, it is critically important that we teach our students to evaluate online materials closely, in much the same way we evaluate popular media such as magazines, television, and billboards. We suggest teaching students to ask the following questions:

- Who created the information at this site?
- What is the background of the creator?
- Knowing who created the site, can you determine why they created it?
- Can you locate a link that tells you what this site is about? What does it say the purpose of the site is?
- When was the information at this site created? How recently was the information updated?
- Where can I go to check the accuracy of this information?
- Are the sources of factual information clearly listed so I can check them with another source?
- If the sources are not clearly listed, how confident can I be about the information at this location?
- Knowing who created this site and what the stated or unstated purpose is, can I tell how this information or the activities here will probably be shaped?
- What biases are likely to appear at this location?

Thinking critically about Internet information will help students and teachers make more informed decisions about the web pages they encounter.

IS LITERACY DEFINING THE WAYS IN WHICH WE USE TECHNOLOGY, OR IS TECHNOLOGY DEFINING THE WAYS IN WHICH WE USE LITERACY?

In considering the research reviewed at the beginning of this chapter, it seems clear that literacy has traditionally defined how we use technology. In the early literacy community, technology's most prominent use has been in the software that supports skills of a singular literacy. However, what is also clear is that when literacy is defined by the limitlessness of ICT, early literacy must be reconceptualized. That is, it is no longer adequate to conceive the period of early literacy as a time when children make discoveries about print only. Rather, it becomes a time when children must make discoveries about the intricacy of multiple sign systems. Although print is one sign system that definitely carries meaning, meaning is also constructed and directed by learners as they negotiate many sign systems in nonlinear ways with ICT.

In reconceptualizing early literacy it becomes vital that teachers recognize the role of instruction in this broader construct. Technology can no longer be viewed solely as a tool to support literacy learning. The role of computers in early literacy learning should not be merely electronic seat work. Instead, teachers should be instructing both *with* and *through* technology by guiding young children as they learn about new literacies.

It is apparent from the work reviewed in this chapter that many teachers have already begun this learning journey with their students. These teachers are leading the field in early literacy and technology through their commitment and imagination. They continually design new projects and create new experiences to afford their students opportunities to learn about literacy from this more encompassing perspective. What seems to be most abundantly clear in considering the role of ICT in early literacy is that early readers and writers are not limited by their developing abilities; rather, the most salient limit they face is related to our willingness to move beyond a singular book literacy to a community that supports and nurtures young readers and writers as consumers and producers of multiple literacies.

REFERENCES

Allington, R. L. (Ed.). (1998). *Teaching struggling readers: Articles from* The Reading Teacher. Newark, DE: International Reading Association.

Anderson-Inman, L., Knox-Quinn, C., & Horney, M. A. (1996). Computer-based study strategies for students with learning disabilities: Individual differences associated with adoption level. *Journal of Learning Disabilities, 29,* 461–484.

Baker, E. A. (2000). Instructional approaches used to integrate literacy and technology. *Reading Online, 4*(1)[Online]. Available: http://www.readingonline.org/articles/baker/ [2000, January 1]

Barker, T. A., & Torgeson, J. K. (1995). An evaluation of computer-assisted instruction in phonological awareness with below average readers. *Journal of Educational Computing Research, 13,* 89–103.

Blachman, B. A. (2000). Phonological awareness. In M. Kamil, P. Mosenthal, P. D. Pearson, & R. Barr (Eds.), *Handbook of reading research* (Vol. III, pp. 483–502). Mahwah, NJ: Erlbaum.

Bolter, J. D. (1991). *Writing space: The computer, hypertext, and the history of writing.* Hillsdale, NJ: Erlbaum.

Boone, R., & Higgins, K. (1993). Hypermedia basal readers: Three years of school-based research. *Journal of Special Education Technology, 12*(2), 86–106.

Bruce, B. C. (1997). Literacy technologies: What stance should we take? *Journal of Literacy Research, 29,* 289–309.

Calkins, L. M. (1994). *The art of teaching writing.* Portsmouth, NH: Heinemann.

Clay, M. M. (1975). *What did I write?* Auckland, New Zealand: Heinemann.

Curtiss, P. M., & Curtiss, K. E. (1995). What 2nd graders taught college students and vice versa. *Educational Leadership, 2,* 60–63.

Eisenwine, M. J., & Hunt, D. A. (2000). Using a computer in literacy groups with emergent readers. *The Reading Teacher, 53,* 456–458.

Foster, K. C., Erickson, G. C., Foster, D. F., Brinkman, D., & Torgeson, J. K. (1994). Computer administered instruction in phonological awareness: Evaluation of the DaisyQuest program. *Journal of Research and Development in Education, 27,* 126–137.

Garner, R., & Gillingham, M. G. (1996). *Internet communication in six classrooms: Conversations across time, space, and culture.* Mahwah, NJ: Erlbaum.

Gee, J. P. (2000). New people in new worlds: Networks, the new capitalism and schools. In B. Cope & M. Kalantzis (Eds.), *Multiliteracies: Literacy learning and the design of social futures* (pp. 43–68). London: Routledge.

Gerzog, E. H., & Haugland, S. W. (1999). Web sites provide unique learning opportunities for young children. *Early Childhood Education Journal, 27,* 109–114.

Harper, J. A., & Ewing, N. J. (1986). A comparison of the effectiveness of microcomputer and workbook instruction on reading comprehension performance of high incidence handicapped children. *Educational Technology, 26*(5), 40–45.

Hastings, E. (2001). *Effects of talking storybooks on word recognition skills and control beliefs of young students with learning disabilities: An exploratory study.* Unpublished doctoral dissertation, Syracuse University, Syracuse, New York.

Higgins, K., & Boone, R. (1990). Hypertext study guides and the social studies achievement of students with learning disabilities, remedial students, and regular education students. *Journal of Learning Disabilities, 23,* 529–540.

International Reading Association. (2001). *Integrating literacy and technology in the curriculum: A position statement of the International Reading Association.* Newark, DE: International Reading Association.

International Reading Association and National Association of Education for Young Children. (1998). Learning to read and write: Developmentally appropriate practices for young children. *The Reading Teacher, 52,* 193–216.

Johnson, G., Gersten, R., & Carnine, D. (1987). Effects of instructional design variables on the vocabulary acquisition of LD students: A study of computer-assisted instruction. *Journal of Learning Disabilities, 20,* 206–213.

Jones, K. U., Torgeson, J. K., & Sexton, M. A. (1987). Using computer guided practice to increase decoding fluency in learning disabled children: A study using the Hint and Hunt I program. *Journal of Learning Disabilities, 20,* 122–128.

Karchmer, R. A. (2001a). Gaining a new, wider audience: Publishing student work on the Internet. *Reading Online, 4* [Online]. Available: http://www.readingonline.org/electronic/elec_index.asp?HREF=/electronic/karchmer/index.html

Karchmer, R. A. (2001b). The journey ahead: Thirteen teachers report how the Internet influences literacy and literacy instruction in their K–12 classrooms. *Reading Research Quarterly, 36,* 442–466.

Kasten, W. C. (1997). Learning is noisy: The myth of silence in the reading-writing classroom. In J. R. Paratore & R. L. McCormack (Eds.), *Peer talk in the classroom: Learning from research* (pp. 88–101). Newark, DE: International Reading Association.

Keene, S., & Davey, B. (1987). Effects of computer-presented text on LD adolescents' reading behaviors. *Learning Disability Quarterly, 10,* 283–290.

Labbo, L. D. (1996). A semiotic analysis of young children's symbol making in a classroom computer center. *Reading Research Quarterly, 31,* 356–385.

Labbo, L. D., & Kuhn, M. (1998). Electronic symbol-making: Young children's computer-related emerging concepts about literacy. In D. Reinking, M. McKenna, L. D. Labbo, & R. Kieffer (Eds.), *Handbook of literacy and technology: Transformations in a post-typographic world* (pp. 79–91). Mahwah, NJ: Erlbaum.

Lachs, V., & Wiliam, D. (1998). Making the computer dance to your tune: Primary school pupils authoring hypermedia. *Journal of Computing in Childhood Education, 9*(1), 57–77.

Leu, D. J., Jr. (2000). Continuously changing technologies and envisionments for literacy: Deictic consequences for literacy education in an information age. In M. Kamil, P. Mosenthal, P. D. Pearson, & R. Barr (Eds.), *Handbook of reading research* (Vol. III, pp. 743–770). Mahwah, NJ: Erlbaum.

Leu, D. J., Jr., Karchmer, R. A., & Leu, D. D. (1999). The Miss Rumphius effect: Envisionments for literacy and learning that transform the Internet. *The Reading Teacher, 52,* 636–642.

Leu, D. J., Jr., & Kinzer, C. K. (2000). The convergence of literacy instruction with networked technologies for information and communication. *Reading Research Quarterly, 35,* 108–127.

Leu, D. J., Jr., & Leu, D. D. (2000). *Teaching with the Internet: Lessons from the classroom* (3rd ed.). Norwood, MA: Christopher Gordon.

Leu, D. J., Jr., Mallette, M. H., & Karchmer, R. A. (2001). New literacies, new technologies, and new realities: Redefining the agenda for literacy research. *Reading Research and Instruction, 40,* 265–272.

Luke, C. (2000a). Cyber-schooling and technological change: Multiliteracies for new times. In B. Cope & M. Kalantzis (Eds.), *Multiliteracies: Literacy learning and the design of social futures* (pp. 69–91). London: Routledge.

Luke, C. (2000b). New literacies in teacher education. *Journal of Adolescent and Adult Literacy, 43,* 424–435.

MacArthur, C. A., Graham, S., Hayes, J. B., & DeLaPaz, S. (1996). Spelling checkers and students with learning disabilities: Performance comparisons and impact on spelling. *Journal of Special Education, 30,* 35–57.

McGee, L. M., & Purcell-Gates, V. (1997). Conversations: So what's going on in research in emergent literacy? *Reading Research Quarterly, 32,* 310–318.

McKenna, M. C., & Watkins, J. H. (1994, December). *Computer-mediated books for beginning readers.* Paper presented at the annual meeting of the National Reading Conference, San Diego, CA.

McKenna, M. C., & Watkins, J. H. (1995, December). *Effects of computer-mediated books on the development of beginning readers.* Paper presented at the annual meeting of the National Reading Conference, New Orleans, LA.

McKenna, M. C., & Watkins, J. H. (1996, December). *The effects of computer-mediated trade books on sight words acquisition and the development of phonics ability.* Paper presented at the annual meeting of the National Reading Conference, Charleston, SC.

McKeon, C. A. (2001). E-mail as a motivating literacy event for one struggling reader: Donna's case. *Reading Research and Instruction, 40,* 185–202.

Medwell, J. (1998). The talking book project: Some further insights into the use of talking books to develop reading. *Reading, 32,* 3–8.

Mikulecky, L., & Kirkley, J. R. (1998). Changing classes: The new role of technology in workplace literacy. In D. Reinking, M. McKenna, L. D. Labbo, & R. Kieffer (Eds.), *Handbook of literacy and technology: Transformations in a post-typographic world* (pp. 303–320). Mahwah, NJ: Erlbaum.

Mitra, A., & Cohen, E. (1999). Analyzing the web: Directions and challenges. In S. Jones (Ed.), *Doing Internet research: Critical issues and methods for examining the net* (pp. 179–202). London: Sage.

The New London Group. (1996). A pedagogy of multiliteracies: Designing social futures. *Harvard Educational Review, 66,* 60–92.

The New London Group. (2000). A pedagogy of multiliteracies designing social futures. In B. Cope & M. Kalantzis (Eds.), *Multiliteracies: Literacy learning and the design of social futures* (pp. 9–37). London: Routledge.

Neuman, S. B., & Dickinson, D. K. (Eds.). (2001). *Handbook of early literacy research.* New York: Guilford Press.

Okolo, C., Cavalier, A., Ferreti, R., & MacArthur, C. (2000). Technology, literacy, and disabilities: A review of the research. In R. Gersten, E. Schiller, & S. Vaughn (Eds.), *Contemporary special education research: Synthesis of the knowledge base on critical instructional issues* (pp. 179–250). Mahwah, NJ: Erlbaum.

Rasinski, T., & Padak, N. (1996). *Holistic reading strategies: Teaching children who find reading difficult.* Columbus, OH: Merrill.

Reinking, D. (1998). Synthesizing technological transformations of literacy in a post-typographical world. In D. Reinking, M. McKenna, L. D. Labbo, & R. Kieffer (Eds.), *Handbook of literacy and technology: Transformations in a post-typographic world* (pp. xi–xxx). Mahwah, NJ: Erlbaum.

Reinking, D., & Chanlin, L. J. (1994). Graphic aids in electronic texts. *Reading Research and Instruction, 33,* 207–232.

Reinking, D., Labbo, L., & McKenna, M. (1997). Navigating the changing landscape of literacy: Current theory and research in computer-based reading and writing. In J. Flood, S. B. Heath, & D. Lapp (Eds.), *Handbook of research on teaching literacy through the communicative and visual arts* (pp. 77–92). New York: Macmillan.

Reinking, D., & Rickman, S. S. (1990). The effects of computer-mediated texts on the vocabulary learning and comprehension of intermediate-grade readers. *Journal of Reading Behavior, 22,* 395–411.

Reitsma, P. (1988). Reading practice for beginners: Effects of guided reading, reading-while-listening, and independent reading with computer-based speech feedback. *Reading Research Quarterly, 23,* 219–235.

Roth, S. F., & Beck, I. L. (1987). Theoretical and instructional implications of the assessment of two microcomputer word recognition programs. *Reading Research Quarterly, 22,* 197–218.

Scrase, R. (1997). Using scanners linked to talking computers as tools for teaching children to read. *British Journal of Educational Technology, 28,* 308–310.

Staton, J. (1988). Contributions of the dialogue journal research to communicating, thinking, and learning. In J. Staton, R. W. Shuy, J. K. Peyton, & L. Reed (Eds.),

Dialogue communication: Classroom, linguistic, social and cognitive views (pp. 312–321). Norwood, NJ: Ablex.

Stoddard, B., & MacArthur, C. A. (1992). A peer editor strategy: Guiding learning disabled students in response and revision. *Research in the Teaching of English, 27*, 76–103.

Teale, W. H., & Sulzby, E. (1986). *Emergent literacy: Writing and reading.* Norwood, NJ: Ablex.

van Daal, V. H. P., & Reitsma, P. (1993). The use of speech feedback by normal and disabled readers in computer-based reading practice. *Reading and Writing: An Interdisciplinary Journal, 5*, 243–259.

Wise, B. (1992). Whole words and decoding for short-term learning: Comparisons on a "talking computer" system. *Journal of Experimental Child Psychology, 54*, 147–167.

11

No More "Madfaces"

Motivation and Fluency Development with Struggling Readers

STEVEN A. STAHL

Listening to a disfluent child can be a nerve-racking experience. Hearing that child stumble over words, hesitate for palpable moments before producing a word, or miscall words wears on a teacher's patience, as it wears on the patience of other children in a group listening. In spite of the recommendations of experts (e.g., Lipson & Wixson, 1997), a teacher is tempted to jump in and correct each miscue as it is made, instead of waiting for the child to self-correct. Worse yet, the teacher is tempted not to ask the child to read orally, depriving the child of practice needed to become fluent.

As much as we praise such children for their effort, they know themselves that they are struggling. This self-knowledge, which may be accurate, may impair their ability to grow as readers. When we know, rightly or wrongly, that we cannot do something well, we are inclined to avoid that activity. For example, I *know* that I cannot do ballroom dancing. Therefore, I avoid situations where I would have to. In my life, this is easy, but for children who *know* that they cannot read, avoidance is more difficult. An extreme case is the child who develops passive failure, who basically shuts down and refuses to read, especially in public. A child whom I am tutoring, Brian, is like that. When I first met him, he would put on his "madface" when asked to read, especially material that was difficult for him. This shutdown was in strong contrast to his ordinary personality, which is open and friendly.

Although we tend to view only the lowest-achieving readers in a class as disfluent, an oral reading study done by the National Assessment of Educational Progress (Pinnell, 1995) found that 44% of fourth graders tested could not read a grade-level passage with adequate fluency. Many of these children could read the passage accurately. Seventy-seven percent could read it with 94% or greater accuracy. This suggests that there is a large population of children who cannot read fluently, and a significant segment who can read accurately but not fluently (21% of the fourth graders in this sample). Although Brian was one of the lowest-performing children in his grade, there were many others who read disfluently.

MOTIVATION AND THE STRUGGLING READER

Faced with repeated failure in reading, the struggling reader tends to be turned off to reading. Beyond a mere rejection of reading as an activity, struggling readers often develop a belief system about reading that can impair their future progress. Struggling readers tend to believe that good reading is a result of talent, rather than effort (Johnston & Winograd, 1985). Furthermore, they believe that others have that talent, but they do not. Thus, when you ask struggling readers about why they are not succeeding, they are more likely to say that they are "dumb" rather than that the task itself is difficult. Without talent for reading, effort seems futile. Continued failure in reading can lead to a condition termed *learned helplessness* (Butkowsky & Willows, 1980), in which the child learns that he or she cannot succeed. The notion of learned helplessness gives the label "struggling reader" an unwanted irony. These children are having reading difficulties partly because they do not struggle, but instead give in to a mistaken belief that they cannot succeed.

We have found some struggling readers who have "learned" that they cannot succeed as early as the second half of first grade. They learn that they cannot succeed by being assigned texts that are easier than those of their peers, by being given instruction that stresses decoding rather than comprehension, by being interrupted more often during reading, and so on (Allington, 1983). In addition, the programs, pull-out and push-in, that we use to help children with reading problems further convince them that they are different from the rest of their class.

To teach a struggling reader requires not only quality instruction, but also a deliberate effort to help the child unlearn these learned helplessness behaviors. Effective teachers of struggling readers not only need to know reading instruction, but also need to sell children on the idea that they can succeed. Thus,

- Children with reading problems tend to see themselves as incapable of reading as well as their peers. If we are to help them become good readers, we need to convince them that they can be good readers.
- Children with reading problems need to see concrete progress.

CONVINCING STRUGGLING READERS

For a struggling reader, the evidence of failure is all around. Struggling readers read simpler texts, read less text over the course of the school year (Allington, 1984), are corrected more often (Allington, 1983), and are generally held to lower expectations. The cognitive effects of this policy of "slow it down and make it concrete" (Allington, 1991, p. 19) are well documented. Stanovich (1986) suggests that because struggling readers read less text, they do not become as fluent as their normally achieving peers. Because struggling readers thus tend to read more slowly, they read less and less text relative to their peers. Furthermore, struggling readers tend to read less difficult text, in terms of vocabulary and syntax, than their peers. Because they read less difficult text, they are exposed to fewer difficult words and thus learn fewer word meanings from context. As with reading fluency, the result is that the gap between instructional levels of struggling and average readers tends to grow. These gaps are cumulative and grow larger every year. Stanovich terms this gap a "Matthew effect," after a passage from the Book of Matthew (25:29) in which it is stated that the rich get richer and the poor get poorer.

There are reasonable explanations for why teachers use less difficult texts for struggling readers. It does not make sense to have children read texts in which they are miscuing on 20%, 30%, or more of the words. When a child reads a text that is extremely difficult, he or she cannot read enough of the words to make sense of even the gist, so there is no context created while reading. We have all experienced this insufficiency when we happen upon a technical article in a journal for which we lack background and vocabulary. In this situation, an extremely difficult text is no more than a bunch of words. For this reason, it has been recommended since at least the 1940s (Betts, 1946) that children not receive instruction in material that is at their frustration level. Given the context of the time in which the recommendation was made, this was reasonable advice. It may not be so at this time, given what we know.

Betts (1946) named three levels of relative difficulty: an *independent* level, at which a child should be able to read a book without assistance; an *instructional* level, at which a child should be able to read with teacher assistance, and a *frustration* level, at which a child would be frustrated if so assigned. The independent level has been conventionally described as the level at which a child reads with 99+% accuracy and 80+% comprehension. The instructional level has been defined as the level at which a child can read with 95 to 98% accuracy and 70% comprehension. The frustration level is defined as accuracy below 90% and comprehension 60% or below. Since 1946 there has been discussion about these levels, but it has centered on the precise percentages at each level or whether semantically acceptable miscues should be counted (see Wixson & Lipson, 1997, for a complete discussion). What has not been discussed, at least not to the degree it deserves, is the relation between relative difficulty level and instruction.

Betts (1946) not only developed the notion of instructional level, he also popularized the Directed Reading Activity (DRA) as a framework for facilitating children's reading of stories. The traditional DRA has been used, at least from the 1940s through the 1990s, in the majority of basal reading programs. The DRA begins with a teacher providing background information, reviewing vocabulary from the story, and providing a purpose for reading prior to reading. Children read the story by section, usually a page. In the original DRA, this reading was to be silent; in reality, it was usually oral. After the children read a section, the teacher asks some questions, which the children must answer and, in the original form of DRA, they then re-read the part of the story in which the answers are to be found. Following this reading, the teacher asks post-reading questions, which lead the children back through the story, and may do an extension activity such as an art or writing project and/or a skills lesson.

This is relatively minimal instruction. The effects of background knowledge preparation are relatively small (Luiten, Ames, & Ackerson, 1980), even when the instruction is focused on key concepts. In practice, background knowledge preparation has been observed to be unfocused or focused on tangential concepts (B. Taylor, personal communication, May 20, 2002). Vocabulary instruction is an important means of improving both oral reading and comprehension, but teachers typically cover 10 words or so out of stories of 200 or 300 words or more. In a 200-word story at a child's instructional level (95% accuracy), about 10 words would be unknown prior to reading. Thus, for this level of instruction, Betts's (1946) levels seem about right.

Text Difficulty

However, there are other ways to look at text difficulty. Adams (1990) estimates that 50% of the words in children's textbooks are among the 109 most frequent words in the English language. This figure is based on a word count of children's textbooks K–12. For younger children, these high-frequency words are likely to account for a larger percentage. Thus, a child who knows these high-frequency words will know at least half of the words in a text. Inasmuch as high-frequency words nearly always signal sentence structure rather than content, this still leaves the child with a considerable task. Consider the following passage, taken from the first two pages of a story in the beginning of a third-grade basal reader.

> My grandfather was a young man when he left his home in Japan and went to see the world. He wore European clothes for the first time and began his journey on a steamship. The Pacific Ocean astonished him. (Say, 1993/ 2001, pp. 16–17)

A child with rudimentary reading abilities (e.g., first-grade level) would be able to read many of the words in these two pages, but might miss "grandfather," "young," "Japan," "world," "wore," "European," "clothes," "journey," "steamship," "Pacific," "Ocean," and "astonished." These 12 words are only 31% of the total but contain nearly all the message. Considering that the story goes on for 20 more pages, teaching all the difficult vocabulary in isolation is out of the question.

Supportive Reading Instruction

The aforementioned story would ordinarily be far out of reach for the child who is reading significantly below grade level. In a more supportive reading situation, a struggling reader might be able not only to make sense of the story, but also to gain from reading it. Consider a structure such as that used in Fluency-Oriented Reading Instruction (Stahl, Heubach, & Cramond, 1997) or an Oral Recitation Lesson (Hoffman, 1987). In these lesson formats, the teacher begins by reading the story to a group of struggling readers. The teacher then discusses the story, using either a recitation format or graphic organizers. In such a format, words such as "grandfather," "Japan," and "journey" would be covered. In addition, the child would be exposed to the other words. This initial reading may be followed by echo-reading, in which the teacher reads a section of the text and the children echo it back. This echo-reading would familiarize the child with more of the unknown words. Throughout the rest of the week, the child would read the story repeatedly, with a parent or other proficient reader at home and with a partner. The cumulative effect of this instructional support is that children can use the class text for instructional material. In fact, we found that with this structure, second-grade children were able to benefit from reading text that they read with only 85% accuracy, well within Betts's frustration level (see Tables 11.1 and 11.2).

This approach represents a different philosophy about struggling read-

TABLE 11.1 Fluency-Oriented Reading Instruction

Fluency-Oriented Reading Instruction has three components—a redesigned basal reading lesson, a home reading component, and a choice reading (i.e., reading books of their own choosing) time during the day. The redesigned basal reading lesson uses a story from the child's reading text. This text can be difficult for children reading below grade level. With the support given by the program, however, children who enter second grade with some basic reading ability can profit from a conventional second-grade text.

1. The teacher begins by reading the story aloud to the class and discussing it. This discussion puts comprehension right in the forefront, so that the children are aware that they are reading for meaning. The teacher then reviews key vocabulary, does comprehension exercises, and conducts other activities around the story itself.

2. Sometimes the teacher echo-reads the story. The teacher reads a section of the text aloud—this section may be a sentence, a paragraph, or longer. Students echo the section back, pointing to each word as they say it. This is a useful introduction for a difficult text. It is optional and may be used only for a group of children whom the teacher thinks will have problems reading the selection.

3. The story is then sent home and read with the child's parents (or other readers) listening. For children who struggle, the story is sent home additional times during the week. Children who do not have difficulty with the story do other reading at home the rest of the week.

4. The next day, the children re-read the story with a partner. One partner reads a page while the other monitors the reading. Then they switch roles until the story is finished. Partner reading can take more than one day, if needed, for longer stories.

5. Following partner reading, the teacher does some extension activities and moves on to another story.

Although this lesson was an important part of the program, it was not the only reading that children did. The children were also required, as part of homework, to read at home. This was monitored through reading logs. Recognizing that children cannot always read at home, the goal is that the children read at home an average of 4 days a week for at least 15 minutes per day.

Time was also set aside for children to read books that they chose. These were usually easy to read and were read for enjoyment. Children sometimes read with partners during this period, as well. This time ranged from 15 minutes in the beginning of the school year to 30 minutes by its end.

ers than the traditional *keep it simple and make it concrete* philosophy that has dominated remedial instruction. Rather than give struggling readers material that they can read easily, these fluency-oriented lesson structures attempt to provide instructional scaffolding so that the child can benefit from more difficult material. The scaffolding is done through repeated reading, and with each reading, children learn more of the words and gain greater prosody (Dowhower, 1987).

This different philosophy views children not in terms of their relative

TABLE 11.2. Oral Recitation Lesson

The Oral Recitation Lesson format reflects an approach that combines a number of procedures into a single lesson plan. An Oral Recitation Lesson has two parts: A Direct Teaching phase and a Mastery phase.

Direct Teaching

1. For a regular-length story, the teacher begins by reading an entire story to the group. The teacher then discusses the story as a whole, either using questions or developing a group story map (Beck & McKeown, 1981).

2. The teacher next reads the story aloud, either sentence by sentence or paragraph by paragraph (use your judgment). Students follow along in their books. After each sentence is read, students echo back the reading. The teacher and the students proceed through the story this way.

3. The teacher divides the story into parts and assigns a section to each student. Each student practices his or her assigned section and performs it for the group. As an alternative, students can choose their parts, based on interest.

4. The teacher and the students proceed to the next story. The teacher may assign work sheets, work on skills, and/or do other activities.

Mastery

The students practice the stories covered in the Direct Teaching phase until they are able to read them with 99%+ accuracy and at least 85 words per minute (or at another acceptable level of fluency). This practice is done on their own. The teacher works with the students when they feel they are ready.

Students progress more quickly through the Direct Teaching phase than the Mastery phase, so a child may be on story # 5 in the Direct Teaching phase, but have mastered only story #3. Students do this mastery work during independent work time, in place of some seat work.

---

abilities, or as good readers and poor readers, but in terms of the amount of scaffolding each child will need in order to read material of an appropriate difficulty. Some children will need no scaffolding and be able to read third-grade material, say, with minimal instruction. Others will need as many as five to seven repetitions in order to read the material satisfactorily. Still other children will not be able to read grade-level material no matter what instruction is provided. In our research (Stahl et al., 1997) we found that almost all of the children who entered second-grade reading at a primer or higher level were reading at grade level at the end of the year, but only half of those starting below the primer level were reading at grade level at year's end. Some children, those who could recognize only a few letters at the beginning of the year, were not included in the study because the difficulty of the reading material was judged to be too great for their abilities. A useful construct is Vygotsky's (1978) notion of the zone of proximal development (ZPD). Vygotsky's ZPD is the zone between the level at which a given child can work independently and that at which the child can work with maximum support. There are tasks that one cannot do, even with maximum support. The supported reading discussed here needs to be within that zone, so that the child can succeed.

Reciprocal Teaching (RT) (Palincsar & Brown, 1984) is not a fluency-oriented approach, but it also enables children to read material that may ordinarily be too difficult. Reciprocal Teaching was developed for children who can recognize words accurately, if not fluently, but cannot comprehend at an appropriate level. In Reciprocal Teaching, each child in a small group, usually of struggling readers, takes a turn being the teacher, directing the reading of a short section of text. The children proceed through the text, practicing the comprehension strategies of predicting, questioning, summarizing, and clarifying. In their meta-analysis, Rosenshine and Meister (1994) found that Reciprocal Teaching produced significant effects on both teacher-developed and standardized measures of reading comprehension. In Reciprocal Teaching, the scaffolding is provided by the short text segments, by the use of a number of strategies, and by teacher guidance. The teacher's role in RT is to prompt the students for appropriate questions, predictions, and so on, and to provide a model for how the students are to act as teachers.

Thematic Units

Another approach to integrating children of all reading abilities into a classroom community is the use of thematic units. These can be used to teach reading and, more naturally, social studies and science. Given the availability of wonderful informational texts on a variety of subjects, many of which are written at easy reading levels, children of many different reading levels can benefit from instruction based on a single thematic unit. For a unit on the growth cycle of frogs, for example, the teacher can assemble books on many levels. Groups of children can use these books to research questions about the life cycle of frogs or fill out graphic organizers containing the same information. The simpler books contain the main points about frog metamorphosis; the more difficult books contain more details. Children can work through a set of books in two ways. Struggling readers may gravitate toward the easier books and make their contributions to the group project through their reading of these books. (They should not be assigned such books, but instead should be free to choose any book, regardless of difficulty.)

Struggling readers may also begin with the easier books and progress through more difficult books. As with repeated reading, providing the easy books familiarizes the child with much of the vocabulary and concepts that would be found in the more difficult books, thus taking some of the difficulty from those books. Consider the following from a Level 1 reader:

The tale of a tadpole begins in a pond. Mother frog lays her eggs next to a
lily pad. Each tiny egg is wrapped in clear jelly. (Wallace, 1998, pp. 4–5)

The basic vocabulary—"tadpole," "pond," "eggs," "jelly"—will be repeated in texts of greater difficulty. Thus, a child who reads this book and
learns these concepts will have an advantage when reading more elaborated
texts, inasmuch as these basic concepts will be repeated in any text dealing
with this subject. Some of these ideas are used in Concept-Oriented Reading Instruction (Guthrie et al., 1996). The progression from easier to more
difficult texts on the same topic can be done individually as well as in a
group context. Working with struggling readers outside of class, as in a
pull-out setting, with easier texts can be a way of supporting them in working with difficult textbooks in their class.

Looking Like a Reader

Another consideration for the struggling reader is the need to look and feel
like a reader. Children with reading problems, especially when they are severe, can be reading several grade levels below their grade placement, like
Brian, fourth grader reading at a second-grade level. Often their reading
ability is outside of the zone of proximal development, making reading
grade-level texts inappropriate.

However, even if grade-level texts cannot be used, a child's maturity
level must be respected. For older children, this means using books that do
not look obviously childish, except in rare circumstances. There are many
chapter books, for example, written at the second-grade or even high-first-
grade level that might be used with older struggling readers. Not only are
these books likely to be more intellectually engaging for such readers (who
need this kind of engagement as much as normally achieving children), but
they are more like the type of reading done by the child's peers.

High Interest–Low Vocabulary books can also be used with older
struggling readers. Again, such books do not look obviously childish, but
allow the struggling reader to practice reading meaningful and interesting
text without feeling self-conscious. The drawback to these books is that if
children are kept in books that are too easy, they will not make adequate
progress. These books should be used, but their use should be monitored
so that when the child is ready, more challenging material will be provided.

As indicated earlier, books of an appropriate level are often childish in
appearance. One approach to giving children practice in such books is to
use them for Buddy Reading (Labbo & Teale, 1990). In Buddy Reading, an
older child practices reading a book so that it can be read to younger children. An older struggling reader can be a buddy to a kindergartner or first
grader. In that situation, reading (and even practicing) a first-grade-level

book may appear appropriate to one's peers. Having a buddy to read to can be a way of saving face for a child with severe reading problems.

Children with reading problems gain from working as readers or as tutors with younger children. Reading to younger students is a good way for children to practice their reading in a natural task. The teacher selects a book that may be interesting to younger children. It should be short, colorful, with few sentences on a page. The struggling reader practices reading the book until it feels comfortable. Then the student reads to a younger child, to the benefit of both. For older children reading at a very low level (a sixth grader reading at a first-grade level), allowing them to pick out books to read to kindergartners, say, is a practical way of allowing them to practice appropriate material and maintain their self-esteem.

Being a Member of the Classroom Community

Fluency-oriented approaches, Reciprocal Teaching, and the use of thematic units have been found to produce significant growth in reading achievement. However, the motivational aspects of these approaches should not be ignored. In these cases, children can read the same material as their peers, which breaks one of the barriers between struggling readers and their normally achieving peers. The result seems to be increased motivation and achievement.

Effective teachers make all children part of the same classroom community. In some classes, children do not know who the good readers are (Stahl, Suttles, & Pagnucco, 1996). In other classes, the boundaries are clear and everyone knows the pecking order. Reading different material than their peers can confirm the belief of children with reading problems that they cannot achieve as well as their peers. Indeed, unless children read material of a third-grade level, say, they will never be able to achieve at that level. As Stanovich (1986) pointed out, the gap between normally achieving and struggling readers will widen over the school years.

MAKING PROGRESS CONCRETE

Another motivational consequence of underachievement in reading is the need to make achievement growth concrete. Children with reading problems have been praised, often for accomplishments they know are below those expected for other children in the class. Thus, praise loses its value. This is not to say that the children should not be praised. Of course children should be praised for their accomplishments. Our experience, though, is that struggling readers need concrete reminders of their progress, proof that they are growing as readers.

We have used a simple activity in our clinic for many years with a great deal of success. Called "Three Strikes and You're Out," it is a basic flash card activity. Words that children miscall during reading are noted and put on 3″ × 5″ index cards. These are added to a word bank. The children can practice words from each other's word banks during individual reading time. We have used a "Three Strikes and You're Out" procedure, in which words that the child correctly identifies on three different occasions are retired from the word bank. The occasions do not have to be consecutive. As words are retired, they are taken from the word bank and put into a bank of retired words. Retired words can be revisited, but ordinarily are left to accumulate. As the bank of retired words grows, the child sees concrete evidence of growth in word learning. The activity takes very little time, but seems to be a favorite among children and teachers.

One of the nice things about "Three Strikes" is that it is a cumulative activity. That is, the number of words will always grow, never diminish. On weekly tests, for example, children's scores will vary, so that even if a child is improving week by week, there will be peaks and valleys. With the use of "Three Strikes," even if a child learns five words in one session and one word in the next, the pile of retired words always grows. "Three Strikes" can be graphed to show continuous progress (see Figure 11.1).

This continuous-progress type of graph can be used for number of books read as well. It can take the form of the graph shown in Figure 11.1, or it may be a column graph in which a column is made by pasting cut-out pictures of books with the titles of the book read. Care must be taken that these activities do not become competitive. Competition stifles the initiative of struggling readers, because they lose most of the time. For that reason,

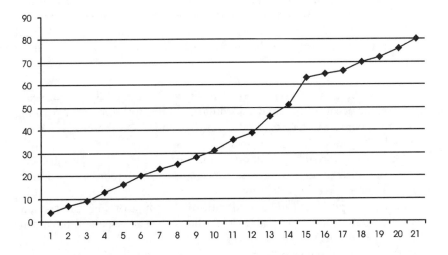

FIGURE 11.1. Number of words learned.

individual charts may be more effective than group charts; moreover, the charts should not be displayed, for fear of making the book reading competitive.

Another activity that lends itself to charting is "Repeated Readings" (Kuhn & Stahl, in press). Literally, this means that students read the same text repeatedly until a desired level of fluency is attained. We use a specific procedure in the Reading Clinic, as follows:

1. Choose a passage to read that is slightly above the child's instructional level, but one that the child may be interested in reading. This method may be used with grade-level materials for a child reading significantly below grade level.
2. Take a 100-word excerpt from this passage. (You may use different lengths, but the math is more difficult.)
3. Have the child read the passage aloud, marking all the miscues that the child makes. Time (using a stopwatch or a watch with a sweep second hand) and tape-record the reading. Mark the child's speed and error rate on a chart.
4. Review the child's miscues with the child. This may be done using the tape or through discussion. Some children like listening to themselves on the tape; others do not. If you use a tape, do not overuse it.
5. Have the child re-read the passage. Mark the child's errors and time on the chart.
6. Have the child continue until a speed of 100 words per minute with 0 or 1 miscue per 100 words is achieved. If this takes more than seven tries, you may want to discontinue and use an easier passage. This will usually take more than one session. Chart each attempt.
7. Go on to another section at the same level. When the child can read relatively fluently for the first time, go on to a more difficult passage.

We use the type of graph shown in Figure 11.2 for "Repeated Readings." Again, because the child is ordinarily going to improve in reading, the graph is cumulative, so the child sees that with every reading, improvement is being made.

This is the approach used in our clinic with one-on-one tutoring. It can be used in a classroom setting with a peer tutor, who records, or a Buddy Reader (Labbo & Teale, 1990) from an upper grade who works as a tutor. An alternative approach can be used with small groups or an entire class, as well as with an individual child. Select a book or a passage and have children read orally for 3 minutes. At the end of 3 minutes, have the child(ren) mark the last word they read with a pencil. You might have a group discus-

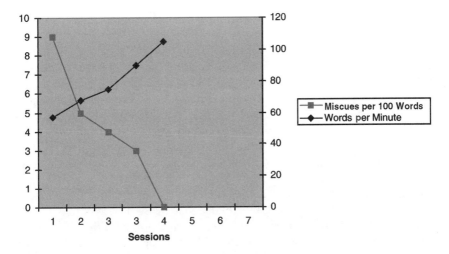

FIGURE 11.2. "Repeated Readings" chart.

sion about three words the children had problems with. Then have them read the passage again, again for 3 minutes. Have the child(ren) mark the last word they read. They should have been able to read more. The procedure can be repeated a third time. This is also a cumulative activity. As children read faster with practice, the marks should move farther down the page, again providing concrete proof of progress.

MOTIVATING THE STRUGGLING READER

To reiterate:

- Children with reading problems tend to see themselves as incapable of reading as well as their peers. If we are to help them become good readers, we need to convince them that they can be good readers.
- Children with reading problems need to see concrete progress.

Motivating reading instruction for a struggling reader must rely on cooperation rather than competition. Children with reading problems do not successfully compete with their peers, and they can be devastated by competition. They respond with shame, negativity, or even a "madface." Brian and I work in the second-grade hallway, away from his fourth-grade peers, so that they do not see him working in the second-grade texts that are a challenge for him to read. I choose chapter books, such as *The Stories Julian*

Tells (Cameron, 1981) to work with him, because chapter books are what fourth graders read.

Integrating struggling readers into the fabric of the classroom can be difficult. Indeed, struggling readers probably know that they are not achieving as well as their peers no matter how much effort is expended. But we can minimize some of the obvious differences by providing differential support rather than different materials and by using thematic units with a wide variety of materials at different reading levels so that the child with reading problems is doing the same things as other children in the class and is contributing to class learning. This is an ideal, but one worth striving for.

The use of graphs and other concrete records to show children how well they are doing is more realistic. Graphing can be integrated into a number of different activities. Our experience in the Clinic is that graphs and piles of cards are powerful motivators, more powerful than just praise or even rewards. Graphs remain as evidence long after the M&Ms are eaten. Graphs can also be used for parent conferences; they are just as good at showing parents a child's progress.

Reading is going to be difficult for some children. Making it easy, through simple texts and a slow pace, does not motivate children to read more. Instead, "keeping it simple" can convince children that they lack talent in reading and that they should not try. To motivate children with reading problems, we need to convince them that they can succeed at reading with appropriate effort. With their effort, and powerful instruction, all children can become part of the reading community—without a madface.

REFERENCES

Adams, M. J. (1990). *Beginning to read: Thinking and learning about print.* Cambridge, MA: MIT Press.

Allington, R. L. (1983). The reading instruction provided readers of differing reading abilities. *The Elementary School Journal, 83,* 549–559.

Allington, R. L. (1984). Content coverage and contextual reading in reading groups. *Journal of Reading Behavior, 16,* 85–96.

Allington, R. L. (1991). The legacy of "slow it down and make it concrete." In J. Zutell & S. McCormick (Eds.), *Learner factors/teacher factors: Issues in literacy research and instruction. Fortieth yearbook of the National Reading Conference* (pp. 19–30). Chicago: National Reading Conference.

Beck, I. L., & McKeown, M. G. (1981). Developing questions that promote comprehension: The story map. *Language Arts, 58,* 913–918.

Betts, E. A. (1946). *Foundations of reading instruction.* New York: American Books.

Butkowsky, I. S., & Willows, D. M. (1980). Cognitive–motivational characteristics of children varying in reading ability: Evidence for learned helplessness in poor readers. *Journal of Educational Psychology, 72,* 408–422.

Cameron, A. (1981). *The stories Julian tells.* New York: Pantheon.

Dowhower, S. L. (1987). Effects of repeated reading on second-grade transitional readers' fluency and comprehension. *Reading Research Quarterly, 22,* 389–406.

Guthrie, J. T., Van Meter, P., McCann, A. D., Wigfield, A., Bennett, L., Poundstone, C., Rice, M. E., Faibisch, F. M., Hunt, B., & Mitchell, A. M. (1996). Growth of literacy engagement: Changes in motivations and strategies during concept-oriented reading instruction. *Reading Research Quarterly, 31,* 306–332.

Hoffman, J. (1987). Rethinking the role of oral reading. *Elementary School Journal, 87,* 367–373.

Johnston, P. H., & Winograd, P. N. (1985). Passive failure in reading. *Journal of Reading Behavior, 17,* 279–301.

Kuhn, M. R., & Stahl, S. A. (in press). Fluency: A review of developmental and remedial practices. *Journal of Educational Psychology.*

Labbo, L. D., & Teale, W. H. (1990). Cross age reading: A strategy for helping poor readers. *The Reading Teacher, 43,* 363–369.

Lipson, M. Y., & Wixson, K. K. (1997). *Assessment and instruction of reading and writing disability: An interactive approach.* New York: Longman.

Luiten, J., Ames, W. S., & Ackerson, G. (1980). A meta-analysis of the effects of advance organizers on learning and retention. *American Educational Research Journal, 17,* 211–218.

Palincsar, A. S., & Brown, A. L. (1984). Reciprocal teaching of comprehension-fostering and comprehension-monitoring activities. *Cognition and Instruction, 2,* 117–175.

Pinnell, G. S. (1995). *Listening to children read aloud: Data from NAEP's Integrated Reading Performance Record (IRPR) at Grade 4.* Washington, DC: National Assessment of Educational Progress.

Rosenshine, B., & Meister, C. (1994). Reciprocal teaching: A review of the research. *Review of Educational Research, 64,* 479–530.

Say, A. (2001). *Grandfather's journey.* New York: McGraw-Hill. (Original work published 1993)

Stahl, S. A., Heubach, K., & Cramond, B. (1997). *Fluency oriented reading instruction.* Research Report No. 75. Athens, GA: National Reading Research Center, University of Georgia and University of Maryland.

Stahl, S. A., Suttles, C. W., & Pagnucco, J. R. (1996). The effects of traditional and process literacy instruction on first graders' reading and writing achievement and orientation toward reading. *Journal of Educational Research, 89,* 131–144.

Stanovich, K. E. (1986). Matthew effects in reading: Some consequences of individual differences in the acquisition of literacy. *Reading Research Quarterly, 21,* 360–407.

Vygotsky, L. S. (1978). *Mind in society: The development of higher psychological processes.* Cambridge, MA: Harvard University Press.

Wallace, K. (1998). *Tale of a tadpole.* New York: Dorling Kindersley.

12

How Can I Help Them Pull It All Together?

A Guide to Fluent Reading Instruction

MELANIE KUHN

One of the primary advances in literacy learning occurs when readers who are painstakingly sounding out words develop such familiarity with print that they come to be seen as fluent (Chall, 1996). Such fluency occurs when learners make the transition from purposeful decoding of words to a rapid, accurate, and expressive rendering of texts. Unfortunately for a number of learners, this transition does not occur readily (Allington, 1983; Rasinski & Padak, 1996; Reutzel, 1996). These readers seem to get stuck in a word-by-word reading pattern. This not only prevents them from reading text expressively, it also prevents them from focusing on its meaning. Yet fortunately, there are a number of effective strategies that teachers can implement to aid their students' transition to fluent reading. This chapter discusses the importance of fluency in the reading process and presents a number of strategies that are designed to develop fluency among students who are in the process of making this transition.

FLUENCY AS A FACTOR IN THE READING PROCESS

Although there is no single precise definition of fluency (Hoffman & Issacs, 1991), there does appear to be a consensus regarding its three primary components: accuracy in decoding; automaticity in word recognition; and the appropriate use of stress, pitch, and suitable phrasing, or the prosodic elements of language. Given that the ultimate goal of reading is comprehension (e.g., Anderson, Hiebert, Scott, & Wilkinson, 1985), it is important to assess the role of fluency in the construction of meaning. There are two primary ways in which fluency contributes to a reader's understanding of text (Kuhn & Stahl, 2000). The first stresses the contribution of automatic word recognition, and the second focuses on prosody.

Contribution of Automatic Word Recognition to Comprehension

Proficient readers have certain features in common when it comes to word recognition; they not only read accurately, they have also achieved automaticity. In other words, they no longer need to purposefully decode the vast majority of words they encounter in text. Given that automatic word recognition is a requisite factor among skilled readers, the question becomes, In what ways does this automatic word recognition lead to reading comprehension? According to a number of authors (LaBerge & Samuels, 1974; Perfetti, 1985; Stanovich, 1980), individuals have a limited amount of attention available for reading. This being the case, attention expended on one component of reading is, necessarily, unavailable for another. When reading, individuals necessarily perform two interdependent tasks: They must identify the words present in a text while also constructing its meaning. Given that these two processes occur simultaneously, the greater the amount of attention expended on decoding, the less that remains available for comprehension. To ensure that readers have enough attention to understand texts adequately, it is necessary for them to develop their decoding to the point where each word is recognized instantly. Once they have reached this point, they will have freed up the attention necessary to focus on the meaning of what they are reading.

Regarding fluency development, the question that follows is, How do learners make the shift from decoding accurately but deliberately, to decoding automatically? According to a number of authors (e.g., Allington, 2001; Anderson et al., 1985; Cunningham, 2000; Rasinski & Padak, 2001), the best way to ensure that this transition occurs is through extensive practice. As with any skill that requires the coordination of a series of smaller steps to create a unified action, it is practice that allows a learner to become a skilled reader. For readers, this practice consists primarily of having successive exposures to print. In other words, the key to students' development of automatic word recognition is the provision of extensive opportunities to read a wide range of connected text. As words become increasingly familiar to the learner, less and less attention needs to be directed toward decoding them, with automatic word recognition the result. However, there is an important aspect of fluency that remains to be addressed, that of prosody.

Contribution of Prosody

Although automatic word recognition accounts for accurate and effortless decoding, it does not actively account for the role of prosody in fluent reading (Kuhn & Stahl, 2000). In regard to fluency, there is a tacit understanding that it involves more than simply reading the words quickly and accurately; it also involves expressive reading. Implicit in the term *reading with expression* is the use of those prosodic features that account for the tonal and rhythmic aspects of language (Dowhower, 1991). These prosodic features include pitch or intonation, stress or emphasis, tempo or rate, the rhythmic or regularly recurring patterns of language, and the use of appropriate phrasing.

Prosody's Role in Fluent Reading

It is commonly noted that children who have not achieved fluency read either in a word-by-word manner or by grouping words in ways that deviate from the phrasing that occurs naturally in oral language (Allington, 1983; Dowhower, 1991; Rasinski, 1989; Reutzel, 1996; Schreiber, 1991). Conversely, appropriate phrasing, intonation, and stress are all considered to be indicators of fluent reading (Chall, 1996; Chomsky, 1976, 1978; Dowhower, 1991; Rasinski & Padak, 1996; Schreiber, 1991). Such prosodic renditions of a text provide clues to an otherwise invisible process by acting as indicators of the reader's comprehension. By grouping text into meaningful phrases, fluent readers make written text sound like oral language. This use of expression further indicates their understanding of what is being read, because readers can begin to apply appropriate phrasing to a text only when they are capable of making sense of it. It is this prosodic reading, in conjunction with accurate and automatic word recognition, that makes for a fluent rendering of a text.

FLUENCY STRATEGIES

Given a working understanding of fluency as discussed earlier, it is possible to identify a variety of strategies that allow teachers to assist students in developing both automatic word recognition and prosody. By implementing these strategies, it is then possible to assist students in making the transition from purposeful decoding to an expressive rendering of text.

Unassisted versus Assisted Interventions

The strategies discussed in this chapter fall into two overarching categories, those that build on independent learning and those that provide learners with models of fluent reading. According to Dowhower (1989), interventions that have fluent reading development as their primary goal can be classified as unassisted or assisted reading strategies. Unassisted strategies rely on learners' ability to improve their accuracy, rate, and prosody without a model, whereas assisted readings provide a direct model of fluent reading in the form of a mentor, a tape recording, or another form of speech feedback, such as a computer. Both categories of strategies have been shown to be effective in assisting students' fluency development; they are discussed here according to the type of intervention provided.

Unassisted Interventions

Unassisted Repeated Readings

Perhaps the best known of the strategies designed to support fluency development is that of repeated readings. This unassisted strategy, which relies on independent practice, was developed by Dahl (1979) and Samuels (1979). These authors noted that classroom practice consists primarily of students reading new material each day in the hope that this will lead to an improvement in their word recognition skills. However, it struck them that this was not necessarily the most effective way to increase students' automaticity. Instead, the authors considered it a distinct possibility that students might have greater success in developing automatic word recognition if they increased their practice on a given passage. Dahl and Samuels believed that not only would this lead to improvements in the students' fluency on the practiced material, but that these improvements in automatic word recognition would transfer, occurring when the practiced words were encountered in previously unread texts as well. Growth in fluency was to be measured through an increase in reading rate, something that was demonstrated in a number of studies (see Dowhower, 1989).

Implementing Repeated Readings

The implementation of repeated readings is quite straightforward, making it easy to use. The procedure is designed as an individualized approach for students who are decoding accurately but slowly even when encountering words that should be familiar and therefore recognized instantly. The strategy has two simple components. The first involves the selection of a text that is at the high end of the student's instructional level or (approximately 95–93% accuracy) or even a little beyond, but that is of interest to the student. The second involves recording the number of words read per minute along with the numbers of miscues made on the passage (see Figure 12.1). As the number of words read per minute increases, the number of miscues decreases until an optimal level is achieved. The student practices re-reading the passage until he or she reaches a rate of words per minute and a number of miscues predetermined by the teacher. The procedure itself is as follows:

- Select a short sample from the passage (100–200 words). Make a copy for yourself and the child.
- Have the child conduct an initial reading of the text aloud. Mark any miscues that are made and, using a stopwatch, time the initial reading. Determine the number of words read per minute and the number of miscues, and mark them on the chart.
- Review the miscues with the child.
- Have the child re-read the passage, and record the new words per minute rating along with the number of miscues.

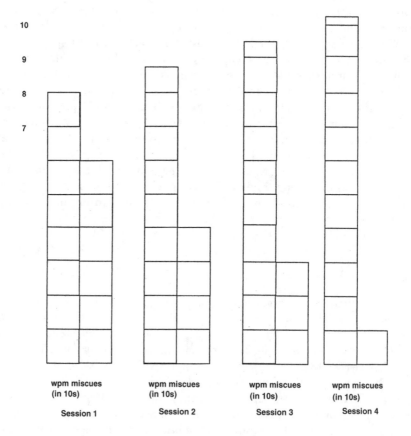

FIGURE 12.1. Chart for recording Repeated Readings passages. From Ash and Hagood (2000). Reprinted by permission of the authors.

- Continue until the child is reading at a rate of approximately 100 words per minute and is making 1 or 2 miscues per 100 words (you may wish to divide this practice time into two or three sessions). It is important to emphasize speed over accuracy for these passages, because the goal is to establish automatic word recognition. If it takes the child more than seven attempts to achieve this goal, you may wish to move to an easier passage.
- Once the child is fairly fluent, go on to another selection at the same level. When the child has reached the point where he or she can read a selection relatively fluently on the initial reading, select a passage at a slightly more difficult level.

The repeated reading procedure has been shown to be highly effective for students who are considered to be slow readers over the course of numerous interventions (e.g., Dahl, 1979; Herman, 1985; Rashotte & Torgesen, 1985; Weinstein & Cooke, 1992). Generally, the students involved in using this strategy enjoy seeing the gains they make through their tracking of the changes in their reading and experience gratification when making visible improvement over a short period of time. However, some authors (O'Shea, Sindelar, & O'Shea 1985, 1987) were concerned about whether students would automatically focus on the meaning of the text when directed to read for improved rate and accuracy, or whether greater improvements in comprehension would occur when they were directed to focus on the meaning.

To answer this question, the authors conducted two studies that demonstrated similar, although not identical, outcomes. They found that in working with third graders who were making the transition to fluent reading, the students cued for comprehension demonstrated a better understanding of the story than their counterparts. Conversely, those cued for speed read at significantly higher rates than those cued for comprehension. However, for struggling readers, both the students cued for comprehension and those cued for rate made similar gains in speed of word recognition, but those cued for comprehension demonstrated a better understanding than those cued for rate. Given these results, repeated readings may prove even more effective when students are cued for comprehension, rate, or both, depending on which component a teacher thinks would provide the most benefit for a given student.

Paired Repeated Readings

Repeated readings have proven to be a highly effective strategy for improving the fluency of a reader. However, if the teacher also serves as the recorder of the students' rates and miscues, it may prove difficult for him or her to work with more than one or two students over the course of the day.

An alternative to this procedure is paired repeated reading (Koskinen & Blum, 1984, 1986). Given that most teachers' days provide only a limited amount of time for individual instruction, Koskinen and Blum (1984, 1986) devised paired repeated readings as an alternative that would allow students to work with one another to improve their reading fluency. As with traditional repeated readings, students practice reading a passage as a means of improving their word recognition. However, the procedure provides several variations from the original strategy.

- Rather than working one-on-one with the teacher, the students work with one another in pairs. The teacher provides training for the students in regard to how best to provide positive feedback. This allows each student within the pair to act as a coach for the other and ensures that comments contribute to his or her partner's improvement.
- Students select an approximately 50-word passage from material they are currently using as part of their classroom reading. Koskinen and Blum (1986) suggest that the two students working in each pair select different passages from a given text so as to minimize "direct comparison of reading proficiency" (p. 71).
- Students read through their passages silently and decide between themselves who is to read the passage aloud first (creating an alternating schedule may also serve to minimize disputes).
- The student who is to go first reads his or her passage aloud to the partner three times. After each reading, the reader assesses his or her own performance, recording how well each rendition went on a self-evaluation sheet.
- The partner listens carefully to each of the readings and, after the second and third renditions, comments on the ways in which the performance has improved. She or he records these improvements on a listening sheet.
- The pair switch roles and the procedure is completed with the new reader.

Because paired repeated reading is designed for use with an entire class or reading group, it is possible to integrate this procedure into the literacy curriculum quite easily, especially in comparison to the individualized version outlined earlier. This method seems to have many of the benefits of the original procedure, as students' ability to read and reread a single passage has been shown to improve their automatic word recognition, which, in turn, leads to improvements in their fluency. As with the original procedure, it is likely that these improvements in the practiced passages will transfer to previously unread material. Furthermore, given that there is a ready audience with this method, it is easy to incorporate expression as part of the criteria with which the passage is evaluated by both the reader and the listener.

Readers' Theater

Another approach that has virtually universal appeal among students is the use of readers' theater (Allington, 2001; Bidwell, 1990; Henning, 1974; Optiz & Rasinski, 1998). An advantage of this approach is that any reading material can be used, including poetry and nonfiction (Hoyt, 2000), which tend to be underutilized in the primary grades (Duke, 1999). A second advantage is that it provides a real purpose for the practice that comes from repetition. There are two ways to conduct this activity. The first is to use plays that have been written specifically for children, examples of which are often included in the literature anthologies and basal readers used in many classrooms or are available in the school or public library. The second option involves rewriting a text or a portion of a text as a performance piece. Unlike traditional plays, readers' theater pieces are not designed for all-out performances. There is no need to provide props, sets, or costumes to integrate readers' theater into the literacy curriculum. In fact, the students are not even required to memorize their lines. Rather, the students are expected to provide an expressive rendition of the text simply through their reading of the material out loud. This is accomplished through practicing the text while keeping in mind the nuances of the part(s). Because there are no external clues to aid in the development of the performance's meaning, the interpretation is entirely dependent on the reader's ability to bring the text to life through the use of appropriate expression.

As with the previously outlined strategies, this method is designed to promote the automatic word recognition that is essential to fluency development. However, with readers' theater, there is a greater emphasis on the importance of using appropriate expression to relay the meaning of the text. The procedure incorporates several distinct steps that make it adaptable as both a small-group and a whole-class activity:

- Select material that you consider would lend itself to being adapted and performed aloud, or allow the students to make a selection themselves, with the provision that it be easily adapted as a script that can be readily performed.
- Read the text to the students or have them read through it independently.
- Divide the students into groups. Provide them with copies of a play or a script based on a text that you have rewritten yourself. Alternately, students can rewrite a story as a script themselves. (Depending on how

much effort you want the students to expend on each project, the re-writing component can become a major factor in a lesson plan, incorporating elements of a writing workshop.)

- Ensure that each student has a role that she or he will be responsible for performing. (Alternately, you can have students read portions of the text in pairs or as a chorus.)
- Provide the students with sufficient time to practice their parts in the performance. This can be accomplished by allowing students an opportunity to read their passages both silently and aloud. Furthermore, they should be encouraged to solicit and contribute positive feedback from their fellow performers in order to make their renditions more effective for their audience.
- Once the students have incorporated feedback and established fluency with the piece, they should perform their interpretations of the roles for their fellow classmates.

As with paired repeated reading, students should be provided with an opportunity to critique their own performances, using a form for self-evaluation. Furthermore, their fellow students should be given an opportunity to provide positive feedback regarding the performance or interpretation of a given piece.

Assisted Interventions

Assisted Readings

As with unassisted fluency strategies, assisted strategies emphasize practice as a means of improving accuracy, automatic word recognition, and prosody. Furthermore, they provide extensive exposure to print. However, unlike the unassisted methods discussed earlier, these strategies provide a learner with a skilled model of fluent reading prior to any attempt on the student's part to read the text independently. Such models allow learners to hear the way an expressive reader interprets a text, thereby giving them a sense of what they should be striving for in their own oral reading. According to Allington (1983), one of the greatest disadvantages struggling readers face is the lack of models of fluent reading. Learners are often placed in groups based on reading ability. For struggling readers, this translates into groups in which disfluent readers serve as the only exemplars. Alternately, reading may be conducted as a whole class. However, when this is the case, the format used is often that of round-robin reading. This method presents the text as a series of disparate units rather than as a unified whole, and although some of the readers may provide a fluent rendering of the story, others provide only halting and disfluent examples of oral reading for their classmates.

Integrating Fluency into Classroom Reading

There are several ways in which to counter the aforementioned unconstructive examples of oral reading. Possibly the easiest to implement involves the integration of choral and echo reading into the literacy curriculum (Hoffman & Issacs, 1991; Kuhn, 2000; Stahl, Heubach, & Cramond, 1997). Choral and echo reading of a story, a strategy that is already undertaken in many classrooms, can be used effectively not only as a means of introducing a particular text, but as a way of promoting fluency development as well. Rather than have the students read the material in a round-robin format, the teacher does an initial reading of the text and proceeds to have a discussion about the story. This allows for comprehension to be addressed at the beginning of the lesson and to be emphasized as the primary purpose for reading. The teacher then asks students to read the story along with him or her in a choral or echo rendering of the text. This component can be repeated several times, depending on the difficulty and length of the selection. Students can then be paired for partner reading of the text, as discussed earlier, or they can read the text independently inasmuch as scaffolding of the text has already been provided. Students can reread the text to identify their favorite passages, to provide their own interpretations of the reading, or to provide evidence for answers to questions that have been set by the teacher. All of these activities contribute to both fluency development and comprehension in reading a given text.

Neurological Impress Method (NIM)

There are several other ways to integrate models of fluent reading into the classroom curriculum. The neurological impress method (NIM) was devised by R.G. Heckleman (1966, 1969) as a strategy that would lead to improvements in reading fluency. In its initial design, the method required that the teacher and student read simultaneously at a rapid rate. The student was to sit in front of the teacher, both were to hold the book, each holding a side, and the teacher was to read into the student's ear. The teacher was to slide a finger under the words as they were read and could vary the pace so that sometimes the reading was faster and louder and sometimes it was slower and softer. This joint reading was to continue until the teacher noticed that the student was becoming tired or uncomfortable. Although this procedure appears to be quaint, given our current vantage point, and is unlikely to be implemented as described, it did prove to be successful. Furthermore, there are several aspects of the method that are replicated in a number of other fluency strategies. These include having the skilled reader and student engaging in choral reading, requiring the text to be pointed at as it is being read in order to promote the connection between oral and written language, and the modeling that is provided through the skilled reader's varied rendition of a text.

Although the NIM has been shown to be an effective procedure (Heckleman, 1966, 1969), it is also labor-intensive because it is designed as a one-on-one strategy. Given that the method requires individualized support, it is more likely to be used in a tutorial session than in traditional classroom settings. This feature was recognized by Hollingsworth (1970, 1978), who attempted to redesign the procedure in a way that was more adaptable to the classroom. His primary goal was to implement the procedure with several students simultaneously. To this end, he created a system that allowed a number of children to listen to a tape recording of a text while simultaneously reading along with individual copies of the passage. The teacher was able to monitor the progress of the group of students, rather than being engaged exclusively with an individual student. Again, the research on this method indicates that it is an effective strategy for readers who need assistance in shifting from purposeful decoding to fluent reading. However, the research also indicates that this strategy will not provide any additional benefits for those students who are already fluent readers.

Reading-While-Listening

The modified NIM that Heckleman describes is very similar to one of the best-known assisted reading strategies, that of reading-while-listening. This strategy was pioneered by Carol Chomsky (1976, 1978). Chomsky worked with five third graders identified by their teacher as struggling readers. Although the two girls and three boys had had extensive instruction in decoding strategies, they seemed unable to apply their knowledge to connected text. Each of the children was reading 1 to 2 years below grade level, and all professed an intense dislike of reading. Chomsky believed that the best way to counter these difficulties was to expose the children to significant amounts of text in an accessible format. To achieve this, she tape-recorded two dozen books ranging in reading level from second to fifth grade. Given that the students were able to decode individual words but unable to put these strategies to use with connected text, the recorded books were at the upper end of their instructional level and might even have been considered challenging for the children. The students were asked to listen repeatedly to the tapes while reading along with the text until they were able to render the material fluently. The children selected their own books from among the choices offered and set their own pace for the assisted readings.

Initially, the process was slow and the children had some difficulty coordinating their eye movements with the voices on tape, but as they became increasingly familiar with their texts as well as the process, they found it easier to keep track of the story. The students were eventually able to provide a fluent rendition of the books on tape before moving on to new selections. Furthermore, it took the learners less time to reach mastery on each subsequent selection. Perhaps even more telling, however, was that, according to both parents and teachers, the children were reading independently and were willing to engage in writing activities as well.

A similar use of reading-while-listening was designed by Carbo (1978). However, Carbo's version differed in some elements of its design from that of Chomsky. For example, she used tapes in which the phrasing was emphasized within the story. Children were instructed to slide their fingers under the words as a form of tactile reinforcement as they read, and each page was cued on the tape to minimize the chances of the listeners losing their place within the passage. Carbo worked with eight children classified as learning disabled over a 3-month period, during which time she reported that the students demonstrated an average gain of 8 months' growth in their reading.

These two procedures (Carbo, 1978; Chomsky, 1976, 1978) differ from the modified NIM approach in that there is less direct monitoring by the teacher and the length and frequency of the sessions is determined by the students. A primary concern regarding such read-along techniques is that there is no way to ensure active engagement on the part of the learners. However, given the results of these studies, it appears that students actively participate in the process when they are held accountable for their reading. Furthermore, anecdotal evidence indicates that the students enjoyed the taped stories and displayed pride in their abilities and their success with the material. However, it is important to stress that these activities do not simply parallel what usually takes place in a listening center; in such centers, stories are listened to in conjunction with a text primarily for enjoyment or to develop emergent literacy skills. In contrast, students who use the reading-while-listening procedure are held accountable for the material they are reading and are expected to develop fluency with each passage before moving forward with a new selection.

ASSESSING READING FLUENCY

An important consideration in the development of fluent reading is to ascertain how well your students are reading both before and after an intervention and, initially, to determine whether students need to work on fluency development at all. There are two scales that assist listeners in assessing the fluency levels of students' oral reading: the Multidimensional Fluency Scale (Zutell & Rasinski, 1991), which addresses phrasing, smoothness, and pace, each as a distinct component, and the National Assessment of Educational Progress's (NAEP) Oral Reading Fluency Scale (1995), which provides a generalized measure of expression and phrasing but is less detailed with each of the categories. The NAEP scale (see Figure 12.2) assesses oral reading on a four-point scale, starting with reading that is primarily word-by-word and does not maintain a sense of syntax, or grammar, and advancing to primarily expressive reading that incorporates appropriate phrasing and in which meaningful interpretation is present and syntax is maintained. The assessment of readers' fluency is not nearly as universal as the assessment of word recognition, but it seems that the NAEP scale may be easily implemented in most classrooms. However, for a more detailed assessment, the scale devised by Zutell and Rasinski (1991) provides a clearer picture and may help the teacher to determine the particular elements to focus on for a particular child.

CONCLUSIONS

There are a number of intervention procedures designed to promote fluency development; in regard to those discussed in this chapter, several generalizations can be made. To begin with, all the methods outlined here are, to a greater or lesser degree, effective in assisting readers making the transition

Level 4

Reads primarily in larger, meaningful phrase groups. Although some regressions, repetitions, and deviations from text may be present, those do not appear to detract from the overall structure of the story. Preservation of the author's syntax is consistent. Some or most of the story is read with expressive interpretation.

Level 3

Reads primarily in three- or four-word phrase groups. Some smaller groupings may be present. However, the majority of phrasing seems appropriate and preserves the syntax of the author. Little or no expressive interpretation is present.

Level 2

Reads primarily in two-word phrases with some three- or four-word groupings. Some word-by-word reading may be present. Word groupings may seem awkward and unrelated to larger context of sentence or passage.

Level 1

Reads primarily word-by-word. Occasionally two-word or three-word phrases may occur, but these are infrequent and/or they do not preserve meaningful syntax.

FIGURE 12.2. National Assessment of Educational Progress's Oral Reading Fluency Scale.

from laborious decoding to fluent reading. Furthermore, this development encompasses gains in speed and accuracy as well as expressive or prosodic reading. Third, these strategies have proven to be effective as long as students have ample opportunity for practice using connected text. In addition, learners using these methods demonstrate gains when working with relatively challenging texts; the keys here seem to be both the practice noted earlier and the support that is provided through repetitions or the modeling of fluent reading. *How* that modeling is provided, either through the use of taped narrations or through the support of another individual, seems to be less crucial than that it *is* provided. The provision of such modeling seems to allow learners to work within their zones of proximal development (Vygotsky, 1978) and offers the scaffolding that allows them to successfully move beyond the point at which they are able to work independently. Such reading can also be incorporated into meaningful activities with a real purpose, unlike many of the procedures, such as round-robin reading, that have often dominated oral reading in the classroom (see, for example, Allington, 1983; Optiz & Rasinski, 1998; Reutzel, 1996). Finally, these strategies can be adapted so that they can be used effectively as part of the broader classroom reading curriculum, making their integration into the literacy curriculum a distinct possibility for teachers who are attempting to promote fluent reading within their classrooms.

REFERENCES

Allington, R. L. (1983). Fluency: The neglected reading goal. *The Reading Teacher, 36,* 556–561.

Allington, R. L. (2001). *What really matters for struggling readers: Designing research-based programs.* New York: Longman.

Anderson, R. C., Heibert, E. H., Scott, J. A., & Wilkinson, I. A. G. (1985). *Becoming a nation of readers.* Washington, DC: The U.S. Department of Education, National Institute of Education.

Ash, G., & Hagood, M. (2000, May). *This song goes out to Miss Gwynne and Miss Margaret.* Paper presented at the annual meeting of the International Reading Association, Indianapolis, IN.

Bidwell, S. M. (1990). Using drama to increase motivation, comprehension, and fluency. *Journal of Reading, 34,* 38–41.

Carbo, M. (1978). Teaching reading with talking books. *The Reading Teacher, 32,* 267–273.

Chall, J. S. (1996). *Stages of reading development.* Orlando, FL: Harcourt, Brace.

Chomsky, C. (1976). After decoding: What? *Language Arts, 53,* 288–296.

Chomsky, C. (1978). When you still can't read in third grade?: After decoding, what? In S. J. Samuels (Ed.), *What research has to say about reading instruction* (pp. 13–30). Newark, DE: International Reading Association.

Cunningham, P.M. (2000). *Phonics they use: Words for reading and writing.* New York: Longman.

Dahl, P. J. (1979). An experimental program for teaching high speed word recognition and comprehension skills. In J. E. Button, T. Lovitt, & R. Rowland (Eds.), *Communication research in learning disabilities and mental retardation* (pp. 33–65). Baltimore: University Park Press.

Dowhower, S. (1989). Repeated reading: Research into practice. *The Reading Teacher,* 42, 502–507.

Dowhower, S. L. (1991). Speaking of prosody: Fluency's unattended bedfellow. *Theory into Practice, 30*(3), 158–164.

Duke, N. (1999). The scarcity of informational texts in first grade. Ann Arbor, MI: Center for the Improvement of Early Reading Achievement (CIERA).

Heckleman, R. G. (1966). Using the neurological impress method of remedial-reading technique. *Academic Therapy, 1,* 235–239.

Heckleman, R. G. (1969). A neurological impress method of remedial-reading instruction. *Academic Therapy, 4,* 277–281.

Henning, K. (1974). Drama reading, an on-going classroom activity at the elementary school level. *Elementary English, 51,* 48–51.

Herman, P. A. (1985). The effect of repeated readings on reading rate, speech pauses, and word recognition accuracy. *Reading Research Quarterly, 20,* 533–564.

Hoffman, J. V., & Isaacs, M. E. (1991). Developing fluency through restructuring the task of guided oral reading. *Theory into Practice, 30,* 185–194.

Hollingsworth, P. M. (1970). An experiment with the impress method of teaching reading. *The Reading Teacher, 24,* 112–114.

Hollingsworth, P. M. (1978). An experimental approach to the impress method of teaching reading. *The Reading Teacher, 31,* 624–626.

Hoyt, Linda (2000). *Snapshots: Literacy minilessons up close.* Portsmouth, NH: Heinemann.

Koskinen, P. S., & Blum, I. H. (1984). Repeated oral reading and the acquisition of fluency. In J. A. Niles & L. A. Harris (Eds.), *Changing perspectives on research in reading/language processing and instruction: Thirty-third yearbook of the National Reading Conference* (pp. 183–187). Rochester, NY: National Reading Conference.

Koskinen, P. S., & Blum, I. H. (1986). Paired repeated reading: A classroom strategy for developing fluent reading. *The Reading Teacher, 40,* 70–75.

Kuhn, M. R. (2000, November). *A comparative study of small group fluency instruction.* Paper presented at the meeting of the National Reading Conference, Scottsdale, AZ

Kuhn, M. R., & Stahl, S. (2000). *Fluency: A review of developmental and remedial strategies.* Ann Arbor, MI: Center for the Improvement of Early Reading Achievement (CIERA).

LaBerge, D., & Samuels, S. (1974). Toward a theory of automatic information processing in reading. *Cognitive Psychology, 6,* 293–323.

NAEP's Oral Reading Fluency Scale. (1995). *Listening to children read aloud, 15.* Washington, DC: U.S. Department of Education, National Center for Education Statistics.

Optiz, M. F., & Rasinski, T. V. (1998). *Good-bye round robin: 25 effective oral reading strategies.* Portsmouth, NH: Heinemann.

O'Shea, L. J., Sindelar, P. T., & O'Shea, D. J. (1985). The effects of repeated readings and attentional cues on reading fluency and comprehension. *Journal of Reading Behavior, 17,* 129–142.

O'Shea, L. J., Sindelar, P. T., & O'Shea, D. J. (1987). The effects of segmenting written discourse on the reading comprehension of low and high performance readers. *Reading Research Quarterly, 18,* 458–465.

Perfetti, C. A. (1985). *Reading ability.* New York: Oxford University Press.

Rashotte, C. A., & Torgesen, J. K. (1985). Repeated reading and reading fluency in learning disabled children. *Reading Research Quarterly, 20,* 180–188.

Rasinski, T. V. (1989). Fluency for everyone: Incorporating fluency instruction in the classroom. *The Reading Teacher, 42,* 690–693

Rasinski, T. V., & Padak, N. D. (1996). Five lessons to increase reading fluency. In L. R. Putnam (Ed.), *How to become a better reading teacher* (pp. 255–265). Englewood Cliffs, NJ: Merrill.

Rasinski, T. V., & Padak, N. D. (2001). *From phonics to fluency: Effective teaching of decoding and reading fluency in the elementary school.* New York: Addison-Wesley Longman.

Reutzel, D. R. (1996). Developing at-risk readers' oral reading fluency. In L.R. Putnam (Ed.), *How to become a better reading teacher* (pp. 241–254). Englewood Cliffs, NJ: Merrill.

Samuels, S. (1979). The method of repeated reading. *The Reading Teacher, 32,* 403–408.

Schreiber, P. A. (1991). Understanding prosody's role in reading acquisition. *Theory into Practice, 30,* 158–164.

Stahl, S. A., Heubach, K., & Cramond, B. (1997). *Fluency- oriented reading instruction.* Reading Research Report No. 79. Athens, GA: National Reading Research Center.

Stanovich, K. E. (1980). Toward an interactive-compensatory model of individual differences in the development of reading fluency. *Reading Research Quarterly, 21,* 360–407.

Vygotsky, L. S. (1978). *Mind in society: The development of higher psychological processes.* Cambridge, MA: Harvard University Press.

Weinstein, G., & Cooke, N. L. (1992). The effects of two repeated reading interventions on generalization of fluency. *Learning Disability Quarterly, 15,* 21–28.

Zutell, J., & Rasinski, T. V. (1991). Training teachers to attend to their students' oral reading fluency. *Theory into Practice, 30,* 211–217.

13

Bridging the Gap between Learning to Read and Reading to Learn

NELL K. DUKE
V. SUSAN BENNETT-ARMISTEAD
EBONY M. ROBERTS

In this chapter we argue that a critical responsibility for early literacy education is to bridge the gap between learning to read and reading to learn. The traditional separation of learning to read, in grades pre-K–3, and reading to learn, in grades 4 and up, may aptly *describe* what happens to children in American schooling, but it does not *justify* it. Extant research does not support this separation and, to the contrary, there are a number of arguments against it.

Our discussion centers on informational texts. Although it is certainly possible to read to learn texts that are not informational (for example, one can read to learn about fairy tales by reading fairy tales), informational texts are primary texts for reading to learn. It is difficult to imagine a read-to-learn classroom (or for that matter, we argue, a comprehensive learn-to-read classroom) that does not include informational text.

The chapter is organized around three key points:

- Informational text is scarce in primary grade classrooms.
- Available research does not justify the scarcity of informational text in primary grade or other early childhood classrooms.
- There are a number of arguments for greater attention to informational text in early childhood classrooms, although more research is certainly needed.

We discuss research relevant to each of these points, and conclude with suggestions for instructional leaders in this area.

SCARCITY OF INFORMATIONAL TEXT

Data from several different sources converge on the point that informational text is scarce in primary grade classrooms. One such source of data is the analyses of the text genres represented in basal reading series. The proportions we found reported in studies within the last two decades ranged from a high of 33.8% factual articles[1] in eight basal reading series for grade 2 (Schmidt, Caul, Byers, & Buchman, 1984) to a low of 12% nonfiction in five basal reading series for grade 1 (Hoffman et al., 1994). In the most recent analysis of which we are aware, Moss and Newton (1998) examined six grade-2 basal reading series copyright 1995 to 1997. They found a mean of 16% of selections that could be classified as informational literature.

One study (Flood & Lapp, 1986) examined the presence of expository text in three standardized reading tests, as well as in the tests and materials from basal reading programs (K–6). Flood and Lapp (1986) found that 38% of the selections in the standardized reading tests were expository (not reported by grade level), as compared with 16% of the selections in the basal readers and 38% of the selections in basal tests. The authors note the considerable discontinuity between the genres included in the basal readers themselves and the genres included in the tests children will take.

Another source of data regarding the scarcity of informational text in the primary grades are surveys about the presence or absence of informational text in primary grade classrooms. In a recent survey of 126 primary grade teachers, Yopp and Yopp (2000) found that only 14% of materials primary grade teachers reported reading aloud on a given day were informational. A survey of 83 primary grade teachers conducted by Pressley, Rankin, and Yokoi (1996) indicated that only 6% of material read throughout the school day (not only read aloud) was expository. Notably, the latter sample was composed particularly of primary grade teachers nominated by language arts supervisors as the most effective in their jurisdictions. It is possible that such teachers use more or less expository text than a more typical group of primary grade teachers.

Direct classroom observation has also been used as a source of data about the amount of informational text experience offered to children in

---

[1]A version of this chapter appears in Duke, N. K., Bennett-Armistead, V. S., & Roberts, E. M. (2002). Copyright 2002 by the International Reading Association. Reprinted by permission.

early schooling. Kamberelis (1998) observed all assigned and self-selected reading and writing in three classrooms, one in each grade K–2, for a 4-month period. He found that science reports/books were read by the children far less often than stories and were also far less often the genre of assigned classroom writing. In raw terms, fewer than 20 science reports/ books were used in language arts instruction in each classroom; fewer than 10 science reports/books were assigned for writing. Duke (2000) conducted an observational study of 20 first-grade classrooms in both low- and high-socioeconomic-status (SES) school districts. The study revealed a scarcity of informational text not only in classroom written language activities, but also in classroom libraries and on classroom walls and other surfaces. Informational text was particularly scarce in classrooms in the low-SES school districts studied.

Notably, evidence suggests that informational text has not always been so scarce in primary grade classrooms. On the contrary, analyses of reading materials available to young children throughout the history of American literacy instruction indicate that at some points in time informational text has enjoyed some prominence. The first such period occurred at and around the birth of the nation in 1776. Until this time, children's readers in this country contained primarily religious selections. After the American Revolution, readers included many selections intended to emphasize national pride, unification, and citizenship. Some informational selections were included for the purpose of instructing children about their environment, affairs of the state, and the workings of the new government (Smith, 1986).

With the rise of industrialism and the perceived link between education and worker productivity (*Fifth Annual Report*, 1842), instructional materials included more informational text. By 1870, McGuffey readers not only offered many childhood stories but also included nature-based text and histories (Venezky, 1982). An examination of a midcentury reader, Wilson's *School and Family* series, shows a heavy emphasis on informational text (Smith, 1986). Moralistic, character-building stories were also prevalent, but attention to scientific study in particular is evident.

By the end of the 19th century, however, the tide turned away from inclusion of informational texts in instructional materials in reading. As part of a set of reforms intended to prompt a return to classicism, Charles Eliot, then president of Harvard University, called for the elimination of readers in favor of *real literature*. Eliot argued that children should be exposed to quality materials rather than watered-down offerings in readers. This influence, more than any other, shifted early reading materials toward narrative literature and away from expository text. The desire to appeal to the child's imagination became a driving force in textbook publishing (Venezky,

1982). By the 1920s, narrative, particularly realistic narrative, held abso-
lute dominance in materials for reading instruction. Smith's (1986) analysis
of 10 popular primers published in the 1920s shows that more than 80%
of the pages were devoted to realistic fictional narrative; no pages were devoted to informational text.

Informational text never regained its foothold in emergent reading instruction in the 20th century, although it did enjoy fleeting periods of increased interest during this period. The Activity Movement of the 1930s led
to a significant focus of attention on factual materials in some schools
(Smith, 1986); after the first World War there was a brief emphasis on content reading throughout schooling (Venezky, 1982); and between 1950 and
1962 the *Developmental Reading Series* published by Bond and Fay broke
from its peers in including attention to a wide variety of genres. But beyond
limited exceptions such as these, informational text has remained rare in
materials used for reading instruction.

AVAILABLE RESEARCH DOES NOT JUSTIFY
THE SCARCITY OF INFORMATIONAL TEXT

At least three beliefs seem to underlie inattention to informational text in
primary grade or other early childhood classrooms—that young children
cannot handle informational text, that young children do not like informational text, and that young children should first learn to read and then (at
about fourth grade) read to learn. In this section we demonstrate that none
of these beliefs is supported by available research in this area.

Unsupported Belief 1: Young Children Cannot Handle Informational Text

The first unsupported belief is that young children cannot handle informational text, that narrative genres are the primary, if not the only, means by
which young children can understand and communicate in the world
around them. This view has certainly been held by a number of researchers
and theorists (e.g., Britton, Burgess, Martin, McLeod, & Rosen, 1975;
Egan, 1986, 1993; Moffett, 1968; Sawyer & Watson, 1987). The extent to
which it is held by classroom teachers, publishers, or other groups has not
been well documented, though it perhaps can be inferred by the textual
choices made by these groups.

We could locate no research to support the assertion that young children are unable to handle informational text, nor could we find evidence in
support of the primacy of narrative genres for young children. However, we
located several studies offering evidence that young children *can* learn from
and about informational text if given opportunities to interact with such

forms. In a landmark study in this area, Pappas (1991a, 1991b, 1993) asked kindergarten-aged children, on three occasions, to pretend to read information books and storybooks that had been read to them immediately before. For both the information books and the storybooks, children's pretend readings showed increasing similarity to the books read to them in terms of a number of language features. This suggested that the children were able to learn about information book language, given exposure to informational texts.

In a related study, Duke and Kays (1998) asked kindergarten-aged children to pretend to read an unfamiliar information book before and after a 3-month period of exposure to other information books through teacher read-aloud. Children's pretend readings on the second occasion reflected greater knowledge of several important features of informational text, such as the use of timeless-present-tense verb constructions and generic noun structures (*Firefighters fight fires* versus *The firefighter is fighting a fire*). Again, these results suggest that young children can learn the language of informational text and reflect that knowledge in a pretend reading context.

Some data from the Duke and Kays (1998) study and a study by Moss (1997) suggest that young children can learn content, as well as language, from informational texts. In the Duke and Kays study, children reflected content knowledge derived from informational texts in their journals. For example, after hearing the book *Potato* (Watts, 1988) read aloud, one child drew a detailed picture of a potato plant sprouting and explained the process in some depth. After hearing the book *Earthworm* (Soutter-Perrot, 1993), another child drew a picture of earthworms, depicting the segmented structure of their bodies. Characteristics of all-terrain vehicles, facts about spiders and their prey, and different types of ocean animals are other examples of the content found in children's journals following information book read-alouds. In another study, Moss examined first grade children's retellings of an informational text (Selsam, 1973) read to them. Eighteen of the 20 first graders she studied produced retellings scoring 3 or higher (out of 5) on a modified version of the Richness of Retelling Scale (Irwin & Mitchell, 1983). Again, young children appeared to learn content from informational texts.

Newkirk's (1987, 1989) work attests to young children's ability to write informational texts. He documented that young children can produce emergent, as well as more fully formed, informational texts in both home and school contexts, and often do so spontaneously. For example, a first grader wrote:

> This is plutowe. It is the frthest planit away fam the sun. They thought it was nata [neptune's] mon but it wasn.

This is natoon. It is the sakint fwst [second farthest] planet away from the sun.

This is satrne it has 10 mos [moons] and it has most rens [rings] in the solarsistm. (Newkirk, 1987, p. 133)

Sowers (1981) reports a similar finding in a study of first-grade children's writing. However, at least one other study of first-grade children's writing (Chapman, 1994, 1995) found no examples of spontaneous informational writing in the context of writing situations in which students had significant choice about what they wrote. Chapman argues that this can be explained by characteristics of the particular classroom she studied, which focused heavily on personal and imaginative writing, rather than by any inability of the children to produce informational texts.

Work of Kamberelis and his colleagues (Kamberelis, 1998, 1999; Kamberelis & Bovino, 1999) also documents relationships between children's classroom contexts and the extent and quality of their informational writing. He found that children write what they read, that there is a strong relationship between the types of text to which children were exposed at home and at school and their genre knowledge. Children in his study were exposed to a great deal more narrative discourse and meta-discourse than informational or poetic discourse, and, indeed, Kamberelis contends, their ability to write informational (and poetic) text was not as well developed as their ability to write narrative forms. However, it is notable that some kindergarten and most first-grade children were nonetheless able to write texts with features characteristic of informational text. Similarly, a study of four first graders' writing in Family Message Journals indicates that they were able to write informational text, as well as other nonnarrative genres, around science topics (Wollman-Bonilla, 2000).

Korkeamaki, Tiainen, and Dreher (1998) examined not only children's ability to write informational text but also their ability to conduct research with that text—that is, to use informational text to find out about something and then represent their findings in writing. The second graders studied were taught strategies for using informational text in research and were given authentic purposes for applying these strategies to research and write their own informational texts. In this context all but one of the seven focus students studied were able to use the strategies to research and then write informational text.

Studies examining children's discussions around informational text also suggest that they are capable of interacting successfully with such texts. Hicks (1995) documented the ways in which children in first grade participated in sophisticated discussions of informational text in the context of a classroom that included many texts in this genre. Oyler and Barry (1996) showed how students in a first-grade classroom initiated intertextual connections among information books when given opportunity to do so. Donovan (1996) examined first-grade children's ability to talk metalinguistically about informational texts (as well as narratives). She found that these children, who had been in a classroom that included regular exposure to and instruction in both informational and narrative forms, had significant metalinguistic knowledge about informational text, knowledge comparable to that which they held in regard to narrative text. In a particularly compelling case, Maduram (2000) documented remarkably complex responses to informational texts by her daughter beginning at age 3. For example, after hearing several books about dinosaurs, she wondered aloud about the concept of extinction: "People don't know why they died. Where they died, their bones are there" and later "Why are they dead? Maybe lions ate them. . . . Who let them die? Dinosaur drank a lot of water and died" (age 3 years, 11 months).

Another source of data regarding young children's ability to interact with informational text is teachers' own reports. Several teachers have published accounts of using informational text in their early childhood classrooms (e.g., Dalton & Mallett, 1995; Duthie, 1994, 1996; Fisher, 1994; Guillaume, 1998; Kamil & Lane, 1997a, 1997b; Read, 2001; Smith, 1992). Although these accounts differ substantially in their scope and focus, all indicate that students were successful with, and indeed benefited from, inclusion of informational text in the classroom.

Unsupported Belief 2: Young Children Do Not Like Informational Text, or at Least Prefer Other Forms of Text

A second unsupported belief that may underlie inattention to informational text in early literacy is that, whether or not they can handle informational texts, young children do not like them, or at least prefer other genres. One piece of evidence indicating that this belief exists was provided in a study by Kletzien and Szabo (1998). As part of this study the researchers asked six teachers in grades 1 through 3 to predict which text their students would prefer to read between forced choices clearly reflective of informational and narrative genres, such as "All About Soccer" (informational) and "Chris Makes the Team" (narrative). The teachers in the study predicted that their students would prefer the narrative titles much of the time, yet in actuality the students preferred the informational titles at least half the time (see later discussion). Just how widespread this belief is, however, is not well established in the existing research literature.

Available evidence does not support the notion that young children do not like informational text or even that they prefer other text forms. In most cases, available research simply is not relevant to the question.

For example, many of the studies on reading interests and preferences have not included young (pre-K–2) children, and many have investigated preferences for particular topics, rather than genres (Monson & Sebesta, 1991). (Genre preferences cannot be easily inferred from topic preferences—books about animals, for example, can be narrative or informational in form.)

Of the studies that have investigated genre preferences among pre-K–2 children, results are mixed. Robinson, Larsen, Haupt, and Mohlman (1997) found that kindergarten and prekindergarten children chose modern and traditional fantasy narrative more often than informational text when given the option of several different genres of text. But Kletzien and Szabo (1998) found that grades 1–3 children preferred information books at least as often as narratives, with boys generally choosing information books more often than girls. The variation in these and other studies of reading preferences may be explained by a host of factors, including differences in methodologies used, age of subjects, consideration or lack of consideration of gender effects, subjects' familiarity or lack of familiarity with the texts assessed, and so on (see Kletzien, 1999, for a review).

A study by Horowitz and Freeman (1995) suggests that the ways in which texts are used in the classrooms studied may have an impact on children's attitudes toward them. In their study, a second-grade class, in which discussion followed a read-aloud, preferred an informational science book to a narrative science book; in a second-grade class with no discussion following the read-aloud, the narrative science book was preferred. As discussed in the previous section, research on children's writing also suggests that classroom context impacts genre preferences.

As the reader may have inferred, an equal or greater preference for informational texts is consistently reported among the single-case and single-classroom accounts of children's interactions with informational text reviewed in this chapter (e.g., Caswell & Duke, 1998; Kamil & Lane, 1997a, 1997b; Pappas, 1991a, 1991b, 1993). However, this finding may reflect a selection bias in that the studies reviewed all focused, at least in part, on informational text. It is possible that a review of single-case and single-classroom accounts of children's interactions with narrative text would show different preferences. What we can be reasonably sure of is that there are at least some children who greatly prefer informational texts, some who greatly prefer narrative genres, and many who do not have clear genre preferences. Indeed, of just twelve 8-year-old children studied by Cooper (1995), three said they chose to read nonfiction almost exclusively, five said they read mainly fiction, and the remaining four said they had no preference. Neither the belief that young children universally prefer narrative texts, nor that they universally prefer informational forms, is supported by extant research literature.

Unsupported Belief 3: Young Children Should First Learn to Read and Then (at about Fourth Grade) Read to Learn

The two unsupported beliefs discussed previously may feed into a third un-supported belief—that children must learn to read before they can read to learn. To our knowledge, the popular articulation of this belief derives from Jeanne Chall's (1983) classic work *Stages of Reading Development.* How-ever, the intent in Chall's work was more to *describe* the stages children go through in reading development than to argue that these are the stages chil-dren *should* go through in reading development. There may be an empirical basis for *describing* stages of reading development as such—as discussed earlier in this chapter, at the time of Chall's writing, as now, informational text was scarce among beginning reading materials—but there is no empiri-cal basis for saying that it therefore *should* be such. That is, there are no studies demonstrating that providing students with opportunities to read to learn prior to grade 4 negatively impact their reading development, or that waiting to do so until grade 4 positively impacts it.

Just as there is no research supporting a learn-to-read-then-read-to-learn sequence, there is little research supporting an alternative model. That is, we have little research demonstrating that providing students with op-portunities to read to learn prior to grade 4 positively impacts their reading development. There is one study (Kamil & Lane, 1997a, 1997b) of three first-grade classes and then one continuing-to-second-grade class (all taught by the same teacher) for which roughly half of the literacy instruction was conducted using informational text. The authors concluded that these students made normal or above average progress and that it is not only possible but desirable to teach students at the first-grade level about infor-mational text genres, features, and uses. Although this does provide evi-dence relevant to Unsupported Belief 1 (that is, it suggests that it is at least possible for young children to develop as readers in the context of both in-formational and other genres of text), it does not tell us whether these chil-dren, with this teacher, would have had greater, or lesser, reading achieve-ment without the informational text, or how generalizable the findings in this case study would be to other classes and settings. We are ourselves cur-rently conducting a large-scale experimental study of the impact of diversi-fying the genres that children read and write in grades 1 and 2 to include more informational text, but results of the study are not yet available. Thus, at this time we can only make educated guesses about the long-term impact of providing young children with opportunities to read to learn. We discuss the basis of some of those guesses in the following section.

ARGUING FOR GREATER ATTENTION TO INFORMATIONAL TEXT IN EARLY LITERACY

In the absence of studies assessing the long-term impact of including informational text in early literacy, scholars have drawn on evidence of other kinds to argue for such inclusion. Many of these arguments have been reviewed elsewhere (e.g., Caswell & Duke, 1998; Dreher, 2000; Duke, 2001), so we discuss them only briefly here.

The most obvious argument for greater attention to informational text in early literacy is that it will make children better readers and writers of informational text (e.g. Christie, 1984, 1987). Fundamental to this argument is the supposition that more and earlier exposure to informational text will result in greater abilities to read and write informational text (Duke, 2000). Studies in which children's knowledge of informational text has appeared to develop following exposure (e.g., Duke & Kays, 1998; Pappas, 1993) seem to support this supposition, as do general patterns in which children seem to read and write better those forms of text to which they have had ongoing exposure (e.g., Kamberelis, 1998; Purcell-Gates, 1988; Purcell-Gates, McIntyre, & Freppon, 1995). Sometimes cited along with this argument are statistics on American students' relatively poor informational reading and writing abilities, coupled with the relatively important role of informational literacies in American society (e.g., Duke, 1999; Moss, Leone, & DiPillo, 1997).

A cluster of arguments for greater attention to informational text focus on other types of knowledge and skills that may help to develop, in particular content area knowledge, vocabulary, and comprehension (e.g., Dreher, 2000; Guillaume, 1998). In regard to content area knowledge, as discussed earlier in this chapter, there is some limited evidence that young children can learn about the world around them through informational texts. Certainly among older children there is a relationship between informational reading and writing abilities and content area achievement (e.g., Bernhardt, Destino, Kamil, & Rodriguez-Munoz, 1995). Specialized vocabulary is a key feature of informational text (e.g., Duke & Kays, 1998), and there is evidence that even young children do learn vocabulary from text, including text read aloud (e.g., Elley, 1989). Studies showing that teachers and/or parents attend more to vocabulary and comprehension when interacting with children around informational texts seem to buttress the claim that informational text has vocabulary-building potential, and they also raise the possibility that general comprehension skills may be further developed through these texts (Lennox, 1995; Pellegrini, Perlmutter, Galda, & Brody, 1990; Smolkin & Donovan, 2000).

Taking the skill-building arguments one step further are those who suggest that greater attention to informational text early on may indeed buttress overall literacy development. The datum most often cited in support of this argument comes from results of the National Assessment of Educational Progress (NAEP). Results showed that fourth-grade children who report reading storybooks, magazines, and nonfiction had, on average, higher reading achievement than children who reported reading only two of these types, who in turn had higher achievement than children who reported reading only one. The interpretation (e.g., Dreher, 1998/1999) is that reading a greater variety of texts may make one a better overall reader or writer (note, however, that it is not possible to establish causality on the basis of these data).

A number of mechanisms have been suggested by which informational text may buttress overall literacy development. One relates to the notion discussed previously, that informational text may build background knowledge, vocabulary, and comprehension skills, which may, in turn, support reading of all kinds. A second relates to interest. It appears that at least some children have high levels of interest in informational texts or topics addressed therein. For those children, the presence of informational text in the classroom may be motivating. That motivation, in turn, may encourage children to read more or to read more productively (e.g., Caswell & Duke, 1998). A third possible mechanism by which informational text may support overall literacy development relates to home literacies. Informational text is read widely outside of schools (Venezky, 1982). The presence of informational text in early schooling may help children make links between home and school literacies and develop a more comprehensive understanding of what counts as literacy (see Duke, 2001, for further discussion). This may be particularly important for children from homes in which narrative reading or writing in not common (e.g., Caswell & Duke, 1998).

SUGGESTIONS FOR INSTRUCTIONAL LEADERS

Although arguments for including informational text in early literacy have much to recommend them, there has yet to be a large-scale evaluation of the impact of actually doing this. Our best guess at this time is that incorporating informational text in early literacy education will not harm, and will likely be beneficial, to young learners. Thus, we suggest that instructional leaders proceed, albeit provisionally, with encouraging greater attention to informational text in their schools and classrooms.

An important next question arises as to the particular instructional techniques or approaches to using informational text in early childhood classrooms that have been shown to be effective. Again, there is considerably more research needed. However, we can make some general recommendations informed by the research reviewed earlier in this chapter. We suggest incorporating informational texts into the following instructional routines in early childhood classrooms:

- *Read-aloud.* Studies suggest that young children learn language and content from informational texts read aloud to them (Duke & Kays, 1998; Moss, 1997; Pappas, 1991a, 1991b, 1993). A number of resources list informational texts that are appropriate and appealing for read-aloud in early childhood settings (e.g., Bamford & Kristo, 1998; Camp, 2000; Reese & Harris, 1997).
- *Independent reading.* Some studies suggest that some children prefer to read informational texts (e.g., Cooper, 1995; Kletzien & Szabo, 1998) and that capitalizing on children's reading preferences may have a number of benefits (Caswell & Duke, 1998). Research by Dreher and Dromsky (2000) suggests that independent reading of informational texts can be encouraged by making a significant proportion of informational texts available to children in their classroom libraries and by including these books in read-aloud. Under such circumstances, second graders in their study ended up selecting informational texts for independent reading about half the time.
- *Writing.* Studies have shown that young children can write informational and emergent informational forms if given the opportunity. This result appears to pertain to writing tasks with assigned topics (Kamberelis, 1998, 1999; Kamberelis & Bovino, 1999), as well as to journaling (Duke & Kays, 1998; Wollman-Bonilla, 2000) and writers workshop contexts (Chapman, 1994, 1995; Newkirk, 1987, 1989).
- *Research.* Research by Korkeamaki and colleagues (1998) suggests that given appropriate instruction and scaffolding, second-grade children can engage in research using informational texts as a source of data and information. Cudd and Roberts (1989) and Lewis, Wray, and Rospigiliosi (1994), among others, provide classroom-tested suggestions for helping young children engage in research with informational text.
- *Discussion and response.* Several studies suggest that discussion around informational text can also be included in early childhood classrooms. Children in Hicks's (1995) research engaged in discussion, interweaving hands-on experiences and informational texts, on a science topic (for further discussion of the interplay of hands-on experiences and texts in science, see Palincsar & Magnusson, 2000). Children in the Oyler and Barry (1996) study made connections and comparisons between different informational texts. Children in Donovan's (1996) research engaged in explicit talk about informational texts and how they differ from storybooks.

Although more work is needed, there are resources currently available to provide further guidance in incorporating informational texts in early childhood classrooms. In addition to the references cited in the preceding list, there are published accounts by teachers who have used informational text in their classrooms (Dalton & Mallett, 1995; Duthie, 1994, 1996; Fisher, 1994; Guillaume, 1998; Kamil & Lane, 1997a, 1997b; Read, 2001; Smith, 1992) as well as books focusing on a broader range of different genres (e.g., Green, 1992; Derewianka, 1990; Jan, 1991; Littlefair, 1991). Whatever your resources, a commitment to providing young children with the opportunity to read to learn, as well as learn to read, constitutes an important part of early literacy education.

ACKNOWLEDGMENT

A portion of this work was supported under the Education Research and Development Centers Program (PR/Award No. R305R70004), as administered by the Office of Educational Research and Improvement, U.S. Department of Education. However, the contents do not necessarily represent the positions or policies of the National Institute on Student Achievement, Curriculum, and Assessment, the National Institute on Early Childhood Development, or the U.S. Department of Education, and you should not assume endorsement by the U.S. government.

REFERENCES

Bamford, R. A., & Kristo, J. V. (1998). *Making facts come alive: Choosing quality nonfiction literature K–8*. Norwood, MA: Christopher-Gordon.

Bernhardt, E., Destino, T., Kamil, M., & Rodriguez-Munoz, M. (1995). Assessing science knowledge in an English/Spanish bilingual elementary school. *Cognosos, 4*, 4–6.

Britton, J., Burgess, T., Martin, N., McLeod, A., & Rosen, H. (1975). *The development of writing abilities*. London: Macmillan.

Camp, D. (2000). It takes two: Teaching with twin texts of fiction and nonfiction. *The Reading Teacher, 53*, 400–408.

Caswell, L. J., & Duke, N. K. (1998). Non-narrative as a catalyst for literacy development. *Language Arts, 75*, 108–117.

Chall, J. S. (1983). *Stages of reading development*. New York: McGraw-Hill.

Chapman, M. L. (1994). The emergence of genres: Some findings from an examination of first-grade writing. *Written Communication, 11*, 348–380.

Chapman, M. L. (1995). The sociocognitive construction of written genres in first grade. *Research in the Teaching of English, 29*, 164–192.

Christie, F. (1984). Young children's writing development: The relationship of written genres to curriculum genres. In B. Bartlett & J. Carr (Eds.), *Language in Education conference: A report of proceedings* (pp. 41–69). Brisbane, CAE, Australia: Mt. Gravatt Campus.

Christie, F. (1987). Factual writing in the first years of school. *Australian Journal of Reading, 10,* 207–216.

Cooper J. (1995). Children reading non-fiction for pleasure. *Reading, 29,* 15–21.

Cudd, E. T., & Roberts, L. (1989). Using writing to enhance content area learning in the primary grades. *The Reading Teacher, 42,* 392–404.

Dalton, J., & Mallett, M. (1995). Six year olds read about fire-fighters. *Reading, 29,* 22–25.

Derewianka, B. (1990). *Exploring how texts work.* Rozelle, NSW, Australia: Primary English Teaching Association.

Donovan, C. A. (1996). First graders' impressions of genre-specific elements in writing narrative and expository texts. In D. J. Leu, C. K. Kinzer, & K. A. Hinchman (Eds.), *Literacies for the 21st century: Forty-fifth yearbook of the National Reading Conference* (pp. 183–194). Chicago: National Reading Conference.

Dreher, M. J. (1998/1999). Motivating children to read more nonfiction. *The Reading Teacher, 42,* 414–417.

Dreher, M. J. (2000). Fostering reading for learning. In L. Baker, M. J. Dreher, & J. T. Guthrie (Eds.), *Engaging young readers: Promoting achievement and motivation* (pp. 94–118). New York: Guilford Press.

Dreher, M. J., & Dromsky, A. (2000, December). *Increasing the diversity of young children's independent reading.* Paper presented at the National Reading Conference, Scottsdale, AZ.

Duke, N. K. (1999). *Using non-fiction to increase reading achievement and world knowledge.* Occasional paper of the Scholastic Center for Literacy and Learning, New York.

Duke, N. K. (2000). 3.6 minutes per day: The scarcity of informational texts in first grade. *Reading Research Quarterly, 35,* 202–224.

Duke, N. K. (2001, March). *Reading to learn from the very beginning: Informational literacy in early childhood.* Paper presented in the Early Literacy Instruction for Children At Risk: Research-Based Solutions conference, Ann Arbor, MI.

Duke, N. K., Bennett-Armistead, V. S., & Roberts, E. M. (2002). Incorporating informational text in the primary grades. In C. M. Roller (Ed.), *Comprehensive reading instruction across the grade levels* (pp. 40–54). Newark, DE: International Reading Association.

Duke, N. K., & Kays, J. (1998). "Can I say 'once upon a time'?": Kindergarten children developing knowledge of information book language. *Early Childhood Research Quarterly, 13,* 295–318.

Duthie, C. (1994). Nonfiction: A genre study for the primary classroom. *Language Arts, 71,* 588–595.

Duthie, C. (1996). *True stories: Nonfiction literacy in the primary classroom.* York, ME: Stenhouse.

Egan, K. (1986). *Teaching as storytelling.* Chicago: University of Chicago Press.

Egan, K. (1993). Narrative and learning: A voyage of implications. *Linguistics and Education, 5,* 119–126.

Elley, W. B. (1989). Vocabulary acquisition from listening to stories. *Reading Research Quarterly, 24,* 174–187.

Fifth Annual Report of the Secretary to the Board of Education of Massachusetts. (1842). (Testimony of Horace Mann.)

Fisher, B. (1994). Writing information books in first grade. *Teaching PreK–8, 25*(3), 73–75.

Flood, J., & Lapp, D. (1986). Types of text: The match between what students read in basals and what they encounter in tests. *Reading Research Quarterly, 21,* 284–297.

Green, P. (1992). *A matter of fact: Using factual texts in the classroom.* Armadale, Victoria, Australia: Eleanor Curtain Publishing.

Guillaume, A. M. (1998). Learning with text in the primary grades. *The Reading Teacher, 51,* 476–486.

Hicks, D. (1995). The social origins of essayist writing. *Bulletin Suisse de Linguistique Appliqué, 61,* 61–82.

Hoffman, J. V., McCarthey, S. J., Abbott, J., Christian, C., Corman, L., Curry, C., Dressman, M., Elliott, B., Matherne, D., & Stahle, D. (1994). So what's new in the new basals? A focus on first grade. *Journal of Reading Behavior, 26,* 47–73.

Horowitz, R., & Freeman, S. H. (1995). Robots versus spaceships: The role of discussion in kindergartners' and second graders' preferences for science text. *The Reading Teacher, 49,* 30–40.

Irwin, P. A., & Mitchell, J. N. (1983). A procedure for assessing the richness of retellings. *Journal of Reading, 26,* 391–396.

Jan, L. W. (1991). *Write ways: Modelling writing forms.* Melbourne, Australia: Oxford University Press.

Kamberelis, G. (1998). Relations between children's literacy diets and genre development: You write what you read. *Literacy Teaching and Learning, 3,* 7– 53.

Kamberelis, G. (1999). Genre development and learning: Children writing stories, science reports, and poems. *Research in the Teaching of English, 33,* 403–460.

Kamberelis, G., & Bovino, T. D. (1999). Cultural artifacts as scaffolds for genre development. *Reading Research Quarterly, 34,* 138–170.

Kamil, M. L., & Lane, D. (1997a, March). *A classroom study of the efficacy of using information text for first-grade reading instruction* [Online]. Paper presented at the annual meeting of the American Educational Research Association, Chicago. Available: http://www-leland.stanford.edu/~mkamil/Aera97

Kamil, M. L., & Lane, D. (1997b, December). *Using information text for first grade reading instruction: Theory and practice* [Online]. Paper presented at the annual meeting of the National Reading Conference, Scottsdale, AZ. Available: http://www.stanford.edu/~mkamil/nrc97b.htm

Kletzien, S. B. (1999, December). *Children's reading preferences and information books.* Paper presented at the National Reading Conference, Orlando, FL.

Kletzien, S. B., & Szabo, R. J. (1998, December). *Information text or narrative text? Children's preferences revisited.* Paper presented at the National Reading Conference, Austin, TX.

Korkeamaki, R., Tiainen, O., & Dreher, M. J. (1998). Helping Finnish second graders make sense of their reading and writing in their science project. *National Reading Conference Yearbook, 47,* 334–344.

Lennox, S. (1995). Sharing books with children. *Australian Journal of Early Childhood, 20*, 12–16.

Lewis, M., Wray, D., & Rospigiliosi, P. (1994). " . . . And I want it in your own words." *The Reading Teacher, 47*, 528–536.

Littlefair, A. B. (1991). *Reading all types of writing: The importance of genre and register for reading development*. Milton Keynes, UK: Open University Press.

Maduram, I. (2000). "Playing possum": A young child's responses to information books. *Language Arts, 77*, 391–397.

Moffett, J. (1968). *Teaching the universe of discourse*. Boston: Houghton Mifflin.

Monson, D. L. & Sebesta, S. (1991). Reading preferences. In J. Flood, J. M. Jensen, D. Lapp, & J. R. Squire (Eds.), *Handbook of research on teaching the English language arts* (pp. 664–673). New York: Macmillan.

Moss, B. (1997). A qualitative assessment of first graders' retelling of expository text. *Reading Research and Instruction, 37*, 1–13.

Moss, B., Leone, S., & DiPillo, M. L. (1997). Exploring the literature of fact: Linking reading and writing through information trade books. *Language Arts, 74*, 418–429.

Moss, B., & Newton, E. (1998, December). *An examination of the informational text genre in recent basal readers*. Paper presented at the National Reading Conference, Austin, TX.

Newkirk, T. (1987). The non-narrative writing of young children. *Research in the Teaching of English, 21*, 121–144.

Newkirk, T. (1989). *More than stories: The range of children's writing*. Portsmouth, NH: Heinemann.

Oyler, C., & Barry, A. (1996). Intertextual connections in read-alouds of information books. *Language Arts, 73*, 324–329.

Palincsar, A. S., & Magnusson, S. J. (2000). *The interplay of firsthand and text-based investigations in science education*. (Report No. 2-007). Ann Arbor, MI: Center for the Improvement of Early Reading Achievement.

Pappas, C. C. (1991a). Fostering full access to literacy by including information books. *Language Arts, 68*, 449–462.

Pappas, C. C. (1991b). Young children's strategies in learning the "book language" of information books. *Discourse Processes, 14*, 203–225.

Pappas, C. C. (1993). Is narrative "primary"? Some insights from kindergartners' pretend readings of stories and information books. *Journal of Reading Behavior, 25*, 97–129.

Pelligrini, A. D., Perlmutter, J. C., Galda, L., & Brody, G. H. (1990). Joint reading between black Head Start children and their mothers. *Child Development, 61*, 443–453.

Pressley, M., Rankin, J., & Yokoi, L. (1996). A survey of instructional practices of primary teachers nominated as effective in promoting literacy. *Elementary School Journal, 96*, 363–384.

Purcell-Gates, V. (1988). Lexical and syntactic knowledge of written narrative held by well-read-to kindergartners and second graders. *Research in the Teaching of English, 22*, 128–160.

Purcell-Gates, V., McIntyre, E., & Freppon, P. (1995). Learning written storybook language in school: A comparison of low-SES children in skills-based and whole language classrooms. *American Educational Research Journal, 32*, 659–685.

Read, S. (2001). "Kid mice hunt for their selfs": First and second graders writing research. *Language Arts, 78,* 333–342.

Reese, D. A., & Harris, V. J. (1997). "Look at this nest!" The beauty and power of using informational books with young children. *Early Child Development and Care, 127–128,* 217–231.

Robinson, C. C., Larsen, J. M., Haupt, J. H., & Mohlman, J. (1997). Picture book selection behaviors of emergent readers: Influence of genre, familiarity, and book attributes. *Reading Research and Instruction, 36,* 287–304.

Sawyer, W., & Watson, K. (1987). Questions of genre. In I. Reid (Ed.), *The place of genre in learning: current debates* (pp. 46–57). Geelong, Victoria, Australia: Deakin University, Centre for Studies in Literary Education.

Schmidt, W. H., Caul, J., Byers, J. L., & Buchmann, M. (1984). Content of basal selections: Implications for comprehension instruction. In G. G. Duffy, L. R. Roehler, & J. Mason (Eds.), *Comprehension instruction: Perspectives and suggestions* (pp. 144–162). New York: Longman.

Selsam, M. (1973). *How kittens grow.* New York: Scholastic.

Smith, F. (1992). Reading the bear facts: Information books and learning in the primary classroom. *English in Education, 26,* 17–25.

Smith, N. B. (1986). *American reading instruction.* Newark, DE: International Reading Association.

Smolkin, L. B., & Donovan, C. A. (2000). *The contexts of comprehension: Information book read alouds and comprehension acquisition.* (Report No. 2-009). Ann Arbor, MI: Center for the Improvement of Early Reading Achievement.

Soutter-Perrot, A. (1993). *Earthworm.* Mankam, MN: Creative Editions.

Sowers, S. (1981). *A case study observing the development of primary children's composing, spelling, and motor behaviors during the writing process.* Washington, DC: National Institute of Education, U.S. Department of Education. (ERIC Document Reproduction Service No. 218653)

Venezky, R. L. (1982). The origins of the present day chasm between adult literacy needs and school literacy instruction. *Visible Language, 16,* 112–127.

Watts, B. (1988). *Potato.* Englewood Cliffs, NJ: Silver Burdett Press.

Wollman-Bonilla, J. E. (2000). Teaching science writing to first graders: Genre learning and recontextualization. *Research in the Teaching of English, 35,* 35–65.

Yopp, R. H., & Yopp, H. K. (2000). Sharing informational text with young children. *The Reading Teacher, 53,* 410–423.

14

Immersing Children in Nonfiction
Fostering Emergent Research and Writing

RENÉE M. CASBERGUE
MARY BETH PLAUCHÉ

In recent decades there has been an explosion in nonfiction literature for young children. From simple picture books with single-word labels on each page to more complex informational picture books with tables of contents and indexes, children now have a broad array of nonfiction literature written specifically for them. In parallel with the emergence of nonfiction genres for young children, research devoted to children's abilities related to expository text—both their reading and writing of it—has increased exponentially.

It was not long ago that general consensus decreed expository reading and writing to be beyond the capability of young children (Britton, Burgess, Martin, McLeod, & Rosen, 1975; Egan, 1993; Moffett, 1968; Sawyer & Watson, 1987). Many researchers discussed the primacy of story writing among young children, asserting that informational (transactional) writing was too difficult for them (Adams, 1990; Mayher, Lester, & Pradl, 1983; Wells, 1986). Temple, Nathan, Burris, and Temple (1988) concurred with these sentiments, stating, "In terms of children's development as writers, it appears that most children write first, and continue to write most easily, in the expressive mode" (p. 131). These authors suggested that transactional or expository writing is inherently more difficult for young children than expressive writing because "to write successfully in the transactional mode requires a writer to maintain in her mind her topic, purpose, and audience" (Temple et al., 1988, p. 210)—all tasks deemed too hard for children in the primary grades.

Despite the widespread belief that young children should be engaged primarily with narrative texts and immersed in expressive writing, some early literacy scholars long ago began to question that conventional wisdom. Bissex (1980) and Newkirk (1984) both offered examples of their children's writing to demonstrate that, even at ages 5 and 6, the youngsters were able to produce nonnarrative pieces to serve multiple transactional purposes. Additional research identified many types of expository writing produced by children in early primary grades, ranging from labeling and listing to simple paragraphs (Dyson, 1982; Harste, Woodward, & Burke, 1984; Newkirk, 1987, 1989).

More recently, researchers' attention has turned to examining children's exposure to informational text and the influence of that exposure on multiple aspects of literacy learning. Pappas (1991a) argued for the inclusion of more informational books in classrooms for young children as a means to facilitate children's development of strategies for dealing with the expository language structures inherent in those books. Her analysis of the language used by kindergarten children as they engaged in repeated pretend readings of both stories and informational books revealed that the children were just as capable with both genres and that they used appropriate expository language to *read* the informational books (Pappas, 1993). Shine and Roser (1999) found that even preschoolers were able to distinguish among genres of text and vary their responses accordingly. Other research has confirmed that the genres of text to which children are exposed do, in fact, influence their language learning and writing development (Duke & Kays, 1998; Kamberelis, 1998, 1999; Pappas, 1991b) and that as early as first grade, some children are able to talk about the differences they notice between informational and storybook genres (Donovan, 1996).

Despite this compelling evidence that emergent readers and writers are able to handle informational books and produce their own expository writing, recent research has documented the relative scarcity of informational text in classrooms for young children. Duke (2000a) examined the extent to which children in classrooms she observed were exposed to informational text in classroom libraries, environmental print, and activities designed to engage children with expository text. She found that a relatively small portion (12%) of books available in classroom libraries was informational and that no more than 10% of environmental print included informational text. Most telling, children participated in activities designed around informational text for an average of only 3.6 minutes per day. The statistics were even more startling for classrooms of children of low socioeconomic status (SES), where only 6% of library books were informational and children were directly engaged with expository text for an average of 1.4 minutes per day (Duke, 2000b).

Teachers' apparent reluctance to encourage children's use of nonfiction may be due to the widespread belief that young children prefer storybooks to informational texts. Research has demonstrated, however, that at least through third grade, children are as likely to state a preference for informational picture books when given a choice of reading materials (Kletzien & Szabo, 1998). Teachers may also hesitate to engage children with nonfiction because of a mistaken belief that children must first learn to read before they are able to read to learn. Yet Caswell and Duke (1998) have presented compelling evidence that reading informational text may be a key to assisting struggling reader-writers in learning to read. Their case studies of two young boys who were struggling to master storybook reading revealed that informational books related to topics they found interesting kept the boys sufficiently interested to persevere in their reading attempts. Furthermore, they were motivated to engage in a greater volume of reading than they had been willing to do when only narratives were offered.

This brief review of research related to young children's ability to read and learn from nonfiction literature and their ability to produce expository writing offers significant support for the inclusion of expository books in preschool and primary classrooms. In fact, a number of scholars have called for in increase in the amount of nonfiction to which children are exposed in early childhood (Chall, Jacobs, & Baldwin, 1990; Dreher, 1998/ 1999, 2000; Hiebert & Fisher, 1990). Of course, exposure alone is not sufficient to maximize the benefits of informational books for young children. Teachers must also provide opportunities for children to participate in activities specifically designed to engage them with those books. The sheer number of new informational titles published in recent years, however, presents a dilemma. How are teachers to select the most appropriate books for young learners? How are they to use the different types of books now available? How might teachers scaffold children's interactions with nonfiction books to support their learning from them and their ability to write in the genres they discover?

TYPES OF NONFICTION FOR YOUNG CHILDREN

Nonfiction titles for young children take many forms and cover a wide range of reading levels. Unlike the early attempts to determine the difficulty level of text based on readability formulas, which focused on measuring word difficulty and sentence complexity, are the multifaceted systems most publishers now use, which level books according to such features as degree of decodability, amount of predictability, text length, size and layout of print, vocabulary and concepts presented, language structure, text structure, language patterns, and supportive illustrations (Fountas & Pinnell,

1996; Hoffman et al., 1994). Leveled books for the youngest readers typically include single words or simple sentences that correlate directly with a picture on each page. Beyond the earliest leveled books are simple picture books that contain more text per page and require more ability to decode print. The most complex picture books require a significant ability in independent reading. The pictures in these books are illustrative of the text and carry less meaning than those in simpler picture books. These more complex books also present significantly more content, often incorporating multiple concepts within a single page. (See Table 14.1 for a list of examples of each type of text.)

Although publishers target specific grade levels for each type of book, in reality, all levels offer benefits for young readers of any level of ability. It is important for teachers to recognize that even children with early emergent literacy skills can enjoy and acquire information from complex books,

TABLE 14.1. Examples of Nonfiction Picture Books for Young Children

---

Examples of early leveled books

For shared, guided, and independent reading:
  Pebble Books, Capstone Press, Monkato, MN
  Little Red Readers, Sets 1, 2, *and* 3, Sundance Publishing, Littleton, MA
  Social Studies Emergent Readers, Scholastic, New York
  Sails Nonfiction, Rigby, Crystal Lake, IL

Examples of simple picture books

For reading aloud and sharing pictures:
  All Aboard Books, Platt & Munk, Grosset & Dunlap, New York
  DK Books, Dorling Kindersley Ltd., London
  Franklin Watts First Library, Franklin Watts, Grolier, New York
  Golden Look-Look Books, Golden Book, Western Publishing, Racine, WI
  Jerry Pallotta Alphabet Book Series, Charlesbridge Publishing, Watertown, MA
  Let's-Read-and-Find-Out-Books, Harper Trophy, New York
  Rookie Read-About Science Books, Children's Press, Grolier, New York
  SNAPSHOT Books (ages 4–8), Covent Garden Books Ltd., London
  Various titles by Gail Gibbons, Holiday House, New York
  Worldwise Books, Franklin Watts, Grolier, New York

Examples of complex picture books

For partial read-aloud and independent exploration of pictures and captions:
  DK Books, Dorling Kindersley Ltd., London
  Eyes on Nature Series, Kidsbooks, Chicago
  Eyewitness Junior Series, Alfred A. Knopf, New York
  Eyewitness Series, Alfred A. Knopf, New York
  SnapShot Series (ages 6–10), Covent Garden Books, New York

---

and the most sophisticated readers can learn from early leveled books. What matters is how children's interactions with the books are scaffolded by teachers and their peers so that they are able to reap the benefits each type of book offers while overcoming the challenges it may present.

Young students may learn a great deal from complex picture books in which they are able to read only a few words. They become savvy in the strategic use of pictures to decipher meaning in ways that teachers may not recognize. By astutely studying pictures and reading the occasional accessible words of the text, young children often pick up surprisingly large amounts of information. Though the text of many simple nonfiction picture books may not be geared to the youngest readers, these books have an important place in primary classrooms as well. They help students develop a degree of sophistication and independence about what they are learning, which transfers well to their own writing in both informal and teacher-directed projects.

Conversely, young students who are able readers benefit from picture books with limited text, in which they concentrate more intently on the information they can learn from the pictures. The success of the best early leveled book series arises from the format of the books, which rely heavily on exceptionally fine photographs or illustrations with limited textual information. The reader is invited to first learn from the picture, to refine that knowledge by reading the accompanying text, and then to pursue more difficult books.

BENEFITS AND CHALLENGES OF DIFFERENT TYPES OF BOOKS

A benefit of early leveled books is that they may be read independently by beginning readers. Such books allow for ease of locating information, thus building confidence. They also provide a simple model of nonfiction picture books that children can easily emulate in their own writing. A drawback of many early leveled books is that they offer relatively little content because the text is so abbreviated. As a result, children get little or no exposure to technical or content vocabulary appropriate to a given topic.

One way to address the challenges presented by such books is to choose only those with intriguing, detailed pictures that present new and interesting information. The images, whether photographs, realistic drawings, paintings, or collages, should be correct. The accuracy of the images is essential, especially because younger readers will attend most directly to the illustrations. Books with illustrations that sacrifice accuracy for quick accessibility should be avoided. Teachers can also expand on the text to make up for the information that is lacking by reading the book aloud once to establish the pattern of the written language and to facilitate subsequent independent reading. Then they can share the text again with lots of discussion of each picture, orally supplying the appropriate content vocabulary and making up for any information that is lacking.

Simple picture books also offer both benefits and challenges for young children. These books may be read independently by more advanced readers, and they provide challenging material for less able readers. Unlike the early leveled books, they offer significant information in both text and pictures and include appropriate technical vocabulary. Such books also offer a more complex model of nonfiction for children to emulate. Of course, these books may be too challenging for some readers, resulting in difficulty locating and understanding the information presented. Teachers can facilitate children's engagement with these books by choosing those with a good balance of pictures and text. In particular, selecting books in which the text is well supported by the pictures will enable children to locate those pages containing the information they want. As with early leveled books, repeated reading by the teacher that includes discussion enables all children to gain information even from books that are beyond their reading capability.

Complex picture books potentially offer both the greatest benefits and the most challenges for young children. These books present a wealth of information and interconnected concepts about specific topics, and they address more subtopics in significant detail than do simple picture books. They also make extensive use of appropriate technical vocabulary. However, these books are often too lengthy and complex to be read aloud in their entirety. The sheer amount of content they incorporate may be overwhelming to beginning readers. These books give much more information via text as opposed to pictures, requiring higher levels of competency with print.

Teachers who use complex picture books successfully choose book series that follow a predictable format across topics to facilitate children's location of the information they seek. The simple tables of content and indexes included in many of these series serve to scaffold children's learning, rendering the texts more accessible for younger readers. When introducing these books, teachers can do a "picture walk" to familiarize children with their content and format, then read selected portions of each page aloud to point out to the children the subtopics that are addressed. During subsequent readings of the book, children may specify which parts they want to hear based on pictures that intrigue them. Finally, children can be encouraged to make use of the pictures and attempt to read captions to glean information as they use the books independently.

Regardless of their age or ability, exposing students to a broad range of informational books and scaffolding their understanding through discussion are critical to the development of their successful use of nonfiction texts. These texts must be read to students and then be available for independent reading and browsing; they must also be discussed. Students learn how to find meaning in nonfiction works through questioning by their teachers and through their own perusal and sharing of books with peers. Young children are typically first drawn to the pictures and derive most of their information there. The supporting text read to them by their teacher or with peers gives them a jumping-off point to consider other elements in the pictures that provide content. The vocabulary and technical language included in nonfiction texts must not only be explained, but must also be amplified for students. Discussion leads to questioning, questioning leads to further examination of the pictures and text, and that examination constitutes the students' own research for their expository writing. Of course, not every nonfiction work needs this level of discussion, but students must have the tools to analyze what they read. They learn these skills through their own analysis of nonfiction works.

SUPPORTING EMERGENT RESEARCHERS

A benefit of immersing children in nonfiction is the genre's potential to encourage the emergence of research abilities in even the youngest children. That research skills can and should be taught in early elementary classrooms is not commonly recognized. Though young children's research does not take the form typical of older students' investigations, in which material is read, notes are taken and organized, and a final piece of writing or project is produced, it has a definite place in the primary classroom. Children's earliest research is more closely related to discovery learning in which students encounter material in books, in the natural world, or through historical artifacts, and want to know more. The search for meaning in nonfiction picture books of all kinds is indeed research for these students, as they begin by relying mostly on pictures and gradually learn to read in greater depth to get at extended meanings to inform their own writing.

Teachers can support students' efforts in this early expository writing by emphasizing the content of their pieces as well as the quality of the writing. When teachers respond to the content of expository writing, they enable students to view their writing as meaningful and important. Furthermore, they reinforce students' understanding that the learning and reporting of new information has inherent value. Such response from a teacher also provides an opportunity for children to examine the accuracy of what they have learned from their exploration of nonfiction.

EXPOSITORY WRITING IN THE CLASSROOM

Teachers who value expository writing and recognize its importance in children's learning provide many opportunities for students to engage in meaningful reading and writing across content disciplines. They use nonfiction picture books to enrich and support students' entrance into the expository writing process and incorporate writing into all aspects of the curriculum through both formal, structured activities and more casual ones. Their goal is that students see expository writing as a natural extension of their learning that builds their knowledge while creating a record of what they learn. As children begin to write, often following formats in texts to which they are exposed, their subject matter knowledge is increased and becomes more firmly established. Ideally, students have opportunities to practice expository writing in both formal and informal pieces throughout the academic year. These opportunities are easily incorporated into a strong, developmentally appropriate writing program

One of us (M.B.P.) teaches in a multi-age classroom for children in kindergarten through second grade. This classroom structure allows us to illustrate how activities that engage children in informational writing can be successful with youngsters of widely varying experiences and capabilities. The key to the success of these activities is the teacher's recognition that children respond in vastly different ways to the same writing activities, depending on their literacy development, their understanding of the reading and writing processes, and their interest in and prior knowledge of the topics they are invited to explore.

Informal writing can be fostered best in classrooms set up in accordance with standard early childhood classroom practices. Centers with objects from nature, artifacts, and picture books that students may look at independently encourage them to make the connection between the natural world and the print that explains it. For example, first graders Carson and Max observed several plastic mounts of spiders and had available picture books on spiders including early leveled texts, simple picture books, and more complex, text-driven books with pictures. They looked through the books to find pictures of spiders they found interesting and then read the text to investigate further. Once each child chose his favorite spider and researched it, he drew its picture and chose the most interesting fact to record. The children's independent completion of this activity, with minimal teacher oversight, was supported by the provision of a structured form on which to record their findings. As is apparent in the writing they produced, both children were successful in locating interesting information about the spiders of their choice (see Figure 14.1).

This very informal writing project includes important elements of expository writing techniques. Students observed, researched, and recorded information by making a scientific drawing and then writing about it. (The term "scientific drawing" is helpful in that it cues students that they are to make an exact copy of what they observe, as distinct from creative drawing.) This project is simple for teachers to construct and provides a model for similar center activities related to any number of topics.

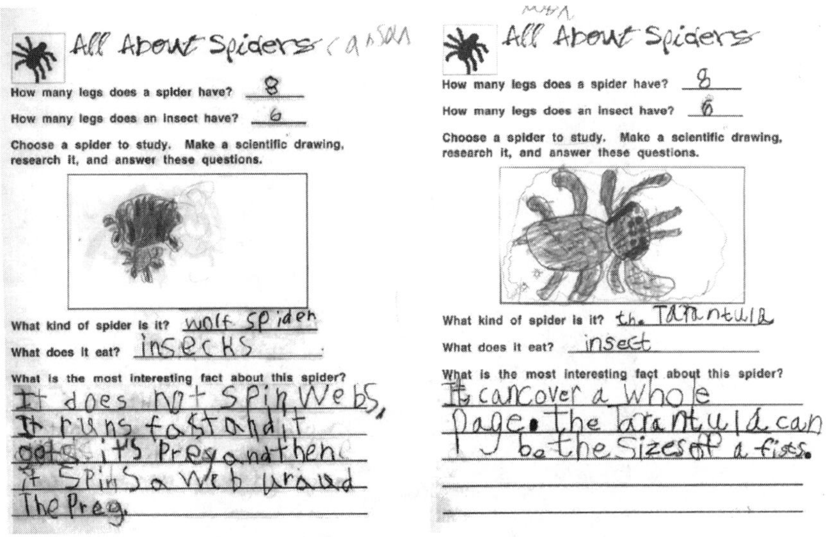

FIGURE 14.1. Carson's spider writing: It does not spin webs. It runs fast and it gets its prey and then it spins a web around the prey. Max's spider writing: It can cover a whole page. The tarantula can be the size of a fist.

Many other opportunities for more extensive expository writing arise naturally in this classroom. Biographies and historical fiction offer a variety of possibilities for both formal and casual expository writing activities. There are currently many biographies for very young children that increasingly present historical figures as real human beings with real human successes and failings. When teachers read these picture books to their students, they foster discussion and further expansion of the concepts presented. The illustrations evoke the correct historical period, and students learn to employ their beginning research skills as they note differences in dress, architecture, transportation, cityscapes, and daily life. The discussions drawn from historical narratives and the questions they provoke from students provide a fertile ground for expository writing.

After a brief discussion about George Washington and his importance, the teacher placed a number of picture book biographies with a variety of reading levels at a center (see Figure 14.2); students researched by browsing through the books, reading, and examining the pictures. The final component of the project was to draw a picture of Washington and to write one interesting fact. The resulting expository pieces were posted on a small bulletin board above the center as each was completed. As students did the project, they conferred—reading, discussing, and planning what each thought was most interesting, and over time comparing what they had written to new entries as they were posted. Although the activity was not

FIGURE 14.2. George Washington research center.

strictly collaborative, it had many collaborative elements as students expanded on their own knowledge through their conversations about George Washington. The expository writing that Lindsey, a first grader, and Taylor, a second grader, produced in response to this activity (see Figure 14.3) was only a sentence or two, but the learning that preceded getting that information on paper was the result of a great deal of research and planning.

A similar project, which engaged the children in learning about Abraham Lincoln and his presidency, resulted in longer, more formal expository products. Over a period of several days, the children were engaged in significant discussions about Lincoln, the Civil War, and the plight of slaves before emancipation. The teacher complemented these discussions by reading aloud from a variety of books related to the topic. Each book that was shared was placed at the writing center for the children's reference, and the children were asked to draw a picture of Abraham Lincoln and write about him and his presidency. Michelle, a kindergartner, demonstrated her recognition that Lincoln wrote, read, and studied like most children—a fact extracted from a simple biography that included a description of how his

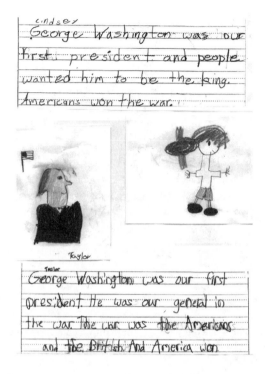

Lindsey

George Washington was our
first president and people
wanted him to be the king.
Americans won the war.

Taylor

George Washington was our first
president. He was our general in
the war. The war was the Americans
and the British. And America won

FIGURE 14.3. Lindsey's and Taylor's Washington writing.

childhood days were spent—as well as her knowledge that he was a president who freed the slaves (see Figure 14.4). John, a second grader, clearly had a more sophisticated understanding of the meaning of the Emancipation Proclamation and Lincoln's role in keeping the Union intact (see Figure 14.5). His illustration revealed even deeper meaning and a more visceral and personal connection to events from long ago, as he drew the president weeping about the Civil War and lamenting, "I don't like it when people die."

Yet another activity that resulted in children's researching of a topic and reporting their findings was part of an ongoing study of life in Japan. The classroom library contained numerous books about Japan, including both fiction and nonfiction picture books of varying levels of difficulty. The students had been immersed in learning about Japanese culture through reading and being read to from these books, exploring Internet sites, examining artifacts, learning geography, and participating in numerous class discussions. When they were asked to write about something they had learned about Japan for inclusion on a bulletin board display, the results clearly

FIGURE 14.4. Michelle's Lincoln writing: Abraham Lincoln loves to write and read and study too. And he freed the slaves. He was nice. He was president.

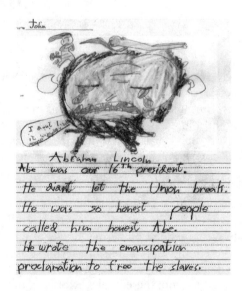

FIGURE 14.5. John's Lincoln writing: Abe was our 16th president. He didn't let the Union break. He was so honest people called him honest Abe. He wrote the Emancipation Proclamation to free the slaves.

demonstrated their developing expository writing skills and their increasing store of knowledge about Japan.

Alex, a kindergartner, spent most of his writing time drawing a complex picture of sumo wrestlers (see Figure 14.6). The text he wrote says simply "sumo wrestling" in invented spelling; it is evident from his picture, however, that he knew what sumo wrestlers do, how they dress, how they are built, and the ceremony attached to sumo wrestling in Japanese culture. Anya, another kindergartner, also spent a significant amount of time on her drawing (see Figure 14.7), and her writing indicates her knowledge that Japanese people wear kimonos for ceremonial purposes "on special days." Her drawing reflects the vivid colors of authentic kimonos, as well as the "obi" sash that flares out behind the wearer's waist, suggesting that she had taken note of more details than she chose to reflect in her writing alone. In contrast, Catherine, a second grader, revealed most of her knowledge in her text rather than in her picture, which serves to illustrate the centrality of her writing rather than conveying additional meaning (see Figure 14.8). She wrote in a sophisticated expository style, using present tense and making generalizations about Japanese people and their culture, and concluding with a cause–effect statement suggesting that the cherry blossom festival is a logical extension of the Japanese love of nature.

An additional opportunity for expository writing occurs in the cre-

FIGURE 14.6. Alex's Japan writing: Sumo wrestling.

FIGURE 14.7. Anya's Japan writing: Japanese people wear kimonos too on special days.

ation of classroom books that are compilations of work by all the students in a classroom on a single topic. While studying ancient Egypt, for example, students were immersed in information about everything from the construction of the pyramids to irrigation techniques and the mythology of Ra, the sun god. They built models of the Nile and, through reading and discussion, learned about its significance in the development of Egyptian civilization. They created their own cartouches and wrote their names in hieroglyphs; they constructed a model of a pyramid using sugar cubes, a long and tedious project much like the building of the pyramids themselves. Through this in-depth study, the students covered a broad range of topics related to Egyptian life. As a culminating activity, the children created a class book to document some of what they learned—a book that would be used as a research tool by future classes. Each child's contribution consisted of a watercolor illustration of the subtopic he or she had chosen, as well as a written entry that was drafted, revised, and edited with the use of a simple word processing program on the classroom computer. Written products ranged from simple statements like Elliott's, which said, "Pyramids had limestone on top of them and Egyptians pushed the bricks up on logs," to Katie's detailed description of the job of scribes: "Scribes wrote on papyrus for pharaohs. They wrote on tombs and temples. When pharaohs died they

In Japan the Japanese like nature. They like cherry blossoms so much they have a cherry blossom festival.

FIGURE 14.8. Catherine's Japan writing: In Japan the Japanese like nature. They like cherry blossoms so much they have a cherry blossom festival.

made them into mummies. They wore a skirt. When they sat down it made a table to write on." Both children painted pictures that illustrated the basic concepts they described. Manya Jean made a more direct connection between her picture and text, using her writing as a caption for her painting. She wrote, "This is a pharaoh. A pharaoh wore lots of jewelry. The pharaohs were the king of Egypt and carried a crook and a flail." All of those details are clearly visible in her drawing. The resulting book is a treasured addition to the classroom library to which the children readily turn for enjoyment and information.

EFFECTS OF IMMERSION IN NONFICTION

Although the effects of immersing young children in nonfiction picture books are not yet fully documented in the research literature, our observations of the ways in which children use nonfiction books and the related writing they produce leads us to conclude that students in primary grades can only benefit from exposure to a balance of narrative and expository texts. In a classroom where expository writing is valued, students have continuous access to nonfiction and fiction books. These include straightforward nonfiction works, science and history series, biographies, historical fiction, wordless (or nearly wordless) picture books, and reference books such as atlases, encyclopedias, and dictionaries. When students have access to this wealth of material, it is used and consulted on a regular basis. In classrooms where writing is habitual and frequent, students often use the information they learn in nonfiction picture books to produce expository writing spontaneously in daily, unprompted writing experiences. First and second graders who are steeped in learning through research and expository writing often ask to research a topic and write down what they learn during daily silent reading. The students themselves decide to take these notes, which are neither requested nor seen by the teacher. The research and writing that result are often shared among peers and encourage further research and writing. For the students, the purpose of the writing is to keep a personal record of things they find interesting.

The resulting expository writing that occurs in these classrooms where students have access to a wide array of books on topics that pique their interest is impressive. Expository writing becomes commonplace and routine as students are exposed to numerous models to emulate in the nonfiction books available to them. Because expository writing is a natural and expected aspect of the curriculum, students are quite comfortable with it and produce well-researched pieces with ease. The facility with which they write comes from practice and experience in nonthreatening activities. The students view expository writing as nothing more than writing about something real. When teachers allow students to concentrate on content first and create an environment in which the information presented is given as much importance as the quality of the writing, students become very willing, indeed eager, to document the things they learn. The pride young children feel when they are recognized for doing research is quite powerful and spurs them on to share what they learn through expository writing.

REFERENCES

Adams, M. (1990). *Beginning to read: Thinking and learning about print.* Cambridge, MA: MIT Press.

Bissex, G. (1980). *GNYS AT WRK: A child learns to write and read.* Cambridge, MA: Harvard University Press.

Britton, J., Burgess, T., Martin, N., McLeod, A., & Rosen, H. (1975). *The development of writing abilities.* London: Macmillan.

Caswell, L. J., & Duke, N. K. (1998). Non-narrative as a catalyst for literacy development. *Language Arts, 75,* 108–117.

Chall, J., Jacobs, V., & Baldwin, L. (1990). *The reading crisis: Why poor children fall behind.* Cambridge, MA: Harvard University Press.

Donovan, C. A. (1996). First graders' impressions of genre-specific elements in writing narrative and expository texts. In D. J. Leu, C. K. Kinzer, & K. A. Hinchman (Eds.), *Literacies for the 21st century* (pp. 183–194). Chicago: National Reading Conference.

Dreher, M. J. (1998/1999). Motivating children to read more nonfiction. *The Reading Teacher, 42,* 414–417.

Dreher, M. J. (2000). Fostering reading for learning. In L. Baker, M. J. Dreher, & J. T. Guthrie (Eds.), *Engaging young readers: Promoting achievement and motivation* (pp. 94–118). New York: Guilford Press.

Duke, N. K. (2000a). 3.6 minutes per day: The scarcity of informational texts in first grade. *Reading Research Quarterly, 35,* 202–224.

Duke, N. K. (2000b). For the rich it's richer: Print experiences and environments offered to children in very low- and very high-SES first grade classrooms. *American Educational Research Journal, 37,* 441–478.

Duke, N. K., & Kays, J. (1998). "Can I say 'once upon a time'?" Kindergarten children developing knowledge of information book language. *Early Childhood Research Quarterly, 13*(2), 295–318.

Dyson, A. (1982). *Drawing, talking, and writing: Rethinking writing development.* Berkeley, CA: Center for the Study of Writing.

Egan, K. (1993). Narrative and learning: A voyage of implications. *Linguistics and Education, 5,* 119–126.

Fountas, I., & Pinnell, G. (1996). *Guided reading: Good first teaching for all children.* Portsmouth, NH: Heinemann.

Harste, J. C., Woodward, V. A., & Burke, C. (1984). *Language stories and literacy lessons.* Portsmouth, NH: Heinemann.

Hiebert, E., & Fisher, C. (1990). Whole language: Three themes for the future. *Educational Leadership, 46*(6), 62–64.

Hoffman, J., McCarthey, S., Abbott, J., Christian, C., Corman, L., Dressman, M., Elliot, B., Matherne, D. & Stahl, D., (1994). So what's new in the "new" basals? *Journal of Reading Behavior, 26,* 47–73.

Kamberelis, G. (1998). Relations between children's literacy diets and genre development: You write what you read. *Literacy Teaching and Learning, 3,* 7– 53.

Kamberelis, G. (1999). Genre development and learning: Children writing stories, science reports, and poems. *Research in the Teaching of English, 33,* 403–460.

Kletzien, S. B., & Szabo, R. J. (1998, December). *Information text or narrative text? Children's preferences revisited.* Paper presented at the National Reading Conference, Austin, TX.

Mayher, J. Lester, N., & Pradl, G. (1983). *Learning to write/writing to learn.* Montclair, NJ: Boynton/Cook.

Moffett, J. (1968). *Teaching the universe of discourse.* Boston: Houghton Mifflin.

Newkirk, T. (1984). Archimedes' dream. *Language Arts, 61,* 341–350.

Newkirk, T. (1987). The non-narrative writing of young children. *Research in the Teaching of English, 21,* 121–144.

Newkirk, T. (1989). *More than stories: The range of children's writing.* Portsmouth, NH: Heinemann.

Pappas, C. C. (1991a). Fostering full access to literacy by including information books. *Language Arts, 68,* 449–462.

Pappas, C. C. (1991b). Young children's strategies in learning the "book language" of information books. *Discourse Processes, 14,* 203–225.

Pappas, C. C. (1993). Is narrative "primary"? Some insights from kindergartners' pretend readings of stories and information books. *Journal of Reading Behavior, 25,* 97–129.

Sawyer, W., & Watson, K. (1987). Questions of genre. In I. Reid (Ed.), *The place of genre in learning: Current debates* (pp. 46–57). Geelong, Australia: Deakin University, Centre of Studies in Literary Education.

Shine, S., & Roser, N. L. (1999). The role of genre in preschoolers' response to picture books. *Research in the Teaching of English, 34,* 197–251.

Temple, C., Nathan, R., Burris, N., & Temple, F. (1988). *The beginnings of writing.* Newton, MA: Allyn & Bacon.

Wells, G. (1986). *The meaning makers: Children learning language and using language to learn.* Portsmouth, NH: Heinemann.

15

Organizing Expository Texts
A Look at the Possibilities

CAROL VUKELICH
CHRISTINE EVANS
BONNIE ALBERTSON

The teachers at the Primary School returned from their fall retreat excited about their schoolwide writing project plans. For the rest of the fall, through workshops and book club discussions, they would continue to build their knowledge about how to teach expository text writing. Then, immediately after the winter break, they would all—every classroom, every grade (K–4)—focus on teaching their students to write expository texts about animals, with each student selecting the animal of his or her choice. And they did—they taught their students how to generate interesting questions about their animals, how to find resources (e.g., books, people, the Internet) to answer their questions, how to take notes and not copy or plagiarize, how to organize their notes into categories, and how to use what they knew about writing (great leads, variety in sentence structure, correct punctuation and capitalization, etc.) to craft their reports. The teachers, administrators, parents, and children were delighted with the process and the children's products. However, as the teachers reflected on their maiden foray into teaching expository texts, they realized that they had not taught their students about a very important aspect of informative text writing: the organizational structures of expository texts.

Certainly, it is common for features of narrative texts to be used in expository texts (particularly in resource materials, like picture books, written for young children). But how the ideas are bound together and developed in an expository text is different from the way they are bound together in a narrative text. And, unlike narrative texts that use a consistent structure (setting, initiating event, internal response, attempt, consequence, and reaction), expository texts use any one (or often a combination) of several structures. Children need to recognize and be able to use expository text structures in order to write quality expository-type pieces.

Young children have numerous experiences with narrative (fiction) text structure. Most of what they read in their basal readers or literature anthologies fits this category. Furthermore, Marcia Freeman (1997) suggests that 9 out of 10 books teachers read aloud to their young students are narratives, and Nell Duke (2000) provides the detail of just how much—or how little—young children are involved with expository text in their classrooms: approximately 3.6 minutes a day. In addition, Duke discovered that expository "texts of any kind comprised a mean of only 9.8% [of the books] in the classroom libraries" (p. 213). Ruth and Hallie Yopp (2000) quote numerous literacy experts who target teachers' failure to provide young children with sufficient experiences with expository texts as a causal factor in the *fourth-grade slump* in children's reading performance. These students have not received what J. David Cooper (1997) argues is imperative: the need to "know the basic differences between narrative and expository texts" in order to "construct meaning" (p. 102). In addition to helping mitigate the difficulty students have in reading expository texts later in life, other researchers (e.g., Caswell & Duke, 1998; Duthie, 1994; Guthrie & McCann, 1997) argue that expository texts offer children opportunities to develop areas of interest and further develop areas of expertise. Researchers (e.g., Duke & Kays, 1998) also report that exposure to expository texts results in young children possessing greater knowledge of several textual features (like the use of timeless present tense verb construction and generic noun structures) characteristic of exposition.

To become good expository text readers and writers, children need numerous experiences with quality models of these kinds of texts to develop an ear for expository text (Freeman, 1997). Freeman (1997) reminds us of the important role of models in other arenas of life: The aspiring artist sits in front of Mona Lisa with sketch pad in hand, trying to copy her mystic smile; the 4.5 tennis player studies Venus Williams's forehand stroke in hope of achieving more power in her own forehand. Clearly, it is no less important for children to experience quality expository text models to help them develop knowledge of this genre.

EXPOSITORY TEXTS AS MODELS OF AUTHORS' USE OF WRITING CRAFTS

As teachers read to and talk with their students about the books the children are reading, they can draw the children's attention not only to the

book's content (the answers to their questions), but also to the ways the author employed the crafts of expository text. The following examples are illustrative of the ways in which teachers share expository text with students.

- *Expository texts can provide models of how to use a cliff-hanger as an
  effective lead.*

  "Listen to how Beth Nadler began *The Magic School Bus Inside Ralphie:
  A Book about Germs* (1995). 'Having a teacher like Ms. Frizzle can
  make a kid nervous. Stange things always seem to happen when she's
  around' (p. 1). What a great cliff-hanger lead! What do you think those
  strange things might be? Are you eager to find out? Maybe you'll begin
  one of your pieces with a cliff-hanger lead."

- *Expository texts can provide models of how to incorporate many interesting details into pieces.*

  "I think Gail Gibbons is a master at providing wonderful details. Listen
  to all the details she gives us in just this little section of *Sea Turtles*
  (1995). 'Sea turtles migrate, or travel, to the place where they will have
  their young. Sometimes they migrate more than 1000 miles to nest.
  They do this every two or three years in the late spring or summer. They
  mate in warm seawater' (p. 15). How many details did she provide?"

- *Expository texts can provide models of effective endings.*

  "As a writer I always have difficulty ending my pieces. Then I read one of
  Jerry Pallotta's books, the *Furry Alphabet Book* (1991), and I thought,
  'What a great ending!' Here's what Pallotta wrote: 'What's going on
  here? Hey, stop eating the book! Sorry, Naked Mole Rat. You are a
  mammal, but you do not have any fur, and you are also quite ugly. You
  should not be in this book, not even at The End' (pp. 29–30). Maybe I
  should look carefully at how my favorite expository writers ended their
  pieces and try ending my pieces like one of these authors."

- *Expository texts can provide models of variety in sentence length and
  structure.*

  "The easiest way you can tell whether your piece is strong in sentence fluency is to read it aloud. Listen to the way Gail Gibbons (1993) writes
  about frogs. 'Frogs have enemies. Foxes, snakes, rats, birds and other
  creatures eat frogs when they can catch them. A sudden leap is a quick
  escape from danger. For protection, some frogs have skin glands that
  make them taste bad or make them poisonous. Sometimes their skin
  color hides them from enemies' (p. 20). What did you notice about the

kinds of sentences Ms. Gibbons uses? And what did you notice about the different ways Ms. Gibbons began these sentences?"

- *Expository texts can provide models of figurative language.*

  "When Cynthia Rylant wrote *The Whales* (1996), she described the whales by comparing them or their actions to something else quite different. Authors help readers form mind pictures by comparing characters, actions, or places to something really different. Listen to what Cynthia Rylant says about whales: 'So many whales in the seas, swimming like birds, rolling in the underneath sky. . . . They are floating like feathers in the deep blue green. They are floating like feathers in a sky' (pp. 17, 25, 27). To what did Ms. Rylant compare whales?"

- *Expository texts can provide models for teaching voice or style in writing.*

  "I was wondering how I was going to teach you about voice in writing, and I came across this really fun book by Steve Parker called *It's an Ant's Life* (1999). It starts like this: 'I've got a few minutes to spare, so I can finally start my journal. Some of us have been given a short rest from work. But, like all ants, I like to stay busy, so I've only got time for a few facts about me and my friends' (p.1). I thought to myself, 'That's just what voice is.' Voice sounds as though a person (or an ant) wrote it. Not just any person (or ant): a particular person (or ant). The writing has personality."

Expository texts, then, can serve as effective models of these and any number of other writing crafts. Children learn about writing by interacting with published texts and by becoming aware of the techniques these mentors used to craft their texts.

There is a craft central to the writing of expository texts missing from the preceding examples. This craft is how the information and ideas are organized—or knit together or clumped—in expository texts. What is missing here, and was missing from the Primary School's teachers' initial teaching of exposition, is instruction in the organizational schemes authors use to write expository pieces.

Guiding children in the close reading of informative texts will not necessarily teach them how to write such texts (Berthoff, 1983). Ann Berthoff advises teachers to "teach reading so that the mind is actively engaged in seeing 'how words work.' [Then] anything and everything that is learned in reading will be transferable to learning how to write" (p. 167). Echoing Berthoff's advice, Rob Tierney, John Readence, and Ernest Dishner (1995) add that text structures should not be taught in isolation. That is, as students learn to recognize text structures, they should also have an opportunity to write using these same text patterns. Students who understand these text structures not only can comprehend expository texts better, but are also able to select the most appropriate text structure to use in their writing of expository texts, to select the one structure that will most effectively communicate information to their audiences. The question, then, is, how can teachers help their young learners to develop a sense of the organizational structures of expository texts and the signal words associated with each structure?

KINDS OF EXPOSITORY TEXT STRUCTURES

There are many kinds of expository text structures. That is, there are many organizational patterns that writers purposely select to communicate meaning effectively. We define the expository text structures commonly used in texts written for young children in the following sections. We credit Randall Decker and Robert Schwegler (1998), as well as Gail Tompkins (2000), with helping us frame these definitions. We also borrow an idea from Stephanie Harvey (1998), an idea she gathered from a reading workshop led by Jan Dole, a professor at the University of Utah, to provide readers with an example of each text structure. Jan asked her group to use each text structure to build sentences around the term *goose bumps*; we build our sentences around the term *jury duty* (a term of significance to one of us [C.V.] as we wrote this chapter).

Description

Children come to a consideration of description in expository texts having had many experiences with description in narrative texts. Most students have experienced using their five senses, using metaphors and similes, taking on the persona of a character (personification), and playing with sound words (onomatopoeia) to make their stories and poems come alive for readers. Description is important in informative texts as well. The purpose of description in expository writing is the same as it is in narrative writing: to give readers a picture of what the subject under investigation looks like, acts like, sounds like, feels like. Writers often describe a topic by using examples and by explaining the characteristics and features that illustrate the topic for readers. Description also frequently involves offering definition, analogy, or classification of the topic under investigation.

Jury duty means that you go to the courthouse to join others who have been summoned—and you wait, and wait, and wait. You wait for your name to be called to leave the small, dark room in the basement to go upstairs to the courtroom. You wait for the many lawyers to decide whether you will be one of the chosen 12. You wait while the lawyers exchange many pieces of paper and confer with their clients. It feels like time wasted, lots of people's time wasted.

Sequence (or Process Analysis)

Again, young children come to consider sequence in expository texts having had numerous experiences with sequence in narrative texts. "What happened first in this story? next? last?" In informative writing, sequencing explains the procedures that produce a specific outcome or product. Most often, steps are detailed in chronological order. Teaching young children to write using sequence translates to helping students explain the steps in a process with sufficient detail to give readers the necessary information. This is a challenging task for young children. Because they are egocentric, they assume that if *they* understand the process, surely *you* do too.

> Getting called to serve on *jury duty* is a nerve-racking experience. First, you get a threatening-sounding note from the government telling you where and when to report. Next, the day comes, and you trudge through snow to find a long line outside the courthouse door. "Take your hands out of your pockets. Walk when the sign says 'Walk.' Go to the basement to the room labeled 'Jury Assembly Room.' Wait." Then you watch the videotape on the jury process. Finally, you can go home; you have done your civic duty, but the court doesn't need you. The cases have been resolved.

Compare–Contrast

Noting similarities and differences in objects, events, or qualities is a critical skill for young readers and writers. But getting students to compare *logically* and *purposefully* can be difficult. Comparison involves noting similarities and differences between and among subjects of the same general classification. Comparison is usually accomplished in one of two ways: block comparisons, in which two items are compared for similarities and then for differences; or the Ping-Pong or point-by-point comparisons, in which similarities and differences between two subjects are compared alternately one feature at a time. In general, for young children, the first method is easier. Regardless of the method chosen, quality comparisons end with the writer making clear to readers what the significance or importance of the comparison is.

Jury duty means people watching, and this can sometimes be fun and other times boring. Some people had hats on; other people did not. Some people chatted with lots of people in the room; other people were very quiet. Some people's names were called to go to a courtroom; other people's names were never called. But despite all our differences, we were all there to perform our civic duty.

Cause–Effect

Sequencing tells *how* something happens; causality explains *why* something happens. Especially with informative texts, it is important for students to understand the results of any action or undertaking. Understanding what action or actions resulted in a particular outcome involves analyzing those actions, a challenging task for young students. Again, using models that illustrate cause and effect clearly, often with the aid of pictures and graphs, can help young students understand simple causality. From a very young age, it is important for students to understand that events often have multiple causes or multiple effects and that to draw overly simplistic conclusions about causality is illogical.

When I saw the return address on the envelope notifying me about *jury duty*, I started to sweat (polite people call it perspire). *Jury duty* makes me nervous because I know I could spend a lot of time sitting in a courtroom. Then I would fall behind with my real job, and I would become very anxious.

Problem–Solution

Similar to cause and effect in many ways, the problem–solution text structure also requires that students first have an understanding of chronology. With problem–solution, students must thoroughly understand and explain the problem before proposing a logical and plausible solution. However, recognizing and writing a problem–solution is not very difficult for young children. They are familiar with the narrative structure whereby a character wants something (a problem), so the character does something (solution), and as a result the character gets what he or she wants.

Serving on *jury duty* was not something I wanted to do; it would be inconvenient and time-consuming. I could just ignore the summons, or I could lie on the questionnaire to get myself released. Or I could just show up and hope I am not picked for a long trial. The latter solution was the most viable option. Fortunately, my nervousness disappeared just as soon as the judge said, "Thank you for your time today, but we will not need your services."

Exemplification (or Reason and Example)

Exemplification is possibly the most frequently assigned type of informative writing given to students as they progress through the grades. Even at an early age, students learn to support a main idea or thesis with reasons and examples. Reasons and examples can range from facts and statistics to narrative firsthand accounts. Learning how to balance these different types of reasons and examples to suit an audience's needs is important. Other issues with which older students must grapple include how to select *relevant* reasons/examples, the *order* in which the reasons/examples should be placed, how many reasons are sufficient, and how much *explanation* must accompany these reasons/examples. For the youngest writers, the first challenge is to help them recognize reasons and examples that support a main idea.

> *Jury duty* can be a waste of time and money for lots of people. One hundred twenty people sat in a room from 9:00 to 11:00 A.M. before anyone was called to report to a courtroom. One man talked about how he would not receive any pay from his real job while he completed his jury duty. Yet *jury duty* pays only $25.00 for a full day and nothing for the first day. "How will I feed my family?" he worried. But whether or not people find the experience convenient or worthwhile, we cannot "just say no" to *jury duty*.

In most texts, no single text structure dominates an entire book, chapter, or article. Indeed, most quality informative texts mix structures. The key is that writers mix their use of the various text structures purposefully. Students who understand the purposes behind these text patterns will not only comprehend expository texts more easily, but will also have more strategies at hand when writing informative pieces.

Exposing children to each of these text structures is important. Providing models of each for children to emulate is important. And these models must reflect what Ellen Keene and Susan Zimmermann (1997) call "considerate text," that is, a text "written in a way that its content and format are familiar and predictable" (p. 87). Cueing children's attention to the structure(s) used in each model is also important. Table 15.1 lists informational books representing the various expository text structures. Note that most are newly released picture books. We hope readers will add their old favorites to our list. (Readers will find Gail Tompkins's [2000] list helpful as well.)

TABLE 15.1. Organizing Expository Texts: A Look at the Possibilities

	Description	Sequence/ process analysis	Comparison	Cause– effect	Problem– solution	Exemplification
How Tall, How Short, How Faraway			All			
A Weed Is a Flower		All			pp. 20, 21	
The Wedge	All					
Building a House		All				
Desert Giant	pp. 1–7	pp. 9–13				
Discovering Mars	p. 16	p. 29	p. 21			
The International Space Station	pp. 6–19				p. 21	
A River Ran Wild	All			p. 17		
Animal Dads	All					All
Stop Drop and Roll		pp. 19–21		p. 17	pp. 8–10	pp. 1–3, 12
Feathers for Lunch	All					
Frogs	pp. 8–16	All		p. 1		
Sea Turtles	All					
Why Frogs Are Wet	pp. 8–14, 16, 17	pp. 5–7, 15	pp. 18, 19			
Apollo 13: Space Race		All			pp. 38, 39	
The Five Senses	All					All
Animals Eating	All		pp. 14, 15, 28, 29			
Jamestown		All			p. 9	
Desert Trek						All
Elephant Quest	pp. 23, 27, 28					
Crocodile		p. 24				
Rats and Mice	pp. 7–9, 16, 17	pp. 20, 23, 35	pp. 5, 6	pp. 11–13, 15, 18	pp. 13, 19, 24	pp. 3, 18, 33
Struggle for a Continent				pp. 15–18		
How to Dig a Hole to the Other Side of the World		All		pp. 12–16		
Children Around the World	All		All			
The Magic School Bus Inside Ralphie		p. 13			pp. 20, 21, 24–28	

(*continued*)

269

TABLE 15.1. (*continued*)

	Description	Sequence/ process analysis	Comparison	Cause–effect	Problem–solution	Exemplification
Megatooth	pp. 3–6, 23, 24	pp. 26, 27	pp. 12–20	pp. 21, 25		
Volcano!	pp. 10, 11, 18, 19			pp. 6–9		
The Furry Alphabet Book	All					
It's an Ant's Life	pp. 1–3	pp. 9, 10	p. 4		p. 15	pp. 11, 12
Bugs Are Insects	pp. 7, 14		pp. 8, 12			pp. 10, 16, 19, 22, 25, 27
Make Me a Peanut Butter Sandwich		All				
The Whales	All					
How to Be a Nature Detective			pp. 10, 13, 17		All	
Who Works Here?: Fast-Food Restaurant	All	pp. 26, 27				
Berry Smudges and Leaf Prints	pp. 2–5, 9, 13, 17, 21	pp. 6, 7, 10, 11, 14, 15, 18, 19				
What Happens to a Hamburger?	pp. 6, 17, 20	pp. 10, 12, 14, 18		pp. 11, 29		
The Brain	pp. 12, 13, 15, 17		p. 13		p. 26	p. 21
Lightning	pp. 15, 19	p. 5	p. 3			p. 18
Wolves	pp. 11, 13, 16, 17, 20, 22, 23	p. 26	pp. 4, 5			
Follow the Dream					pp. 12–17	
People			All			
The Robins in Your Backyard	pp. 6, 8	p. 10	pp. 15, 16, 24			
Metamorphosis		pp. 3–10	p. 3			
The Wolf Girls					All	

Certainly, picture books provide young children with important models of expository text structures. There is, however, another important model source: children's writing. Teachers should provide children with opportunities to read and emulate the work of other children. And, of course, teachers can guide children's use of these models just as they would guide children's use of published works by adult authors. In Figures 15.1 through 15.9 we provide student models representing different expository text structures that teachers may use with their young writers. Rather than labeling the text structure evidenced in each piece in the figures, we invite readers to try their skill at labeling the text structures employed by the child writer in each. (The answers to this challenge appear following the References section.)

INSTRUCTION IN TEXT STRUCTURES

Sharing models with children, inviting them to emulate these models, and cueing them to the features of the chosen text structure is not a sufficient scaffold for all children. Most young children need more supports; in order to develop a schema for expository text, they need instruction in the text structures. As Carol Sue Englert and Troy Mariage (1991) note, teachers need to scaffold children's reading and writing activities so that students can recognize and use cues related to expository text structures to plan, organize, draft, and monitor their production of expository texts. They remind us that each expository text structure serves a different purpose, each "answers [a] different text structure question and is signaled by various semantic and syntactic techniques" (pp. 332–333). They illustrate with the compare–contrast text structure. This structure answers the questions, "What is being compared and contrasted? What qualities are being compared? How are they alike? How are they different?" (p. 333). They continue:

> The structure and the answers to these questions are signaled semantically through an expression of the macrostructure in a summary sentence (e.g., "Shetland sheepdogs and collies are similar in several ways, but they are strikingly different dogs"), as well as signaled syntactically through the inclusion of signal or key words such as *alike, different than, in contrast to,* and *similar to.* (p. 333)

A map (or frame or graphic organizer; the terms are used interchangeably) can be drawn for each text structure. (See Table 15.2 for an example of a map for each of the text structures defined earlier and for the signal or key words associated with each structure.)

"The sheep is important because you get wool. You can make mittens and sweaters and lamb chops and jackets."

FIGURE 15.1. *Sheep Are Important,* by Stephanie (age 5).

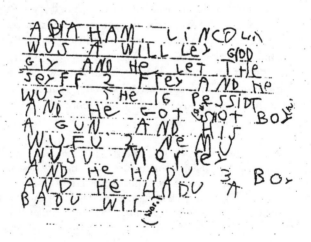

"Abraham Lincoln was a really good guy and he let the slaves free and he was the 16th president and he got shot by a gun. And his wife's name was Mary and he had 3 boys and he had a bad war."

FIGURE 15.2. *Abraham Lincoln,* by Keenan (age 5).

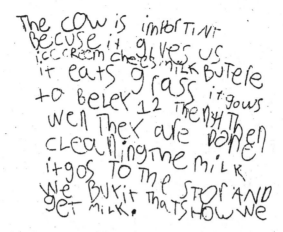

"The cow is important because it gives us ice cream, cheese, milk, butter. It eats grass. It goes to belly 1 and 2 then 3 and 4. Then when they are done cleaning the milk it goes to the store and we buy it. That's how we get milk."

FIGURE 15.3. *Cows Are Important*, by Brandi (age 5).

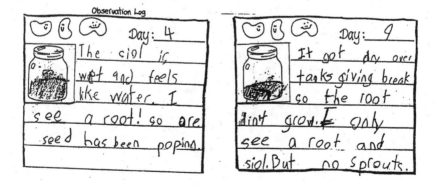

FIGURE 15.4. *A science Observation Log entry*, by Brad (age 6).

I think my Police Department, my hospital and my Fire Department are the most important parts of my community. First, the police are important because the streets wouldn't be safe. They also help guard valuables so people don't steal them. I think if it weren't for the police, my community wouldn't be very big. Also, my hospital is important because what would a community be without health care? Everyone would be ill. I don't think many people would live at Cherry Woods without the hospital. Last but not least the Fire Department is an important part of my community. Without them fires would be everywhere. If it weren't for them Cherry Woods wouldn't be safe.

FIGURE 15.5. *My Community*, by Brad (age 7).

Basketball –Soccer

Basketball and soccer are two sports first and second graders can play.
They are fun to play. In soccer you use your feet of it is a hand ball. In basketball you use your hands. In soccer you dribble with your toes and go down the field. In basketball you dribble with your hands and dribble down the court. Even though they are different they are both fun

FIGURE 15.6. *Basketball–Soccer*, by Alexandra (age 7).

Damge to the ozone layer is breaking apart very quickly. The levels may drop by 3 per tccnt in the next to years. The ozone is breaking aprat because pollution, mainly the chemicals used in refrigirators. Scients think the summer months will be very harmful! Here are some things we can do to help:
Try to find a natural substituite for the harm fule chemicals. Not cut down alot of trees and plant new ones! Not stay out in the sun for a long time or wear sun block

FIGURE 15.7. *Pollution*, by Chandra (age 8).

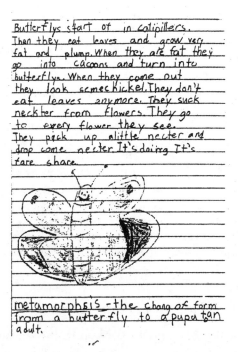

ButterFlys start of in calipillers.
Then they eat leaves and grow very
fat and plump. When they are fat they
go into cacoons and turn into
butterflys. When they come out
they look semes hickel. They don't
eat leaves anymore. They suck
neckter from flowers. They go
to every flower they see.
They pick up alittle necter and
drop some necter. It's daireg It's
fare share.

metamorphsis - the chang of form
from a butterfly to a pupa tan
adult.

FIGURE 15.8. *Butterflies*, by Thomas (age 8).

How to Work a
Jigsaw Puzzle

The first thing you have to do
to work a jigsaw puzzle is
dump out all the pieces and turn
them so you can see the color.
The second thing you do is
put together the the outside (†)
of the puzzle. After you do
that is finish the puzzle. You
can look at the box to help
you.

FIGURE 15.9. *How to Work a Jigsaw Puzzle*, by Valerie (age 8).

Why teach text structures? Englert and Mariage (1991) advise:

> Text structure knowledge is an important tool for teaching students to think about texts and writing. Text structure provides an important scaffold that can guide students in the writing process, as well as providing them with common language tools for analyzing, interpreting, and negotiating their texts. (p. 339)

Other researchers provide additional reasons. For example, Lea McGee (1982) discovered that awareness of text structure is related to children's comprehension and recall of important textual information.

Thus, awareness of text structure is important, and teachers can guide young children in the use of these structures to analyze expository texts they read and to plan expository texts they write. Several instructional strategies have earned researchers' support because of their positive effect on children's reading and writing performance. Here we describe an effective strategy for use with young children.

A Text Structure Analysis and Mapping Teaching Strategy

Following a read-aloud of an expository text, the teacher may display a large model of the appropriate text structure map, like one of those illustrated in Table 15.2. Then the teacher and children can map the text. Such visual representations help to illustrate the relationships among the text's ideas. In essence, the teacher is making the text's grammar visible to the children. Teachers can walk the students through the text structure by asking questions that focus their attention on the key aspects of the structure. It is also important, according to John Readence, Tom Bean, and Scott Baldwin (1998), to point out any words that signal, or cue, the reader regarding what the text structure is. Teachers may also want to verbalize the text structure summary pattern, such as the patterns used by Bonnie Armbruster, Thomas Anderson, and Joyce Ostertag (1989, p. 133). In Table 15.2 we include the kinds of questions teachers might ask as both readers and writers, cue words, and the summary patterns teachers might use for the various text structures.

A teacher would not teach all the text structures at one time; children need multiple experiences with each kind of text structure to acquire an ear for each structure. Yet a glance at Table 15.1 will reveal that the authors of many outstanding expository children's books use more than one text structure in the writing of a single book. One such children's book is Sandra Markle's (2001) *Outside and Inside Rats and Mice*. The teacher may elect to use a book such as Ms. Markle's more than once to illustrate various text structures. To do so, the teacher should decide which text structure

TABLE 15.2. Expository Text Structures

Text structures	Text structure map	Cue words	Questions to help students map a text structure when reading	Structure summary/pattern	Questions to help students choose text structure for their writing
Description	Object/event described: What I see: • Setting/surrounding • How something acts • What something looks like • What I hear • What I smell • What I feel • What I taste *Note:* Not all senses are used for all descriptions	above around beside in back (front) of off throughout across behind between inside on (onto) to the right (left) of against below by into outside under among beneath down near over	• What does ____ look like? • What does ____ smell like? • What does ____ sound like? • What does ____ feel like? • What does ____ act like? • What does ____ taste like? • Does the author describe other things that are similar to ____?	____ is a ____ and ____. It has ____ and ____. It smells like ____, it sounds like ____, and it feels like ____, and it tastes like ____. It looks (acts) a lot like ____. If you watch ____, you might see it ____ or maybe it will ____.	• Does your reader need to know what your topic looks like, sounds like, feels like? • Does your reader need to know how your topic acts? • Does your reader need to know what other things your topic is like? If the answer is "Yes," then *description* will be a good text pattern for you to use in your writing.

(continued on next page)

277

TABLE 15.2. (*continued*)

Text structures	Text structure map	Cue words	Questions to help students map a text structure when reading	Structure summary/ pattern	Questions to help students choose text structure for their writing
Sequence/process/analysis	Step/Event 1 ↓ Step/Event 2 ↓ Step/Event 3 ↓ Step/Event 4 etc.	first to begin with before as soon as second next then until when . . . as soon as immediately at last finally after later soon until as a result	• What directions did the author give you? • What steps were needed? • What words did the author use to cue you to the next step?	_____ is made like this. First, _____. Second, _____. Next, _____. Last, _____. These are the steps needed to make (to understand how) a _____ or _____ happened like this. First, _____. Next, _____. Then, _____. Finally, _____. This is how _____ happened.	• Does your reader need to understand how your topic works or is put together? • Would your reader need "how to" directions to understand your topic? If the answer is "Yes," then *sequence* will be a good text pattern for you to use in your writing.

278

| Compare–contrast | Venn diagram (for younger children)

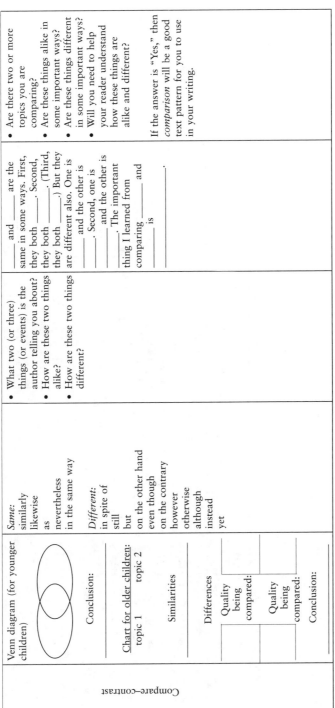

Conclusion:

__Chart for older children:__
topic 1   topic 2

Similarities

Differences

Quality being compared:

Quality being compared:

Conclusion: | *Same:*
similarly
likewise
as
nevertheless
in the same way

Different:
in spite of
still
but
on the other hand
even though
on the contrary
however
otherwise
although
instead
yet | • What two (or three) things (or events) is the author telling you about?
• How are these two things alike?
• How are these two things different? | ___ and ___ are the same in some ways. First, they both ___. Second, they both ___. (Third, they both ___.) But they are different also. One is ___ and the other is ___. Second, one is ___ and the other is ___. The important thing I learned from comparing ___ and ___ is ___. | • Are there two or more topics you are comparing?
• Are these things alike in some important ways?
• Are these things different in some important ways?
• Will you need to help your reader understand how these things are alike and different?

If the answer is "Yes," then *comparison* will be a good text pattern for you to use in your writing. |

(continued on next page)

TABLE 15.2. (continued)

Text structures	Text structure map	Cue words	Questions to help students map a text structure when reading	Structure summary/pattern	Questions to help students choose text structure for their writing
Cause–effect	Simple cause–effect CAUSE → EFFECT Multiple *effects* CAUSE → EFFECT → EFFECT → EFFECT Multiple *causes* CAUSE CAUSE → EFFECT CAUSE	as a result because so consequently so that for	• How did the author describe how _____ started? • What happened as a result of _____? • What did _____ do and what happened as a result _____?	Because of _____, _____ happened. The result of this was _____. *or (for multiple causes)* Because of _____, and _____, _____, and _____ happened. *or (multiple effects)* Because of _____, _____ and _____ happened.	• Would your reader understand what caused or started _____? • Does your reader need to know what will happen with _____? If the answer is "Yes," then cause–effect will be a good text pattern for you to use in your writing.

280

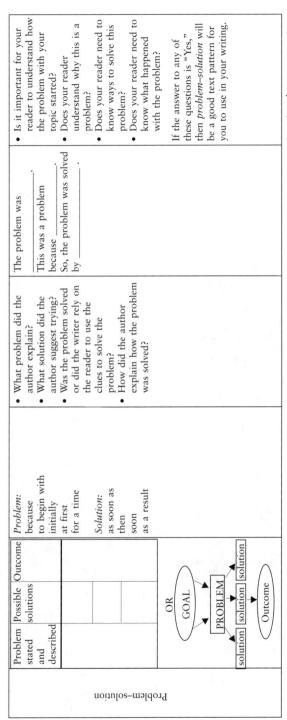

Problem stated and described	Possible solutions	Outcome

OR
GOAL → PROBLEM → solution → Outcome
(solution, solution, solution)

Problem-solution

Problem:
because
to begin with
initially
at first
for a time

Solution:
as soon as
then
soon
as a result

- What problem did the author explain?
- What solution did the author suggest trying?
- Was the problem solved or did the writer rely on the reader to use the clues to solve the problem?
- How did the author explain how the problem was solved?

The problem was _____.
This was a problem because _____.
So, the problem was solved by _____.

- Is it important for your reader to understand how the problem with your topic started?
- Does your reader understand why this is a problem?
- Does your reader need to know ways to solve this problem?
- Does your reader need to know what happened with the problem?

If the answer to any of these questions is "Yes," then *problem-solution* will be a good text pattern for you to use in your writing.

(continued on next page)

TABLE 15.2. (*continued*)

Text structures	Text structure map	Cue words	Questions to help students map a text structure when reading	Structure summary/pattern	Questions to help students choose text structure for their writing
Exemplification	Primary students are too young to be taught about inductive and deductive reasoning; however, textual maps can help students see that sometimes reasons and examples follow or support a main idea, and other times the main idea evolves from the details: (main idea) → (reasons and/or examples) OR (reasons and/or examples) → (main idea)	for example again another in addition along with as well as for instance finally	• What reasons did the author give to prove the main idea? • What examples did the author give to prove the main idea? • What reasons and examples help you understand the author's main idea better?	_____ is _____. I know this because _____. Also _____ is _____ because _____. Finally, _____ is _____ because _____. These are the reasons that _____ is _____.	• Does your reader need to have examples to understand your topic? • Does your reader need reasons for your topic? If the answer is "Yes," then *exemplification* will be a good text pattern for you to use in your writing.

282

to teach and then construct a large version of an appropriate text map such as those described in Table 15.2. The teacher can then direct students to the specific passage in the book and ask questions that will enable them to complete the organizer and identify the cue words.

Sandra Markle's book (2001) offers wonderful examples of comparison. For instance, on page 5, she compares rats with mice:

> Look at the white-footed mouse, on the left, and the cotton rat on the right. The rat is much bigger. The main difference between mice and rats is size. Rats may be as much as fifteen times bigger than mice. Whatever their size, mice and rats have many things in common—one is big front teeth.

With such a relatively short passage, teachers can easily demonstrate the use of a Venn diagram, with similarities being "big front teeth" (and on the next page, the author also names the lack of a thumb as another similarity between mice and rats) and differences having to do with size (rats may be "fifteen times bigger than mice"). After directing students to cue words such as *than* and *in common*, the teacher can help them complete the diagram. Then the teacher can say to the students something such as, "So what can we say is most important to understand when comparing the appearance of rats and mice?" Through such questioning, the students may arrive at a conclusion about the significance of the comparison: Although mice are much smaller than rats, they have other features in common.

Outside and Inside Rats and Mice (Markle, 2001) also provides an excellent example of sequence on page 20:

> Like you, a rat gets the energy it needs to run and be active from its food. Look in the mirror and open your mouth. Digestion, or the breaking down of food, begins here. First, rats chew, grinding the food between their molars. Then a special liquid called saliva floods the food, starting to break it down.
>
> Next the mashed wad is swallowed. Then, more digestive juices go to work, breaking down the food in the stomach and the small intestines. Finally, the food is broken down into chemical building blocks, or nutrients, ready to use. These nutrients pass into the bloodstream and are carried to all parts of the rat's body.

Once the teacher has reviewed some of the difficult vocabulary (e.g., *molars* and *nutrients*) in this segment, the students will probably need relatively little assistance separating the text into discrete stages, especially with the teacher asking them to identify particular cue words that can help them: *first, then, next, finally* (students may want to lump the final stage "These nutrients pass into the bloodstream and are carried to all parts of the rat's body" with the previous sentence because there is no cue word to signal a separate stage). The teacher may engage the students in a discussion about whether a cue word is *always* necessary or evident.

In another section of her book (page 13), Sandra Markle utilizes a problem–solution text structure:

> Rats can't sweat the way you can to cool off. So as a rat heats up, blood flow near the surface of its tail increases. Heat escapes from the blood through the skin, cooling off the rat.

The teacher can ask, "What problem does the rat have because he cannot sweat?" By cueing the students to "sweat," the teacher is scaffolding the students in an effort to help them identify the problem—keeping cool. Once the students have identified the problem as keeping cool, they can go beyond the text to explain *why* this is a problem by identifying the rat's unstated ultimate goal of maintaining a healthy temperature. They then can locate the solution described in the text: The blood flow increases near the surface of the tail so that the heat can escape through that surface. The teacher then asks, "Which line in this story tells us the result of the solution described?" and the students can locate the final line, "cooling off the rat."

A final example from Sandra Markle's book deals with cause–effect (p. 11):

> The rat is grooming its fur after swimming across a stream. . . . By grooming, the rat spreads its natural body oil over its fur. This lets the hair shed water, keeping the rat's skin dry and warm.

Students must first understand the reasons for the rat's grooming its fur. After making sure that students know what "grooming" means, the teacher may ask, "*Why* is the rat doing this?" The students may immediately jump ahead to the effect: "to keep the rat's skin dry and warm." Because this is the result, the teacher can go ahead and put this response in the "effect" bubble of the graphic organizer. But the students have not identified what specifically has *caused* this effect. By asking, "*Why* does the skin stay dry and warm?" the teacher forces students to explain that the rat is spreading oil over the fur, which acts as a coating to keep out the cold and wet. They can then fill in the cause bubble of the text map.

By referring to Table 15.1, teachers can locate other longer segments from *Outside and Inside Rats and Mice*, as well as other picture books, for teaching these and other text structures through models the students will enjoy. The students can then be invited to use literature as models for their own informative writing.

From Drafts to Publication

What *form* will the final draft take? Will the draft be published as an informational picture book? If so, will it be an alphabet book, or a pattern book, or a biography? Maybe it will be published as a feature article in a magazine. Perhaps it will be presented as a speech or sung as a song. Perhaps it will be written in a journal format. Some teachers may even venture bravely into guiding their students through the multigenre research process (Romano, 2000). Whatever the form, children need to see models of how other writers moved beyond their notes to publication. They need to see how other writers used photographs, captions, labels on illustrations, different types of print, and other features of expository text writing to help the reader. Does their text need a table of contents, a glossary, or an index? Again, mentors are important. Children learn by trying what others have done before them.

Who will be the *audience* for the expository pieces? The Primary School children wrote their expository books for each other and their parents. (The principal organized authors' teas and the Parent Teacher Association had an ice cream social at which children in each classroom read their pieces to family and friends.) Tracy Novack's second graders wrote their reports for their school's kindergartners. Writers are willing to invest much more energy in their work when they know their pieces will be read or heard by a real audience, by others beyond the teacher.

SUMMARY

In this chapter we have focused on expository text structures: what they are, how teachers can help children discern the text structures used in the pieces that are read to them and that they read, and how teachers can help children use these text structures in their crafting of expository text pieces. We recognize that we have *not* provided teachers with information on how to guide their students' topic selection; or how to help them frame the questions to guide their data/information collection; or how to connect children, some of whom are not yet reading, with the authentic resources and sources that will answer their questions; or how to conduct interviews or read and take notes; or how to get all those notes into an order that will allow the children to select a text structure to begin drafting. Just as Jerry Pallota decides on the final page of *The Furry Alphabet* (1991) that naked mole rats do not belong in his book of mammals because they have no fur, these other important features of getting ready to write do not belong in this chapter. A number of writers, such as Stephanie Harvey (1998) and

Tony Stead (2002), have written whole books on these aspects of expository text reading and writing. We think they did it better in their books than we could have done in this chapter, and we refer readers to these important resources. Yet although others provide teachers with direction on the *how* of engaging in the process of guiding children's expository text reading and writing, we are convinced that too little has been written about how expository texts are organized and how to support children's development of this important knowledge. When children read and write expository texts without the knowledge they need, their reading comprehension and writing development is hampered. It is not surprising that the Primary School's teachers' inaugural foray into teaching expository text reading and writing did not include text structure lessons—teachers also need mentors to guide their expository text teaching plans.

REFERENCES

Armbruster, B., Anderson, T.H., & Ostertag, J. (1989). Teaching text structure to improve reading and writing. *The Reading Teacher, 42,* 130–137.

Berthoff, A. E. (1983). How we construct is how we construe. In P. Stock (Ed.), *Forum: Essays on theory and practice in the teaching of writing* (pp. 166–169). Upper Montclair, NJ: Boynton/Cook.

Caswell, L. J., & Duke, N. K. (1998). Non-narrative as a catalyst for literacy development. *Language Arts, 75,* 108–117.

Cooper, J. D. (1997). *Literacy: Helping children construct meaning.* Boston: Houghton Mifflin.

Decker, R. E., & Schwegler, R. A. (1998). *Decker's patterns of exposition 15.* New York: Longman.

Duke, N. (2000). 3.6 minutes per day: The scarcity of information texts in first grade. *Reading Research Quarterly, 35,* 202–224.

Duke, N., & Kays, J. (1998). "Can I say 'once upon a time'?" Kindergarten children developing knowledge of information book language. *Early Childhood Research Quarterly, 13,* 295–318.

Duthie, C. (1994). Nonfiction: A genre study for the primary classroom. *Language Arts, 71,* 588–595.

Englert, C. S., & Mariage, T. V. (1991). Shared understandings: Structuring the writing experience dialogue. *Journal of Learning Disabilities, 24,* 330–342.

Freeman, M. S. (1997). *Listen to this: Developing an ear for expository.* Gainsville, FL: Maupin House.

Guthrie, J. T., & McCann, A. D. (1997). Characteristics of classrooms that promote motivations and strategies for learning. In J. T. Guthrie & A. Wigfield (Eds.), *Reading engagement: Motivating readers through integrated instruction* (pp. 128–148). Newark, DE: International Reading Association.

Harvey, S. (1998). *Nonfiction matters: Reading, writing, and research.* York, ME: Stenhouse.

Keene, E. O, & Zimmermann, S. (1997). *Mosaic of thought: Teaching composition in a reader's workshop.* Portsmouth, NH: Heinemann.

McGee, L. M. (1982). Awareness of text structure: Effects on children's recall of expository text. *Reading Research Quarterly, 17,* 581–590.

Romano, T. (2000). *Blending genre, altering style: Writing multigenre papers.* Portsmouth, NH: Heinemann.

Readence, J. E., Bean, T. W., & Baldwin, R. S. (1998). *Content area reading: An integrated approach* (6th ed.). Dubuque, IA: Kendall/Hunt.

Stead, T. (2002). *Is that a fact?: Teaching nonfiction writing K–3.* York, ME: Stenhouse.

Tierney, R. J., Readence, J. E., & Dishner, E. K. (1995). *Reading strategies and practices: A compendium.* Boston, MA: Allyn & Bacon.

Tompkins, G. (2000). *Teaching writing: Balancing process and product* (3rd ed.). Upper Saddle River, NJ: Prentice-Hall.

Yopp, R. H., & Yopp, H. K. (2000). Sharing informational text with young children. *The Reading Teacher, 53,* 410–423.

SUGGESTED BOOKS FOR CHILDREN

Adler, D. A. (1999). *How tall, how short, how far away.* New York: Holiday House.

Aliki. (1988). *A weed is a flower: The life of George Washington Carver.* New York: Simon & Schuster.

Armentrout, P. (1997). *The wedge.* Vero Beach, FL: Rourke Press.

Barton, B. (1981). *Building a house.* New York: William Morrow.

Bash, B. (1989). *Desert giant: The world of the saguaro cactus.* New York: Scholastic.

Berger, M. (1992). *Discovering Mars: The amazing story of the red planet.* New York: Scholastic.

Brandley, F. M. (2000). *The international space station.* New York: HarperCollins.

Cherry, L.. (1992). *A river ran wild.* Orlando, FL: Harcourt, Brace.

Collard, S. B. (1997). *Animal dads.* New York: Scholastic.

Cuyler, M. (2001). *Stop, drop, and roll.* New York: Simon & Schuster Books for Young Readers.

Ehlert, L. (1990). *Feathers for lunch.* New York: Scholastic.

Gibbons, G. (1993). *Frogs.* New York: Scholastic.

Gibbons, G. (1995). *Sea turtles.* New York: Holiday House.

Hawes, J. (2000). *Why frogs are wet.* New York: HarperCollins.

Herman, G. (1995). *Apollo 13: Space race.* New York: Grosset & Dunlap.

Hewitt, S. (1999). *The five senses.* Danbury, CT: Children's Press.

Hickman, P. (2001). *Animals eating: How animals chomp, chew, slurp, and swallow.* Tonawanda, NY: Kids Can Press.

Knight, J. (1998). *Jamestown.* New York: Troll Communications.

Le Rochais, M. (1999). *Desert trek.* New York: Walker.

Lewin, T., & Lewin, B. (2000). *Elephant Quest.* New York: HarperCollins.

London, J. (2001). *Crocodile: Disappearing dragon.* Cambridge, MA: Candlewick Press.

Maestro, B., & Maestro, G. (2000). *Struggle for a continent: The French and Indian Wars*. New York: HarperCollins.

Markle, S. (2001). *Rats and mice*. New York: Atheneum Books for Young Readers.

McNulty, F. (1979). *How to dig a hole to the other side of the world*. New York: HarperCollins.

Montanari, D. (2001). *Children around the world*. Tonawanda, NY: Kids Can Press.

Nadler, B. (1995). *The magic school bus inside Ralphie: A book about germs*. New York: Scholastic.

Nicholson, C. P. (2001). *Volcano!* Tonawanda, NY: Kids Can Press.

O'Brien, P. (2001). *Megatooth*. New York: Henry Holt.

Pallotta, J. (1991). *The furry alphabet book*. New York: Scholastic.

Parker, S. (1999). *It's an ant's life: My story of life in the nest*. Pleasantville, NY: Reader's Digest Children's Publishing.

Robbins, K. (1992). *Make me a peanut butter sandwich: And a glass of milk*. New York: Scholastic.

Rockwell, A. (2001). *Bugs are insects*. New York: HarperCollins.

Rylant, C. (1996). *The whales*. New York: Scholastic.

Schaefer, L. (2001). *Who works here? Fast-food restaurant*. Chicago: Heinemann.

Selsam, M. E. (1995). *How to be a nature detective*. New York: HarperCollins Children's Books.

Senisi, E. (2001). *Berry smudges and leaf prints*. New York: Dutton Children's Books.

Showers, P. (2001). *What happens to a hamburger?* New York: HarperCollins.

Simon, S. (1993). *Wolves*. New York: HarperCollins.

Simon, S. (1997). *The brain: Our nervous system*. New York: Scholastic.

Simon, S. (1997). *Lightning*. New York: Scholastic.

Sis, P. (1991). *Follow the dream: The story of Christopher Columbus*. New York: Knopf.

Spier, P. (1980). *People*. New York: Bantam Doubleday Dell.

Willis, N. C. (1998). *The robins in your backyard*. Middletown, DE: Birdsong Books.

Woelfein, L. (1995). *Metamorphosis*. New York: Penguin Books.

Yolen, J., & Stemple, H. (2001). *The wolf girls*. New York: Simon & Schuster.

ANSWER KEY TO FIGURES

Figure 15.1.   Exemplification (note how the examples in the text match the picture).

Figure 15.2.   Description (the author describes who Abraham Lincoln was, what he was like, and what he did).

Figure 15.3.   Sequence.

Figure 15.4.   Cause–effect.

Figure 15.5.   Exemplification.

Figure 15.6   Compare–contrast.

Figure 15.7.   Problem–solution.

Figure 15.8.   Sequence.

Figure 15.9.   Sequence.

Part V

Conclusion

16

Caution, Apply with Care
Recommendations for Early Literacy Instruction

DIANE M. BARONE

> Every time a new orthodoxy hits the school system and we
> throw out the old to bring in the new, we are in danger of
> losing our way.
>   —FOX (2001, p. 105)

This quote has made me rethink the work I do with teachers. Frequently, I
recommend new literacy strategies that I think are important to put in place
in their classrooms. It has also made me reflect on my research in schools
where I have had an opportunity to observe teaching and learning in the
primary grades, especially in schools considered at risk. In my observations,
I have learned how hard it is to bring a new literacy strategy into a classroom and that it takes time for teachers to make it a significant part of their
curriculum (see Chapter 1 in this book). Teachers ask, "How does it fit in
with what I already do?" or "Where will I find the time to do one more
thing in my already jammed curriculum?" And if the new strategy is not
seen as beneficial, it quickly moves to the margins of the classroom and
then departs silently under the door.

It is no easy task for a teacher to make adjustments to his or her literacy curriculum. Each change requires a close examination of the classroom
organization and how it must be modified for the new strategy. For example, asking children to engage in discussion about a book usually means
breaking the class into small groups so that each child has a chance to contribute to the discussion. When students are organized into small groups,
the teacher is responsible for finding appropriate learning activities for

those children not involved. And he or she must also determine a rotation schedule so that all children have an opportunity to participate in this activity.

In addition to organization, the teacher must consider the strengths and needs of each child in the classroom in forming the groups and in providing appropriate independent learning activities. All of this planning is necessary for the new strategy to be implemented, and it must be carried out for the remaining part of the literacy curriculum as well. Moreover, teachers also have to consider how this activity or strategy meets the district and state standards and how it will potentially affect any testing that is required of the students. It is no wonder that teachers often roll their eyes at the thought of any change to their curriculum. Teachers are resilient, however, and they routinely take on the challenge of revising their established literacy curriculums to fit in new strategies supported by research.

In this chapter, I discuss some of the recommended knowledge or strategies for early literacy that are based in research, such as the alphabetic principle, and describe the complexity of bringing new strategies and content into the classroom. Although there are many aspects of the literacy curriculum to focus on, I narrow the discussion to an exploration of learning the alphabetic principle, oral reading, independent reading, and balancing the literacy curriculum. To enhance these descriptions, many vignettes from my observations are presented. My goal for this chapter is to support a teacher in integrating the newer research-based strategies into his or her classroom while maintaining the successful strategies already imbedded in the classroom literacy curriculum.

LEARNING THE ALPHABETIC PRINCIPLE

Many reports (Adams, Foorman, Lundberg, & Beeler, 1997; Ehri et al., 2001; National Reading Panel, 2000) have documented that phonemic awareness is an important foundation for early reading because it is through this awareness that children come to learn about the alphabetic principle—how sounds map to letters. Because of this importance, children are explicitly taught to manipulate the phonemes (smallest sound units) within words. For example, in preschool, kindergarten, and the primary grades, children can be seen learning about phonemes by listening to and memorizing rhymes, clapping out the syllables in their names, saying the initial sounds in words, and journal writing, among other activities. For most early childhood teachers, these activities are not new and have been present in early childhood curriculums for some time. What is new is the importance assigned to this knowledge and that this knowledge is considered critical to a child's later reading success.

Teachers emphasize phonemic awareness initially by helping children aurally recognize sounds in words and then moving them to segmentation, the ability to separate the sounds in words, such as b – a – t for bat. Teachers move children from an aural knowledge of phonemes to the ability to read and write them. Teachers have long understood the importance of this knowledge for children and have provided various activities for them to acquire it.

The newest addition to the repertoire of strategies designed to support phonemic knowledge is the engagement of children with writing. The work of Calkins (1986), Bissex (1980), and Henderson (1990), among others, demonstrates how young children, before they are aware of conventional spelling, write messages even though their writing may be hard to decipher. Read's work (1975) unlocked some of the reasons behind the patterns seen in the invented writing of children, and teachers and researchers have learned about the typical development of young writers. Moreover, they have learned how children practice and extend their knowledge of phonemes through their writing. Teachers can see and hear young children practice sounds as they go about writing. For example, when I visited a kindergarten, I heard a child say the /m/ sound. Unfortunately, although he knew this sound began the word he wanted to write, he did not know how to make an *M*. He asked his friend, who said, "Like McDonalds." The child then quickly made an *M* on his paper and continued his message. This brief example demonstrates the power of writing to support phonemic knowledge; in addition, it shows the power of children working together to decipher how to actualize this knowledge.

Although this example is eloquent, what I have seen teachers doing recently to help children acquire knowledge of phonemes is directed more explicitly. There is great pressure on teachers to make sure that young children acquire knowledge of phonemes and how to use them to decode words. They are aware of the research that documents the importance of this ability to later reading success (Adams, 1990; Juel, 1988; Stanovich, 1986). Thus, they are trying very hard to make this knowledge available to students, especially to children considered at risk.

The following sections present examples of teachers implementing instruction in phonemic awareness, phonemic segmentation, and phonics in an attempt to help their students acquire the alphabetic principle. Some of the examples describe teachers who have implemented instruction but are not meeting the needs of their students with this implementation, and others describe teachers who have successfully incorporated this instruction into their classrooms. It is important to remember that all of the teachers described here are trying to enrich their curriculums and meet the learning needs of students by bringing new strategies and content into their classrooms.

Unsuccessful Implementation

During a recent study, I observed the literacy instruction in two kindergarten classrooms in a school considered to be at risk because it enrolled predominantly high-poverty children who were learning English as a new language. In one room, Mrs. Castor began each day by having the children
listen to a record, echoing the sounds of each letter. Here is what it sounded
like:

> "A says 'ah,' 'ah,' 'ah.' B says 'buh,' 'buh,', 'buh.' . . ."

Many of the children tried to imitate the record; others waited for it to be
over and just looked around the room while it played. The problem with
this activity was that most of the children did not speak English at all and
could not write their names yet. Thus, although they imitated the sounds,
they had no understanding of how these sounds tied to print or, more important, even what letters were. They were obedient, however, and they
tried to please their teacher each day when the record was played.

In a second kindergarten room, Miss Spencer also spent a large part of
her day on letter–sound lessons. Most of the children in her room were
learning English as a new language. Each student had a journal in which
pages were devoted to specific letters. On the day I observed, the teacher
had the children volunteer words that began with the letter R. A few children did suggest words that began with R, like "rose" and "rope." Unfortunately, the majority of children volunteered random words that did not
begin with this letter. The teacher wrote the correct words on the chalkboard and then drew pictures to represent each word. The children were
expected to copy the words and illustrations from the board. The children
did follow the teacher's directions and tried to replicate the words and
drawings in their journals. However, when I asked several what letter they
were working on, they had no idea. Moreover, when I asked them about
the words they were trying to copy, they could not identify them.

These activities continued throughout the kindergarten year and were
supported with work sheets to help the children learn about sound–symbol
relationships. The teachers were diligent in teaching these skills to their students on a day-to-day basis, and they structured their lessons systematically
so that the children built on the previous teachings of letters and sounds. At
the end of the year when the teachers assessed their students, fewer than 10
of the 80 students in these rooms had developed sound–symbol knowledge
and most children recognized fewer than 10 letters. Clearly, the teachers'
instruction was systematic, but it did not take into consideration the
strengths and needs of the children in the room. They needed to be involved

in aural exploration of language through rhymes and ditties before focusing on more formal aspects of letter–sound relationships. They also needed opportunities to become familiar with the alphabet before considering sound–symbol relationships.

Successful Implementation

The following examples come from kindergarten classrooms where the majority of students were high-poverty children of African American heritage. Mrs. Campbell could be considered an exemplary teacher, as described by Ladson-Billings (1994). She was aware of her students' out-of-school experiences, and she knew their parents as well. She began each morning with conversations with the children. As the children and teacher chatted, she recorded some of their conversations on chart paper. As she wrote, she had children help her with the writing. They suggested what letter to use or how to spell a word. Each sentence began with the name of the child who offered it. When one or two sentences were recorded, the children reread the message with the teacher's support. Then Mrs. Campbell asked children to go to the chart to find a word or a letter. They marked the letter or word on the chart. Every child was able to participate, because each could find his or her name. These messages were displayed in prominent places so that the children could re-read them throughout their kindergarten day. At the end of a week, the messages were bound into a book for the children to explore as well.

As the year progressed, Mrs. Campbell moved the children to more explicit exploration of letters and sounds. For example, she presented the letter *S* to the children. As in the preceding example, the children volunteered words that began with the letter presented. Following this brainstorming activity, the children, in pairs, looked through magazines and found pictures that began with *S*. They glued the pictures on a paper and attempted to write the words that accompanied them. The teacher was concerned only that the children had the initial *S* correct, and she looked at how they represented the words to get ideas for building her next lessons.

This lesson was dramatically different from those discussed earlier: The children were not copying, they were engaged in meaningful activity in which they had to discover the pictures that accompanied a letter and then use their letter–sound knowledge to represent the appropriate words. Following from this activity, Mrs. Campbell formed short-term groups that either continued to work on initial consonants or moved to an exploration of short vowels and what follows. For children in the latter group, Mrs. Campbell helped children consider short vowel patterns like *an*, *at*, and *ap*.

In a second kindergarten classroom, Mr. Webster grouped his students around an easel at the beginning of each day. Each child also had a clipboard with paper and a pencil. At the beginning of the year, the children practiced writing the names of the children in the room, one each day. Mr. Webster had the child whose name was to be written come to his easel and help him write his or her name. As the teacher wrote, all of the children wrote on their papers. Once all the names were recorded in this way, the children made comparisons by looking at the initial consonants or vowels in their classmates' names. Then, he moved from names to writing a message from one child each day. Unlike the procedure in Mrs. Campbell's room, the child wrote the message on the chart paper with the help of the teacher. Because Mr. Webster wanted all the children to participate simultaneously, the children wrote with the focal child. Each child had the opportunity to record the message with the help of the focal child and the teacher. Following the writing, the focal child illustrated his or her sentence, and such papers became part of a book for the children to read during free reading time.

While this activity was occurring, Mr. Webster carefully watched his students to see the ease or difficulty they were having with the task. Following the activity, he worked with small groups of students on phonemic awareness or segmentation, depending on their strengths. He often engaged them in aural activities in which they identified a word that did not belong (e.g., *bat*, *bug*, *car*, *bed*). With other groups, he explored sound–symbol relationships or short vowel patterns.

Comparison of Unsuccessful and Successful Implementations

The examples discussed in the preceding sections describe a number of ways in which teachers have incorporated phonemic knowledge into their curriculums. In the first two examples, the teachers were thoughtful in the ways that they brought this knowledge to students. What they did not conceptualize was how this knowledge matched the strengths of their students or how to individualize this instruction for the children. They taught their students in one large group, with no accommodation for individual students' learning needs or the reality that most of their students were learning English as a new language.

In the last two examples, the teachers built their instruction of phonemes around the children's own language and experiences. They moved from what was known by the students to less familiar territory. They expected all of their students to participate and used whole-group sessions for assessment as well. From these activities, they moved to smaller groups in which individual student needs could be met. At the end of the year when the teachers assessed their students, the children in these classrooms had full understanding of the sound–symbol relationships of initial consonants and many of the children understood short vowels and ending consonants.

ORAL READING

When I think back to my days in the primary grades, a very long time ago, I remember best the reading groups to which the children were assigned. Each day, small groups of children met with the teacher and engaged in round-robin oral reading. Following the reading, the teacher asked a few questions about the story, and then the group was dismissed to complete the workbook sheets that accompanied each story (Smith, 1986). When I visit classrooms today, I frequently see students organized into small reading groups that meet with the teacher. Although round-robin reading has not vanished, it is now accompanied by choral or echo-reading. Teachers engage the children with a story by discussing the cover of the book, often a predictable leveled text, and then they orally read the story using one of the strategies mentioned earlier. As the children read, the teacher closely monitors each child to check on his or her ability to decode the words in the story. Sometimes the children are stopped during reading to talk about the story, and sometimes they are asked questions at the end of the story.

These newer reading situations vary, although in subtle ways, from the earlier reading instruction of children when I was a child. Back then, teachers used readiness tests to group children for reading instruction. These teachers typically had one basal to use with all children, and the only variation among groups was the speed with which children moved through the texts (Smith, 1986). Today, teachers have a wider repertoire of ways to assess children (Johnston & Rogers, 2001), which include formal and informal assessment to help with grouping. Although readiness tests are still used in many schools, teachers also use alphabet knowledge, running records, and concepts of print, among other assessments (Johnston & Rogers, 2001). Teachers have a wider variety of materials to use with their students, such as basals, leveled texts, and expository material. In spite of these differences, sometimes the reading groups appear not to have changed much from the 1950s, in that the children are reading orally with a focus on decoding rather than comprehension.

The major concern that has developed in regard to oral reading is that children view reading solely as decoding, rather than a meaning-based process. If teachers spend most of the time with students focused on decoding, then the children come away believing that decoding is reading, rather than understanding the importance of gaining meaning from reading. This worry about the definition of reading becomes clearer in the following examples derived from first- and second-grade classrooms.

Unsuccessful Implementation

Mrs. Denton and Miss Trent co-taught a first-grade class of 32 low-income children. They each worked with three reading groups every day, which were organized according to the ability level of the students. The teachers informally assessed each of their students at the beginning of the year using running records, and they repeated this assessment during the year to check on the literacy growth of the students. The children's groups were then adjusted so that children of the same reading level were placed together. Typically, the students were called to a group and the teacher introduced a new story by a quick look at the cover. The children then read the book aloud together, following the lead of the teacher. When the book had been read, the children reread the story to themselves. As they reread the story, the teacher engaged one child in a running record of his or her oral reading of it. Each day the teacher worked with a different child to accomplish this individually based assessment. These records determined the level at which a child could adequately decode.

This assessment/instruction sequence sounds exemplary, in that the teachers were closely matching instruction to assessment. What was missing was any focus on the individual strengths of students or the understanding of text. For example, when I asked Mrs. Denton about Angel's reading, she said, "He is at level 4." I asked what that meant. Her response was, "He can read words at level 4 without much trouble." When I watched Angel's reading group, it was true that he did not have problems with material assessed to be at this level. His teacher did not ask the children to talk about the book before or after reading, so the focus was only on decoding. Mrs. Denton used the running record as a way to match a child to a reading level, but she did not analyze the ways in which Angel or the other students deciphered a word to build their strengths with word identification. Moreover, she did not focus on an understanding of the story or its characters. Comprehension was particularly important in this classroom, as the majority of children were learning English as a new language and were not familiar with much of the vocabulary or situations portrayed in the stories they read. Therefore, it was not surprising that when I asked Angel to tell me about reading, he said, "It is sounding out the words." When I asked him about a favorite story, he could not identify a book by title. Similar descriptions were provided by the majority of children in the room; for them, reading was decoding.

Successful Implementation

In one of my research studies, I was able to spend a year in the second-grade classroom led by Mrs. Campbell. The majority of her students were poor and African American. She organized her reading so that she provided a whole-class reading activity and small-group reading each day. One day I watched her engage the children with the book *Miss Nelson Is Missing* (Allard, 1977). As the children came to sit on the floor near her, she told them, "Put on your visors so you have extra-special thinking powers." The children took visors from their desks and placed them on their heads before joining the group. Mrs. Campbell encouraged the children to talk about the book before it was begun; she continued this process as they read and at the end of the story. When the story had been read, the children played a game called "Stump the Teacher." They asked her questions about the plot or characters in the story. They were challenged to come up with a question she could not answer. This strategy is similar to ReQuest, an activity designed by Manzo (1969). After this question-and-answer time, she asked them, "Do you think Miss Nelson was a good teacher?" The children did not agree on this issue, and they created a chart with the reasons why and why not. They then returned to their desks to continue the discussion. Through this question, Mrs. Campbell moved her students to think critically about what they read and to support their beliefs with evidence from the book.

When the children worked in small groups, the routine was similar. The only major difference was that the children read books at their instructional levels. Although Mrs. Campbell facilitated the understanding of stories and expository books, she also provided direct instruction in decoding. She sat next to each child as the child re-read a story and listened as he or she read her a page. She made notes of the way the children decoded words and the strategies they used. She then used this information in planning for her next lesson. She also made notes on the children's comments about a story and any troubling vocabulary or comprehension issues. Unlike Angel, when I asked Curtis about reading, he said, "I have too many books to have a favorite. I like myths a lot." Other children in the class talked about favorite books, and they talked about learning to read "by reading a lot."

Comparison of Unsuccessful and Successful Implementations

At the end of the year, the children in the two classrooms discussed earlier had very different ideas about reading. They both had had systematic instruction in decoding grounded in oral reading. However, the children in Mrs. Campbell's room understood that meaning was the important part of reading, not just getting the words right. In addition, Mrs. Campbell was able to articulate the strengths and needs of individual children and did not rely on reading level alone. She was also able to use a running record for more information than just decoding knowledge. She asked children comprehension questions and had them talk to her about what they read so that she had a fuller picture of their reading strengths.

INDEPENDENT READING

Independent reading in early childhood classrooms has become a common event. Teachers structure their day so the children have an opportunity to explore illustrations and read self-selected books. It is during these social and interactive experiences with books that children get to practice and demonstrate their language and literacy competence (Meier, 2000). Moreover, these experiences allow children to be engaged with books that they personally choose to read, unlike other reading situations in which the teacher selects the reading material. Teachers have responded to the positive relationship that has been documented between reading achievement and access to literature (Elley, 1992) by incorporating libraries in their classrooms to facilitate book selection for children.

So why the discussion of independent reading when it is documented to result in increases in reading achievement? I have chosen to include it because in many observations, I see teachers relying on independent reading as their major strategy to develop literacy. Unfortunately, the majority of children in these classrooms have not developed as readers and writers. Access to books has been beneficial to the children as they are engaged with the books, but it has not been sufficient to develop the knowledge they need to develop into readers (McGill-Franzen, Allington, Yokoi, & Brooks, 1999). The following sections give examples that describe unsuccessful and successful implementations of independent reading.

Unsuccessful Implementation

For one academic year, I observed in the first grade of Mrs. Carroll and Mrs. Hagin. They taught low-income children who were learning English as a new language. In this room, the teachers allocated 1 hour each morning for independent reading. They dismissed their students to the library area, where they expected the children to read or look at books. During this time, they conducted running record assessments with individual students and infrequently interacted with the children in the library. During my observations, I targeted several children and watched them closely during independent reading time. The majority of children chose books, looked at them briefly, and then put them back. They spent most of their time talking to friends until a teacher reminded them to look at a book. They were rarely engaged with the books that were chosen, and most of the books were too difficult for them to read without the support of a teacher. The teachers filled the library with beautiful picture books, but the children did not have the ability to read the words in these books. At best, they scanned the illustrations.

At the end of the year, the only children in this first-grade classroom to achieve at grade level in reading and writing were those who had Reading Recovery support. (The teachers used level 16, based on Reading Recovery levels, to determine grade-level achievement.) The remaining children were still struggling with the alphabetic principle and were not able to read text independently. Clearly, independent reading was not successful as the primary strategy to teach these children to read.

Successful Implementation

Mr. Evans taught first grade in a school that enrolled primarily low-income children. In fact, about 40% of the children were homeless. Like the teaching team described in the preceding section, he organized about 1 hour each day for independent reading. The differences in this classroom were that Mr. Evans interacted with his students as they read and he provided numerous books at their independent and instructional levels.

Each day the children chose the books they wanted to read from a tub of books that were at their independent or instructional levels. Mr. Evans moved among them and frequently sat next to a child as he or she shared a book with him. He asked the children questions about the book, such as why it was chosen or what they thought was interesting about what they had read. He did not ask specific comprehension questions, although he engaged each student in extensive dialogue about the book. Following their discussion, the students wrote about their books in their personal journal, to which Mr. Evans responded on a daily basis. He encouraged his students to begin independent reading by rereading the books they had chosen yesterday and then moving on to a new selection.

Mr. Evans's independent reading time was also the major strategy he used to develop readers and writers. He was successful because of his time with each of his students, during which he checked their ability to decode text and understand as well. He made sure that he provided narrative and informational text that his students could read easily or with his help. He often nudged children to try a special book that he knew they "would love." He also pushed his young students by having them write about their reading. Through this writing, the children had an opportunity to practice their knowledge of the alphabetic principle as they wrote about the important aspects of their books. Mr. Evans also found time to respond to their writing with a personal message centered on the ideas shared in their writing. At the end of the year the majority of his students exceeded grade-level expectations, based on informal reading inventory results, and were well on their way to becoming independent readers and writers.

Comparison of Unsuccessful and Successful Implementations

The reasons for the differences in student achievement in the examples presented in the preceding sections were the presence of the teacher and the inclusion of books at students' independent and instructional levels. The teacher was the key to the children's benefiting from the independent reading experiences. Mr. Evans spent time sitting next to children as they read, and he learned about the books and strategies they used when reading. He carefully planned the books that the children could choose from so that they could use their current literacy knowledge and build from it to newer understandings. He saw independent reading as a time for his students to practice the skills and strategies he taught them during other instructional episodes during their day. He used this time as well to informally assess their development and to plan future lessons based on this knowledge.

BALANCING THE LITERACY CURRICULUM

The issue of balance in the literacy curriculum is complex, for it extends beyond the balance of explicit teaching of phonics and meaning-centered activities focused on reading and writing. Although the issue of balance (phonics and comprehension) may be the first one teachers and researchers consider, there are many other instructional issues related to balance. Among these are considerations concerning text (expository and narrative and other genres), fluency and decoding, whole-class and small-group organization, direct instruction and more informal support, heterogeneous and homogeneous grouping, and the philosophical orientation of the teacher. In this section I focus on only two aspects of balance: balance in strategies for teaching and in philosophical orientation.

Balance in Strategies

Teachers are often most concerned with balancing strategies. For some teachers, this means moving away from using direct teaching as the dominant style. For other teachers, it means the opposite, in that they must find time for more explicit teaching in their workshop-oriented classrooms. The key to each of these approaches is the organization and management structures that are its foundation. For example, teachers who engage their students in the explicit learning of how a letter maps to a particular sound need to be cognizant of their students' abilities and to make sure that the lesson is understood by their students. These are also the concerns of teachers who engage their students in workshop lessons. Here, again, the teacher must think carefully about the students' knowledge and how he or she can build from it. However, these approaches require different organization and management structures. In whole-class teaching, it is easy to see when students are disengaged by observing them play at their desks with crayons or pencils rather than listen to the teacher (Hicks, 2002). Although the behaviors are different, it is also easy to observe when a workshop classroom is out of control. For example, students move from activity to activity without any real involvement with it. They chat with friends but they do not commit to the reading or writing that is expected. In both of these situations, the teachers have not prepared the students to work responsibly, and as a result students lose direction and motivation to participate (Kaufman, 2001).

Unsuccessful Implementation

The following examples are grounded in both explicit and more indirect learning opportunities. In both cases, the teachers and students struggled with the organization necessary to support the teaching strategy. These examples come from kindergarten classes with students who were predominantly from low-income backgrounds.

Mrs. Brayton organized her literacy instruction by teaching all of her students at one time. They sat in a circle near her as she taught about the alphabet. When they worked on a specific letter, the children watched as she presented a letter, such as *T*, and words that began with it. Following this instruction, she gave a few children pictures; they were to decide whether their pictures began with a *T*. Frequently, as I observed, I noted children who never paid attention to the teacher and her instruction. They wiggled and talked to their neighbors as Mrs. Brayton reminded them to pay attention. Later, when a few students determined whether their letter began with a specific sound, they still did not pay attention to this matching. During follow-up learning activities, only a few children were able to find pictures that began with the designated letter.

Mrs. Hunt organized her room so that the children worked at centers for all instruction. While she worked with one group, the remaining children were busy with learning activities in the centers. Even though her students were organized into groups, she did not vary the learning expectations at any of the centers or in her work with the children. When she worked with a small group, her instruction centered on sound–symbol relationships; the same relationship was explored for each group. Her students were not as disinterested as those in Mrs. Brayton's class, but many failed to absorb the instruction provided. It was clear in their writing that they still confused many of the sound–symbol relationships that were explicitly discussed.

Both of these examples demonstrate that regardless of organization, teachers must meet the learning needs of their students. These teachers taught skills systematically and carefully prepared for their instruction. Unfortunately, they considered their students as a class and did not match instruction to individual student strengths and needs.

Successful Implementation

The following example is from a first-grade classroom where the teacher combined direct and workshop instruction. She also met the needs of individual students in her instruction.

Miss Moore taught a group of low-income students, many of whom were learning English as a new language. At the beginning of each day she organized a read-aloud with her students. Most of the books she chose for this instruction were simple, predictable text in a big-book format. She started her reading by engaging all of her students in a discussion of the illustration on the cover. Then she read the book, allowing for informal comments by her students. At the end of the reading, she and her students discussed the book. She then re-read the story. Following this reading, she asked individual children to identify letters or words. The more sophisticated children might be asked to find a short- or long-vowel word.

After this whole-group instruction, Miss Moore divided her students into small groups for specific homogeneous instruction. Each group alternated between her and the center activities. When students met with her, she engaged them in a short lesson focused on phonemic awareness or phonics. After this lesson, she introduced a book, at their instructional level, to the children. The children talked about the book and read it silently. Following reading, the children talked about the book. Periodically, Miss Moore asked the children to read a snippet of text from the book to check on decoding strengths. The children were dismissed from this group to complete extension activities that grew from her lesson; sometimes the activities were tied to the story and other times they were connected to the teacher's phonics instruction. After the students had completed these activities, they engaged in library reading or a science activity. As in the examples in the preceding section, the teacher's instruction was systematic, but it also built on each child's learning strengths and needs.

Balance in Philosophical Orientation

The issue of balance in philosophical orientation grows from the decision by teachers to use an eclectic approach to organizating their instruction. I have heard teachers say, "I use a little of this and a little of that. I want to meet the needs of all of my students." Although being eclectic is not necessarily problematic and can help teachers meet the needs of individual students, it can also be detrimental to students if a number of very different philosophical orientations are included in a classroom. The following example illustrates.

Unsuccessful Implementation

Mrs. Herald thought carefully about how she would blend her explicit and more workshop-oriented instruction for the literacy learning of her students. She had many students in her second-grade classroom who were struggling with reading and writing. To meet the needs of these students, she used two very different approaches with them.

Early in the morning Mrs. Herald met with small groups of students, for whom she used a scripted program for phonics instruction. Her students were expected to respond in specific ways to her instruction, which was very directed. She showed them a picture, for example, and they were to say the initial consonant and its sound. If the children lost attention, Mrs. Herald started the lesson again. During this instruction students were not to help each other. Later in the lesson the children wrote words; they were expected to spell them correctly without support from peers, following the concept that she had just taught. This instructional format continued until recess time.

After recess, the students returned to the classroom for writing workshop. During writing workshop Mrs. Herald asked the children to write stories or informational text, spelling the best they could to get ideas down on paper. They were also encouraged to work together on their writing, both for generating ideas and for editing. Her students found this difficult. They often asked each other or the teacher for help with spelling. Spelling got in the way of recording ideas, and they never felt comfortable working together. The children struggled with adapting to the expectations for classroom learning and behavior that were in place before recess and then abruptly changed after recess.

This teacher was indeed eclectic; unfortunately, the instruction before and after recess varied tremendously with respect to the expectations for the students. Before recess, all words needed to be spelled correctly and the children could not help each other—but after recess, students could represent words with their best attempts and work collaboratively. The philosophical shift was too much for the children in this class. They were not able to separate expectations in regard to spelling and collaboration based on the time of day.

Successful Implementation

Rather than providing a new example, I think that the earlier example of Miss Moore is adequate. In the description of her classroom, it was clear that she combined more explicit or formal instruction with less explicit and informal instruction. Although she brought many strategies to her instruction, they were all based on a similar philosophical orientation. She expected students to do their best and use the knowledge they had. Miss Moore did not shift expectations from correctness to best guesses within a day. In addition, her students were able to work and help other students throughout the day. These expectations were consistent even while she varied strategies. Her students were not expected to adjust because of the clock.

FINAL THOUGHTS

The examples given throughout this chapter are meant to highlight the importance and difficulties of bringing new strategies and organizations into the primary classroom. They also demonstrate how thoughtful teachers were in bringing in new strategies and ways of organization, whether they were successful with student learning or not. Clearly, it is important for teachers to retain their own good sense about their students and instruction when adapting these newer strategies in their classrooms. Mem Fox (2001) cautioned teachers when she wrote:

> We teachers tend to put on blinkers. We stop being critical of our own practice and theory and become converts to the latest orthodoxy, and we are so single-minded about it that we can't see the forest for the trees. We put our brains on hold, sneer at anyone who isn't an active convert, and purse our lips as if we are sucking lemons when any of our colleagues hangs on to a good idea from the past. (p. 106)

Fox helps us to see how narrow some of us are when adapting newer strategies, and careless as well through our dismissal of successful strategies. Other writers care more specifically about strategies and caution that a too heavy dose of decoding may limit fluency and meaning-based reading (Heald-Taylor, 2001; Taylor, Anderson, Au, & Raphael, 2000). This dominance was clearly demonstrated in many of the vignettes in this chapter.

As teachers know, teaching children to read and write is a complex process. In addition to balancing literacy content, teachers need to develop structures to support instruction. These structures allow children to share what they know about literacy while simultaneously developing their knowledge and expertise in reading and writing. It is important to keep in mind that teaching children to read and write is not reducible to a simple set of techniques or strategies. Rather, strategies and techniques must be adapted to the contextual experiences of the teacher and learners at the moment of engagement—whereby the student is moved to a newer, more refined level of knowledge and understanding. Teachers must think carefully as they bring new, research-based strategies to their classrooms. They must consider their students and how these newer strategies will benefit them, while they retain successful practices already in place. By so doing, they will not "lose their way" as they enrich the learning experiences of their students.

REFERENCES

Adams, M. J. (1990). *Beginning to read: Thinking and learning about print*. Cambridge, MA: MIT Press.

Adams, M. J., Foorman, B., Lundberg I., & Beeler, T. (1997). *Phonemic awareness in young children: A classroom curriculum*. Baltimore: Brookes.

Allard, H. (1977). *Miss Nelson is missing!* Boston: Houghton Mifflin.

Bissex, G. L. (1980). *Gnys at wrk: A child learns to read and write*. Cambridge, MA: Harvard University Press.

Calkins, L. M. (1986). *The art of teaching writing*. Portsmouth, NH: Heinemann.

Ehri, L., Nunes, S., Willows, D., Schuster, B., Yaghoub-Zadeh, Z., & Shanahan, T. (2001). Phonemic awareness instruction helps children learn to read: Evidence from the National Reading Panel's meta–analysis. *Reading Research Quarterly, 36*, 250–287.

Fox, M. (2001). Have we lost our way? *Language Arts, 79*, 105–113.

Heald-Taylor, G. (2001). *The beginning reading handbook: Strategies for success*. Portsmouth, NH: Heinemann.

Henderson, E. H. (1990). *Teaching spelling* (2nd ed.). Boston: Houghton Mifflin.

Hicks, D. (2002). *Reading lives: Working-class children and literacy learning*. New York: Teachers College Press.

Johnston, P. H., & Rogers, R. (2002). Early literacy development: The case for "informed assessment." In S. B. Neuman & D. K. Dickinson (Eds.), *Handbook of early literacy research* (pp. 377–389). New York: Guilford Press.

Juel, C. (1988). Learning to read and write: A longitudinal study of 54 children from first through fourth grade. *Journal of Educational Psychology, 80*, 437–447.

Kaufman, D. (2001). Organizing and managing the language arts workshop: A matter of motion. *Language Arts, 79*, 114–123.

Ladson-Billings, G. (1994). *The dreamkeepers: Successful teachers of African American children*. San Francisco: Jossey-Bass.

Manzo, A. (1969). The ReQuest procedure. *Journal of Reading, 12*, 123–126.

McGill-Franzen, A., Allington, R., Yokoi, L., & Brooks, G. (1999). Putting books in the room seems necessary but not sufficient. *Journal of Educational Research, 93*, 67–74.

Meier, D. R. (2000). *Scribble scrabble—Learning to read and write: Success with diverse teachers, children and families*. New York: Teachers College Press.

National Reading Panel. (2000). *Report of the National Reading Panel: Reports of the subgroups*. Washington, DC: National Institute of Child Health and Human Development Clearinghouse.

Read, C. (1975). *Children's categorization of speech sounds in English.* Urbana, IL: National Council of Teachers of English.

Smith, N. B. (1986). *American reading instruction.* Newark, DE: International Reading Association.

Stanovich, K. (1986). Matthew effects in reading: Some consequences of individual differences in the acquisition of literacy. *Reading Research Quarterly, 21,* 360–406.

Taylor, B., Anderson, R., Au, K., & Raphael, T. (2000). Discretion in the translation of reading research to policy [Online]. Available: http://www.ciera.org/library/reports/inquiry-3/3-006/3-006/html [2001, November 27]

Index

Page numbers followed by *f* indicate figure, *t* indicate table